T0399255

The Oxford History of the Archaic Greek World

The Oxford History of the Archaic Greek World

Editors: Paul Cartledge and Paul Christesen

This landmark series comprises seven volumes containing 22 in-depth studies of key city-states, sanctuaries, and regions during the Archaic period (c. 750 to c. 480 BCE). Ranging from Massalia in the west to Cyprus in the east and from Cyrene in the south to Lesbos in the north, and fully integrating the literary, epigraphic, and archaeological evidence, these studies present an authoritative and comprehensive portrait of a transformational era that witnessed the emergence of democracy, tragedy, temple architecture, and so many other features commonly associated with ancient Greece.

Volume I: Argos, Chalcis and Eretria, Chios-Lesbos-Samos, Corcyra
Paul Christesen, Sylvian Fachard, Hans-Joachim Gehrke, Jonathan Hall, Giuseppe Lentini, Sarah Murray, Philip Sapirstein, Matt Simonton, and Samuel Verdan

Volume II: Athens and Attica
Robin Osborne

Volume III: Cumae and Pithecusae, Cyclades, Cyprus
Erica Angliker, Grégory Bonnin, Paul Christesen, Matteo D'Acunto, Edward Henderson, Clayton Howard, Alex Karsten, Yannos Kourayos, Alexandra Sfyroera, and Anja Ulbrich

Volume IV: Cyrene, Delphi, Macedonia, Massalia, Metapontion
Zosia Archibald, Hélène Aurigny, Joseph Carter, Adolfo Domínguez, Gerry Schaus, and Michael Scott

Volume V: Miletus, Northwestern Greece, Olympia
Catherine Morgan, Reinard Senff, and Anja Slawisch

Volume VI: Rhodes, Sicyon, Syracuse, Thebes, Western Sicily
Franco De Angelis, Yannis Lolos, Valentina Mignosa, Thomas Heine Nielsen, Adam Schwartz, and Lone Wriedt Sørensen

Volume VII: Sparta
Paul Cartledge and Paul Christesen

The Oxford History of the Archaic Greek World

Athens and Attica

VOLUME II

ROBIN OSBORNE

OXFORD
UNIVERSITY PRESS

Oxford University Press is a department of the University of Oxford. It furthers the University's objective of excellence in research, scholarship, and education by publishing worldwide. Oxford is a registered trade mark of Oxford University Press in the UK and certain other countries.

Published in the United States of America by Oxford University Press
198 Madison Avenue, New York, NY 10016, United States of America.

© Oxford University Press 2023

All rights reserved. No part of this publication may be reproduced, stored in a retrieval system, or transmitted, in any form or by any means, without the prior permission in writing of Oxford University Press, or as expressly permitted by law, by license, or under terms agreed with the appropriate reproduction rights organization. Inquiries concerning reproduction outside the scope of the above should be sent to the Rights Department, Oxford University Press, at the address above.

You must not circulate this work in any other form and you must impose this same condition on any acquirer.

Library of Congress Control Number: 2023940343

ISBN 978-0-19-764442-3

DOI: 10.1093/oso/9780197644423.001.0001

Contents

List of Illustrations

Abbreviations

Athens NM	Athens National Archaeological Museum
EG	Early Geometric
EPG	Early Protogeometric
FGrH	Jacoby, F. 1923–1958. *Die Fragmente der griechischen Historiker.* 3 vols. in 14 vols. Berlin: Weidmann.
IG	*Inscriptiones Graecae.* 1873–. Berlin: Walter de Gruyter.
LG	Late Geometric
LH	Late Helladic
LPG	Late Protogeometric
MG	Middle Geometric
PG	Protogeometric
SEG	*Supplementum Epigraphicum Graecum.* 1923–. Leiden: Brill.

A Note on Chronology

Greeks did not think in terms of centuries as we do. Nor did they have any single chronological system: when Thucydides wants to date the start of the Peloponnesian War he does so with reference to the priestess at Argos, the eponymous ephor at Sparta, and the eponymous archon in Athens (Thuc. 2.2.1). In his account of earlier history in 1.3–19, Thucydides indicates dates by reference to individuals (e.g., Minos) or events (e.g., the Trojan War). Herodotos similarly dates Homer and Hesiod in relation to his own time (2.53). How Thucydides and Herodotos estimated the length of time that had elapsed since past events is unclear, and when, in Book 6, Thucydides produces a series of dates for Greek settlements in Sicily and South Italy with reference to the foundation of Syracuse (6.3–5) the basis for his doing so is again obscure. Later Greek writers attempted to match events of the Archaic period to a unified chronological framework, but there is no reason to believe that they had any secure foundation for their claims.

Ancient material culture is dated by establishing the sequence of artifact styles, above all styles of pottery, preferably on the basis of archaeological stratigraphy. That sequence is then linked to a relatively small number of "fixed points," i.e., archaeological events whose absolute date is established with reference to what seem to be reliable textual evidence, largely Egyptian.

Although the absolute length of time for which a particular artifact style persists is not without interest, what is most important in archaeological dating is sequence and synchrony—that is, the order in which artifacts were made or deposited and the company that those artifacts kept during their lifetime (to use the language of "object biography") or on their journey (to use the language of object itineraries). But as soon as one writes archaeological history, as here, relating historical events to artifact sequences becomes important. To do that directly ("Solon was an early black-figure poet") would give a misleading impression of what it is that we know about Solon's date and how we know it. It is therefore convenient to refer to artifacts and historical events and figures in terms of absolute dates.

The question of which precise absolute dates are appropriate continues to be much debated. My approach here no doubt simplifies realities, but because we think in centuries and half- and quarter-centuries, and because important changes happen to occur at something like whole century intervals, I have taken advantage of that. The consequences of Late Geometric pottery ceasing production in 680 rather than 700 for our understanding is more or less nil unless this later dating changes its relation to other elements of material culture (e.g., early Protocorinthian pottery)—and scholars who move the one also move the other (Rönnberg 2021a: 271–7).

Spelling Divergences

The spellings used for some places and people in this volume diverge from those used in parts of the *Oxford History of the Archaic Greek World* (*OHAGW*). Those divergences are listed below to facilitate searches across the entirety of the digital version of *OHAGW*.

spelling used in this volume	spelling used elsewhere in the *OHAGW*
Acharnai	Acharnae
Aglauros	Aglaurus
Aigisthos	Aegisthus
Aineias Tacticus	Aeneas Tacticus
Alkaios	Alcaeus
Alkmaionidai	Alcmaeonidae
Alkman	Alcman
Amphiaraos	Amphiaraus
amphictyonic	amphictionic
Aristogeiton	Aristogiton
Artemision	Artemisium
Boiotia	Boeotia
Chalkis	Chalcis
Cheiron	Chiron
Constitution of the Athenians	*Ath. Pol.*
Dekeleia	Decelea
Demaratos	Demeratus
Demetrios	Demetrius
Diodoros	Diodorus

spelling used in this volume	spelling used elsewhere in the *OHAGW*
Diogenes Laertios	Diogenes Laertius
Dionysos	Dionysus
Diphilos	Diphilus
Drako	Draco
Enyalios	Enyalius
Ephesos	Ephesus
Ephoros	Ephorus
Erechtheion	Erechtheum
Erichthonios	Erichthonius
Eridanos	Eridanus
Euboia	Euboea
Harmodios	Harmodius
Harpocration	Harpokration
Hellanikos	Hellanicus
Hephaistos	Hephaestus
Herakles	Heracles
Hermippos	Hermippus
Hermokrates	Hermocrates
Herodotos	Herodotus
Hipparchos	Hipparchus
Hippodamos	Hippodamus
Hymettos	Hymettus
Hysiai	Hysiae
Iolkos	Iolcus
Iphikrates	Iphicrates
Kallias	Callias
Karia	Caria
Karystos	Carystus
Kekrops	Cecrops
Keos	Ceos
Kephissos	Cephisus
Kimon	Cimon
Klazomenai	Clazomenae

spelling used in this volume	spelling used elsewhere in the *OHAGW*
Kleidemos	Cleidemus
Kleisthenes	Cleisthenes
Kleomenes	Cleomenes
klerouch	cleruch
Klytemnestra	Clytemnestra
Knossos	Cnossus
Korax	Corax
krater	kratēr
Kratinos	Cratinus
Kroisos	Croesus
Kronos	Cronus
Kylon	Cylon
Kypselos	Cypselus
Kythnos	Cythnos
Kyzikos	Cyzicus
Lampsakos	Lampsacus
Laurion	Laurium
lebes	lebēs
lebetes	lebētes
lekane	lekanē
Lenaia	Lenaea
Leukas	Leucas
Lindos	Lindus
Lokris	Locris
louterion	loutērion
Lykeion	Lyceum
Mardonios	Mardonius
Megakles	Megacles
Megara Hyblaia	Megara Hyblaea
Menelaos	Menelaus
Messina	Messana
Miletos	Miletus
Mounychia	Munichia

spelling used in this volume	spelling used elsewhere in the *OHAGW*
Naukratis	Naucratis
Nearchos	Nearchus
Nisaia	Nisaea
Oikonomika	*Oeconomica*
oinochoe	oinochoē
Oropos	Oropus
palaistra	*palaestra*
Panathenaia	Panathenaea
Patroklos	Patrolcus
Peiraieus	Peiraeus
Peisistratos	Pisistratus
pelike	pelikē
pentekonter	pentecontor
Perikles	Pericles
Phanodemos	Phanodemus
Pharsalos	Pharsalus
Pheidias	Phidias
Pherekydes	Pherecydes
Philochoros	Philochorus
Phokaia	Phocaea
Phrynichos	Phrynichus
Pithekoussai	Pithecusae
Pittakos	Pittacus
Plataia	Plataea
Polykrates	Polycrates
Polyphemos	Polyphemus
Poteidaia	Potidaea
Prokonessos	Proconnesus
Propylaia	Propylaea
Rhamnous	Rhamnus
Sigeion	Sigeum
Sikyon	Sicyon
Skymnos	Scymnus

spelling used in this volume	spelling used elsewhere in the *OHAGW*
Sophilos	Sophilus
Sounion	Sunium
symposion	symposium
Themistocles	Themistokles
Thermopylai	Thermopylae
Thespiai	Thespiae
Thorikos	Thoricus
Triptolemos	Triptolemus
Troilos	Troilus
Troizen	Troezen
Tyrtaios	Tyrtaeus
Xanthippos	Xanthippus
Xanthos	Xanthus

Acknowledgments

BUT FOR THE flattery of Paul Cartledge and Paul Christesen I would never have written this volume. I am grateful to them for the invitation and encouragement and, in particular, to Paul Christesen, who put a truly enormous amount of work into turning this into the text and book that he wanted (and put up with me turning some of it back into the text I wanted). I am equally grateful to Sylvian Fachard for reading the whole text and providing a mass of critical insights and relevant references. The development of my thinking on Archaic Attica has been further shaped by various conference invitations which gave me opportunities to discuss aspects of the account that follows; in particular, I am indebted to Attila Gyucha, Naoise Mac Sweeney, Maximilian Rönnberg and Veronika Sossau, and Bela Dimova and Margareta Gleba and to audiences in SUNY Buffalo, Leicester, Tübingen, and Cambridge.

Note to the Reader

This volume represents one component of the *Oxford History of the Archaic Greek World* (*OHAGW*). All of the 22 studies in *OHAGW* are organized around an identical set of 11 rubrics: (1) sources, (2) natural setting, (3) material culture, (4) political history, (5) legal history, (6) diplomatic history (including warfare), (7) economic history, (8) familial/demographic history (including education), (9) social customs and institutions, (10) religious customs and institutions, and (11) cultural history. Each study begins with an Introduction and ends with a Conclusion.

If you wish to read a specific part of a given study, rather than the entire study from start to finish, we would strongly advise that you first read the Introduction to the study in question—the Introductions in *OHAGW* are designed to provide basic background information that set the stage for the discussion that follows.

The Series Editors' Preface that appears at the beginning of each volume of *OHAGW* offers an overview of the project as a whole and information on transliteration and the spelling of names, places, and titles of literary works. The latter is likely to be helpful if you are accessing *OHAGW* in digital form and wish to search across one or more studies.

Editors' Preface

THIS VOLUME FORMS part of a larger project, the *Oxford History of the Archaic Greek World* (*OHAGW*), that consists of 22 in-depth studies of city-states, sanctuaries, and regions, ranging from Massalia in the west to Cyprus in the east and from Cyrene in the south to Lesbos in the north. All those studies, written by more than 30 eminent scholars with deep expertise in their sites, focus on the period from c. 750 to c. 480 and are aimed at a scholarly audience.

OHAGW is available in both print and digital versions (the latter on the website of Oxford University Press). The 22 studies in *OHAGW* are collected in seven volumes and presented in alphabetic order by site name.

Contents of and Contributors to the *Oxford History of the Archaic Greek World*

Site	Author(s)	Placement in OHAGW
Argos	Jonathan Hall	Volume 1
Athens	Robin Osborne	Volume 2
Chalcis and Eretria	Sylvian Fachard Samuel Verdan	Volume 1
Chios, Lesbos, Samos	Paul Christesen Giuseppe Lentini Sarah Murray Matt Simonton	Volume 1
Corcyra	Hans-Joachim Gehrke Philip Sapirstein	Volume 1
Cumae and Pithecusae	Matteo D'Acunto	Volume 3

Site	Author(s)	Placement in OHAGW
The Cyclades	Erica Angliker	Volume 3
	Grégory Bonnin	
	Paul Christesen	
	Edward Henderson	
	Clayton Howard	
	Alex Karsten	
	Yannos Kourayos	
	Alexandra Sfyroera	
Cyprus	Anja Ulbrich	Volume 3
Cyrene	Gerry Schaus	Volume 4
Delphi	Hélène Aurigny	Volume 4
	Michael Scott	
Macedonia	Zosia Archibald	Volume 4
Massalia	Adolfo Domínguez	Volume 4
Metapontion	Joseph Carter	Volume 4
Miletus	Anja Slawisch	Volume 5
Northwestern Greece	Catherine Morgan	Volume 5
Olympia	Reinhard Senff	Volume 5
Rhodes	Thomas Heine Nielsen	Volume 6
	Adam Schwartz	
	Lone Wriedt Sørensen	
Sicyon	Yannis Lolos	Volume 6
Sparta	Paul Cartledge	Volume 7
	Paul Christesen	
Syracuse	Franco De Angelis	Volume 6
	Valentina Mignosa	
Thebes	Hans Beck	Volume 6
Western Sicily	Clemente Marconi	Volume 6
	Andrew Ward	

Project Design

The primary goal of *OHAGW* is to facilitate study of a broad array of Greek communities during the Archaic period. In pursuit of that goal, the editors of and contributors to *OHAGW* have made a concerted effort to ensure that the studies in *OHAGW* are—individually and collectively—comprehensive, commensurable, and convenient.

There are numerous pre-existing publications that offer comprehensive coverage of the ancient Greek world. One might note in particular the *Cambridge Ancient History*, in its second, revised edition and, more recently, the *Inventory of Archaic and Classical Greek Poleis*, edited by Mogens Herman Hansen and Thomas Heine Nielsen (Hansen and Nielsen 2004). Those and similar works remain valuable resources, not least because they are expansive in their spatial and temporal coverage. Yet that sort of breadth comes inevitably at the expense of depth.

In designing *OHAGW* we sought to find a compromise between breadth and depth that leaned toward the latter. The decision to pursue depth even at the expense of breadth reflects our belief that there is a pressing need for fine-grained studies of specific sites that consolidate large, disparate, and complex arrays of evidence. Scholars studying the ancient Greek world are increasingly adrift on a continually expanding sea of information that is far beyond the capacity of any individual to manage. The bibliographic database provided by *L'année philologique* increases by approximately 12,000 items each year; given that the *L'année philologique* is by no means exhaustive, one might venture the suggestion, as a rough approximation, that on an average day 40 new scholarly books, theses, and articles on ancient Greece are published and take their place in an already luxuriant landscape of secondary literature. Someone interested in, for instance, developing a thorough knowledge of Cyrene would need to put in months, if not years, of work in order to identify, collect, and read the relevant scholarly literature, which includes, but is by no means limited to, reports from dozens of excavations conducted by various teams of American, British, French, Italian, and Libyan archaeologists starting in 1884 (for further discussion, see the *OHAGW* essay on Cyrene by Gerry Schaus). To make matters worse, the bibliography is highly site-specific. An examination of the bibliography for the *OHAGW* studies of the neighboring *poleis* of Samos and Miletus shows that only about 20 percent overlap (i.e., 20 percent of the sources cited in those studies are identical).

With that in mind, we gave contributors the room to explore their sites in depth, with the length of any given study varying from a little under 30,000 words to well over 100,000 words. At the same time, we made certain that *OHAGW* included studies of a sufficiently large and diverse array of cities, sanctuaries, and regions to achieve reasonably broad coverage of the Archaic Greek world as a whole.

Inevitably, trade-offs had to be made to keep the project to a manageable size. Many Greek sites that merit detailed exploration are not treated in *OHAGW*, and the project focuses solely on the Archaic period (see the discussion of the criteria used to select sites and of the decision to focus on the Archaic period as we conceive it). Even with those limitations, the project attained a scale—in the neighborhood of 1.5 million words—that was, at times, daunting.

We also sought from the outset to make *OHAGW* comprehensive in the sense that each study takes into consideration both textual and material evidence. To that end, all contributors were asked to employ an approach that we have chosen to call "archaeohistory." Despite the laudable emphasis on interdisciplinarity in recent decades, there remains a divide between scholars who study ancient Greece largely on the basis of texts and scholars who study ancient Greece largely on the basis of material evidence. That divide is driven, to some extent, by a previously touched upon issue—the sheer volume of the relevant information and the impossibility of familiarizing oneself with even a small fraction of it. Nevertheless, the textual evidence and the material evidence for ancient Greece each has its own particular lacunae and limitations, and their full value is realized only when they are brought into dialog with each other. Much of the best scholarship on the Archaic period produced in the past 30 years is notable for combining successfully literary and inscriptional texts with material evidence such as pottery, coins, and statuary. The term "archaeohistory" reflects our desire to fuse together seamlessly the emphasis on material evidence associated with archaeology and the emphasis on textual evidence associated with history. The commitment to archaeohistory will, we believe, be evident in every study in *OHAGW*.

A second major concern in designing and producing *OHAGW* was to create a collection of studies with a high degree of commensurability to facilitate comparison and contrast across the Greek world. Before discussing that facet of *OHAGW*, it is necessary to raise the question of whether "ancient Greece" is anything more than a modern construct. As the inhabitants of the southern end of the Balkan peninsula, what might be called the Greek homeland, dispersed throughout much of the Mediterranean and Black Sea basins, the different environmental and human ecosystems they encountered led almost inevitably to important differences among the settlements in which they lived. Furthermore, each of those settlements developed its own unique set of sociopolitical institutions and practices, and even communities that were situated relatively close to one another frequently responded in very different ways to similar demographic, political, social, and economic challenges.

The absence of anything resembling a single territorial state embracing a significant fraction of what is typically described as "the Greek (or Hellenic) world" means that "Greek" needs to be construed culturally, not politically, along the lines of a perceived common ethnicity or shared cultural traits. The work of Jonathan Hall (author of the *OHAGW* essay on Argos) in the late 1990s and early 2000s created an awareness that Hellenic ethnic identity was a relatively late arrival—Hall suggested that it emerged in the seventh and sixth centuries BCE (Hall 1997; Hall 2002).

As indicated by its title, this project is based in part on the assumption that there was a sufficiently high degree of shared ethnic identity and cultural traits among certain communities in the Mediterranean to speak meaningfully of the "Greek world" in the Archaic period. Those communities were bound together by a loosely structured but highly active network of commercial, cultural, diplomatic, and military ties. In addition, certain places and events—most notably Olympia and the Olympic Games—attracted participants from Greek communities throughout the Mediterranean and beyond and became sites for the production and inculcation of a deeply embedded sense of belonging to a distinct group (for further discussion see the *OHAGW* essay on Olympia by Reinhard Senff).

Other terminology has also proved awkward. More recent scholarship has emphasized that the term "colonization" is a problematic label for the complex process of long-term, multidirectional cultural exchange and ongoing mobility of individuals and small groups that led to the movement of people outward from the southern end of the Balkan peninsula (see, for example, Mac Sweeney 2017). While communities such as Pithecusae have long been recognized as multi-ethnic (see the *OHAGW* essay on Cumae and Pithecusae by Matteo D'Acunto for further discussion), it now seems evident that ethnic diversity was a feature of many, if not most, communities typically described as Greek.

Our concern with commensurability was motivated by a keen awareness that the study of ancient Greece in the Archaic period entails exploration of simultaneous difference and sameness—we see the complex interplay of diversity and uniformity as one of the most fundamental and fascinating traits of the ancient Greek world. In constructing *OHAGW* we wanted to ensure that the project would greatly simplify the process of comparison and contrast. In doing so we were particularly alert to the fact that, even though there were pre-existing scholarly monographs on sites such as Miletus and Syracuse that are included in *OHAGW* (see, for example, Gorman 2001; Evans 2016), those works took widely varying approaches with respect to the periods of time covered, types of evidence considered, and methodologies used, which in turn makes it difficult to explore divergences and convergences across communities.

To ensure a high degree of commensurability within *OHAGW*, all of its component studies are built around the same 11 rubrics (framed by an introduction and a conclusion): (1) sources of evidence, (2) natural setting, (3) material culture, (4) political history, (5) legal history, (6) diplomatic history (including warfare), (7) economic history, (8) familial/ demographic history, (9) social customs and institutions, (10) religious customs and institutions, (11) cultural history. All those rubrics are covered in every study (although not necessarily in precisely the order given above), so that there is a high level of commonality in the structure and general contents among the various components of *OHAGW*. We have pursued commensurability at a level below that of the rubrics by placing specific types of subject matter that could conceivably fall under more than one rubric under the same rubric in every study. For example, pottery, which might be placed under "material culture" or "cultural history," is consistently placed under the rubric of "material culture."

Both the rubrics themselves and the division of material among rubrics are to a certain extent arbitrary, and we experimented with various arrangements before arriving at the one employed in *OHAGW*. Different arrangements had different advantages and disadvantages, and none was, in our view, perfect. We nonetheless persisted in the use of a consistent set of rubrics primarily because that feature of the project will make it possible to explore diversity and uniformity across the Greek world with much greater ease and in greater depth than ever before. Moreover, the material within each study would perforce need to be subdivided in some fashion, and the absence of a single, shared set of rubrics would have, in effect, resulted in the creation of a different set of rubrics for each of the 22 studies in *OHAGW*. The arbitrary element in the selection and division of material would still be present, but the benefits of a shared organizational template would be lost.

A third key trait we had in mind when designing *OHAGW* was convenience. The scale of *OHAGW* is such that most readers will want to examine specific parts of the project rather than the project as a whole, and we wanted to make it easy for readers to access the material of particular interest to them. The high degree of structural and methodological commensurability among the component studies in *OHAGW* makes it possible to read either vertically (reading a complete study of a single site) or horizontally (reading, for example, the rubric of political history of a number of different sites). Reading vertically will enable scholars to familiarize themselves relatively quickly with a number of different Archaic Greek sites. Reading horizontally will enable scholars to familiarize themselves relatively quickly with how specific institutions and practices manifested themselves from place to place across the Greek world.

Reading horizontally, however, does present certain difficulties: the section on the political history of, say, Metapontion inevitably assumes that the reader is aware of particular items of information such as places, names, and dates that are discussed in earlier sections of that study. (The alternative would have been to construct each rubric as a stand-alone piece, which would have entailed a massive amount of repetition.) To minimize that difficulty, the Introduction to each study discusses essential places, names, and dates that feature in other parts of the study.

Readers who wish to work through *OHAGW* horizontally are strongly encouraged to take the time to read the Introduction to a study before they look at the text under any of the aforementioned 11 rubrics. We have also supplied a generous amount of cross-references throughout each study so that readers working horizontally can easily find more information about a subject treated elsewhere in the study. Each study, moreover, is prefaced by a detailed table of contents.

OHAGW, by its very nature, discusses literally hundreds of places, many of which will not be immediately familiar, even to many specialists in ancient Greece: examples are Parauaia and Tymphaia, which feature in Zosia Archibald's study of Macedonia. Every study in *OHAGW* thus includes a set of maps and site plans that shows the location of sites and buildings featured in the essay, as well as a gazetteer (located at the end of each study) that lists every site and building shown on a map or site plan and gives the relevant map number(s) and grid-square(s).

Finally, we asked all contributors to make their work readily accessible to an audience consisting largely of scholars who have some substantial grounding and serious interest in the ancient Greek world. While, given that audience, there was no need for them to explain the plot of the Homeric poems or the nature of Thucydides' work, we did want to make certain that every part of every study could be understood and appreciated regardless of whether a reader was trained as an archaeologist, historian, philologist, epigrapher, art historian, etc. Our hope is that each study is a self-contained, self-sufficient piece of scholarship that a reader who knows little or nothing about the site in question beforehand can comprehend fully without immediate reference to any other scholarship.

Site Selection

In selecting places to include in *OHAGW* we began by looking for sites that were in some fashion and by some criterion significant in the Archaic period, that had notable physical remains (which had been excavated and published), and for which there was considerable textual evidence, either epigraphic or literary. From among the many places that fulfilled those criteria we assembled a group of approximately 30 places that included various geographies and site types. We make no claim that the sites treated in *OHAGW* constitute a representative sample, in the sense that careful study of the *OHAGW* sites would reveal all the major features of Archaic Greek communities broadly speaking, but we would say that the *OHAGW* sites collectively give some substantial sense of the diversity of the Greek world in the Archaic period.

The exigencies involved in carrying out a large-scale project over multiple years and the manifold hardships created by the COVID-19 pandemic produced a certain degree of attrition, and the roster of sites covered in *OHAGW* is not identical to that which we originally outlined. At a certain point we decided that it was more important to publish the very considerable collection of valuable material that the contributors had produced than to delay publication to add more sites. Our feeling was that adding five or even ten more sites would not bring us across some crucial threshold, and that *OHAGW* could not possibly become an encyclopedic treatment of the Archaic Greek world in any sort of reasonable timespan.

That said, certain sites (such as Aegina) are perhaps conspicuous by their absence. Our hope is that the 22 studies that currently constitute *OHAGW* will find an enthusiastic audience and that in short order it will be desirable and possible to commission additional studies that extend the template that has already been established.

Periodization

The choice to focus on the Archaic period reflects our conviction that it was a critical, formative era in Greek history. As Anthony Snodgrass eloquently argued in his foundational *Archaic Greece: The Age of Experiment* (1980), the institutions and practices that took shape in Greek communities during the Archaic period differed from what came before, and remained influential, even definitive, among Greek communities for centuries thereafter. Indeed, much of what is now seen as distinctive about Greek culture—democracy, stone temples, and nude athletics, to name but a few—first developed within the boundaries of the Archaic period. The history of this period thus merits careful study by anyone interested in the ancient Greek world and its legacy.

The decision to concentrate on the Archaic period raised *ab initio* the question of how to define its temporal boundaries.[1] The traditional periodization of Greek history is a *post eventum* and fluctuating construct, and the Archaic period (which is typically understood as stretching from some point in the eighth century to c. 479 BCE) as a construct has a long history. The perception of events corresponding in time roughly to the beginning and end of the Archaic period as key epochs can be traced all the way back to ancient Greece. According to the Roman grammarian Censorinus (active in the third century CE), Varro (active in the first

---

1. It is not possible here to offer a complete conspectus of the scholarship on the Archaic period as an historical construct. We are not aware of a single publication that covers the full range of possible considerations, but there are several relevant, stimulating books, theses, and articles, among which we would highlight Heuss 1946; Golden and Toohey 1997 (esp. the article by Ian Morris in that volume); Davies 2009; Lange 2015; and Étienne 2017.

century BCE) divided the history of the world into three parts: the "obscure" period (stretching from Creation to the Flood), the mythical period (from the Flood to the first Olympiad), and the historical period (everything after the first Olympiad) (*De die natali* 21.1–3). For Varro, the first Olympiad marked the point at which it was possible to separate fact from legend in accounts of past events.

It is probable that Varro derived his three divisions from a Greek chronographer, possibly Eratosthenes or Castor of Rhodes (see Frances Pownall's commentary on Eratosthenes F1c in the second edition of *Brill's New Jacoby*). Both Eratosthenes and Castor dated the first numbered Olympiad to 776 (Christesen 2007: 173–8, 311–20), and that date has repeatedly featured in modern scholarship on ancient Greece as an important epoch. George Grote, in his 12-volume *History of Greece* (1846–1856), claimed that "the history of Greece falls most naturally into six compartments," the first of which starts in 776. He notes that "I begin the real history of Greece with the first recorded Olympiad, or 776 B.C." (Grote 1846–1856: vol. 1: x–xi, vii). Anne Jeffery set the upper boundary of the Archaic period at 776, in her monograph entitled *Archaic Greece* (Jeffery 1976: 24–8).

The lower boundary of the Archaic period has traditionally been tied to the (second) Persian invasion of the Greek homeland in 480–479. The stature of that event as marking a key historical epoch can be traced to the enduring influence of the *Histories* of Herodotus, for whom any event post-479 BCE was after "ta Mēdika." Diodorus Siculus, for example, so arranged his *Library of History* that Book 11 begins with Xerxes' crossing into Europe in 480. Here again, modern historians have generally followed suit. For example, Grote's second historical "compartment" ends with the defeat of Xerxes' invasion of Greece.

Starting in the eighteenth century, the timespan between roughly the first Olympiad on one hand and the Persian Wars on the other became identified as a distinct period of art history, and it was expositions of art history that provided the currently prevailing terminology. In his *Geschichte der Kunst des Alterthums* (first edition 1764) Johann Winckelmann, working primarily with reference to sculpture, divided Greek art into four chronological phases that formed part of a pattern of growth and decay: der ältere Stil, der hohe Stil, der schöne Stil, and der Stil der Nachahmer; the "ältere Stil" encompassed art from the earliest times up to the work of Phidias (see, for example, Winckelmann 1764: 39, 214, 433–62; Dittmann 1991; Potts 2000: 67–112). The conversion of Winckelmann's "ältere Stil" to "Archaic period" was due primarily to anglophone authors.

Of particular note in that regard are Charles Cockerell and Edward Dodwell, who were familiar with Winckelmann's work and who in 1811 were among a group that discovered several pedimental sculptures at the Temple of Aphaea on Aegina that were seen as the embodiment of the "ältere Stil." Cockerell and

Dodwell wrote about what they called the "archaic style" in Greek art (see, for example, Cockerell 1819: 340; Dodwell 1819: vol. 1: 571, vol. 2: 199, 201; Lange 2015: 154–8 and *passim*). By 1833, Henry Ellis, in a guide to sculptures in the British Museum, could write about "the archaic period, as it is called, of Grecian art" that "extended through eight almost unknown centuries, nearly to the time of Phidias" (Ellis 1833: 100). As archaeological explorations began to produce large quantities of material from what would now be called the Bronze and Early Iron Ages, chronologies were adjusted accordingly, and the starting point of the Archaic period was pushed downward. In Leonard Whibley's *Companion to Greek Studies* from 1905, the sculpture of the Archaic period is placed between 750 and 500 BCE (Whibley 1905: 234).

While there is a long tradition of identifying epochs in the eighth century and in the early fifth century, and thus at the beginning and end of the Archaic period as typically defined, and while the intervening centuries have long been read as a distinct era in the history of Greek art, there is no compelling necessity to identify the time period between the eighth and the early fifth century as a distinct phase of Greek history broadly construed. This is immediately evident from Grote's work: he recognized 776 and 479 as significant dates, but he divided what we call the Archaic period into two distinct "compartments," one running from 776 to c. 560 (the accession of Pisistratus and Croesus) and another running from c. 560 to the defeat of Xerxes in 479. Closer to home, two contributors to *OHAGW*, Jonathan Hall and Robin Osborne, have written surveys of the Archaic period in ancient Greece that begin c. 1200 (Osborne 2009; Hall 2014). This is because, for them, the events of the end of the Bronze Age set in motion a series of changes that played themselves out without any major breaks until the early fifth century.

Scholars who identify the Archaic period as a distinct historical phase and who place its boundaries at the eighth and early fifth centuries have given varying reasons for doing so. For example, Anthony Snodgrass started his account of Archaic Greece in the eighth century because he placed in that time period a "structural revolution" that established the basic economic, social, and political framework within which the multiplicity of Greek communities operated for centuries thereafter (Snodgrass 1980: 13).

We firmly subscribe to the idea that the Archaic period can be reasonably characterized as a distinct historical phase that extended from roughly the middle of the eighth century to roughly the end of the sixth century, and we agree that it was, as Snodgrass put it, "a complete episode in its own right" (Snodgrass 1980: 13). From our perspective, there are two determinant factors: politics and sources. The beginning of the Archaic period is marked by the re-emergence of formal political institutions in the Greek world, including the widespread creation of *poleis*. The end of our Archaic period is marked by the emergence of democracy as a fully developed form of governing a *polis*, completing the set of six forms of governance (monarchy, tyranny, aristocracy, oligarchy, *politeia*, and democracy) identified by Plato and Aristotle (see, for example, *Eth. Nic.* 1160a31–b12; *Pol.* 1279a22–b8). While significant developments in the political life of Greece communities certainly took place in the centuries after the Persian invasions, the basic repertoire of possibilities was established within the timeframe we call the Archaic period.

The Archaic period is also arguably a "complete episode" with respect to the textual sources. The wealth of extant literary and epigraphic texts written in Greek represent a remarkable and—globally speaking—highly unusual resource for the study of the history of a group of people in the pre-modern period. The reappearance of literacy in Greek communities occurred in the eighth century: that and its gradual dissemination, due to the invention of an alphabet, to a much broader segment of the population than had been literate in the Late Bronze Age constitute an epoch in its own right. The Homeric poems, not coincidentally transcribed within a framework of alphabetic literacy, make it possible to explore the Greek world of the eighth century in ways that are simply not feasible for the Early Iron Age.

Moreover, the literary texts of the Archaic period are sufficiently different from those that follow as to form a distinct group: A. R. Burn thus wrote a history of the Archaic period under the title *The Lyric Age of Greece* (Burn 1960), which captures one particular new source of poetic and cultural sensibility. As for the qualitative difference between the Archaic period and what follows, an important variable is the degree to which the literary texts of the former were produced against the background of a society that remained strongly oral in its orientation and social memory (see the discussion and cautionary comments in Thomas 1992). With the appearance of properly historical texts in the early part of the Classical period, the Greeks' approach to their past changed in fundamental ways.

In parenthesis, however, it is important to note that putting political institutions and textual sources front and center is a choice that necessarily excludes other possibilities. As Kostas Vlassopoulos has pointed out, variant perspectives on ancient Greek history, for example, those that emphasize the agency of subaltern populations, entail variant periodizations, each of which is, by definition, partial (Vlassopoulos 2018: 215).

A further consideration that materially shaped our approach to the Archaic period was a desire to give contributors a certain degree of flexibility to adjust the temporal parameters of their studies to fit the contours of their particular site. This was most obviously necessary in the case of sites such as Cyrene and Metapontion, which did not receive any substantial number of Greek migrants until the second half of the seventh century. At the other end of the temporal scale, for many Greek communities within the broader cultural horizon of Hellas, the Persian invasion of the Aegean Greek homeland in 480–479 was an event of at best minor significance. Far more important for most Sicilian Greek communities, for example, was the invasion of their island from Carthage, though as it happens the contemporaneous Battle of Himera in 480 could be considered epoch-making too. Contributors were therefore asked to define the Archaic period in a way that suited their site, while staying roughly within the boundaries of the eighth century and the fifth century. To give but one example, in their study of Syracuse, Franco De Angelis and Valentina Mignosa set the upper limit at the time of the arrival of substantial numbers of Greek migrants, the third quarter of the eighth century, and the lower limit at 461, at which point the last of the Deinomenid tyrants was overthrown and a democratic government established that endured, in one form or another, to the end of the fifth century.

Transliteration and the Spelling of Names, Places, and Titles of Literary Works

We have taken the *Oxford English Dictionary* (*OED*) as our guide in deciding what Greek words (other than names, places, and titles of literary works) to anglicize and what words to transliterate. Ancient Greek words that have a direct equivalent in the *OED* are given as they are in the *OED*, without italics. For example, ἀκρωτήριον has a direct equivalent in the *OED*, "acroterion," that is used throughout *OHAGW*, without italics. On the other hand, χώρα has no direct equivalent in the *OED* and hence is given in transliterated form, italicized and with the long vowels marked with macrons (e.g., "The *chōra* of Metapontion consisted of a series of relatively flat, well-watered natural terraces rising from a coastal plain to a hilly and dissected interior"). Names, places, and titles of literary works presented special challenges and were treated differently.

OHAGW will be available in both print and digital form. Insofar as we view *OHAGW* as a collectivity, we wanted to simplify as much as possible the process of searching across the entirety of the digital version of *OHAGW*, and, to that end, we wanted to be both consistent and predictable in the spelling of Greek names, places, and titles of literary works. The complication of course is trying to find a balance between transliterating in such a way as to be as faithful as possible to original spellings while taking into account established usages (e.g., Korinthos or Corinth?).

We considered producing a complete list of all the Greek names, places, and literary works mentioned in *OHAGW* to serve as a guide for searches, but we decided that the list would be sufficiently cumbersome to locate and use that most readers would not refer to it. Instead, we have implemented the following practices throughout *OHAGW*, a general awareness of which should make it possible to carry out searches without any great difficulty:

(1) Greek names and places that have their own lemma in the *Oxford Classical Dictionary* (*OCD*) are spelled as they are in the *OCD*. Our rationale was that the provision of a lemma in the *OCD* was a reasonably good measure of the prominence of a person or place and hence the likelihood that there was an established usage for the spelling of the person or place in question. In addition, our assumption is that most scholars interested in the ancient Greek world, the intended audience of *OHAGW*, would have easy access to the *OCD*.

(2) Greek names and places that do not have their own lemma in the *OCD* were transliterated into English. We did not, however, provide long marks to distinguish *epsilon* from *eta* and *omicron* from *omega* because that would have produced a rather strange orthographic mixture such as Sappho for Σαπφώ (as per the *OCD*) and Phrynōn for Φρύνων (who does not have a lemma in the *OCD*).

(3) References in the main text to the titles of well-known Greek literary works are typically given in the most common and obvious English translation; for example, the *OHAGW* essays refer to Aristotle's *Politics* rather than Πολιτικά or *Politika* or *Politica*. In parenthetical citations of Greek literary works, the title is given in accordance with the list of abbreviations provided in the *OCD*; for example: "The practices explored by Aristotle in the *Politics* extend beyond the bounds of the Greek world; Aristotle, for instance, claims that political offices are distributed on the basis of height in Ethiopia (*Pol.* 1290b4–5)," to keep the text in parenthetical citations as brief and therefore legible as possible. For literary works not included in the *OCD*'s list of abbreviations, the title used in the main text is also used in parenthetical citations.

(4) We maintained established usages for Greek literary works that are habitually known by titles in Greek transliteration or in Latin translation. For example, Athenaeus' Δειπνοσοφισταί is in the main text of *OHAGW* studies referred to as the *Deipnosophistai* (whereas, in accordance with the *OCD*, it is in parenthetical citations referenced, for example, as Ath. 145b), and the (pseudo-) Aristotelian Οἰκονομικά is referred to as the *Oeconomica* in the main text (and *Oec.* in parenthetical citations).

(5) For more obscure Greek literary works, we have used the title given in the *Canon of Greek Authors and Works* produced by the Thesaurus Linguae Graecae (TLG), both in the main text and in parenthetical citations. For example, the work on prosody produced by Aelianus Herodianus in the second century CE, ἡ καθ' ὅλου προσῳδία, is referred to under the title assigned by the TLG: *De prosodia catholica*. We are less than entirely enthusiastic about

the TLG's practice of latinizing Greek titles, but the TLG does provide a convenient reference point without which all sorts of difficulties would arise. Aelianus Herodianus' work on prosody, for instance, is referenced in ancient sources by three different titles.

In implementing these practices, we found it necessary to make a number of judgment calls, a handful of which are worth specific mention here:

Author	Title in Greek	Title in main text of OHAGW
?	Ἐτυμολογικὸν Μέγα	*Etymologicum Magnum*
Aristophanes	Most of the titles of Aristophanes' plays have been translated into English, with the exception of the *Ecclesiazusae* and the *Thesmophoriazusae*.	
[Aristotle]	All of the titles of the 158 Aristotelian *politeiai* are referred to as the "*Constitution of the . . .*" with the city ethnic in the plural; e.g., *Constitution of the Athenians*.	
Herodotus	Ἱστορίαι	*Histories*
Marmor Parium	n/a	Marmor Parium (rather than Parian Marble or Parian Chronicle)
Pausanias	Ἑλλάδος Περιήγησις	*Guide to Greece*
Polyaenus	Στρατηγήματα	*Strategemata*
pseudo-Scylax	Περίπλους	*Periplous*
pseudo-Scymnus	Περίοδος πρὸς Νικομήδη	*Periplous*
Stephanus of Byzantium	Ἐθνικά	*Ethnica*

The same basic practices were used for the titles of Latin literary works: the titles of more frequently cited texts (e.g., Cicero, *On the Laws*) are given in English translation, whereas less frequently cited Latin works are referred to in the Latin original.

Acknowledgments

Over the course of the decade on which we have worked on this project in one form or another, we have benefited greatly from the assistance of many individuals, institutions, and organizations. First and foremost, we would like to express our profound gratitude to the contributors to *OHAGW*. The need to cover a broad sweep of subject matter, without the possibility of skipping over areas about which one might initially at least be less than fully informed, and to synthesize the textual and material evidence, means, as we have all discovered, that writing a study for *OHAGW* is a Herculean labor. The willingness of *OHAGW*'s contributors to put in the requisite hard work and to persist in the face of manifold difficulties and delays is a testimony to their professionalism and dedication. We have learned an immense amount from reading the studies in *OHAGW*, and we are certain that *OHAGW*'s readers will, like its co-editors, be thankful to the contributors for sharing their remarkable expertise.

This project would not have been possible without support from the Trustees of the A.G. Leventis Foundation. Their generosity made it possible for Paul Christesen to spend the better part of two years in Cambridge working solely on *OHAGW*, and for Paul Cartledge, as an A.G. Leventis Senior Research Fellow (of Clare College, Cambridge), to dedicate much of his time to the project for the past near-decade. The Leventis Foundation also provided funding for two post-doctoral research associates—Drs. Estelle Strazdins and Carol Atack—who made enormous contributions to the almost inconceivable amount of editorial work necessary to bring this project to completion. Paul Christesen's time at Cambridge was also supported by a stipend from Clare Hall, which additionally provided pleasant living quarters and workspace along with a highly congenial intellectual community.

The deans of Dartmouth College's Arts and Sciences faculty have offered invaluable support on a continuing basis. That support made it possible to bring *OHAGW*'s contributors together in Hanover, New Hampshire, for a very productive conference in the spring of 2018 and helped fund leave time for Paul Christesen. Dartmouth also provided a grant that made it possible to hire a copy editor and project manager, Aurora McClain, who handled much of the logistical heavy lifting of the final stage of the project, and to hire two graduate students, Adlai Everett Lang and Evelyn Rick, who helped with editorial work. Another graduate student, Evan Levine, lent us his expertise in establishing the basic design used in virtually all the maps in *OHAGW*. Dartmouth also defrayed the cost of hiring undergraduate students who have been invaluable in moving *OHAGW* along. In addition to Duncan Antich, Ben Bonner, Albert Chen, Gray Christie, Ryan Fraser, Gracie Goodwin, Elizabeth Hadley, Shania Kee, Nathaniel Kramer, Anshul Lalan, Naomi Meron, Brian Morrison, Anindu Rentala, and Thomas Rover, we would like to single out for special mention Tim Hannan, who did most of the organizational work for the aforementioned conference, and Katie Goyette, who did a final round of editing on all of the *OHAGW* essays before they went to Oxford University Press.

Speaking of Oxford University Press, we cannot fail to mention Stefan Vranka, the commissioning editor. Stefan had the vision and patience to move *OHAGW* from concept to reality, and his enthusiastic support proved to be invaluable at every stage. The many colleagues who have offered assistance along the way are too numerous to name here, but we hope that they are aware of our appreciation of everything that they have done and continue to do for us. Last but by no means least, we would like to express our gratitude to our families. Editorial and authorial work take a special toll of their own, and our families have supported us in good times and bad.

BIBLIOGRAPHY

Burn, A. R. 1960. *The Lyric Age of Greece*. New York: St. Martin's Press. 2nd edition, 1978.

Christesen, P. 2007. *Olympic Victor Lists and Ancient Greek History*. Cambridge: Cambridge University Press.

Cockerell, C. R. 1819. "On the Aegina Marbles." *The Journal of the Science and the Arts* 6: 327–41.

Davies, J. K. 2009. "The Historiography of Archaic Greece." In *A Companion to Archaic Greece*, edited by K. Raaflaub and H. van Wees, 3–21. Malden, MA: Wiley-Blackwell.

Dittmann, L. 1991. "Zur Entwicklung des Stilbegriffs bis Winckelmann." In *Kunst and Kunsttheorie 1400–1900. Vorträge gehalten anläßlich des 22. Wolfenbütteler Symposions "Kunstgeschichte von Vasari bis Winckelmann" vom 1.–5.12.1987 und des 24. Wolfenbütteler Symposions "Kunstgeschichte seit Winckelmann" vom 27.11.–1.12.1988*, edited by P. Ganz and M. Gosebruch, 189–218. Wiesbaden: Harrassowitz.

Dodwell, E. 1819. *A Classical and Topographical Tour through Greece during the Years 1801, 1805, and 1806*. 2 vols. London: Rodwell and Martin.

Ellis, H. 1833. *The British Museum. Elgin and Phigaleian Marbles. Volume 1.* London: Charles Knight.

Étienne, R. 2017. "Introduction: Can One Speak of the Seventh Century BC?" In *Interpreting the Seventh Century BC: Tradition and Innovation. Proceedings of the International Colloquium Conference Held at the British School at Athens, 9th–11th December 2011*, edited by X. Charalambidou and C. A. Morgan, 9–14. Oxford: Archaeopress.

Evans, R. J. 2016. *Ancient Syracuse, from Foundation to Fourth Century Collapse*. London: Routledge.

Golden, M., and P. Toohey, eds. 1997. *Inventing Ancient Culture: Historicism, Periodization and the Ancient World*. London: Routledge.

Gorman, V. B. 2001. *Miletos, the Ornament of Ionia: A History of the City to 400 B.C.E.* Ann Arbor: University of Michigan Press.

Grote, G. 1846–1856. *History of Greece*. 12 vols. London: John Murray.

Hall, J. M. 1997. *Ethnic Identity in Greek Antiquity*. Cambridge: Cambridge University Press.

Hall, J. M. 2002. *Hellenicity: Between Ethnicity and Culture*. Chicago: University of Chicago Press.

Hall, J. M. 2014. *A History of the Archaic Greek World, ca. 1200–479 BCE*. 2nd ed. Chichester: Wiley-Blackwell.

Hansen, M. H., and T. H. Nielsen, eds. 2004. *An Inventory of Archaic and Classical Poleis*. Oxford: Oxford University Press.

Heuss, A. 1946. "Die archaische Zeit Griechenlands als geschichtliche Epoche." *Antike und Abendland* 2: 26–62. Now in *id.* 1995. *Gesammelte Schriften in 3 Bänden*. Stuttgart: Franz Steiner, vol. 1: 2–38.

Jeffery, L. H. 1976. *Archaic Greece: The City-States c. 700–500 B.C.* New York: St. Martin's Press.

Lange, A. 2015. "Die Entdeckung der Archaik—Ein ungeschriebenes Kapitel Wissenschaftsgeschichte. Die Etablierung des Terminus technicus "archaisch" in der Klassischen Archäologie in Deutschland." PhD diss., Humboldt-Universität zu Berlin.

Mac Sweeney, N. 2017. "Separating Fact from Fiction in the Ionian Migration." *Hesperia* 86: 379–421.

Osborne, R. 2009. *Greece in the Making, 1200–479 BC*. 2nd ed. London: Routledge.

Potts, A. 2000. *Flesh and the Ideal: Winckelmann and the Origins of Art History*. New Haven: Yale University Press.

Snodgrass, A. M. 1980. *Archaic Greece: The Age of Experiment*. Berkeley: University of California Press.

Thomas, R. 1992. *Literacy and Orality in Ancient Greece*. Cambridge: Cambridge University Press.

Vlassopoulos, K. 2018. "Marxism and Ancient History." In *How to Do Things with History: New Approaches to Ancient Greece*, edited by D. Allen, P. Christesen, and P. Millett, 209–35. New York: Oxford University Press.

Whibley, L., ed. 1905. *A Companion to Greek Studies*. Cambridge: Cambridge University Press.

Winckelmann, J. J. 1764. *Geschichte der Kunst des Alterthums*. Dresden: Waltherischen Hof-Buchhandlung.

I

Introduction

THERE ARE TWO good reasons why there are currently no books about Archaic Athens and Attica. First, it is both virtually impossible and conceptually problematic to divide an Archaic period in Athens and Attica from earlier periods. Athens has a continuous settlement history starting in the Bronze Age, and there is no point in the ever-changing archaeology at which a clean break occurs.[1] Although archaeologists have given different cultural phases different names, usually based on changes in pottery styles, many of these phases are only questionably distinct. This is particularly true of the two points at which scholars have been inclined to stop and start their accounts: the end of the last Bronze Age phase, LH (Late Helladic) IIIC, and the end of Late Geometric (LG). Distinguishing "LH IIIC late" from "Submycenaean" is close to arbitrary, and attempts to contrast LG IIB with Protoattic pottery face issues of changing pot use, as well as of workshops whose production falls into both categories.[2] Although striking changes occur at the time of the LG IIB—Protoattic transition, c. 700, in burials as well as in ceramics, it is as impossible to understand the eighth century without the seventh as to understand the seventh without the eighth.

Finding a place at which to end an account of Archaic Athens is equally problematic. Political histories tend to conclude treatments of the Archaic period either with the Persian Wars, or, in the case of Athens, with the fall of tyranny in 510. But, for Athens, the Persian Wars are much more important for

---

1. On the complications of identifying a "Dark Age," and the politics of that nomenclature, see Kotsonas 2016.

2. For problems involved in distinguishing LH IIIC late from Submycenaean, see Dickinson 2006: 14–15. It is notable that Mountjoy decides to include Submycenaean in her treatment of Mycenaean Athens (Mountjoy 1995, cf. Mountjoy 1999), whereas Privitera (2013) excludes the Submycenaean and ends at the end of LH IIIC. For the Late Geometric–Protoattic transition, see Brokaw 1963; Whitley 1994b: esp. 53; Denoyelle 1996; and the discussion in Section 4.5.3.

The Oxford History of the Archaic Greek World. Robin Osborne, Oxford University Press. © Oxford University Press 2023. DOI: 10.1093/oso/9780197644423.003.0001

their consequences, for what they started, than because they concluded anything; indeed, it is very curious, if time-honored, to end "the Persian Wars" in
479 given that active conflict with Persia continued for another three decades.
The Kleisthenic reforms, which followed the fall of the tyrants and introduced
democracy, certainly belong in the history of Classical Greece, but they cast a
bright light backwards, as well as forward, making it inappropriate to exclude
them from the discussion.

There is, however, a marked cultural change around the time of the Persian
wars. Tragedy was developed as a dramatic form in Athens at the end of the sixth
century (the precise date is disputed), and comedy was developed early in the
fifth century. Our earliest extant tragedy is Aeschylus' *Persians* of 472. In art there
was also a profound transformation, long known as the "Greek revolution," in
the early fifth century; this has usually been treated primarily as a stylistic change,
but in fact it was more far-reaching, affecting the sorts of scenes shown by sculptors and painters, as well as the manner in which those scenes were represented.[3]
Given all this, and since coverage must begin and end somewhere, I swallow my
scruples about periodization and begin my treatment in 800 and continue to
480, treating each date flexibly.

The second reason why there is no current book on Archaic Athens and Attica
is that the body of relevant material evidence available is, by the standards of
Classical archaeology, unusually large. Athens produced pottery in quantity from
the Protogeometric period (tenth century) onward, and in the sixth century that
pottery production was not only still more abundant, but it was also distributed
widely across the Mediterranean. From c. 600 Athenians were also commissioning and making stone sculpture on a large scale. From the middle of that century,
they were minting coins—again in ever-increasing quantities. Add to this the
large and important religious sanctuaries outside Athens—at Eleusis, Sounion,
and Brauron, in particular, as well as the large numbers of burials known from
the Kerameikos cemetery and elsewhere. And for all that we have little Athenian
literature surviving from the Archaic period, beyond the rich corpus of Solon's
poetry, we have significantly more from Athens than from most Greek cities in
the way of traditions about early history, as a result of the activities of the ancient
historians of Attica, the Atthidographers, and of the almost complete survival of
the Aristotelian *Constitution of the Athenians*.

It is hardly surprising, therefore, that no one previously has had the temer-
ity to put all this material together to tell a story about Archaic Athens and
Attica as a whole, covering its material culture as well as its economic, social,

---

3. For further discussion of this change, see Osborne 2018d.

and political history (although Rönnberg 2021a now comes close to doing this). What scholars have done is study different aspects of this story in great detail. That is true of certain particular periods (sometimes swept up in considerations of the whole of Greece in those periods) (Desborough 1972; Jeffery 1976; Snodgrass 2000; Coldstream 2003; Doronzio 2018; Arrington 2021). It is true of the various phases of Athenian pottery, of gravestones and their epigrams, and of free-standing sculpture.[4] It is also true of the burial record, although not yet of patterns of votive deposition (Kurtz and Boardman 1971; I. Morris 1987; Walter-Karydi 2015; cf. Papadopoulos and Smithson 2017).[5] On the historical front, it is true of Athenian constitutional arrangements, of Athenian finance, and of the politics of tyranny.[6] Although scholars have been keen to link the archaeology and the political and economic history in some areas, most notably to understand the reforms of Solon, they have been more generally content to focus narrowly and offer rather minimal contextualization.[7]

Pulling all these studies together, which is what I attempt to do here, is not simply a convenience to other scholars, although I hope that it is that. It is also an intellectual necessity. Political, social, economic, and cultural history are not independent, any more than material culture is independent of intellectual culture or visual culture of literary culture. If these areas of historical and archaeological study do not talk to each other, then they talk nonsense. Increasing attention is currently being devoted to the early history of Attica, as indicated by recent and forthcoming conferences, and while that in one sense makes this a bad moment to be trying to synthesize the various parts, it also makes it a moment at which such an attempt is vital. Building archaeological interpretations on shockingly naïve optimism about what writers composing their accounts hundreds of years later could know about their remote past, or pursuing analyses of artistic and material culture in ignorance of the world revealed in inscriptions or Solon's poetry, is not simply fatuous but dangerous. This book does not remotely claim to be the last word on the subject, but it does hope it might serve appropriately as the first word.

---

4. Protogeometric pottery: Desborough 1952. Geometric pottery: Rombos 1988; Boardman 1998a; Coldstream 2008; Coulié 2013. Protoattic pottery: J. M. Cook 1934–1935; Boardman 1998a; Rocco 2008; Coulié 2013. Attic black-figure pottery: Boardman 1974; Beazley 1986. Attic red-figure pottery: Boardman 1975; Robertson 1992. Gravestones and epigrams: Richter 1961; Jeffery 1962; Kissas 2000. *Kouroi*: Richter 1970. *Korai*: Richter 1968; Karakasi 2003.

5. On cult sites, see also van den Eijnde 2010.

6. Constitution: Hignett 1952. Finance: van Wees 2013. Tyranny: Lewis 1988; Andrewes 1982.

7. Forsdyke 2006 is the most serious attempt to situate Solon archaeologically.

The structure of the *Oxford History of the Archaic Greek World* separates out different aspects of the archaeology and history of each site for clarity of exposition, and does such things as put the history of pottery into the section on material culture but the history of sculpture into the section on cultural history. The order of the sections is indeed somewhat arbitrary, and it would make equally good sense for readers to read Section 8 immediately after Section 3, and Sections 9 and 11 before Section 5. At the expense of some repetition, I have attempted to discuss the different aspects of the Athenian record in terms that enable the overall shape of what is happening in Athens and Attica to be discerned, but inevitably readers will need to cross-reference extensively between sections. Those who like to know what the overall picture looks like before encountering detailed discussion are invited to start with the conclusion.

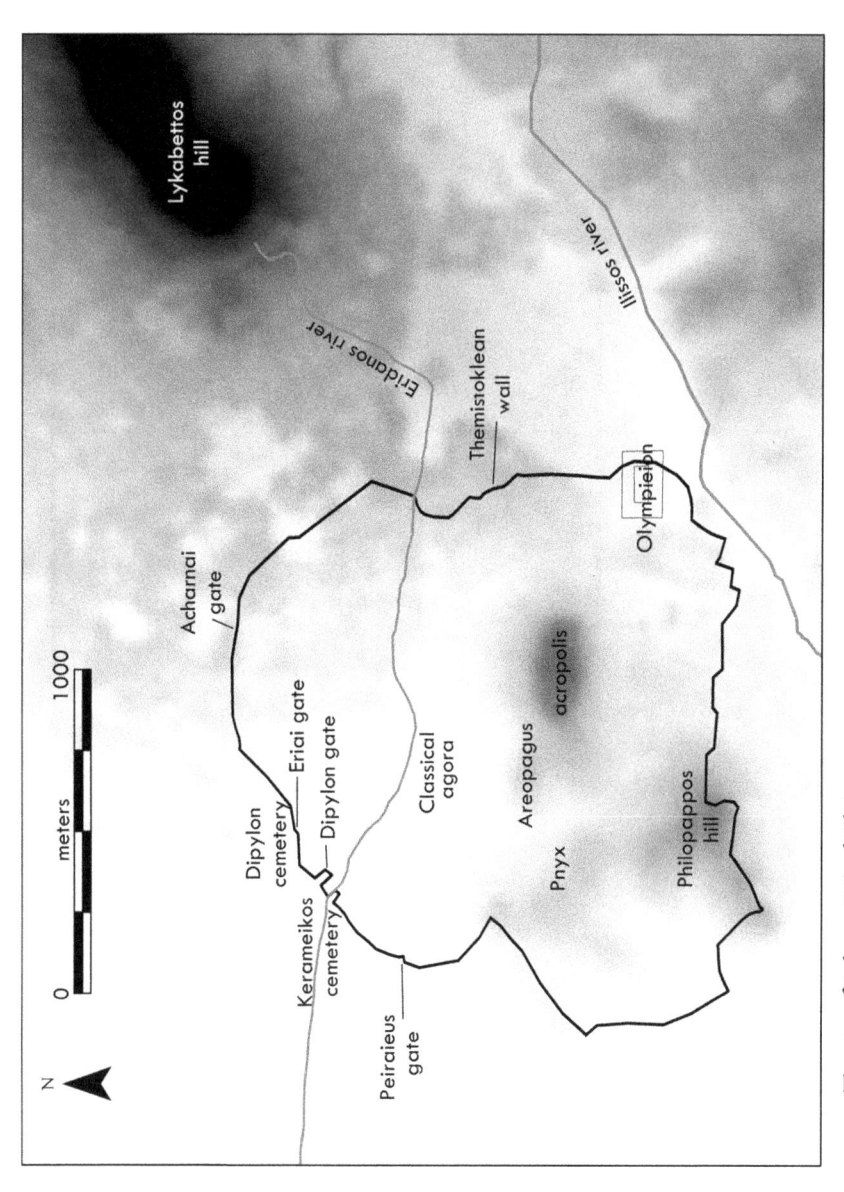

MAP 1 The city of Athens. © Paul Christesen 2022.

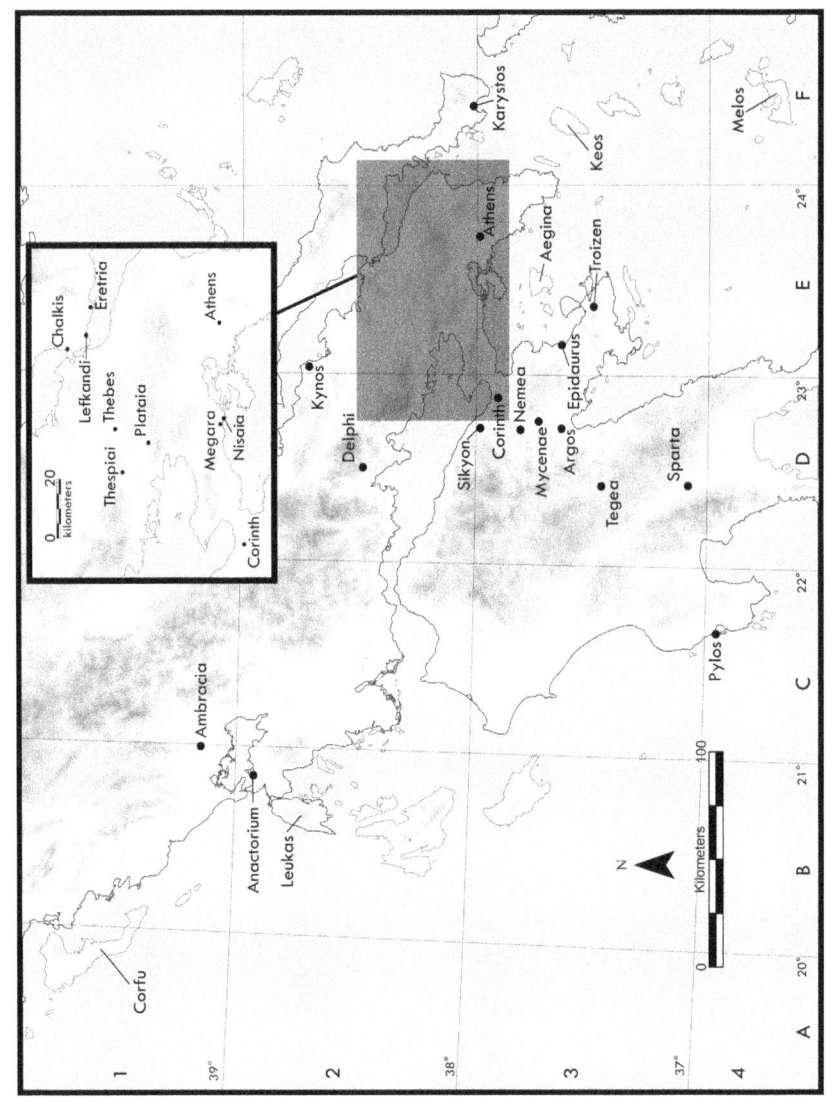

MAP 2   Some key sites in the immediate vicinity of Athens mentioned in this work. © Paul Christesen 2022.

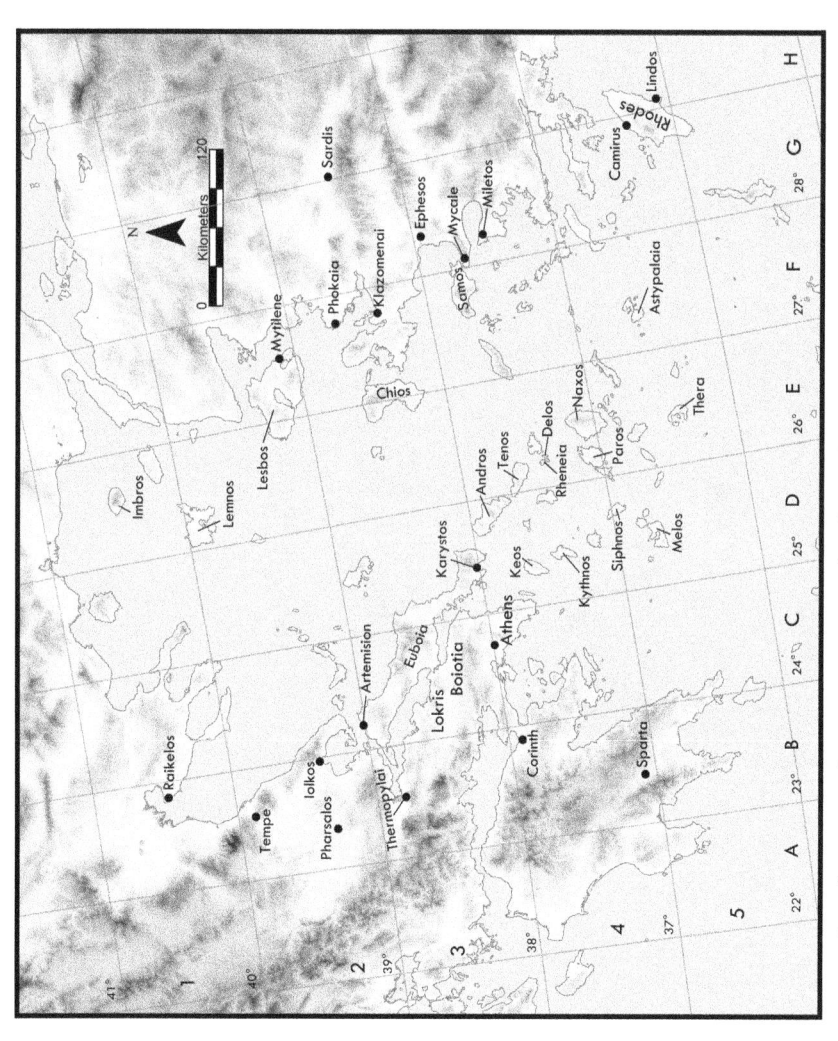

MAP 3 Some key sites in the Aegean mentioned in this work. © Paul Christesen 2022.

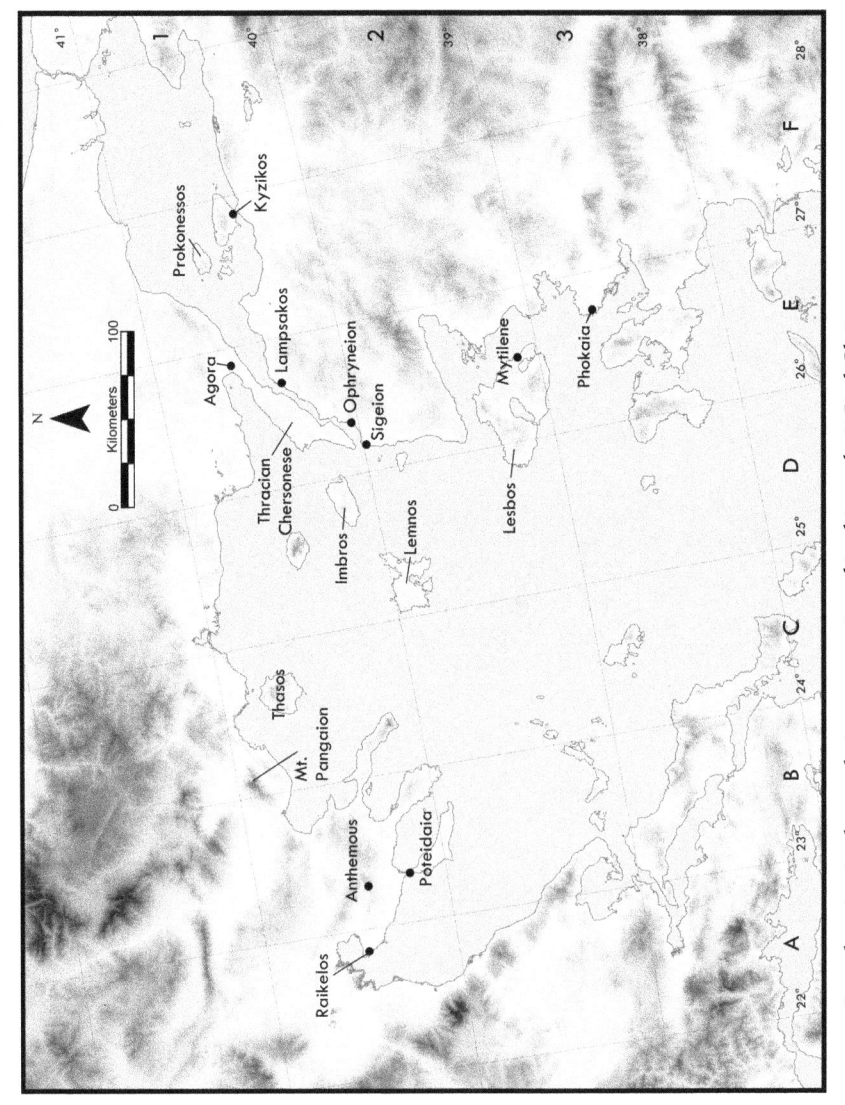

MAP 4   Some key sites in the north Aegean mentioned in this work. © Paul Christesen 2022.

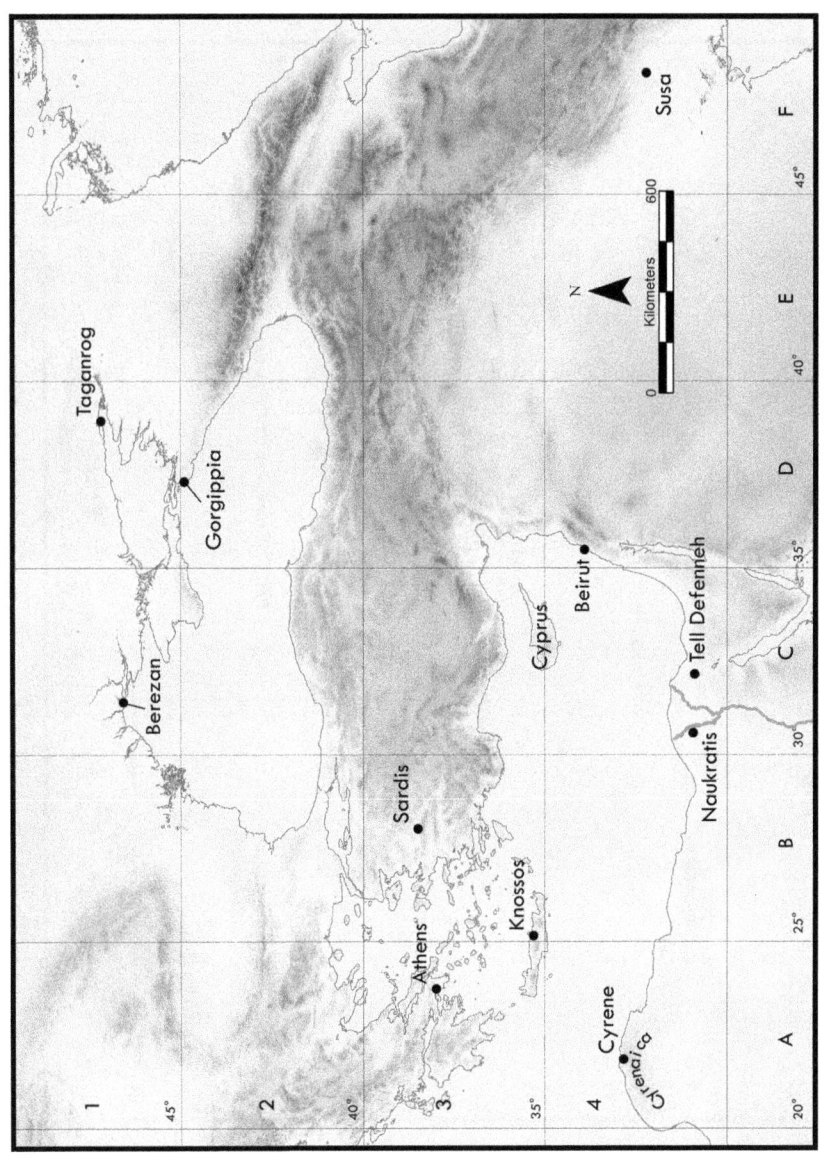

MAP 5 Some key sites in the eastern Aegean mentioned in this work. © Paul Christesen 2022.

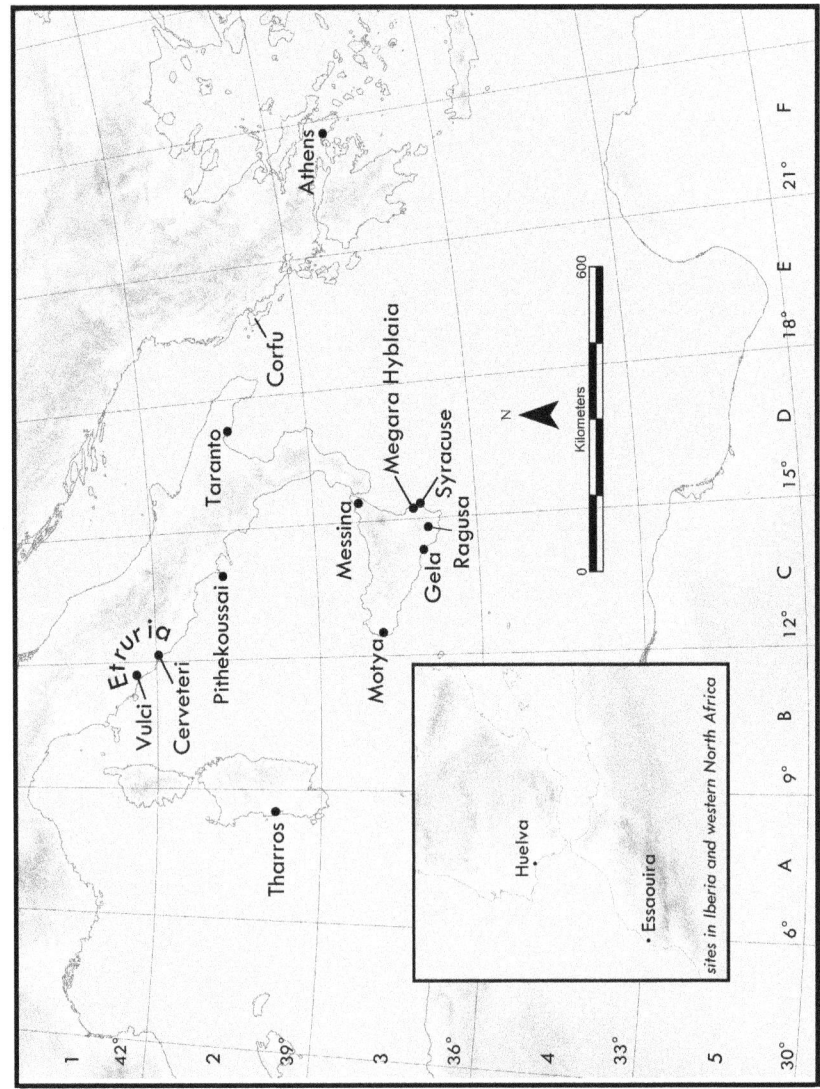

MAP 6 Some key sites in the central and western Mediterranean mentioned in this work. © Paul Christesen 2022.

2

Sources

2.1 Archaeological Evidence: A Brief History of Excavations in Athens and Attica

The monuments on the Athenian Acropolis have been continuously visible since antiquity; the Parthenon, Erechtheion, and Propylaia were all turned into churches, and the Parthenon was subsequently converted first into a cathedral and then, c. 1460, a mosque (Ousterhout 2005: 317).[1] So, too, the Classical temples at Sounion and Rhamnous remained visible. The writings of Cyriac of Ancona, who visited Athens in 1436 and 1444, brought those monuments to the attention of readers throughout Western Europe (Bodnar 2003; Bodnar 2015). The visible ruins of Athens were visited and described in the seventeenth century by, among others, the Marquis de Nointel (1674) and Jacques Spon and George Wheler (1676).[2]

The eighteenth century saw various scholarly missions, the most important being that sent by the Society of Dilettanti in London and led by James Stuart and Nicholas Revett. Stuart and Revett spent two years in Athens (1751–1753) and set about recording the visible antiquities with an unheard-of thoroughness and accuracy; their publications were highly influential on Greek Revival architecture, both in Britain and in America (Stuart and Revett 1762–1830; Stoneman 2010: 121–6). None of the buildings visible to and recorded by them antedated the fifth century BCE. Further expeditions sent by the Dilettanti led to the recording

---

1. For general histories of early travelers to Greece, see Eisner 1991; Stoneman 2010.

2. The Marquis de Nointel was accompanied by Jacques Carrey, who in the span of two weeks produced 55 drawings of the sculptures on the Parthenon (Wheler 1682; T. Bowie and Thimme 1971; Stoneman 2010: 69–81). Carrey's drawings, produced prior to the Venetian bombardment of the Parthenon in 1687, are a particularly valuable source of information about the sculptural program of the Parthenon.

The Oxford History of the Archaic Greek World. Robin Osborne, Oxford University Press. © Oxford University Press 2023. DOI: 10.1093/oso/9780197644423.003.0002

of antiquities at Eleusis (where the plan of the Telesterion was clear), Thorikos, Sounion, and Rhamnous in a volume entitled *The Unedited Antiquities of Attica*, published in 1817 (Porter, Roffe, Armstrong et al. 1817). One of the participants in those expeditions, J. P. Gandy, worked at Rhamnous and explored the small "Temple of Themis," which seems to have been built shortly after 480 and was the oldest building substantially surviving in Attica, as well as the Classical Temple of Nemesis.

The establishment of the Kingdom of Greece in 1833 rapidly led to Greeks taking control of their archaeology, and the archaeology of Athens first and foremost.[3] The Greek Archaeological Society was founded in 1837, and a program of removing later buildings from the Acropolis and reconstructing the classical buildings began. From 1850 onward excavations were undertaken, and it was at this point, as the southeast area of the Acropolis was dug, that substantial quantities of Archaic sculpture were recovered from the pits where what had been destroyed by the Persian sack in 480 had been buried. Later in the century (1885–1890) systematic excavation of the entire Acropolis summit uncovered the foundations of the late Archaic temple of Athena Polias between the Erechtheion and Parthenon.

Excavation of parts of the classical Athenian Agora was undertaken in 1859–1862 and 1898–1902 by the Greek Archaeological Society and in 1896–1897 and 1907–1908 by the German Archaeological Institute, but systematic investigation of the area, by the American School of Classical Studies in Athens, began only in 1931.[4] The Kerameikos cemetery had begun to be systematically explored by the Greek Archaeological Society from 1870 onward, and, in 1913, the Kerameikos was entrusted to the German Archaeological Institute for further investigation (Banou and Bournias 2014; Stroszeck 2014). Both these long-running excavations have yielded enormous quantities of archaeological material that have been, and are still being, published in impressive detail. A key publication venue for the Agora excavations is the *Athenian Agora* series, the first volume of which was published in 1953 and additions to which continue to be made (with volume 38 appearing in 2017). A similar series, *Kerameikos: Ergebnisse der Ausgrabungen*, exists for the Kerameikos; volume 1 appeared in 1939, volume 22 in 2018.

The countryside of Attica (map 7) was meticulously mapped by the Prussian army, under the supervision of the German archaeologist Ernst Curtius and cartographer Johann August Kaupert, between 1875 and 1881, with antiquities picked

---

3. For a detailed account of archaeological activity in Greece since 1828, see Petrakos 2013.

4. An attractive pictorial history of the Agora excavations, including an account of the area in the nineteenth century, is provided by Mauzy 2009.

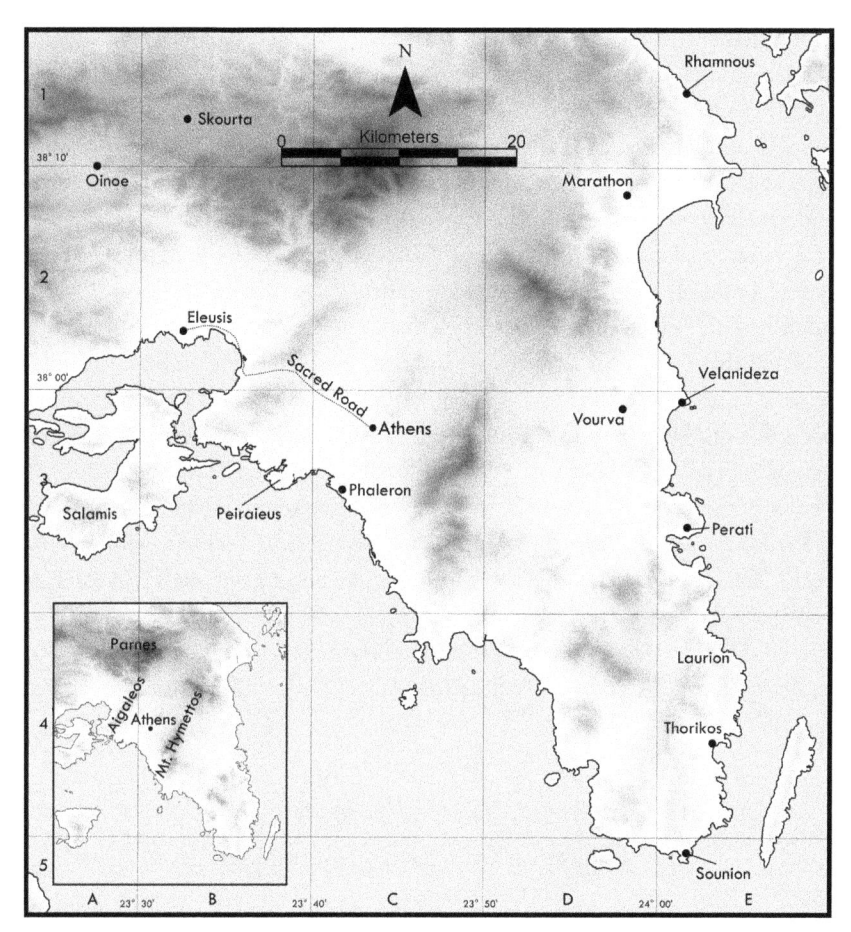

MAP 7 Some key sites in Attica mentioned in Section 2. © Paul Christesen 2022.

out in red. Arthur Milchhoefer wrote commentaries on these maps describing the visible antiquities in careful detail (Curtius, Kaupert, and Milchhoeffer 1881–1900). The Greek Archaeological Society made its first excavations at Rhamnous in 1880 (returning more seriously in 1890–1892), at Eleusis in 1882, at Thorikos in 1888 and 1893 (there had been earlier American excavations there in 1885 and 1886), and at Sounion in 1897. Valerios Staïs, who was responsible for the excavations at Sounion, Thorikos, and the 1890s excavations at Rhamnous, also excavated Archaic burials at Vourva and Velanideza in the Mesogeia,[5] and the tomb of the Athenians at Marathon.

---

5. On the Mesogeia, the plain between the Hymettos and the sea, Pendele and Laurion, see Section 3.1.

During the twentieth and twenty-first centuries the Greek Archaeological Service has undertaken rescue excavations all over Attica, as well as in Athens itself, as the massive expansion of the modern city has brought antiquities to light; since 1960 all such excavations have been reported in *Archaiologikon Deltion*. More extensive excavations have also been conducted in cemeteries at Eleusis, Perati, and Phaleron; in the fort and adjacent settlement at Rhamnous; at the Sanctuary of Artemis at Brauron; and all around Velatouri hill at Thorikos. With the exception of Brauron, for which only annual reports and some specialist studies were published, these extensive excavations have received exemplary publication.[6]

Attica has been much walked over by archaeologists, but it has been the site of relatively little systematic intensive archaeological survey. Hans Lohmann carried out a one-man survey of the area west of Sounion (Lohmann 1993), and surveys have also been carried out along the border between Attica and Boiotia, in particular in the Skourta plain and around Oinoe (Munn and Zimmerman-Munn 1989; Munn and Zimmerman-Munn 1990; Papangeli, Fachard, and Knodell 2018). The extensive remains above ground in the mining region of Laurion have been particularly well recorded, but only small-scale excavations have been conducted there, revealing nothing Archaic.[7] Likewise excavation of rural establishments has been limited in extent and has uncovered nothing from the archaic period.[8]

2.2 Textual Sources

2.2.1 Epigraphic Sources from Archaic Athens

Athens can claim more writing than any other Archaic city, although exactly how much depends upon whether one includes all writing on pottery, both painted and scratched. There are several hundred Archaic epitaphs and dedicatory inscriptions, and thousands of inscriptions on pottery. Athens also claims some of the oldest

---

6. Eleusis: Mylonas 1975. Perati: Iakovidis 1969. Phaleron: Young 1942. For more recent excavations see: https://asu.pure.elsevier.com/en/projects/an-archaeological-study-of-the-ancient-phaleron-cemetery-near-ath-5 (accessed 7/9/20); Ingvarsson, Bäckstrom, Chryssoulaki et al. 2019; Prevedorou and Buikstra 2019; http://phaleron.digital-ascsa.org. Rhamnous: Petrakos 1999a. Thorikos: nine volumes of Preliminary reports (*Thorikos I–IX*, 1968–1990), three volumes of final reports, *Fouilles de Thorikos I–III* (1977–2006).

7. Conophagos 1980 has an invaluable map, but there have been numerous more recent archaeological investigations of particular features (note especially Photos-Jones and Ellis-Jones 1994); see also Goette 2000; Kakavogiannis 2005.

8. For excavations at the Dema house, by the Dema Wall between Parnes and Aigaleos, and at the house on the lower slopes of Hymettos above Vari, see J. E. Jones, Sackett, and Graham 1962; J. E. Jones, Graham, and Sackett 1973.

FIGURE 1 Late Geometric II oinochoe; c. 740; height: c. 23 cm; from a tomb in the Dipylon cemetery. This oinochoe features the earliest long inscription from Attica proclaiming this jug (full of wine?) to be a prize to be given to a dancer. Athens National Archaeological Museum 192.

extensive writing from anywhere in the Greek world, in the form of a graffito on a Late Geometric II oinochoe from the Dipylon cemetery. This graffito around the neck of the oinochoe (see Figure 1) proclaims it to be a prize for "Whoever of the dancers dances most friskily" (the reading and meaning of the final adverb is not certain).[9] Extensive early graffiti, including dedications, some abecedaria and sexual abuse ("bugger" [κατάπυγον]), have been found on sherds from the Sanctuary of Zeus on the peak of Mt. Hymettos (M. K. Langdon 1976: 9–50; see further Sections 9.3 and 11.1). Seventh-century graffiti from Athens and Attica include names, ownership inscriptions (some of these on "SOS" amphoras), and, in one case, a term of abuse ("The boy is sex-mad" [μίσετος]) (H. R. Immerwahr 1990: 11, 13). The earliest certain writing that is painted, as opposed to scratched, on Athenian pottery, and so certainly written in the potter's workshop, dates to the seventh century: there are what are probably mythological names (Antenor and Menela(o)s, see Section 4.5.3), but also one painted ownership inscription ("I belong to –ylos" [–ύλο εἰμί]), and a possible painted dedicatory inscription, but

9. All early Athenian inscribed material is reviewed by Jeffery 1990: 66–78, 431–3. For the Dipylon jug, see H. R. Immerwahr 1990: 7, and, most recently, Binek 2017. See further Section 10.

no signatures (H. R. Immerwahr 1990: 7–10). From the very beginning of black-figure pottery, in the last quarter of the seventh century, identification of figures and signatures of painters and potters are common.

Inscriptions on stone are harder to date than those on pottery, but the earliest seem to be two grave *stēlai*. One of those *stēlai*, found in the Cave of Pan on Hymettos above Vari, bears a single male name in the genitive; the other, the understanding of whose more extensive text is disputed, comes from Athens itself and commemorates a woman (*IG* I³.1194, 1247; H. R. Immerwahr 1990: 23). From the beginning of the sixth century (there are two possibly seventh-century examples) we have inscribed dedications from the Athenian Acropolis and from the sanctuaries at Brauron, Eleusis, Ikarion, Sounion, and elsewhere, and throughout the sixth century we have a rich sequence of funerary inscriptions, many in verse, from all over Attica as well as from Athens itself.[10] Peisistratos' son Hipparchos was responsible for having herms inscribed in verse put up halfway between Athens and each of the demes, and one of these partially survives (*IG* I³.1023; P. A. Hansen 1983–1989: vol. 1: #304; see Section 11.3).

The inscription of public decisions on stone comes only after the democratic reforms of Kleisthenes. The earliest extant decree, concerning the sending of settlers to Salamis, seems to date before 500; four other decrees, all about religious matters, seem more or less certainly to date to the first two decades of the fifth century (*IG* I³.1–5; Section 11.4).[11]

2.2.2 Literary Sources

2.2.2.1 *Literary Sources from Archaic Athens*

From the Archaic period, the only extant literary sources from Athens take the form of poetry, and indeed the only certainly Athenian poet of whom any verses

---

10. The classic publication of Acropolis dedications is Raubitschek and Jeffery 1949. See also Kissas 2000 and *IG* I³.589–687, and for dedications on bronze, *IG* I³.526–8. For dedications from Attica, see *IG* I³.984, 988–92, 1009, 1015, 1018ter, 1024 and Kissas 2000. For Archaic Attic grave epigrams, see Jeffery 1962; P. A. Hansen 1983–1989: vol. 1:1–78; Kissas 2000; and Section 4.4.4 .

11. The basic collection of inscribed material from Archaic Athens and Attica is contained in the volumes of *Inscriptiones Graecae* devoted to inscriptions dated before 403 (*IG* I) of which the latest, third, edition (*IG* I³) dates to 1981, 1994, and (indexes) 1998. English translations of a substantial and constantly growing number of Attic inscriptions can be found at https://www.atticinscriptions.com/. New epigraphic material, and new interpretations of old epigraphic material, are collected annually in the volumes of *Supplementum Epigraphicum Graecum*. Writing painted on pottery is collected in H. R. Immerwahr 1990, but a fuller database is available online at https://avi.unibas.ch.

are extant is Solon. Solon's poetry, unlike the poetry of many Archaic poets, has not been found on papyri from Egypt: we rely entirely on quotations of the poetry by later authors (*in primis* the author of the Aristotelian *Constitution of the Athenians* and Plutarch), most frequently quotations made in the attempt to shed light on Solon's political actions (see Section 12.3).

The earliest Athenian prose writer of whom we know is the genealogist and mythographer Pherekydes, who seems to have written in the decades following the Persian Wars. Pherekydes tells us nothing about Archaic history as such, but the wealth of stories that he was able to collect and put together in his matter-of-fact way gives a potential insight into the world of reference for Archaic Athenians that has yet to be fully exploited, and of which only occasional names on painted pottery and some hero cults otherwise give us even a glimpse.[12]

2.2.2.2 Literary Sources about Archaic Athens

Both great fifth-century historians, Herodotos and Thucydides, had a particular interest in the early history of Athens. Herodotos famously, indeed infamously, was explicit in his judgment that it was the actions of the Athenians that were crucial to the Greeks winning the Persian Wars (7.139). Scholars have considered that the very structure of Herodotos' *Histories*, and particularly its enigmatic ending, was designed to warn Athens about the potential consequences of her fifth-century imperial behavior (Moles 2002; Fowler 2003). If we take that line, then the whole *Histories* is, in a sense, built around Athens, and it is not surprising that special attention is paid to Athens at the time of Kroisos in Book 1 (1.59–64) and to the Kleisthenic creation of Athenian democracy in Book 5 (5.62–78).

Herodotos shows detailed knowledge of Athenian family traditions at various points—the Gephyraioi (the family to which both Harmodios and Aristogeiton belonged, 5.57), the Philaidai (the family of Kimon and Miltiades, 6.103), and above all the Alkmaionidai (the family of Megakles and Kleisthenes). The family history of the Alkmaionidai surfaces at various points in the *Histories*, but particularly at 6.125–131, where Herodotos defends them against the claim that they sent a shield-signal to the Persians at Marathon. Scholars have speculated that Herodotos was particularly dependent upon an Alkmaionid source, and there is no doubt that the Alkmaionidai of Herodotos' time preserved stories about the family past (Thomas 1989: 238–82, esp. 64–82). There are various ancient traditions of Herodotos having spent some time in Athens, and we should reckon him generally well aware of the variety of stories of their past that the Athenians told. However, his enterprise was not to write Archaic Greek history but to explain

---

12. On Pherekydes, see Fowler 2000: 272–364; Fowler 2013: 706–27.

why the encounter between Greeks and Persians turned out as it did. It is perhaps for this reason that Solon figures in Herodotos primarily as a wise adviser, in the context of a historically unlikely encounter between him and Kroisos, rather than as an Athenian law-giver, although Herodotos is clearly well aware of his law-making activities (1.29, 2.177.2).[13]

Thucydides' concern for Archaic Athenian history is even more limited. Although he gives Athens a special place in his opening account of early Greek history (1.2.5), and gives Athens a leading role in some particular trends (abandoning weapons, adopting a more luxurious mode of life, 1.6.3), he has no interest in anything that happened between Theseus' *synoikismos* (2.15, see Section 4.1.1) and the fall of the tyrants, except for the failed coup of Kylon, which he discusses to explain the curses on the Alkmaionidai invoked by the Spartans (1.126, see Section 5.2.1). Neither Solon nor Kleisthenes is mentioned. The one episode of Archaic Athenian history that attracts extended treatment is the killing of Hipparchos, which Thucydides discusses at length to show how little the Athenians knew about their own history (6.53.3–9, cf. 1.20.2; see Section 5.2.3). The building of fortifications around the Peiraieus attracts Thucydides' attention because this had been Themistokles' initiative (1.93.3; see Section 7.1.2).

Athenian tragedy was much concerned with Athens, but it was the Athens of the time of Theseus on which it concentrated (Mills 1997). Historical material was rarely the basis of tragedy, and the only tragedy we know of about Athenian history was Aeschylus' *Persians*, at the center of which was the Battle of Salamis. Attic Old Comedy was more inclined to allude to the historical past, and it was relatively uninterested in Theseus (mentioned just once in extant Aristophanes). Aristophanes alludes on two occasions to Solon and his laws (*Clouds* 1187, *Birds* 1660–1666), and repeatedly to Harmodios and Aristogeiton. Comic fragments suggest that Solon and Harmodios were the main Archaic Athenians referred to by other playwrights too (Kratinos linking Solon with Drako), though Eupolis also mentioned Peisistratos. It was the Battle of Marathon and the generation of those who fought there that Aristophanes most revisited, in at least eight different plays, and Eupolis and Hermippos seem to have referred to them similarly. Salamis comes a poor second in Aristophanes, figuring in just two plays, and no other comic dramatist seems to have mentioned Salamis at all.

This picture of the selectivity of Classical Athenians' engagement with their Archaic history is reinforced by what we find in Plato. Solon again figures significantly, Hipparchos gets a dialog named after him, and the tyrannicide episode is explored. But beyond that there is very little. Nor is the picture seriously different

---

13. For Herodotos on Archaic Greek history more generally, see Osborne 2002.

in the case of Isocrates and Demosthenes. Isocrates makes repeated references to Theseus, and Solon attracts his attention and praise in a number of speeches, as wise man, sophist, and founder of Athenian democracy. Peisistratos is mentioned twice, but his sons not at all. Kleisthenes gets mentioned for the expulsion of the tyrants and the restoration of democracy. Marathon is repeatedly alluded to, but Salamis only once. Demosthenes makes much of Solon and engages also with Harmodios and Aristogeiton; Aeschines refers to Solon and the battles of the Persian wars, but that is essentially all (Clarke 2008: 254–74).

However, the fourth century saw the development of local history as a genre, and a series of writers, most of them Athenians, who have become known as the Atthidographers, set about unearthing the early history of their city.[14] The earliest of these *Atthides* was that of Hellanikos of Lesbos, who is referred to by Thucydides (1.97.2). Hellanikos' history of Athens, the full version of which was published after c. 400, began in Athens' distant past, certainly mentioned events of 407/6, and presumably went down to the end of the Peloponnesian War.[15] The earlier parts of Hellanikos' history seem to have been built around the reigns of the Athenian kings, the later parts around archon years. Thucydides is critical of Hellanikos' chronology of fifth-century events, and his chronology of earlier events is not likely to have been more accurate, but it was surely influential (Hellanikos is regularly quoted down to and beyond Plutarch).

During the fourth century, successive, rival *Atthides* were written by Kleidemos, Androtion, and Phanodemos. These works survive only as quoted by later authors, but were, among other things, important sources for the research student responsible for the Aristotelian *Constitution of the Athenians* (Rhodes 1981: 15–30; Sickinger 2003; for Androtion, see Harding 1994). We know that both Androtion and Phanodemos were engaged in Athenian politics, and what they wrote about early Athenian history was also politically engaged. Kleidemos' *Atthis* was divided into four books, two of which dealt with Athenian history down to Kleisthenes. Androtion wrote eight books, even the second of which took history well down into the fifth century. Phanodemos is known to have written nine books and seems to have been discussing late sixth-century history still in book nine. Certainly, the great majority of surviving quotations of his work

---

14. The classic study of the *Atthis* is Jacoby 1949; the fragments of the Atthidographers are collected in Jacoby's *FGrH* #323a–334 with commentary, in English, in Part III b (Supplement). The fragments are translated, and ordered by event rather than author, in Harding 2008. For a recent discussion, see Thomas 2019: 358–85.

15. For Hellanikos' contribution to the traditions about the Athenian kings, see Fowler 2013: 447–93. On Hellanikos more generally, see Pearson 1942: 1–26; Jacoby *FGrH* 323a; Fowler 2013: 682–95.

concern matters of cult or the kings. One of the political actions of Phanodemos of which evidence survives is a proposal to honor the hero Amphiaraos, and it seems likely that it is the history of Athenian cults that occupied most of the extensive space that he gave to early history. The Atthidographer of whom we have most surviving, Philochoros, who wrote in the third century, devoted fewer than three books of the 17 books of his *Atthis* to Athenian history down to the end of the sixth century (Harding 1994: 9–35).

Many of the quotations that survive from the Atthidographers concern religious festivals or political institutions (e.g., the Areopagus), and it is likely that the *Atthides* traced the origins of these to particular kings or other named individuals and then described their nature. The lexicographer Harpokration, for instance (s.v. Παναθήναια), tells us that both Hellanikos and Androtion traced the Panathenaia back to Erichthonios son of Hephaistos. The way in which the *Atthides* survive, only in later quotations, no doubt reinforces the impression that these works were more compilations of information than connected histories, but at least for the period before the Persian Wars that is what they seem to have been. All the signs are that these works reflected the regular structure of oral history—that is, that there was a "floating gap" between early history, on which much attention was lavished, and recent history (Vansina 1985: 23). Later writers quoted both Androtion and Philochoros on Solon's "Seisachtheia," but it is striking that this is the only explicit discussion of Solon's laws that gets reflected in the fragments. We have clearly lost a great deal with the loss of the works of the Atthidographers, but we almost certainly have not lost a tightly argued narrative history of Athens (for all the recent resistance to terming local historians "antiquarian," Thomas 2019: 143–50, 327, 40).

The importance of the Aristotelian *Constitution of Athens* lies therefore not only in its survival, but also in the fact that its author tried to write a connected history of Athens, with an exclusive focus on the constitution. Something of the agenda of the Aristotelian *Constitutions*, of which there were 158 (according to Diog. Laert. 5.27), can be gathered from Aristotle's own *Politics*, where both Solon (at some length) and Kleisthenes get discussed, but Theseus and the kings go unmentioned, and religious festivals are notoriously ignored.[16] The *Constitution of Athens* seems to have kept very much to this agenda, for although the lost beginning does appear to have discussed the kings, Ion, and Theseus, the focus of the historical part is very much on constitutional changes, from Drako onward. While the four pages or so of early history that we have lost probably derived from the Atthidographers, the extensive treatment of Solon, with long

---

16. For a recent discussion of the relationship between the Aristotelian *Politeiai* and the tradition of *polis* history, see Thomas 2019: 358–85.

quotations from his poetry, is not in the style of any existing Atthidographic fragment, and it may derive from a separate work on Solon also used by Plutarch for
his *Solon*. Much of the treatment of Peisistratos and Kleisthenes derives from a
reading of Herodotos. There is sufficient inconsistency between passages to indicate that the Aristotelian compiler had taken the trouble to amass information
from a range of sources, although whether he did any original historical research
is unclear.

Two much later works are also of some importance. Plutarch's *Lives*, written around 100 CE, are invaluable for showing what stories had built up around
Theseus and Solon. Plutarch was enormously widely read, and his work gives us
the best chance of understanding the world created by the enormous quantities of historical writing of the Hellenistic period, now almost totally lost to us.
Pausanias, who wrote his *Guide to Greece* during the second century CE, was also
very well read, but in addition derived much knowledge from talking to people
at the sites he visited and looking closely at inscriptions.[17] Although the Persian
destruction ensured that at Athens there was little that belonged to the Archaic
period to see, Pausanias remains useful not least for his own clear sense that the
Archaic Greek world looked different.

---

17. For the classic modern discussion, see Habicht 1985; see also Pretzler 2007: 39–42.

3

Natural Setting

3.1 Geography and Geology

In the Classical period the territory of the Athenian state included everything south of the Parnes mountain range and covered some 2,400 sq km, thus constituting the largest territory of any mainland city state, bar only Sparta.[1] Cut off from central Greece by the Parnes range (1413 m) and from the Peloponnese by Mt. Trikeraton (465 m), the territory of Attica was itself divided into distinct plains by mountain barriers (see Map 8; for the relationship of those barriers to early settlement patterns, see Section 4.1.1).

On the western side of Attica lay Eleusis and the Thriasian plain, effectively isolated by the convergence of the Parnes and Aigaleos (469 m) ranges. Parnes and Aigaleos are the oldest of the series of nappes that dominate the geological structure of Attica; they are formed of Triassic limestone of the Pelagonian zone. South of these the underlying rocks are schists and marbles of the Attic–Cycladic belt that also produces the fine marbles of Euboia, Naxos, and Paros (M. D. Higgins and Higgins 1996: 28).

Southeast of Aigaleos, Athens itself lay at the upper, eastern end of a triangular basin formed by faulting and by the erosion of Cretaceous marles and shales, bounded by Hymettos (highest point 1026 m) on the south and east and drained by the rivers Kephissos and Ilissos. The settlement of Athens was itself loosely bounded on the north and west by the river Eridanos and on the east by the river Ilissos; immediately north of the Eridanos the hill of Lykabettos rose steeply. Lykabettos, the Acropolis, and Philopappos (Mouseion) hill are all Late Cretaceous limestones (M. D. Higgins and Higgins 1996: 28).

---

1. The fullest geographical description of Attica is provided by Philippson 1952: 753–939. On the geology of Athens, see M. D. Higgins and Higgins 1996: 28–34.

The Oxford History of the Archaic Greek World. Robin Osborne, Oxford University Press. © Oxford University Press 2023. DOI: 10.1093/oso/9780197644423.003.0003

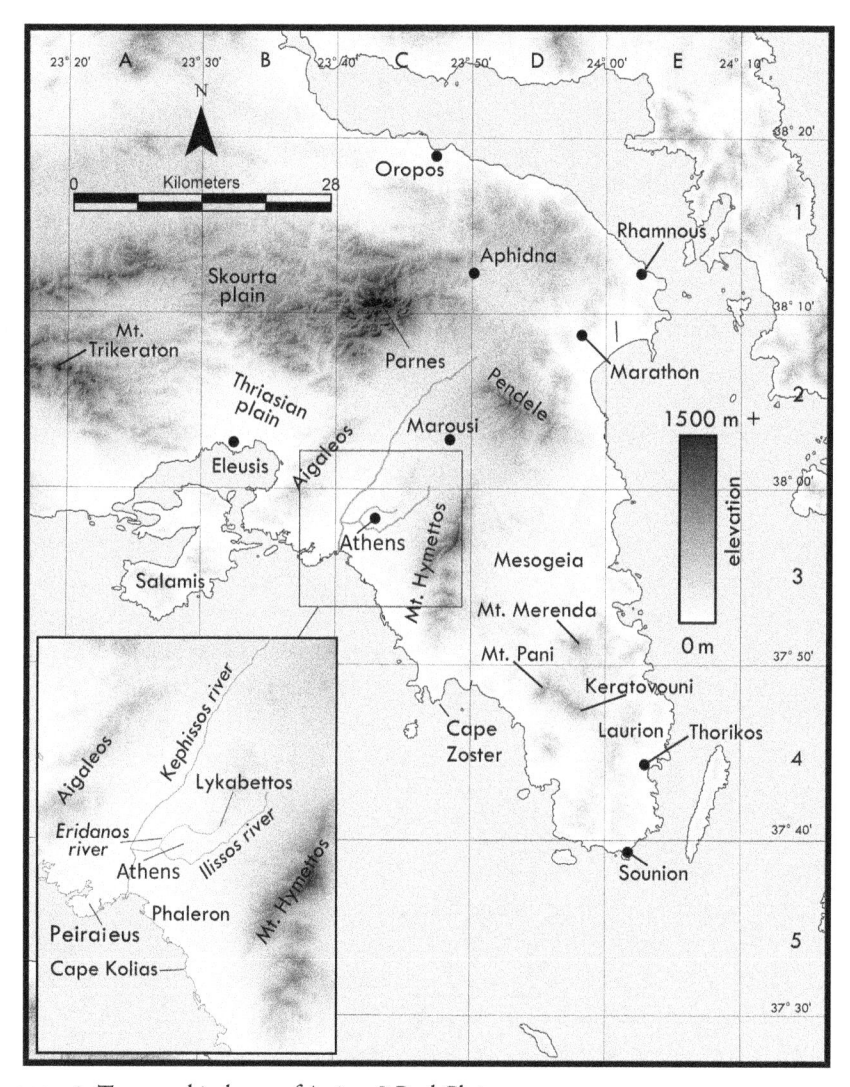

map 8 Topographical map of Attica. © Paul Christesen 2022.

East of Hymettos and bounded to the north by Pendele (highest point 1108 m), to the east by the sea, and to the south by the rising lands that become the mining area of Laurion, lay the Mesogeia, Attica's largest plain. North of the Mesogeia and east of Pendele was the coastal plain of Marathon. North again, between Pendele and Parnes was a relatively narrow corridor past Aphidna, important in antiquity as the corridor through which passed traffic to Euboia via Oropos. The territory of Oropos was controlled by Athens at some points in the Classical period, but not in the Archaic period.

South of the Mesogeia was a landscape of hills with at best small coastal plains; several hills rise to over 600 m (Mt. Merenda 612 m, Keratovouni 650 m, Mt. Pani 635 m), while the hills of the Laurion region are lower, the highest being Vigla Rimbari at 372 m. The geology of the Laurion region consists of alternating layers of marble and schist, between which seams rich in lead and silver were trapped.[2]

Attica was variously enriched by its geology. As well as the silver and lead of Laurion, the Athenians had fine sources of white and gray marble on both Hymettos and Pendele, and extensive ancient quarries remain visible, despite more recent exploitation, although the major Pendele quarries seem to have been significantly exploited only from the end of the sixth century on. Less fine, but adequate for architectural use at Sounion in the fifth century, was the marble from the Laurion area, where again ancient quarries can be traced. Attica, and in particular the area northeast of Athens around modern Marousi (ancient Athmonon) also had extremely fine clay beds, responsible for clay that produces the high quality and distinctive color of Athenian pottery.[3]

The long coastline of Attica offers a number of rival harbors or beaching facilities (Phaleron, Sounion, Thorikos, Porto Raphti (Prasiai), Rhamnous), such that the great harbor of the Peiraieus came into its own only when Athens needed to shelter a large fleet (see Section 8.3). Even today Attica maintains ports, Raphina and Lavrion, on the east coast, and the Peiraieus on the west.

3.2 Vegetation and Climate

It is not easy to gain a picture of the vegetation in Attica in antiquity. Parnes was almost certainly covered with woods, but perhaps not to the extent that it was in the eighteenth and nineteenth centuries and is today. Reduction in arable agriculture has, in Attica as in the rest of Greece, allowed forests to expand (Rackham 1983: 334–5, 38). Charcoal-burning, for which the area of Acharnai is famous because of Aristophanes' *Acharnians*, relied upon the products of the maquis rather than on wood from forests. It was charcoal, similarly, that was required for the enormous smelting activity required by the Laurion mines in the Classical period. (Agriculture is further discussed in Section 8.1.)

Reconstructing ancient climate has attracted much attention, particularly in the context of contemporary climate change, but it is fraught with difficulty, and there is no general agreement as to whether the climate in antiquity was

---

2. This is clearly mapped in Conophagos 1980. See also Morin and Photiades 2005.

3. Attic clay beds, glaze, and pottery production are discussed in Chaviara 2019.

significantly different from today.[4] The strong argument from plant communities is that the climate of the Archaic and Classical periods was broadly parallel to that today, although there is some evidence that winters may have been slightly colder and rainfall slightly more abundant (Grove and Rackham 2001: 141–3). Certainly, there is no reason to think that the seasonal pattern of the climate was different, whatever the case with average temperatures or annual rainfall. In the present-day, Attica is among the driest areas on the Greek mainland, with an average annual rainfall of less than 400 mm, but in temperatures it falls between extremes, with frost and snow rare, other than on the mountains, and summer temperatures relatively moderate. (Climate is further discussed in Section 8.1, in relation to agriculture).

4. Discussion has particularly concerned the possible role of climate change in bringing the Bronze Age to an end; see the useful review by Knapp and Manning 2016: 102–12. For a broader review of Mediterranean climate data over the last six thousand years, see Finné et al. (2011).

4

Material Culture

4.1 Settlement Pattern

4.1.1 The Late Bronze Age through the End of
the Eighth Century

4.1.1.1 The Literary Tradition

The Homeric Catalog of Ships already treats all inhabitants of Athens as
Athenians (*Il.* 2.546–56; Kirk 1985: 179). The Catalog certainly contains knowledge of Mycenaean Greece, since it includes places without eighth- or seventh-
century occupation, but equally clearly it has been "updated" in various ways
that show, in some cases, accumulating ignorance of Bronze Age political geography, and in others the effect of contemporary political geography.[1] Whether,
in the case of Athens, what is reflected is Bronze-Age or eighth-century reality
is arguable. Mycenaean Athens was certainly not the same sort of powerful center that we find at Mycenae and Pylos, but that does not necessarily mean there
was no sense of political unity in Attica in the Late Bronze Age (Papadimitriou
2017; Osborne 2020a; Papadimitriou and Cosmopoulos 2020). According to
their own myth-history, forged in the fifth century, the Athenians had always
lived in Attica, they were "autochthonous," born from the earth itself (Loraux
1986: 149–50, 93–4, 277–8, 331–3; Rosivach 1987; Loraux 1993: 3–22, 37–71;
Pelling 2009). But fifth-century Athenian writers, and plausibly also the sixth-
century Athenians who first celebrated the festival of the Synoikia (literally
"Housing Together"), also believed that the Athenians had not always been
politically united (Parker 1996: 12 n.9) and that there had been a process of

---

1. Most discussions of the catalog have sought to place it firmly in the Late Bronze Age or firmly
in the eighth/seventh century (see Kirk 1985: 169–70), but that seems both unnecessary and
inappropriate; see J. K. Anderson 1995; M. L. West 2011: 111–14.

The Oxford History of the Archaic Greek World. Robin Osborne, Oxford University Press. © Oxford University Press 2023.
DOI: 10.1093/oso/9780197644423.003.0004

synoecism, which was associated with the mythical Theseus (Thuc. 2.15). This synoecism was taken by Thucydides to have been political, not material; that is, a matter of agreeing to have a single decision-making structure, not a matter of physical relocation. What Theseus did, on this story, was to create the political and residential arrangements of Classical Athens, when Athenians were scattered in more than 100 villages across the territory of Attica, but decisions affecting all of them were taken in one place—Athens itself (see further Section 4.1.1.3).

By the fourth century, at latest, Athenians had come to tell a more detailed story in which Athens had originally been inhabited in scattered villages but had been brought together into twelve "cities" by Kekrops as a means of making them more defensible against attack from Boiotians by land or from Karians by sea. This was the story contained in the *Atthis* (= local history of Attica) written by Philochoros c. 300 (see Section 2.2.2.2), but, given the mention of 12 towns in the Parian Marble (on which see Section 5.2), it is likely to go back earlier, possibly to the fifth century (Strabo 9.1.20 = Philochoros *FGrH* 328 F94; Parian Marble *FGrH* 239.20). As quoted by Strabo, Philochoros lists the cities as Kekropia, Tetrapolis, Epakria, Dekeleia, Eleusis, Aphidna, Thorikos, Brauron, Kytheros, Sphettos, and Kephisia (which makes 11, so that scholars have suggested that Tetrakomoi has dropped out after Tetrapolis by haplography). But there is nothing in Strabo's quotation from Philochoros that indicates whether what he says was based on tradition or evidence—scholars have generally believed it was based on neither, but "is a mere construction based on the number twelve."[2]

If this is a "mere construction," it is not an ignorant one. If we take Kekropia to be Athens itself, Tetrapolis to be Marathon (one of the four Kleisthenic demes involved in the Classical cult organization called Tetrapolis—for the question of whether this can be seen to be reflected in Geometric cemetery distribution, see Mazarakis Ainian 2011: 706), and Tetrakomoi, if included, to refer to Phaleron, then of these 12 places, eight can certainly be associated with important Bronze Age remains—Athens itself; Marathon, with its tholos tomb; Eleusis, with a major Late Bronze Age cemetery; Thorikos, with tholos tombs and chamber tombs; Brauron; Kytheros, corresponding to the Mycenaean tombs at Ligori near Porto Raphti (Traill 1986: 51); Sphettos (which can stand for the successive sites of Kiapha Thiti and Vourvatsi just to its south); and Phaleron (Sgouritsa 2007; Osborne 2020a) (see Map 9).

---

2. So Jacoby 1923–1958: 3b Supplement, vol. 1: Text: 396 at the conclusion of a long discussion of other scholars' views of how the number was arrived at.

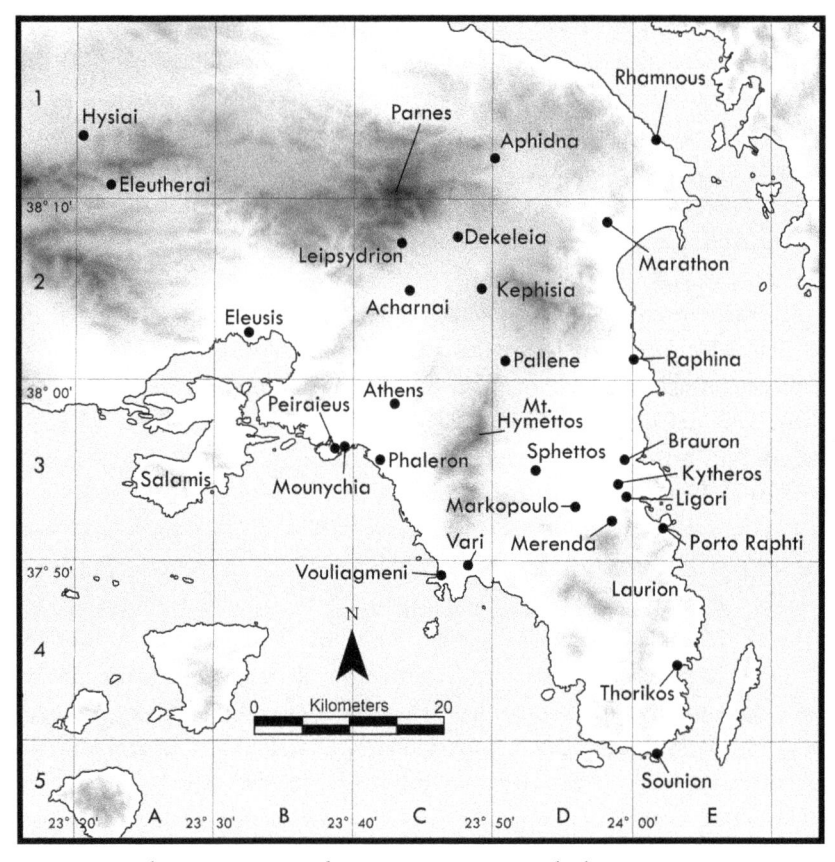

MAP 9 Some key sites mentioned in Section 4.1.1.1. © Paul Christesen 2022.

Although substantial Bronze Age remains continue to be elusive, modern scholars still expect to find evidence of Late Bronze Age settlement as well as Early and Middle Bronze Age burials at Aphidna. Dekeleia features in Herodotos (9.73) in a story about the Tyndaridai invading Attica to rescue Helen from Theseus, and clearly had somehow or other got caught up in this mythical tale, despite the failure of archaeology to date to find remains earlier than Geometric. That leaves only Kephisia, where the earliest known remains are eighth century, and Epakria, located near Tetrapolis by one late lexicon, without known or strongly suspected Bronze Age links. Or, looked at the other way, it leaves only Acharnai, with its tholos tomb, as a major Mycenaean site that has no presence in this list.

None of this rules out Philochoros' list being a construction. The use of the names of pre-Kleisthenic cult groups (Tetrapolis, Tetrakomoi) and of a name, Epakria, which seems also to have been a pre-Kleisthenic name for a group of settlements, corresponds to the story told, which is of Kekrops concentrating settlement in just twelve locations.[3] Such names exhausted, the remaining spaces in the list were then probably filled with the names of settlements known or suspected of having a long past history. But the accuracy of the guesses made by Philochoros' sources suggests that there were enough traditional stories about Attic demes, perhaps partly preserved in relation to local cult celebrations, to convey a broadly accurate, if vague, picture of Athens' past settlement history.

4.1.1.2 The Archaeological Evidence

The complex history of Late Bronze Age settlement in Attica sees some sites cease to show any use after LH IIIB, others survive into the early part of LH IIIC, a very much smaller number continue to have evidence to the end of LH IIIC, and only Athens itself and the Arsenal cemetery on Salamis show evidence from the Submycenaean period (Dimitriadou 2020; Osborne 2020a; Tsalkou 2020; Rönnberg 2021a: 278, 81–2, 336). In early Protogeometric Athens is left as the only site producing evidence, but by late Protogeometric evidence has (re) appeared in some 20 places in Attica (understood here as encompassing Salamis), including Brauron, Eleusis, the southern Mesogeia (Merenda and Markopoulo), Thorikos, and the cult sites at Mounychia and on the peaks of Hymettos and Parnes (Rönnberg 2021a: 278).

The big expansion of sites in Attica comes in the eighth century (D'Onofrio 1995a; van den Eijnde 2010; Osborne 2019b; Rönnberg 2021a: 279).[4] We can demonstrate ninth-century occupation for no more sites than we can tenth-century (and largely at the same sites), but in the eighth century evidence appears from more than three times as many sites. What is important about this expansion is not simply its scale, but its pattern.[5]

The evidence that we have for tenth- and ninth-century settlement in Attica (Map 10) suggests that there were at least seven discrete areas or clusters: (1) Athens itself spreading down to the coast through Palaia Kokkinia, Mounychia, and Phaleron and up to Patissia; (2) Eleusis; (3) Menidi/Acharnai; (4) Geraka/

---

3. For the lexicographical entries, see Jacoby 1923–1958: 3b Supplement, vol. 1: Text: 392–3 and notes.

4. For a full survey of settlement in Attica see now Rönnberg 2021a: 83–166, 278–85 (chronological listing of sites by period), 286–389 (site catalog, organized by area) and Karten 42–8. My account differs in some details from Rönnberg's, partly over the question of what constitutes sufficient evidence of occupation, always a problematic question. The collection of evidence and the maps in Petropoulakou and Pentazos 1973 remain invaluable. Van den Eijnde counts one site (Athens) in the EPG, 16 sites in LPG, 14 sites in EG, 19 sites in MG, and 46 sites in LG.

5. I develop here ideas that I have previously explored in Osborne 2019b.

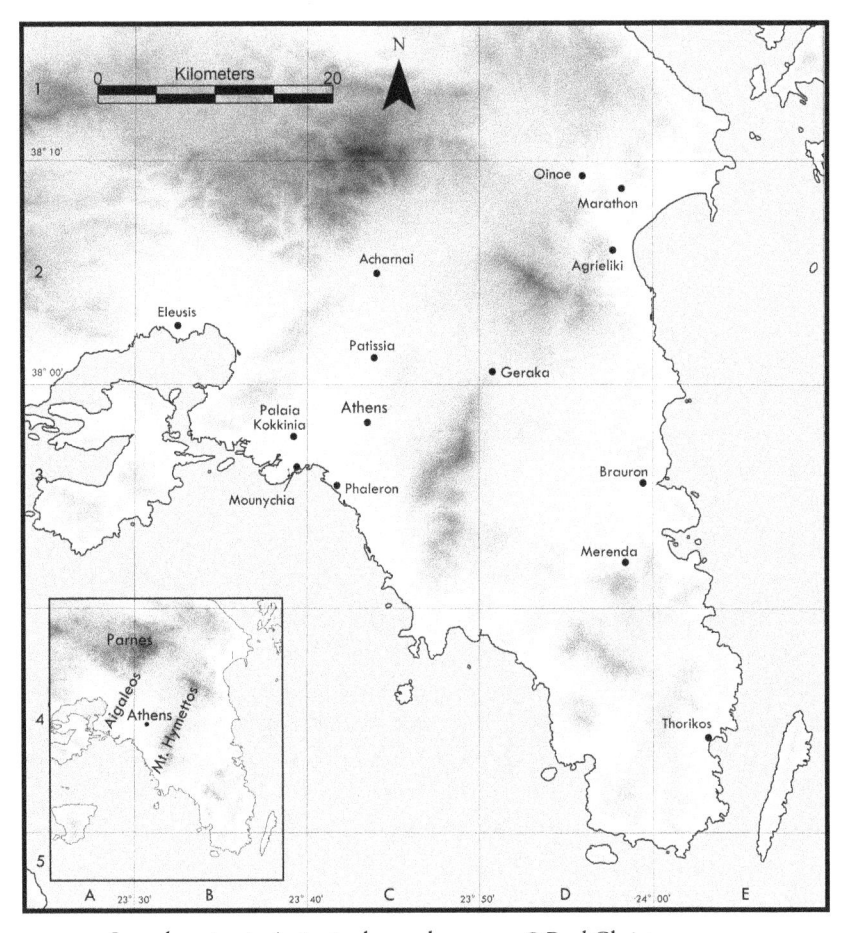

MAP 10 Some key sites in Attica in the tenth century. © Paul Christesen 2022.

Stavros at the northern tip of Hymettos; (5) Marathon with the cult site of Agrieliki above, and nearby Oinoe; (6) Brauron and Merenda, in the southeastern part of the Mesogeia; and (7) Thorikos. There is also evidence of cult activity on the top of Parnes and of Hymettos.

These clusters leave us with great swathes of Attica from which we have no settlement evidence. The whole west coast south of Phaleron, the vast majority of the Mesogeia north of Brauron, and the fertile corridor between Parnes and Pendele show no signs of occupation. This not only contrasts with the later settlement pattern, but also with the Late Bronze Age pattern, which had seen strong occupation of the northern Mesogeia, and of the belt running across Attica at the south end of Hymettos, from Vouliagmeni through Vari, Vourvatsi, and Ligori to Porto Raphti.

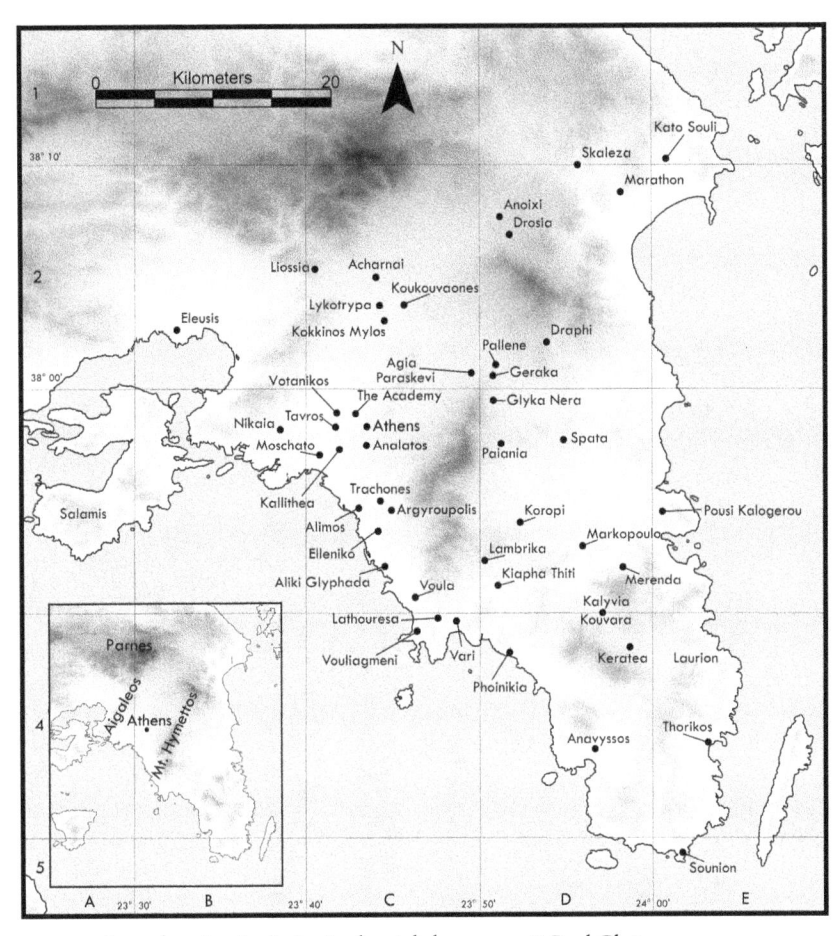

MAP 11 Some key sites in Attica in the eighth century. © Paul Christesen 2022.

In the eighth century the pattern is quite transformed (Map 11) (Rönnberg 2021a: 279). Although in the Thriasian plain there is little further development, and in Salamis only one new site is added to that already in evidence, in every other area settlement distinctly thickens. From Athens itself, activity spreads north to the Academy, Votanikos, and Aigaleos, as well as south and east to Analatos, Kallithea, Tavros, Nikaia, and Moschato. Around Acharnai activity is found to the south at the tholos tomb at Lykotrypa, Koukouvaones, and Kokkinos Mylos, as well as to the west at Liossia. Around Marathon settlement spreads east to Kato Souli, north to Skaleza, and west around the slopes of Pendele to Anoixi and Drosia. In the Mesogeia, occupation reappears at Spata and appears on the western fringe in the foothills of Hymettos at Paiania. South of Merenda on the southern fringe of the Mesogeia, where previously only Thorikos had yielded

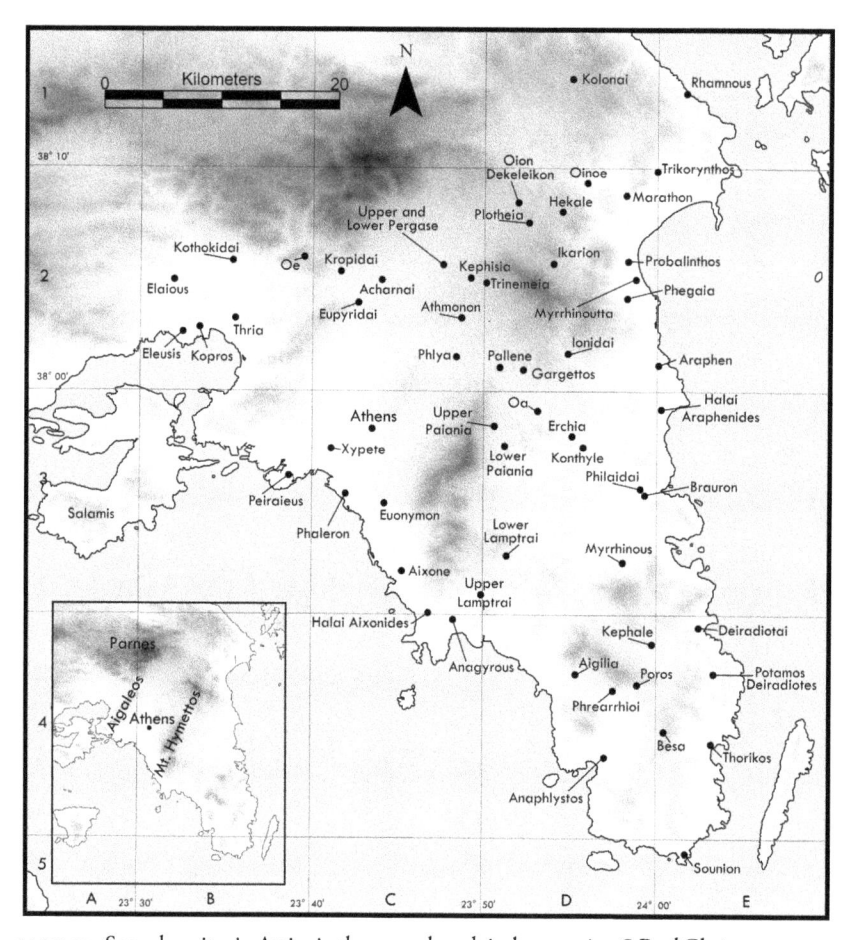

MAP 12   Some key sites in Attica in the seventh and sixth centuries. © Paul Christesen 2022.

evidence, eighth-century material has been found at some dozen sites, including Sounion, Laurion, Anavyssos, Keratea, Kalyvia Kouvara, and Phoinikia.[6]

More remarkably, occupation is found all the way down the west slopes of Hymettos from Argyroupolis and Trachones, through Alimos and Elleniko to Aliki Glyphada, Voula, Vouliagmeni, and round to Lathouresa and Vari. East of Athens the isolated ninth-century occupation at Geraka/Stavros is joined by renewed activity at the important Late Bronze Age site of Glyka Nera, at Pallene, at Draphi to the east, and at Agia Paraskevi to the west. Once more the belt of occupation between Vari and Porto Raphti is restored, with renewed

---

6. For references for all these sites and those mentioned in the next paragraph, see D'Onofrio 1995a: 83–6; D'Onofrio 1997: 79–84; see also I. Morris 1987: 222–33.

occupation at Kiapha Thiti, at Lambrika, at Koropi, and Markopoulo and at Pousi Kalogerou.

4.1.1.3 Overview

How are we to explain either the sheer increase in evidence for human presence, or its pattern? If we go back to the tenth and ninth centuries we have, by all appearances, a number of centers, essentially independent of one another—at most, a cluster of separate settlements seem to be working together locally. And those centers almost all look away from Attica. Eleusis, Thorikos, Brauron, and Marathon all have, in different ways, excellent access to the sea and much less good access to the rest of Attica insofar as they are protected, if not cut off, by rising land. Eleusis enjoys an extensive plain and commands the only land route from Attica to the Peloponnese, and the easiest land route to central and northern Greece. Thorikos has access to only a small fertile plain, although behind are the mineral-rich hills of the Laurion area. Marathon has access to a coastal plain and rich valleys. The only settlement sites from the tenth and ninth centuries that do not enjoy immediate access to the sea in this way are Acharnai and Stavros, both strategically placed to command important land routes—Stavros ("Cross") the east–west and north–south routes in Attica itself; Acharnai the pass leading to Boiotia. None of these places is sited with a view to maximizing collaboration; rather, each is placed to achieve the best competitive advantage.[7]

The eighth-century (in pottery terms, Late Geometric) pattern is quite different. Although the cluster of sites around Marathon and Thorikos, the sites of the southeastern tip of Attica down to Sounion, and the sites of the Thriasian plain remain somewhat separated from other occupation, the rest of Attica comprises a series of strings of sites that are hard to separate. From Athens one string of sites leads north to Acharnai, another string diverges east from this through the gap between Hymettos and Pendele, and a third string runs south down the west side of Hymettos and then curls round to join up with the group of sites that pour south from the southern Mesogeia. Rather than a set of separate settlement chambers,[8] each as concerned with their links out of Attica as with their links within Attica, we have a great spread of sites that make sense only as a set and in relation to each other.

---

7. The eighth-century pattern can usefully be compared to the maps of least-cost paths between Bronze Age sites produced by Fachard and Knodell 2020.

8. "Settlement chamber" is a technical phrase, translating the German "Siedlungskammer," and refers to distinct microregions marked off by mountains or rivers and with sufficient land resources to support a settlement. See Vionis and Papantoniou 2019: 2–3.

If the pattern of the ninth century looks very compatible with the sort of political arrangement presupposed by the story about Kekrops (a series of essentially independent communities clustered in different settlement chambers), the pattern in the eighth century is hard to understand without presupposing something like the *synoikismos* that came to be ascribed to Theseus—i.e. political unification.[9] Neither in terms of the nature of the occupation uncovered by archaeology at these numerous sites, nor in terms of their patterning do these sites suggest the existence of separate political centers. Marathon, Eleusis, and Thorikos aside, occupation otherwise runs in such continuous chains that neighboring sites must be reckoned to be collaborative not competitive.

What changed in the eighth century? The most interesting feature of the change in settlement pattern is that it is a change from a pattern that looks outward, with each of the settlement chambers having its own route out to a wider world, to a pattern that looks inward. I have talked above of settlement radiating out from Athens, but equally we can see the settlements as linking into Athens, and they do so from north, east, south, and southwest. Although the language of strings will not apply to the sites scattered across Attica south of the Mesogeia, the remarkably even spread of sites is more suggestive of equal dependence on a distant center than of any local focus. We must conclude that Athens was able to supply something that other settlements needed—not something they needed on an hourly, daily, or even weekly basis, but something that they could reckon to access at a distance (for the effects upon the settlement remains in Athens itself see Section 4.3).

What was it that Athens supplied? If we think in terms of economics, Athens' advantage is unlikely to have been that it provided a market for daily provisions, but it might have been that it could provide for needs that were more occasional (supplies of metals, for instance, or of fine pottery or jewelry or similar sorts of "luxury" or semi-luxury items). If we think of other possible centralized "services," it might in part have been that Athens could supply religious needs, privileged access to the gods, but it is likely to also have been in part political and military. One of the things for which the spread of occupation provides evidence is for a sizeable population—indeed it may be that the increase in settlement numbers provides our best evidence for the rate of population growth (see I. Morris 1987: 156–7) and the larger the population

---

9. What follows is argued against the claims of G. Anderson 2003: esp. 19–21 (cf. also Flament 2011). At issue in discussions of *synoikismos* is, in part, what is entailed by political unification (cf. also Rönnberg 2022). For further discussion of the data here in connection with issues of different sorts of regionalism in Attica, see Osborne 2022.

the greater the need for a source of order and of protection (on demography, see Sections 4.4.2 and 9.1).

Whatever the nature of the political organization(s) of Attica as a whole in these years, there can be no doubt at all what changed in the eighth century was in part political—for how could such a growth in the archaeological visibility of settlements occur without raising political questions? We might reasonably ask whether political change was merely a consequence or actually a cause that produced the efflorescence of eighth-century evidence.

It is important to be clear about what it is that is happening in the eighth century. That is, we are certainly dealing with an archaeological phenomenon—that vastly more sites produce evidence that can be dated to the eighth century than produced evidence that could be dated to the ninth. But this does not necessarily mean that sites that produce eighth- but not ninth-century evidence were not occupied at all in the ninth century. It only means that any occupation failed to leave traces diagnostic of a ninth-century date. In fact, a great deal of evidence is uncovered in Attica, as elsewhere in the Greek world, that simply cannot be dated. Dating demands the discovery of manufactured items that change significantly over time. Walls built out of local stone, or graves that contain only a skeleton and are covered with a slab of stone, cannot be dated (particularly given the problems with the carbon-14 calibration curve during the so-called Hallstatt plateau, which lasts from c. 800 to 400).

What produces evidence that *can* be dated is both a certain degree of wealth, so as to be able to access items that are subject to changing fashion, and a certain desire to leave a mark. Some items are found by archaeologists because they were lost in antiquity, but the great majority of what archaeologists find was deliberately deposited, most obviously as grave goods, as dedications to the gods, or as rubbish. What we are seeing in the eighth century, therefore, is that people occupying a far greater range of sites across Attica wanted to make themselves visible.

Why were they making themselves visible? They may have been making themselves visible because previously they were not there at all; that is, that increased evidence of occupation from across Attica correlates directly to increased occupation across Attica. But that is certainly not the only possibility. The growth of the desire to make themselves visible might equally be a product of economic prosperity, and a consequent increase in disposable wealth. But again, having greater wealth is not likely on its own to motivate depositing it visibly. At some level or other, increased visibility was surely related to politics, that is to bids for a share of the limelight, and therefore of power, by either groups or individuals—this is true not only of conspicuous burial and conspicuous dedications, but even of increased deposit of non-perishable goods as rubbish, which is an indication of levels of consumption and the rapidity with which goods go out of fashion. As we will see (Sections 4.4.2 and 4.4.3), the case for significant political change during the eighth century is strong.

Whereas we have no tenth- or ninth-century remains substantial enough to give any impression of what a settlement of that period in Attica was like, one site gives us a very vivid picture of a late eighth-century settlement. This is the site of Lathouresa, on a low hill immediately west of the modern village of Vari (the Classical deme of Anagyrous) at the south tip of Hymettos. In June and July 1939 Greek archaeologists uncovered the walls of some 23 different buildings, or at least rooms, clustered closely together on the east spur of Lathouresa hill. They thoroughly excavated eight of those buildings, including a well-built circular structure, 7.8 m in diameter, that crowned the top of the hill. Hundreds of votive objects were collected from inside and around the circular building, including large numbers of seated figurines, bronze fibulas and earrings, and one Mycenaean-era silver ring carved with a running deer. The small finds seem to have been lost in the turmoil of the years that followed the excavation, but the remains of the buildings have been closely re-examined (and a certain number of additional finds of clay objects made).

The buildings seem to have been constructed facing inward, with their back walls forming a continuous wall at least around the eastern end of the spur. Several of the buildings are apsidal, others more rectilinear, but, with the possible exception of the round building, which may have been added in the sixth century, they appear to have been largely, if not wholly, constructed at the same moment in the late eighth century. The finds reported from the excavation indicate that offerings certainly continued to be made at the round building until the end of the sixth century, but whether the whole site continued in occupation is less clear. Without the small finds, and without an excavation of the buildings on the south side of the cluster, it is impossible to be certain what we have here, but it seems most likely that we have a late eighth-century settlement consisting of not more than a dozen families, perhaps fewer, established in a secure and commanding position. The cult center that they established then continued to attract votives, and indeed further building activity, long after the rest of the settlement seems to have been abandoned.[10] Whether other settlements in Attica looked like Lathouresa in the eighth century we have no way of knowing.

---

10. The buildings are meticulously described in Lauter 1985b (who, however, mistook a circuit wall created by the excavators for an original feature); on the round building see Seiler 1986: 7–24. The excavators' notebooks were then used in Mazarakis Ainian 1995 to nuance the interpretation. See also Alexandridou 2017b: 290 and Section 4.4.3.

4.1.2 The Seventh and Sixth Centuries

4.1.2.1 The Archaeological Evidence

Just as most sites in Attica occupied during the ninth century had been occupied in the tenth, so most sites occupied in the seventh century (see Map 12 and Rönnberg 2021a: 280–1) had been occupied in the eighth. Although there are a number of places that have produced evidence from the eighth century (or more generally from the Geometric period) but none from the seventh century, the vast majority of these are cases where the quantity of Geometric pottery is small. It is, however, notable that the seventh century shows through particularly strongly at cult sites, a number of which are more or less clearly separated from any settlement (Osborne 1989: 303–9; D'Onofrio 1995a: 71–4 with fig. 4; Rönnberg 2021a: 253–5). By contrast, the number of known cemeteries thins out (see discussion in Sections 4.4.2 and 4.4.3). There is strong evidence for a change in the way in which Athenians envisaged and related to the world, which will be discussed later (Section 4.5.3), but that seems to have had relatively little impact on the overall pattern of settlement. Nothing about the settlement pattern as such indicates whether the settlement chambers that may have been politically distinct in the eighth century—Marathon, and Eleusis in particular—remained distinct. It will require different evidence to answer that question.

Although we can comment in some detail on the development of particular sites, particularly sanctuaries (Section 11.3) in the sixth century, it is not possible to construct an archaeological map of settlement for that century. The pottery of the sixth century has so much in common with that of the fifth that, without substantial parts of pots being preserved, assigning dates to sites is problematic, and it is not possible to have much confidence that when archaeologists have identified fifth-century occupation they have not overlooked that there is sixth-century occupation also. However, for settlement in Attica at the end of the sixth century we arguably have a quite different source of information.

4.1.2.2 The Evidence of the Kleisthenic Demes

In 508/7 Kleisthenes persuaded the Athenians that they should radically alter their constitution. The details of his reforms will be discussed in Section 5.2.4; what is important about them here is that they determined political representation on a Council of 500 by assigning a fixed quota of places to every "deme" (community), that is, every village in Attica (and the separate communities within the town of Athens). We have neither the list of villages nor the quotas preserved from the sixth century, but we know both from the fourth century, and although a case can be made for some change having been necessary in the interim, it is extremely likely that the vast majority of the 139 demes known from the fourth century have their origins in the sixth century. If that is so, then the map of deme locations (we know where most, although not all, of the demes were), gives us a map, not of every site with sixth century activity, but of where all significant communities were located.[11]

If we work on this assumption, that the map of demes is essentially a map of settlement across Attica in the last decade of the sixth century, what do we find?[12] There is a great deal of continuity, as we might expect. The cluster of sites around and inland from the Bay of Marathon is reflected in a cluster of demes—Marathon, Trikorynthos, Oinoe, Probalinthos. The cluster of sites around the northeast foothills of Hymettos is reflected in a cluster of demes, including Pallene and Gargettos. The cluster of sites at the south end of Hymettos is reflected in the demes Aixone, Halai Aixonides, Anagyrous, and the two Lamptrai demes. The sites at the southeast of the Mesogeia, from Brauron south through Merenda are reflected in the cluster of demes of Philaidai, Angele, Kytheros, Myrrhinous, and Hagnous. The large demes of south Attica, Kephale, Phrearrhioi, Anaphlystos, along with the smaller demes of Thorikos and Sounion, all mirror earlier signs of human presence of one sort or another.

But alongside the continuity there are striking changes. In the plain of Athens itself, both to the west and south and to the north of the city, the pattern of demes is as dense as or, especially northwest of Athens, denser than, the pattern of earlier sites. In and around the Thriasian plain we find not only Eleusis and Aspropyrgos (ancient Thria), but plausibly also the demes of Elaious, Kothokidai, and Oe. In the western foothills of Pendele we find not only Kephisia but also Upper and Lower Pergase, Trinemeia, and Athmonon. Most strikingly of all we find the central Mesogeia occupied by activity not simply at the site of the deme Erchia, but also at Oa, and probably Konthyle and Ionidai. On the eastern edge of the Mesogeia there is settlement not simply at Brauron and Marathon, but also in between at Halai Araphenides, Araphen, Phegaia, and perhaps Myrrhinoutta.

---

11. Producing a representative for the Council demanded a certain population size, so some demes may have been made up of a number of separate "hamlet" settlements rather than a single nucleated village (there is some evidence of this for Aphidna, in particular). That the precise configuration of demes and bouleutic quotas altered between Kleisthenes and the fourth century, from which our data on the quotas comes, is in my view quite likely, but since no reform of the system is ever alluded to in text, it is probably safe to think that it primarily consisted of varying the precise number of *bouleutai* returned by a given community; see the discussion in Osborne 2009: 283–8.

12. I follow the deme locations suggested by Traill 1986: 125–40, although I am not persuaded by the *trittys* divisions suggested there (Traill 1975 remains, in my view, more plausible).

4.1.2.3 Overview

What are we to deduce from these changes? The first thing to note is that, although some "cities" of the old Dodecapolis (Athens itself, Eleusis, Aphidna, Marathon) remain major centers, returning 10 or more Councilors to the fourth-century Council of 500, the pattern of demes would not lead one to guess that these had once had special status. A number of other places jostle for attention at the top of the village size hierarchy—Acharnai returns 22 to the *boulē*; Aixone and Lower Paiania 11; Alopeke (in the modern suburb of Daphni, just southeast of the classical city), Anaphlystos, and Euonymon 10. As far as the other members of the supposed Dodecapolis are concerned, the largest of these was Kephisia, returning six to the Council, whereas Kephale, Lower Lamptrai, Phaleron, and Phrearrhioi returned nine; Peiraieus and Rhamnous eight; and Erchia, Thria, and Xypete seven.

Equally when we look to unevenly distributed resources—major sanctuaries or theaters, for instance—it is again not the old Dodecapolis that is prominent. Athens itself, Eleusis, Brauron, and Thorikos did indeed have major sanctuaries, and Marathon was the site of a significant festival of Herakles (*IG* I^3.3, cf. [Arist.] *Constitution of the Athenians* 54.7 with Rhodes 1981 ad loc), and so, too, Athens and Thorikos had theaters. However, Classical theaters have been also found at Acharnai, Euonymon, Ikarion, Peiraieus, and Rhamnous and are known from textual sources at Aigilia, Aixone, Halai Araphenides, Myrrhinous, and Paiania. A conservative list of sites of major Classical sanctuaries includes Halai Aixonides (Cape Zoster), Halai Araphenides, Pallene, Peiraieus (Mounychia), Rhamnous, and Sounion (Whitehead 1986: 219–20; Paga 2010). Few of these facilities will date back, in any form, to 600, but where they developed gives a good indication that the places of the old Dodecapolis did not head any hierarchy.

The places that the eighth- and seventh-century settlement pattern leaves as possibly independent local centers, commanding their own separate settlement chambers (Eleusis, Marathon, Thorikos), no longer look at all plausibly separate when seen against the array of Kleisthenic demes. Eleusis is linked in by a continuous string of settlement east through the gap between Aigaleos and Parnes (Kopros, Thria, Oe, Kropidai, Eupyridai) as well as through the string of settlement along the Sacred Road running from Athens to Eleusis. Marathon is linked northwest to Aphidna, west to the string of small demes along the north of Pendele (Hekale, Kolonai, Plotheia, Oion Dekeleikon), and south along the coast. Thorikos is linked in northward through Potamos Deiradiotes to Deiradiotai, northwest through Poros to Kephale, west through Besa to Anaphlystos, as well as south to Sounion.

The second thing that the changes show is not simply that during the sixth century settlement in Attica expanded, by comparison to that archaeologically visible in the seventh century, but that it expanded in certain particular areas. It expanded in the edges of the Thriasian plain and in the gap between Aigaleos and Parnes, in the west foothills of Pendele, and in its eastern foothills down to the sea, and on the western slopes of Hymettos. Whereas there had been a Geometric cemetery at Paiania but no seventh-century archaeological trace, there were now not only separate settlements at Upper and Lower Paiania (the latter growing quite large), but also at nearby Oa. All these are areas of marginal land, but the new settlements are far from all being small—though not rivaling Lower Paiania in size, places such as Oe in the Thriasian plain, Athmonon and Phlya in the west foothills of Pendele, and Halai Araphenides on the east margin of the Mesogeia, all returned four to six councilors in the fourth century. Even if the land occupied in the sixth century was not prime, it was clearly able to support a substantial population.

What the plotting of settlements cannot do is tell us what brought about the settlement expansion. Rising population must have played a part, and the occupation of more marginal land indeed strongly suggests that population pressure was a significant factor (although the fact that Athens seems to have been involved in no overseas settlement [see Section 7.3] suggests that the population pressure was not severe). But was population the only factor or did social, economic, and political changes also play a part? Certainly, the disappearance of anything that might be thought to be empty zones, dividing one cluster of settlements from another, strongly suggests that by the sixth century at least all Athenians thought of the whole of Attica as a single unit, and that there was nothing preventing settlement at any point where settlement might prove profitable.

4.2 Settlement Organization of Major Sites in Attica Outside of Athens

If we can plot sixth-century settlements on to the map with some degree of confidence, we must admit that we have little idea what a sixth-century settlement looked like. The Classical village communities that have been excavated at Rhamnous, Thorikos, and Halai Aixonides have given no good evidence of their Archaic predecessors. Archaeologically, the distinctive nature of sixth-century Attic communities emerges only from their burial practices (on which see Section 4.4.4).

We can fairly say that we know nothing about the settlement organization of any settlement site in Attica outside of Athens in the Archaic period, with the exception of Lathouresa, discussed in Section 4.1.1.3. For the case of the Peiraieus, the development of which was essentially Classical, see Section 8.3. For the Archaic sanctuary sites, see Section 11.3.

4.3 Settlement Organization of Athens

There is little doubt that what marked Athens out from the beginning was the Acropolis (156 m). Human habitation from the Bronze Age onward was on the slopes around the Acropolis, in the area further defined by the rivers Ilissos (which flows westward from Hymettos, runs south of the Acropolis, and eventually joins the Kephissos) and Eridanos (which flows westward from Lykabettos hill, runs to the north of the Acropolis, and eventually joins the Ilissos prior to the juncture of the Ilissos and the Kephissos) and by Philopappos or Mouseion Hill (147 m). These natural features effectively divided human activity into three areas, the Acropolis itself, the Ilissos valley, and the Eridanos valley (see Map 13).[13]

In the earliest Iron Age (Submycenaean) the Acropolis itself, complete with its impressive Mycenaean fortifications, which remained largely intact, was the central place of residence and was also a place of burial (Gauss and Ruppenstein 1998: 41 for summary; Bohen 2017: 14, 51, 89–90; Doronzio 2018: 12–16; Dimitriadou 2019: 112). The evidence of burial on the Acropolis is slight during the Protogeometric period and up through the Late Geometric period, when the quantity of pottery massively increases and the existence of pottery with scenes of *prothēsis* and of other characteristic funerary vessels indicate continued funerary use. Clear signs of cult activity reappear in Late Geometric for the first time since the Mycenaean period, and from the end of the eighth century on the evidence from the Acropolis is entirely compatible with purely cult activity: burials ceased and if some people continued to live on the Acropolis, their residence has left no clear trace. (For the history of the Acropolis as a cult site, see below and Sections 11.1 and 12.1.)

Already in the Submycenaean period, however, Athens was very much more than just the community on the Acropolis. Extensive cemetery remains are found northwest, south, and east of the Acropolis (Rönnberg 2021a: 281–2). To the northwest, Submycenaean burials are found on the south, west (on Kolonos Agoraios, the rise just to the west of the Classical agora) and north (straddling the Eridanos) sides of the later Classical Agora, as well as across the Eridanos in both the Kerameikos and Dipylon cemeteries (Ruppenstein and Lagia 2007).[14] To the east burials are found in the area of the center of the modern city, Syndagma

---

13. For a history of the study of Athenian topography, see Greco 2014: 1522–40. For the underlying geology, see Section 3.1.

14. The Dipylon cemetery is distinct from, and c. 400 m northeast of, the Kerameikos Cemetery; the Dipylon cemetery is located in the immediate vicinity of the Eriai Gate (see n. 17 of this chapter), the Kerameikos Cemetery in the immediate vicinity of the Dipylon Gate.

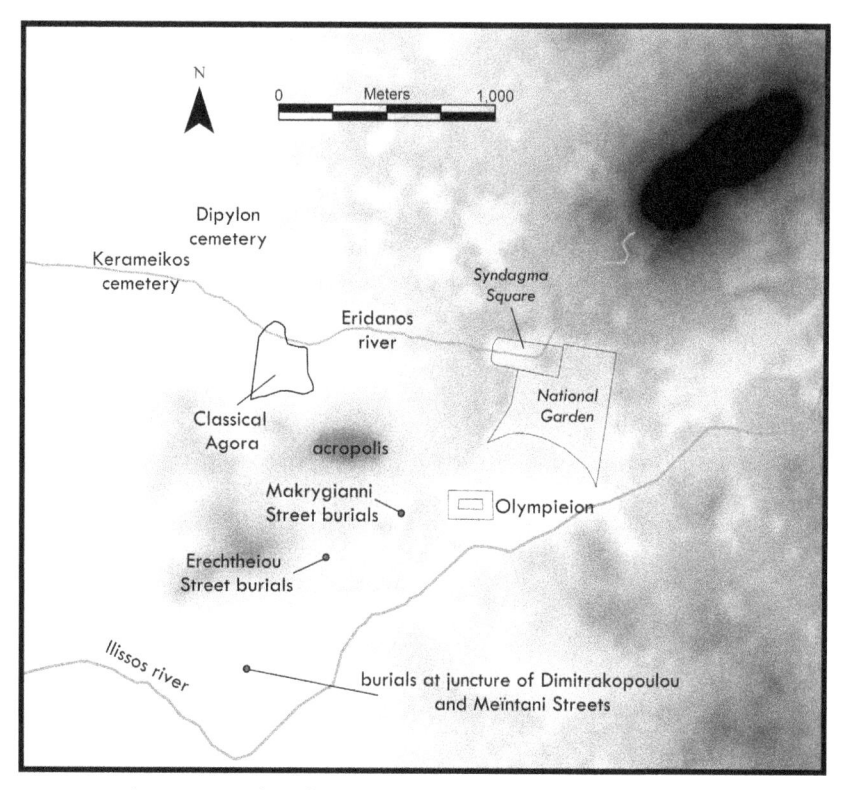

MAP 13 Submycenaean burial sites in Athens mentioned in Section 4.3. © Paul Christesen 2022.

Square, and indeed beyond in the northeast corner of the National Garden. To the south burial sites are scattered down the Ilissos valley from immediately south of the (much later) Olympieion, through sites on Makrygianni and Erechtheiou Streets to a cemetery at the junction of Dimitrakopoulou and Meïntani Streets. Direct settlement evidence is hard to find, but these burial plots must all relate to local communities, scattered over an area of about 250 ha.[15]

In the Protogeometric period burial evidence continues in all these areas and is now also found for the first time in the area of the later Kynosarges gymnasium (southeast of the Acropolis and across the Ilissos) and in Nileos St, to the west of the Classical agora (Rönnberg 2021a: 282) (Map 14). Further burial areas are added during the ninth and eighth centuries, including in the area of the modern district of the Plaka (just to the north and east of the Acropolis), but few old plots

---

15. The evidence is extensively discussed in Dimitriadou 2019: 19–70, and is conveniently summarized in Dimitriadou 2017: 986–7.

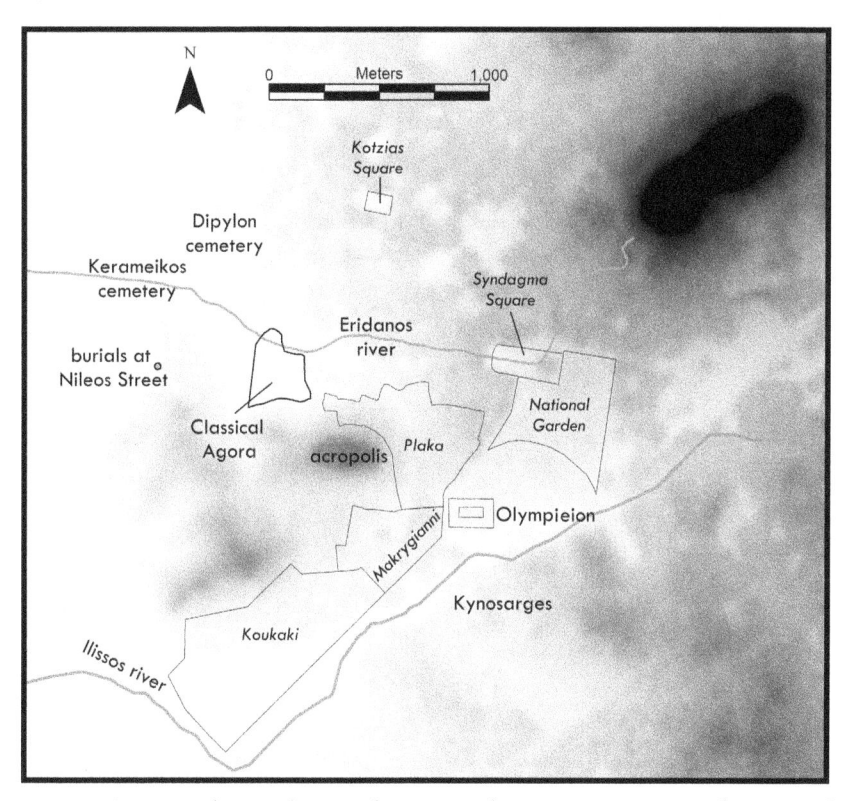

MAP 14 Areas in Athens with attested activity in the Protogeometric period mentioned in Section 4.3. © Paul Christesen 2022.

are abandoned (despite the change from secondary cremation to inhumation as the prevailing burial practice, see Section 4.4) (Rönnberg 2021a: 282–3). The only exception is in the Agora area, where the central area and the area north of the Eridanos are not used for burials after Submycenaean, and in the central Agora area a number of wells are sunk. Other positive evidence for habitation or craft activity is limited to a very small number of wells north of the Eridanos and near Syndagma Square, and to retaining walls that indicate craft workshops in the area of the modern Makrygianni and Koukaki districts (Dimitriadou 2019: 117–20 for the Agora; Dimitriadou 2019: 120–2 for other habitation and workshop evidence). All of this suggests that in the eighth century settlement covered a very broad area, spreading northwest from the Acropolis, through the later Agora and up to the areas from the Kerameikos to the area of present-day Kotzias Square (the site of the later Acharnai Gate in the Themistoklean wall), on the one hand, and all the way down the Ilissos valley, and across into Kynosarges, on the other (Dimitriadou 2019: 71–164). On the whole, it looks as if we have local communities burying separately, except in as far as the Dipylon cemetery has outstandingly rich finds (see Section 4.4.2 for further discussion of the Dipylon cemetery).

Around 700, radical changes occurred (Doronzio 2018: 55–282; Dimitriadou 2019: 165–238). The Mycenaean fortifications of the Acropolis continued to dominate its appearance, and Athens as a whole, throughout the Archaic period, but what was happening on the top of the Acropolis changed. As we will see (Section 11.1), from the late eighth century we have a wealth of bronze dedications that indicate that the Acropolis had become an important sanctuary. From the seventh century, although the quantity of votive material is reduced, two limestone column-bases survive that are likely to have been part of a temple building. In the sixth century the evidence for temple buildings multiplies massively with remains of walls, architectural elements, and a lot of sculpture. By the end of the century the Acropolis was densely covered with buildings and free-standing sculpture (see Sections 11.1 and 12.1.2, as well as Boersma 1970: 13–17; Hurwit 1999: 99–121; Klein 2015). If significant numbers of Athenians continued to live on the Acropolis in the seventh century (Holtzmann 2003: 41–2 suggests there was a small military post), they certainly departed in the sixth.

Around the Acropolis the story is harder to disentangle, not least because of the dense modern occupation of the area. Down to the early eighth century, burials had appeared in clusters—in the area of the Classical Agora (from the slopes of the Areopagus through to the banks of the Eridanos river); in the Kerameikos and Dipylon cemeteries; in the area of Kotzias and Syndagma Squares; in the Koukaki and Makrygianni districts to the south and southeast of the Acropolis; and in the Kynosarges area southeast of the Acropolis. Then during the Late Geometric period burial spread, so that in the later eighth century "cemeteries can be identified over virtually the entire area of the walled Classical city" (Dimitriadou 2017: 988) (Map 15).[16] It seems that what had been distinct communities had, by the end of the eighth century, ceased to be distinct in the same way.

At the end of the eighth century that sense of a single community then expresses itself by ceasing to bury, with relatively few exceptions, within the settlement area later bounded by the classical "Themistoklean" defensive wall. Cemeteries all around the Acropolis are abandoned, so that only the Tholos cemetery continues in use in the Agora area, only the west slope of the Areopagus is used for burial, and to the south of the Acropolis only the Erechtheiou Street burial places go on being

---

16. Dimitriadou's map indicates that some exaggeration is involved in this statement, but it is significant that this is how she perceives the situation. Dimitriadou's map (opposite p. 986) supersedes Morris's maps (I. Morris 1987: 64) where both the clustering and the subsequent spread are rather less obvious. See also, and particularly for the continuing story into the Archaic period, Dimitriadou 2019 with maps 3.47–9.

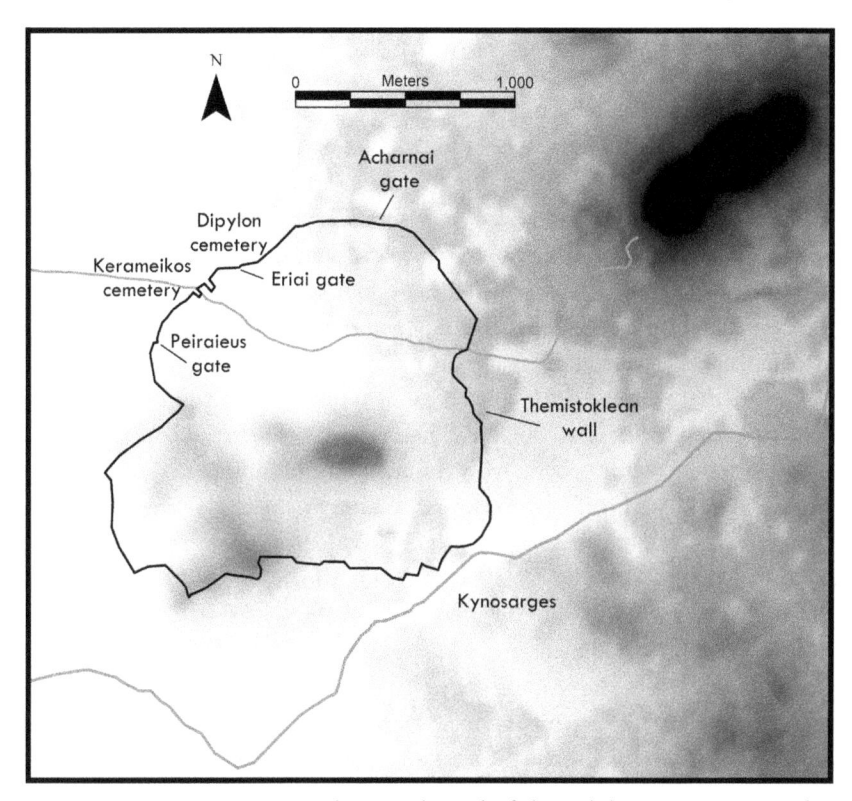

MAP 15 Major cemeteries in Athens at the end of the eighth century mentioned in Section 4.3. © Paul Christesen 2022.

used, with those in Makrygianni discontinued. That left a core area of about 200 ha for residence and work spaces. That is some indication of community organization and of a distinction between the space of the living and the space of the dead.

The main cemeteries are now those along what would be the northern stretch of the later Themistoklean wall—the Kerameikos and the cemeteries at the Peiraieus Gate, Eriai Gate ("Dipylon cemetery"), and Acharnai Gate—as well as the Kynosarges cemetery. There are signs of competitive funerary display across these cemeteries, initially in the form of high-quality pottery used as grave markers and, from the end of the seventh century, of *kouroi*, sphinx monuments, or relief *stēlai*.[17] There was evidently enough of a single coordinated community to agree to separate burial from settlement, but enough separation for each neighborhood to have its own cemetery and its own prosperous inhabitants.

---

17. Kerameikos: *kouroi*. Eriai Gate: the Nettos Painter's name amphora. Acharnai Gate: sphinx funerary sculpture and the Panathenaic Burgon amphora. From graves at Panepistemiou

Beyond burials there is little to report for the seventh century, outside the Acropolis (for which see Sections 11.2 and 11.3), except for the Agora (Rönnberg 2021a: 285). Numerous remains of craft activity from the Archaic period, including potters' debris and debris from the production of bronze statues, have been found here, and near the later Tholos was a potter's kiln.[18] It seems that through the seventh and into the sixth century the Agora was the chief area of pottery production in Athens, before potters moved out to the Dipylon Gate and the area to its northwest during the sixth century (Baziotopoulou-Valavani 1994). But the area was certainly not exclusively occupied by potteries, but rather multi-functional, with settlement evidence and evidence for cult activity also clear in the record, and sufficient fragments of drinking vessels with their owners' names inscribed on them to suggest contexts of communal male drinking (Doronzio 2018: 201–6).

In the sixth century, along with the monumentalization of the Acropolis, we see in the second half of the century building in the Sanctuary of Dionysos Eleuthereus, south of the Acropolis, the Eleusinion on its north slopes, and at the Olympieion (see further Section 11.3) (Map 16). The limited evidence for craft activity elsewhere in the city includes two unfinished female statues, apparently destined for a pediment, from Lekka Street 23–5, northwest of Syndagma Square. To the southeast of the city there is good textual evidence for the sixth-century foundation of a gymnasium at Kynosarges in the vicinity of a sanctuary of Herakles already established there (at uncertain date) (Doronzio 2018: 55–292, esp. 239–45 on Kynosarges; Dimitriadou 2019: 165–238).

But where did early Athenian magistrates operate? Some scholars think that the evidence for cult and for people gathering in the area of the later Classical Agora sufficient to support the idea that the site of the Classical Agora was the civic and commercial center of the city throughout the Archaic period (Baurain-Rebillard 1998: 135; Kistler 1998: 162–76; Doronzio 2018: 202–6, 10). However, the location of the Sanctuary of Aglauros, in consequence of the discovery of an inscription, has helped to strengthen arguments that the Prytaneion in which Solon's laws were said by Pausanias to be still on display in his time, and therefore

---

9: Orientalizing pottery. From the Syndagma Square end of Mitropoleos St: the torso of a tomb *kouros*. From the hillock by the Olympieion: fine pottery by the Analatos, Nettos, and Gorgon Painters. Kynosarges cemetery: the Protoattic "Kynosarges amphora" (Section 4.5.3). Makrygianni: a *kouros* head and a separate torso. Erechtheiou 25: fine tomb bases. From Nileos St: a marble sphinx. The name "Eriai Gate" is retained here to designate the gate at Leokoriou Street because of the widespread use of the appellation in the extant scholarship. It is now apparent that neither the gate at Leokoriou Street nor any other gate in Athens bore that name (Theocharaki 2020: 355–6).

18. Papadopoulos 2003: 272–80 supported by Dimitriadou 2017; for arguments to the contrary, Doronzio 2018: 163–212.

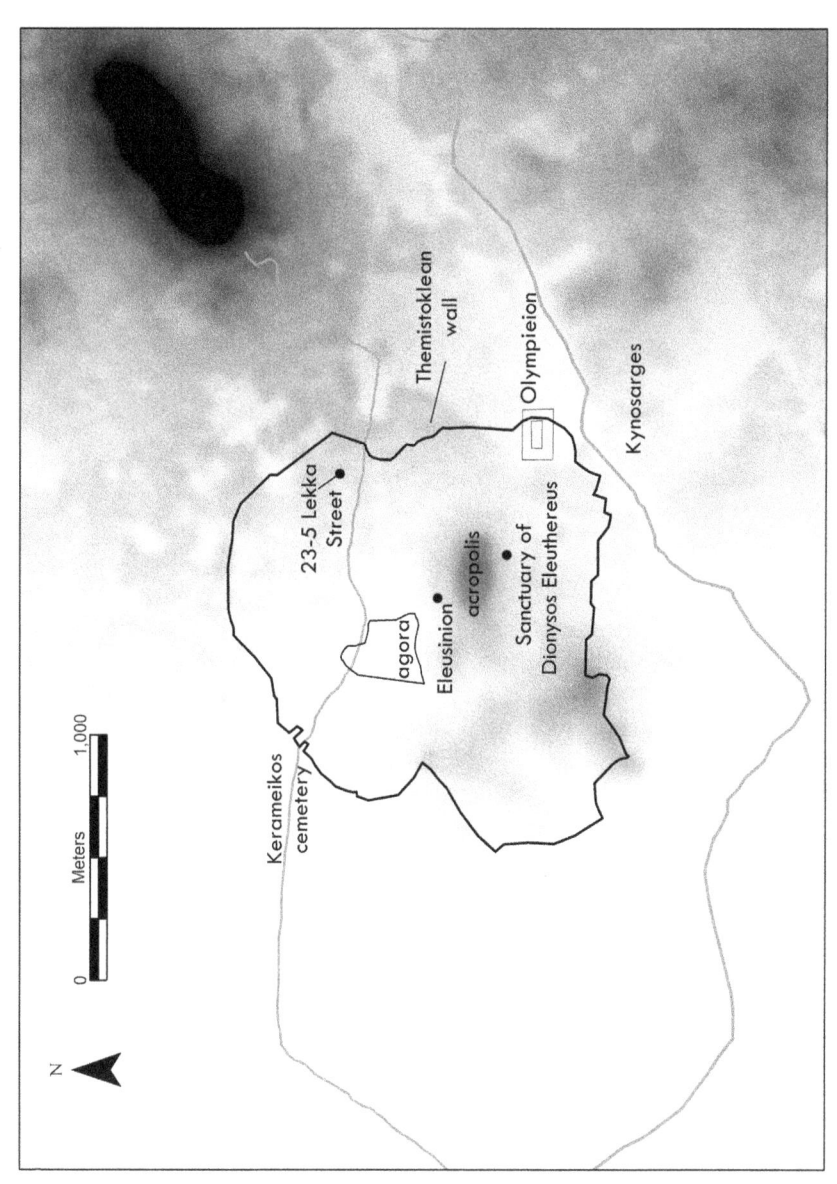

MAP 16 Some important sites in sixth-century Athens. © Paul Christesen 2022.

the Archaic center of civic government, lay just to the northeast of the Acropolis (Shear Jr. 1994: 226–8; Papadopoulos 2003: 282–5; Schmalz 2006; Osborne 2007a; Kavvadias and Matthaiou 2014). The great advantage of this will have been that it was halfway between the main residential areas north and south of the Acropolis. Thucydides (2.15.3–4) draws attention to the importance of the area south of the Acropolis and to the number of sanctuaries, including that of Dionysos "in the Marshes" there. That sanctuary is likely to have been at the junction of Makrygianni with Chatzichristou and Veïkou Streets, but we have no archaeological evidence to offer any history (Travlos 1971: 332–3).

Whether the site of Archaic civic government was also the place where the people as a whole met, let alone whether it was ever called the "agora," and exactly when the shift in the siting of civic office occurred remains unclear. The site of the Classical Agora may have been used for meetings long before any civic offices were based there, and the most plausible story is of the potters moving out of the area of the later Agora in perhaps the third quarter of the sixth century, and the area then being smartened up. We can trace various private buildings along the west side of the Agora. At the southwest corner, a long narrow building (labeled Building A in the original excavation report) appears to go back to the seventh century, close to an iron-working establishment (see Figure 2). Then, in the course of the sixth century, the following were built just to the north: a two-room structure (Building C) from the start of the century, associated with a pit containing sixth-century domestic pottery; and half-century later, a still smaller three-room structure (Building D) (Thompson 1940: 3–15; L. Johnstone and Graff 2018: 10–11).

Building A was replaced sometime after 550 with a large structure with many rooms and a large colonnaded court (Building F). This was a very impressive building, but still a private residential building. In the same period a temple of Apollo Patroos was constructed on the west side of the Agora, along with what may have been a temple of Zeus Agoraios, and there was building on the Eleusinion site near the Agora (see Section 11.3). But only c. 500 were any buildings constructed that are clearly for public but secular use: the Old Bouleuterion, built for the Kleisthenic Council of 500, and, more or less contemporaneous with that, the Stoa Basileios (Royal Stoa) (see Figure 3). Both these buildings seem to have been architecturally pioneering—the Stoa is the earliest stoa we know of from a civic rather than a sanctuary context, and the Council chamber the earliest to appear in any city (the *bouleuterion* at Olympia may be partly earlier). At this point it is clear that the area has acquired a civic role (Shear Jr. 1994: 228–39, Camp II 2001: 32–6).

The importance of the area for the community seems, however, to antedate its governmental functions. This emerges from various infrastructural works, and in particular works to do with drainage and the water supply. In the final quarter of the sixth century the Eridanos river, at the point where it flows between the Agora and the Kerameikos, seems to have been made to run through pipes

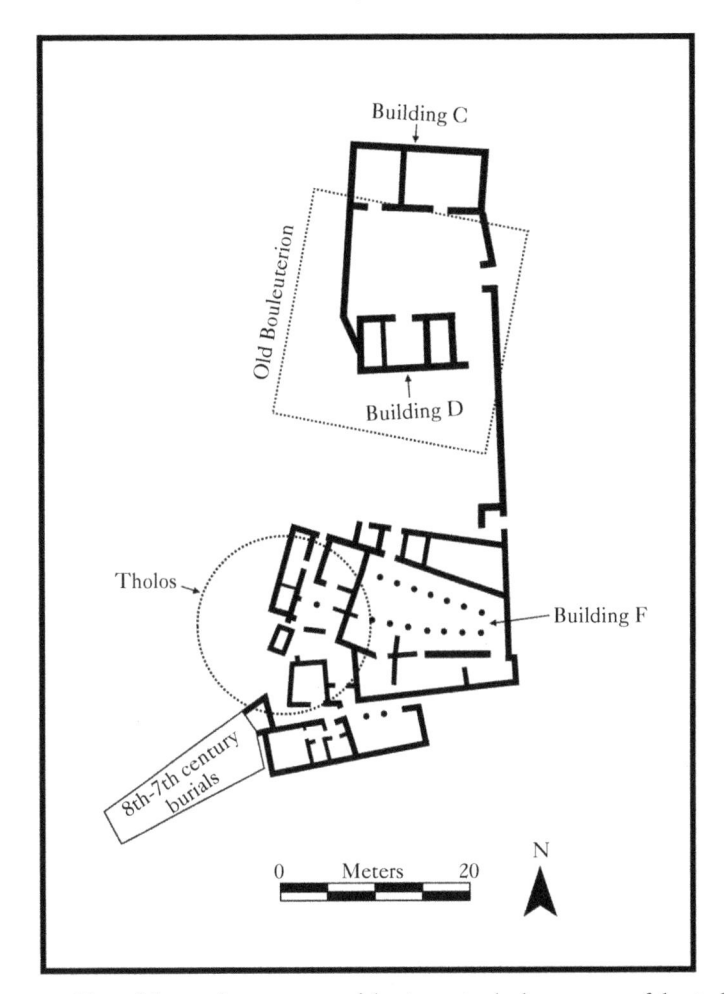

FIGURE 2 Plan of the southwest corner of the Agora in the last quarter of the sixth century, after L. Johnstone and Graff 2018: Figure 1B; later structures in the area are shown in dotted outlines.

and the resulting dry streambed was filled in. More or less at the same time, aqueducts were built bringing water from the upper Ilissos valley. The aqueduct branched to bring water both to the southwest slopes of the Areopagus and to the southeast corner of the Agora where a small fountain house was constructed, plausibly the fountain house that appears in literary accounts as Enneakrounos (Thuc. 2.15.4, Paus. 1.14.1; Camp II 1986: 42–4; Tölle-Kastenbein 1986; Tölle-Kastenbein 1994a). After the decision was taken to turn the west side of the agora over to civic use, a great drain was constructed in the early fifth century to remove surface water from what had now become a public square into the Eridanos (Ammerman 1996).

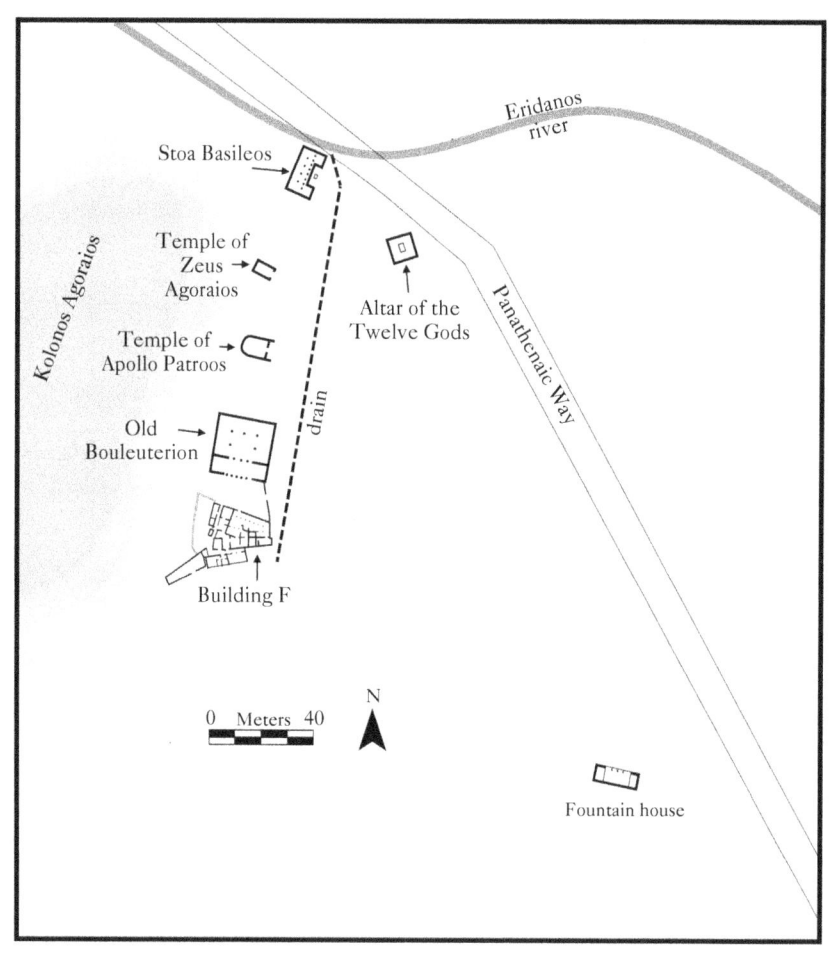

FIGURE 3 Plan of the Agora c. 500.

The importance of the Agora area already in the last quarter of the sixth century emerges also from what happens at the northwest corner, close to the Eridanos. Here the grandson of Peisistratos, when archon in 522/1 is said by Thucydides (6.54) to have set up the Altar of the Twelve Gods, which became the central milestone of the city. It is to c. 500 that the extant Agora boundary stones date (Camp II 1986: 40–2, 48; Papadopoulos 2003: 288–9).

The shift of the center of gravity from the area east and south of the Acropolis to the area north and west can be seen in what happens with cemeteries.[19] The

---

19. It has sometimes been thought that the assembly place on the Pnyx also dates to the Kleisthenic period, but excavations revealed no material by which to date the earliest rock-cut

burial grounds southeast of the Acropolis that went back to the ninth century and continue through to the sixth century disappear, whereas the Kerameikos cemetery to the northwest further expands at this period, and a new cemetery area appears in the fifth century northeast of the Acropolis, in Syndagma Square (I. Morris 1987: 62–9 with fig. 17–18; Dimitriadou 2019: 165–238). That may coincide with further development in the area east of the Acropolis. Certainly, the Peisistratids had begun work on a massive temple at the Olympieion site, and the younger Peisistratos is also associated with the Sanctuary of Apollo Pythios (not definitively located but certainly close to the Olympieion; Hesychius s.v. ἐν Πυθίῳ χέσαι). But the fact that the Olympieion was never finished may indicate that it is not merely the development of the modern city that means that we have little knowledge of this eastern part of the town.

One of the factors that may have influenced the development of the Classical Agora is the growing importance of the Peiraieus. While Phaleron was Athens' most important access to the sea, the route out of the city from south of the Acropolis was most important. But from the Peiraieus the easiest route into the city came in from the west, and thus more or less directly into the Classical Agora (Papadopoulos 2003: 285–8). The mixed character of the Classical Agora, as commercial center as well as civic center, was fundamental.

What was undisturbed by the decision to move civic functions to the Classical Agora was the pre-eminence of the Acropolis. As we will discuss in Section 11.3, the Athenians had invested heavily, and more or less continuously, through the sixth century in constructing temples and erecting substantial dedications to mark their devotion to Athena on the Acropolis. That investment increased rather than decreased at the end of the sixth century, with bigger and now public dedications (above all the bronze monument celebrating the victory over the Boiotians and Chalkidians in 508, on which see Section 7.1.2) and with a monumental propylon (gateway building), as well as with the beginning of the massive all-marble predecessor of the Parthenon on the southern part of the plateau.

The story that we tell of the development of Archaic Athens has many gaps (Greco 2014: 1542–6). The burial history is relatively well known because subterranean burials survive even when an area is continuously built over. But residential remains survive very much less well, and we have extremely poor evidence for any residential buildings until the Classical period. In consequence, we do not know how tightly nucleated residence at Athens was. There are two pointers

---

features, and it is conceivable that the Pnyx only became the Assembly place in the course of the fifth century, at the date at which a boundary stone was inscribed (*IG* I³.1092); see Thompson 1982: 136–7; G. R. Stanton and Bicknell 1987: 74–6.

toward a somewhat dispersed pattern. One is the somewhat dispersed pattern of cemeteries, and the other is the Classical division of the city into five separate demes. As elsewhere in Attica, Kleisthenes' reforms recognized existing reality rather than effecting change, and it is likely that his urban demes reflected existing separation between different communities.

Whether those communities were united within a single fortification is also unclear. Immediately after the Persian Wars the Athenians rapidly created a wall around their city, the so-called Themistoklean wall, enclosing some 211 ha. (Thuc. 1.89–93). As we have seen, the distribution of cemeteries strongly implies that from around 700 the line along which the Themistoklean wall was built was seen as the line dividing residential parts of the city from parts where burying the dead was appropriate. There were certainly earlier fortification walls close to the Acropolis, but whether there was an Archaic city wall either along the line of the Themistoklean wall or elsewhere remains unclear—there are simply no archaeological traces (Lauter and Lauter-Bufé 1975; Frederiksen 2011: 133).

4.4 Burial Practices and How Those Evolved over Time

Throughout the Archaic period there are broad patterns to burial practices across Attica, but there is also much local variation (stressed by Rönnberg 2021a: 167–92). Even when, for example, at the end of the eighth century the quantity of evidence is large, it is often extremely hard to tell whether variations are a product of local differences or are occasioned by the particular individuals being buried (by their age, by their family line, or by their wealth) (Alexandridou 2016). At some points it is plausible that there is something of a divide between the town of Athens and the rest of Attica, but more frequently variation is as manifest within Athens itself as over Attica as a whole (for the changing distribution of burial sites within Athens, see Section 4.3). In what follows I tell essentially a single story about changing burial customs within Attica over time, but I attempt to indicate when there are striking differences between different burial sites.

4.4.1 Before 800

In Late Bronze Age Attica, as more generally in the Mycenaean world, the dead, or at least the dead of significant status, had primarily been disposed of by inhumation in collective burials, predominantly in chamber tombs, although tholos tombs are known in Attica from Acharnai, Marathon, and Thorikos. But a number of single burials in cist or pit tombs are found in the Late Bronze Age

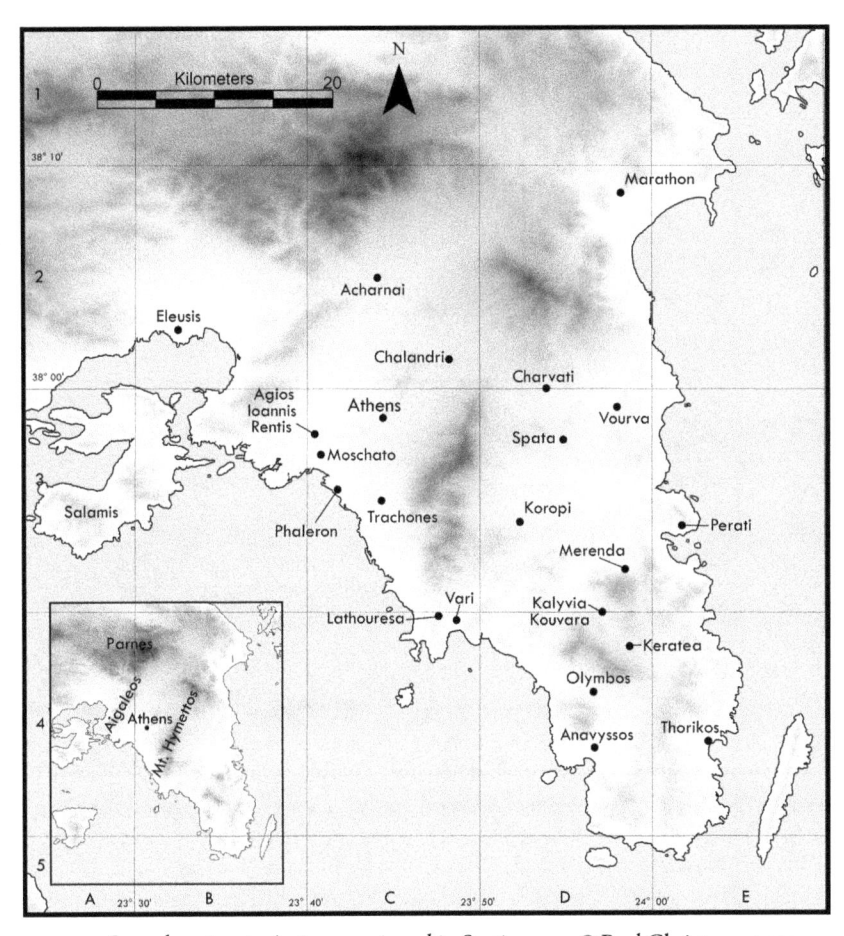

MAP 17 Some key sites in Attica mentioned in Section 4.4. © Paul Christesen 2022.

cemeteries at Athens, and also at Eleusis, throughout the LHIIB–LHIIIB period (S. A. Immerwahr 1971: 103). In the LHIIIC and Submycenaean periods cremation began to be found alongside inhumation (see Table 1). Scholars refer to the form of cremation practiced in this period as "secondary cremation," that is cremation where the body is first burned on a pyre and the charred bone fragments are then gathered and buried in a second location ("primary cremation" refers to burning the corpse in the tomb itself, with the bones then left as they had been cremated rather than gathered and placed in an urn). At the LHIIIC cemetery at Perati on the east coast of Attica, where 10 of the chamber tombs contained some cremated remains (and where, by contrast to later practice in Athens itself, the bone had been crushed after cremation and before placement in an urn), there

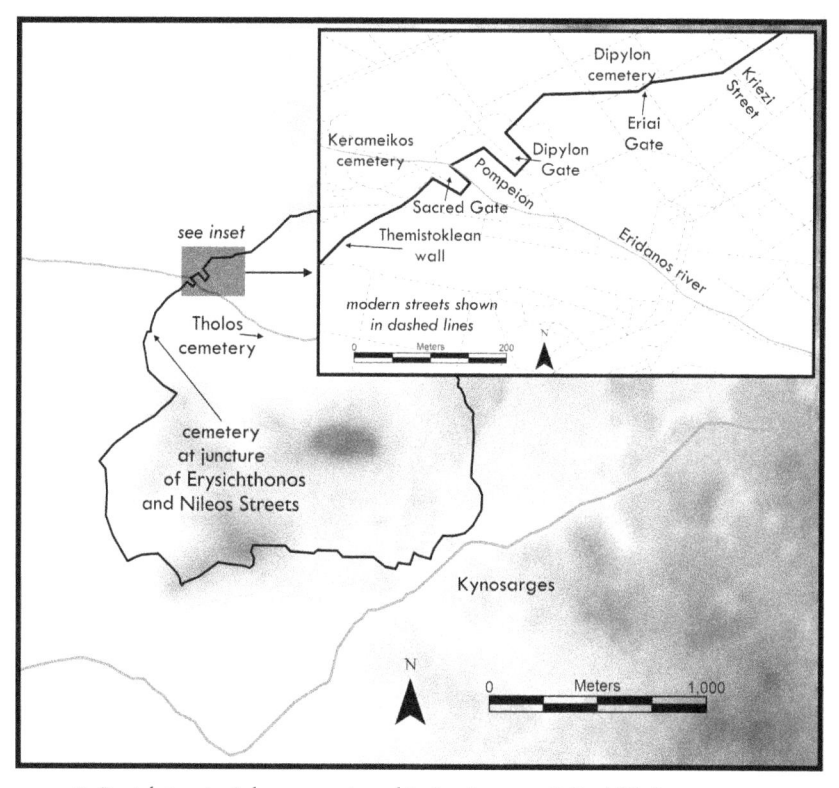

MAP 18 Burial sites in Athens mentioned in Section 4.4. © Paul Christesen 2022.

were 26 pit burials in addition to the chamber tombs, and a total of 61 tombs had just one burial in them; in the Submycenaean cemeteries of the Pompeion (in the Kerameikos area) and at the Arsenal site on Salamis, individual burials were the norm (Kurtz and Boardman 1971: 31–3; Dickinson 2006: 179–80; Ruppenstein and Lagia 2007; Papadopoulos 2017: 679–80, 86–7).

In the Protogeometric period, starting in the middle of the eleventh century, cremation gradually took over as the dominant mode of disposing of the adult dead, although inhumation continued to be practiced. Single burial is the norm, although in a small number of cases two individuals have been found in the same grave, either deposited together (e.g., mother and child groups) or occasionally apparently as the result of re-use of the grave. Cremation graves most commonly consist of a rectangular pit with a round hole in the bottom for the urn ("trench and hole" cremations), regularly an amphora, in which the cremated remains are deposited, and sometimes a second hole for remains of the pyre. The shape of the amphora used as a cinerary urn seems to have been determined by the sex of the deceased: in the Agora there is, among those cases where the bone remains enable

Table 1 Athenian Burial Practices, Submycenaean to c. 500.

Period/ Pottery style	Type of Burial	Grave Goods	Type of Commemoration
SM 1100	**Adults:** Single supine inhumation in cists and pits. Some secondary cremation with bones placed in neck amphora. **Children:** Pit burials and some cists in separate cemeteries.	Few grave goods. Pottery mainly lekythoi. Some simple jewellery. Some iron objects at end of period. Wide disparities in quantity of goods.	No preserved commemorative features. Some possible mounds.
PG 1000	**Adults:** Secondary cremation becomes dominant, but there are also some simple cremations and cremations in the burial pit. Trench and hole arrangement, for ash urns—neck amphoras for men, belly amphoras for women. **Children:** Inhumed in separate cemeteries.	Regularly found. Fewer lekythoi; cups, jugs, and bowls most common. Metal artifacts take new forms. Some sex discrimination in metal goods: some gold jewellery, some weapons. Distinct pottery assemblage for children. Richest graves female, but disparities less wide.	Mounds. LPG marker vases (kratēres for men in Kerameikos, belly amphoras for women) and stone markers.
EG/MG1 900–800	**Adults:** Trench and hole cremation; neck and shoulder-handled amphoras for men, belly amphoras for women, showing signs of special commissioning (types of decoration found only in vessels from graves). Some metal cauldron ash urns. Some inhumations after 850.	Few burials lack grave goods. More gold and jewellery (especially in women's graves), more exotic goods (ivory, faience, imported bronzes). Iron and bronze more elaborate. Some weapons.	More kratēres (perhaps commissioned) and block markers. Fifty percent of marker pots found in situ have their bases pierced. Plots enclosed.

(continued)

Table 1   Continued

Period/ Pottery style	Type of Burial	Grave Goods	Type of Commemoration
	Children: Almost disappear. Inhumations in pithoi for younger children, in pits for older.		
MGII/LGI 750	**Adults:** Inhumation becomes more common. Secondary cremation continues, but belly-amphoras no longer used as ash urns. Total number of burials rises steeply in LGI. Dipylon cemetery emerges as exceptional. **Children:** Still almost invisible. Pithos inhumation for younger children, cist inhumation for older.	Decline in number. Gold limited to few graves (Isis grave) with maximum consumption of gold bands in LGI. Pot and metal grave goods of limited range of types, but pot shapes and decoration not unique to graves, similar to sanctuaries. Weapons rare except in Dipylon cemetery.	Monumental and highly decorated grave markers—kratēres, giant oinochoai, pitchers, belly amphoras, neck amphoras. Marker an indicator of sex. Figurative scenes on some markers (but not on oinochoai or pitchers).
LGII 700	**Adults:** Transition to inhumation almost complete. Secondary cremation also locally found, with primary supine cremation in some places. **Children:** Adolescents, children, and infants (buried in pots) reappear in large numbers in adult cemeteries—even in adults' graves.	Further decline. Metal items fewer; no iron weapons. Some elaborate ivories. Distinctive grave goods for young women. offering trenches (*Opferrinne*) appear with distinctive contents: terracotta figurines, clay cauldrons on stands, neck amphoras with figured scenes. Some sacrificial pyres.	Kratēres, belly-amphoras, pitchers and oinochoai disappear as grave markers. Some graves monumental but unmarked. Some neck amphora markers, but these smaller.
Protoattic 650	**Adults:** Numbers of burials decrease. Primary cremation normal. Mass pit burials at Phaleron. **Children:** Adolescents inhumed, children in pithoi.	Goods in graves end c.700. Now *Opferrinne* only, with "banquet service" of pots. Possible sacrificial pyres at Vari.	Smaller plots and cemeteries. Mounds increase in size, and then mud-brick structures appear. Pots still used as grave markers; stele funerary markers in late seventh century

Table 1   Continued

Period/ Pottery style	Type of Burial	Grave Goods	Type of Commemoration
Black-figure 600	**Adults:** Inhumation returns in simple pits, especially after 550; some secondary as well as primary cremation. Some wooden coffins. **Children:** Inhumed in separate cemeteries, pots for young, tubs/coffins for older. A few cremations.	Numbers of *Opferrinne* decline, with just cups, bowls, and jugs.	Cemetery and plot size increases. Mounds and built tombs marked by pots and sculpture. Sculpted markers increase in magnificence; use of sphinxes declines. Painted plaques fixed to tombs. Some inscribed epigrams.
Early red-figure 500	**Adults and Children:** Cemeteries increase in size and new cemeteries begin. Both primary and secondary cremation (with various ceramic and metal vessels used as ash urns) and inhumation found. Tile graves appear. Some use of sarcophagi. **Adults:** Burial numbers increase greatly. **Children:** Burial numbers come close to matching those for adults. Pot burials and burials in clay tubs frequent.	Small in number, low in quality. Lekythoi standard, along with cups and jugs.	Grave *stēlai* vanish; *kouroi* survive only in Attica/for non-Athenians. Burial plaques cease.

determination of sex, no exception to the rule that women's bones are deposited in belly and shoulder-handled amphoras, men's bones in neck-handled amphoras (although neck-handled amphoras not used as cinerary urns are also found in some graves) (Papadopoulos 2017: 669 and fig. 5.12).

Although "trench and hole" cremations are "secondary" cremations, in the sense that the cremated remains are gathered and placed in a vessel serving as an urn, in some cases, and in some groups of graves in most cases, traces of burning show that the pit itself was the site of the cremation, rather than a pyre constructed beside the pit, but with the bones, ash, and grave goods then separated and the bones placed in an urn. There are also some cases of what have been called "simple cremations," where a pyre was built over the pit itself, and the cremated bones were deposited directly in the pit, along with charcoal, ash, and burned sherds of pottery, without an urn. The various sorts of cremation are found side by side with inhumation in the same cemetery, and there is no difference in grave goods between the two burial practices. Although some graves are distinguished by the presence of gold spirals, the distribution of grave goods does not show massive variation (Kurtz and Boardman 1971: 34–40; I. Morris 1987: 120–2; Liston 2017: 509; Papadopoulos 2017: 607–32).

Toward the end of the tenth century, pots (and stone blocks) began to be used as markers on graves, and shortly afterward pots of monumental size begin to appear as markers. Throughout the ninth century a very high proportion of graves in the Kerameikos were marked with vases, and, uniquely, kraters were common markers on male graves there (I. Morris 1987: 122–4, 51; see also Section 4.5.1). Outside Athens evidence from Merenda and Anavyssos suggests that marker vases were adopted only in the eighth century, and that their use remained restricted to a limited number of graves (I. Morris 1987: 152; see also Flament 2011: 79).

Very large cemeteries disappeared after 900, although it is unclear whether this represents community fission or is a product of social selectivity in burial (on which see Sections 4.4.2 and 9.1). In the second half of the ninth century (MG I [850–800]) inhumation began to return as a major burial practice— although to different extents in different cemeteries (cremation continues to dominate the Kerameikos and the Kriezi Street cemeteries in Athens) and at first primarily for children. The number of graves known is smaller than in the Protogeometric period, but the quantity of gold and other luxury goods, including imported ivory, faience, and imported Phoenician bronze work, increases markedly. Jewelry and other items of personal adornment, along with pots of Attic Fine Handmade Incised Ware, are, in the Agora, almost all found in the graves of women, but elsewhere the pattern is less clear (Whitley 1991: 116–37; Papadopoulos 2017: 667–78). The first use of inhumation in the Kerameikos was exceptional: uniquely for this period, a wooden sarcophagus contained an individual marked as a warrior by the presence of a sword, but also including a gold diadem, large enough (49.5 cm long) to encircle the head but actually placed on the right wrist, and having a belly-handled amphora (regularly a marker of women's graves) as a grave marker (Schlörb-Vierneisel 1975: 7–8; I. Morris 1987: 123; Alexandridou 2016: 334).

Graves that include weapons (daggers or swords) are found throughout the Early Iron Age in Athens down to the middle of the eighth century (LG 1), but their distribution seems to be skewed. The practice is much more common in graves in the northern part of the city—in the southern part of the city the practice both starts later and is much less frequent. Within the northern part of the city, in the Kerameikos the practice is predominantly an eleventh- and tenth-century one, with 15 examples from those centuries, as against six from the ninth century and at most one from the early eighth century; three eleventh-century examples are inhumations, but subsequently all, except the burial discussed above, are cremations. In Kriezi Street there are two eleventh-century examples, three ninth-century, and one perhaps early eighth-century; again all are cremations. In the Agora, there is just one example datable before 900 and four in the ninth century, all cremations. The skeletal remains from these Agora burials indicate that the men involved were active and in the prime of life, and in one case bits from horse bridles correlate with vertebral herniations characteristic of horse riders. More strikingly still, while the practice elsewhere largely dies out by around 800, there is a sudden burst of burials including a sword or dagger in the Dipylon cemetery in the middle of the eighth century (see further Section 4.4.2); in this case two of the four burials were certainly, and the other two probably, inhumations (D'Onofrio 2011, with an invaluable catalog at 659–63; Liston 2017: 512; Papadopoulos 2017: 653–4).[20]

All these variations must be seen against an overall background of ninth-century uniformity. We have a high degree of local variation, but no structured variation. There is no over-arching way of signaling hierarchy common to all cemeteries. Rather we seem to have local practices in which individual burials distinguish themselves in relation to their particular burying group. Archaeologically visible burials dip to their smallest numbers in the latter half of the ninth century with child burials hardly attested. The presence of gold and of imported material in graves points to communities able to access exotic material and to willingness to allow such goods to be put out of circulation, and the presence of marker vases points to a desire to enable on-going memory of some deceased members of the group, but the impression is that competition was highly localized.

---

20. On weapon burials, see more generally Whitley 2002.

4.4.2 The Eighth Century

For the first half of the eighth century little changes in Athens or Attica as far as the preserved record goes. Inhumation becomes more common, and the traditional trench and hole cremation disappears, with both cremations and inhumations now found in rectangular trenches surrounded by a ledge to support flat covering slabs, and both marked by ever more monumental and highly decorated pots. Those pots now include figured decoration (Section 4.5.2), initially mourning women referencing the funerary ritual. The classic depiction of the laying out of the corpse, with a scene of armed warriors marching below it, first appears in the MG II in the early eighth century. Belly-handled amphoras cease to be used as cinerary urns but remain as grave markers. But not all graves had markers, since alongside the continuation of graves marked with pots indicative of the sex and status of the deceased, there are other graves that had no markers and in which the deceased was inhumed with a large quantity of pots and metalwork (Whitley 1991: 137–62).

In the middle of the eighth century (LG I) two things happen that significantly change the picture. The first is that the number of graves known, both from Athens and from Attica, massively increases (see Figures 4a and 4b). Numbers from the early eighth century had been closely comparable to numbers in the ninth century, but the number of burials per year in LG I is close to three times the number during EG and MG (I. Morris 1987: 72–3, 218–19). The second is that one cemetery stands out from all the others for the magnificence of its burials. This is the so-called Dipylon cemetery close to the ancient Eriai Gate.[21] Unfortunately the earliest excavations here were poorly recorded, but this cemetery produced the largest and most elaborate marker vases (including the "Dipylon Amphora" [Athens NM 804]), most of them the products of a single workshop. Those vases are notable for representing a high proportion of all known LG I pots with battle scenes (Ahlberg 1971a). What is more, these graves included four burials with swords, half a century or so after such burials had ceased to be made in the Kerameikos or the cemeteries of the Agora area. So distinctive a cemetery is a quite new phenomenon (Snodgrass 1987: 148–53; Coldstream 2008: 29–33; D'Onofrio 2011: 659).

In the final third of the eighth century (LG II) the picture changes again, and in equally radical ways. The number of adult burials per year remains at a level more or less comparable to that in LG I, but the number of child burials, practically all of

---

21. What is now called the Dipylon cemetery was thus, contrary to what one might expect, not located in the immediate vicinity of the Dipylon Gate (the Dipylon Gate being the site of the Kerameikos cemetery). For the name Eriai gate, see n.17 in this chapter.

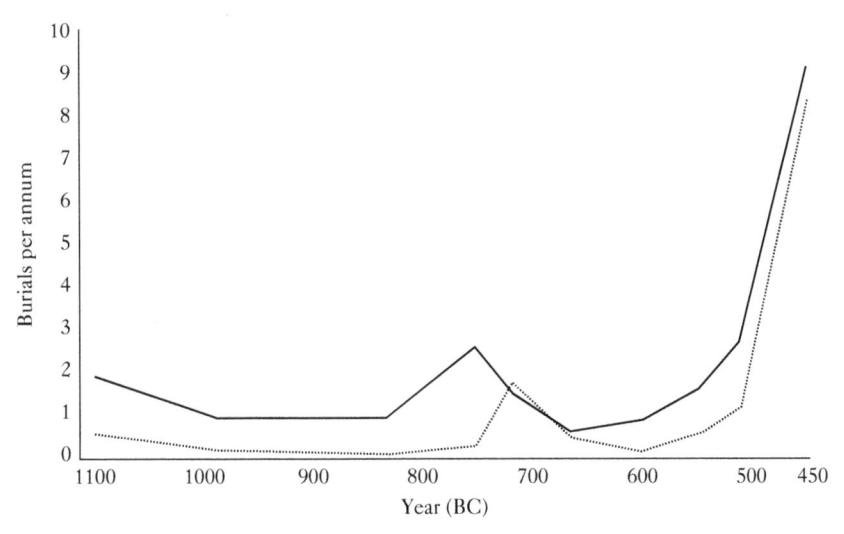

FIGURE 4a Changing numbers of burials in Early Iron Age and Archaic Athens and Attica. Based on I. Morris 1987: fig. 22.

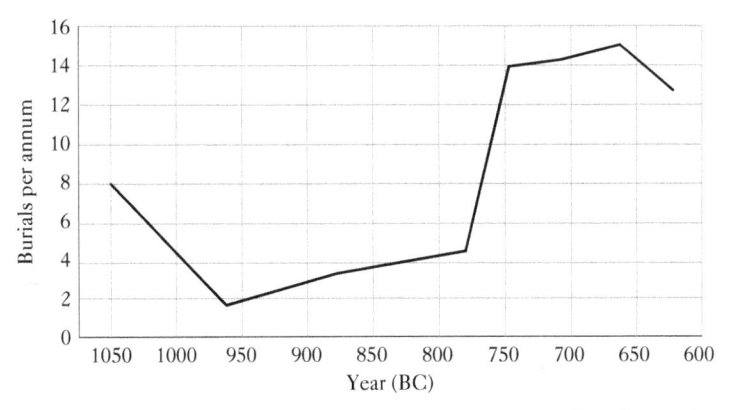

FIGURE 4b Changing numbers of burials in Early Iron Age and Archaic Athens and Attica (including 300 Phaleron graves in the first half of the seventh century, and 350 in the second half). Based on Rönnberg 2021: Diagramm 15.

them pot-burials (*enchytrismoi*), increases by a factor of more than 10, so that more child burials (as far as can be seen, equally divided between girls and boys) than adult burials are known from this period. Indeed, in some cemeteries the number of adult burials declines sharply, and they become preponderantly child cemeteries. This is a phenomenon not limited to Athens but strikingly manifested in Attica at Anavyssos and Eleusis (I. Morris 1987: 82–5, 219; Haentjens 1999; Alexandridou

2016: 334). Cremation continues to decline as a practice in this period, more or less disappearing from cemeteries in Athens north of the Acropolis, but it persisted as the general practice in cemeteries south of the Acropolis. In Attica, the picture is distinctly mixed; the large cemeteries at Anavyssos, Eleusis, Merenda, and Thorikos employed primarily inhumation, but elsewhere cremation continues at various sites including Acharnai, Palaio Phaleron, Kalyvia Kouvara, and Trachones. Alongside secondary cremation, primary cremation where the body is cremated supine in the tomb and the cremated bones are left where they were burned, a practice that seems to have been first adopted in the southeast Aegean and to have spread to Attica perhaps via Euboia, occurs (first at Trachones with bodies not fully cremated) (Alexandridou 2016: 335–47).[22]

Not surprisingly, the massive increase in the number of burials has attracted much attention. Anthony Snodgrass, who first quantified the increases, suggested that it indicated a massively rising population, but Ian Morris subsequently demonstrated that when the pattern for child-burial was separated from that for adult burial a purely demographic explanation became implausible. There are two main reasons for this. The first is that we are reasonably confident (on the basis of comparative demography) that roughly one-half the population died before reaching adulthood, and so if graves perfectly reflected the living population we would find as many child graves as adult graves for each period; in fact, we generally find far fewer child graves, but in the late eighth century we do briefly find numbers of child and adult graves matching, indicating that the proportion of burials visible to us changes from period to period for reasons unconnected with size of population. The second reason is that the rise in the number of child burials in the eighth century actually comes later than the rise in the number of adult burials, whereas in any population growth caused by increased fertility the number of child burials should rise first.

Morris himself explained the change in the eighth century as a change to including the whole of the population in visible burial (followed in the seventh century by a reversion to the social exclusion of many children and other undistinguished members of the community). This is unconvincing, not least because initially numbers of child burials continue to rise when numbers of adult burials have already begun to fall, and then child and adult burials decline at the same rate. This pattern where more children are being recognized as of appropriate status for burial when an increasing proportion of adults is being considered not of appropriate status for burial is hard to understand in social

---

22. In Athens itself cases of primary cremations are very rare. The rich Late Geometric cemetery at Kephisia divides equally between inhumation and secondary cremation (Schilardi 2011: 476).

terms, which suggests that this social explanation is not the right one (Snodgrass 1977: 10–16; Snodgrass 1980: 21–4; I. Morris 1987; Osborne 2009: 73–5; Duplouy 2019: 93–106).

But if the changing numbers of burials are not a map either of population change or of social inclusion and exclusion, what is their significance? We need to allow the possibility that the change in the number of known burials is not in fact a consequence of there having been a change in the number of people buried at all but is a result of what archaeology happens to have discovered. We should note, for instance, that the decline in the numbers of burials in the seventh century (see Section 4.4.3) that Morris observed in 1987, has been reversed by recent discoveries—most particularly by the more than 1,700 burials excavated at Phaleron, a large proportion of which date to the seventh century (see Section 4.4.3) (Rönnberg 2021a: 199–201 and Diagramme 11–15; Rönnberg 2021b; for another recent seventh-century cemetery publication, see Arrington, Spyropoulos, and Brellas 2021). But if the changing number of burials is itself an artifact of discovery, the fact that more eighth-century burials have been discovered is itself significant.

One way of thinking about archaeologically discoverable burials is in terms of location. What affects the proportion of a local population buried in a particular cemetery is the proportion of the local population for whom it was important to signal in death that they belonged to the group buried there. So burial practice may not reflect how people thought about their place in society as a whole but rather how people thought about a place in a particular local group. The more sociable a society is, the more likely it is that in death, as in life, families wish to show off before a sizeable social group; the more families are socially self-sufficient, the more likely that they will bury on their own land or very locally. There is no doubt that cemeteries became larger in the eighth century, and the reason why the Phaleron cemetery so changes our picture of the seventh century is again its vast size.

We have observed that there was a marked increase in the clustering of settlement around Athens in the eighth century (see Section 4.3), and we have interpreted that as signaling the changing importance of Athens within Attica. But the growth of settlements nearby may have increased the importance residents attached to displaying their links to their particular local settlement. It is not hard to see that as belonging to a particular place became more important, belonging to a particular family became less important; parents might continue to be concerned to signal that they and their children belonged to that local group at the same time as they become less concerned to mark that they belonged to the same group as their own parents and grandparents. In other words, the explanation for the archaeologically visible changes in burial numbers may be less about class anxieties (either way—to be included or to exclude) than with anxieties about local identities.[23] The changes in burial numbers would, on this view, go together with the marked change in the settlement pattern.

In the last third of the eighth century sacrificial pyres containing much pottery and figurines make their first appearance, both within Athens and in Attica. In the Kerameikos the earliest offering trenches are found, initially in association with inhumations but then regularly with primary cremations (Houby-Nielsen 1996: 44–6; Kistler 1998: 31–8, 149–52 and catalog 81–5; Alexandridou 2015b; Alexandridou 2016: 335). Offering trenches (sometimes referred to as *Opferrinne*) involved digging a trench close to the burial, piling wood in the trench, building over the trench a table with pots and other offerings on it, and setting fire to the wood and burning the table and the gifts (see Figures 5 and 6). All that was done with the grave open, and, when the grave was filled, the remains from the trench pyre were swept into the offering trench, and it too was filled, sealed, and at least partly covered by a mound built over the grave. Although limited to the Kerameikos, and a single case at Chalandri in Attica, in the late eighth century, offering trenches appeared subsequently in the Agora and at Vari, Vourva, and Marathon, although remaining uniquely Athenian, not found elsewhere in Greece (Houby-Nielsen 1996: 45–6; Alexandridou 2016: 335, 53).

Changes in grave goods are also marked in the last decades of the eighth century. Throughout the tenth and ninth centuries graves with metal grave goods had been three times as common as graves without metal objects, but in the second half of the eighth century the situation is reversed, with almost twice as many graves lacking metal objects as containing them. Some types of metal goods disappear altogether, notably iron daggers, swords, and spearheads, and the absolute number of metal objects in graves drops between LG I and LG II, with, correspondingly, a very uneven distribution of metal objects across LG II graves. The quantity of pottery is reduced also, and in some contrast to LG I, pottery in graves consists largely of domestic items. Overall, the distribution of grave goods is more inequitable in the second half of the eighth century than it had been at any time since the early twelfth century (I. Morris 1987: 140–4; Whitley 1991: 162–80; Belletier 2003).

Richly equipped burials for women were relatively common in the ninth and early eighth century (Whitley 1996), but in the late eighth century we lack such graves for older women. There are, however, some rich graves of girls and young women, and these are marked by a different set of grave goods: the hair spirals, model boots, and dolls that seem to be markers of childhood disappear to be

---

23. Cf. Alexandridou 2016: 354 on the importance of kinship groups at this period.

FIGURE 5 Reconstruction of a seventh-century primary cremation and associated offering trench in the Athenian Kerameikos cemetery, in cross-section (Kerameikos VI:1, Analge XI.11). From Houby-Nielsen 1996: Figure 1.

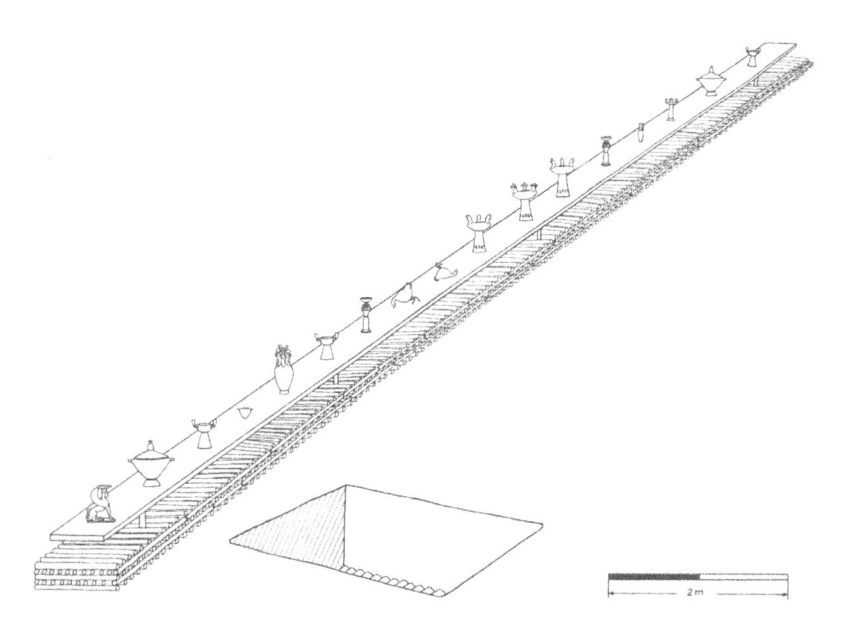

FIGURE 6 Reconstruction of a seventh-century primary cremation and associated offering trench in the Athenian Kerameikos cemetery, perspective drawing (Kerameikos VI:1, Analge XI.11). From Houby-Nielsen 1996: Figure 5.

replaced by model pomegranates, baskets, gold bands, and figurines of Demeter's daughter Kore. But graves of this type date no later than the beginning of LG II (S. Langdon 2003; S. Langdon 2008: 132–3, 41–3; Alexandridou 2016: 349–52). And, although at this point in time the burials with the most elaborate grave goods tend to be of those of females, men's graves may have been more visible. No LG II pots used as markers have been found in situ, but a significant number of large pots with burial scenes on them have been found, and the vast majority of these show a male corpse (Ahlberg 1971a: 32–3; Boardman 1998a: 173).

Not only is there inequality between graves at the end of the eighth century, but also between cemeteries, with cemeteries at Kynosarges and a newly created burial site at the juncture of Erysichthonos and Nileos Streets showing distinctly more wealth than the Kerameikos, and cemeteries in Attica, at Acharnai, Koropi, Merenda, and Spata wealthier than any Athens cemetery (I. Morris 1987: 143, cf. 52).

4.4.3 The Seventh Century

Close to 700, burial practice in Athens changed again, and in dramatic ways.[24] Until the recent Phaleron excavations, whose full publication we still await, the total number of burials known per year dropped to under half what it was during LG II, and the overall proportion of child burials to adult burials dropped from 4:3 to 4:7. With the exception of Thorikos, which has four adult burials for every six child burials, cemeteries divide clearly between those dominated by child burials and those dominated by adult burials (I. Morris 1987: 220). Although the Phaleron graves radically change this picture numerically, what happens outside Phaleron remains highly significant. Spatially, the tendency already visible in the later eighth century for sites outside the later walled area of the city to be preferred for burial becomes virtually absolute, with only the so-called "Tholos" cemetery in the area of the Classical agora and the west slopes of the Areopagus remaining in use for burials in the core area of the city, although sporadic burials continue south of the Acropolis (I. Morris 1987: 64–7; Dimitriadou 2019: 165–238).[25] Primary cremation takes over as the dominant burial rite for adults. Inhumation/pot-burial remains normal for children (D'Onofrio 2017: 278).

The Kerameikos, by far the most important cemetery known at this period, has entirely primary cremations apart from one multiple secondary cremation

---

24. Seventh-century burial practices are now thoroughly discussed by Arrington 2021: 107–55, who lists all Protoattic burials at 227–52.

25. For important late Archaic tomb bases from Erechtheiou Street, see Stavropoulos 1965.

and one adult inhumation. Although some objects are deposited in the grave itself, twice as many and more elaborate objects are deposited in the offering trenches and pyres on which items other than pottery seem to have been burned also occur. The pottery from offering trenches in the Kerameikos is dominated by drinking and pouring vessels and effectively constitutes a banquet service (Kistler 1998). Everything about the material from these offering trenches, including the scenes that appear on the figured pottery, connects them with men. So, too, most of the surviving seventh-century pots used to mark graves in the Kerameikos were kraters, the shape that had earlier invariably marked a male grave. The possibility that primary cremation and offering trenches were restricted to male burials is a real one (Houby-Nielsen 1992: 347–59). But there are strong parallels as well with the offerings made during this period of time to heroes, and these suggest that offering trenches may pick out those buried close by as approaching the condition of the heroes whose cult begins to be visible at just this time (see Section 11.1) (D'Onofrio 1993; Whitley 1994a: 217–26; Houby-Nielsen 1996: 51–5).[26]

Variability in offerings in the trenches is high, with strong evidence of bespoke objects, and the most impressive Kerameikos burials in the seventh century, in the "Rundbau" plot, include elaborate metal objects of eastern origin. The mounds constructed over the graves grow larger in the course of the seventh century, some reaching 10 m in diameter (and one in the sixth century attains 30 m in diameter). In the Kerameikos some use is also made of a small rectangular earth marker (which the excavators refer to as an "Erdmal"), measuring 2 to 4 m on the long side, 2 to 3 m on the short, and 0.5 m high, and some at least of these were covered with lime plaster (Kurtz and Boardman 1971: 81; I. Morris 1987: 129; Gaspari 2007–2008).

In the middle of the seventh century the first stone *stēlē* marker appeared in the Kerameikos, and from the late seventh century a series of impressive *stēlē* markers survives, both from Athens itself and from numerous sites in Attica (Kurtz and Boardman 1971, 79–89; I. Morris 1987: 152–3; see Section 12.1.3).[27] Although few have been found in situ, these tall and narrow *stēlai* seem to have stood not on the top of the tomb like earlier markers but at the side of the tomb, closest to the road where people might pass, see, and read.

The appearance of the stone *stēlē* does not simply change the medium with which the grave is marked, but also comes to alter the whole function of the marker (Richter 1961; Jeffery 1962; D'Onofrio 1988; Kissas 2000). The great grave markers of the Late Geometric period depicted the laying out of the corpse

---

26. See also Kistler 1998, who stresses assimilation to eastern elites rather than heroes.

27. For the earliest *stēlē*, see Jeffery 1962: 123 #1 and fig. 7.

and put the burial ritual into a wider context by juxtaposition with processions of soldiers, battles, or ships. The Protoattic and early black-figure pots that marked graves in the seventh century seem frequently to have placed the dead into a mythological context, or to have put Orientalizing monsters on display on the tomb. The earliest narrow *stēlai* acted as supports for sphinxes, making the association with being snatched away by death virtually explicit (cf. the appearance of the Gorgon on some *stēlē* shafts), and appear to have had the name of the deceased but no figurative decoration on the shaft.

Outside Athens, the richest seventh-century cemeteries in Attica are from Vari, where the southeast cemetery was used from the Late Geometric period on and the north cemetery began to be used in the seventh century (Kallipolitis 1963; Kallipolitis 1965; Alexandridou 2009; Alexandridou 2011: 34–8; Alexandridou 2012b; Alexandridou 2017b). Particularly interesting at Vari is a funerary enclosure from the third quarter of the seventh century containing eight primary cremations and six *enchytrismos* burials, all but two of children or adolescents. Apart from two graves with a single aryballos each, there were no grave goods, but over the graves was a layer of offerings including various small Corinthian oil containers, a number of figurines (dogs, horses and riders, chariot wheels, shields), two askoi, and, famously, a terracotta bier complete with driver, mourners, and a small child. This collection of material is rather different from the material found in offering trenches, but it resembles the remains of sacrificial pyres, raising the question of whether we might be dealing here with tomb-cult (there are close parallels with material deposited in the seventh century at an abandoned Late Geometric building on the Areopagus that had been constructed on the site of ninth-century burials [D'Onofrio 2001], with material found on sacrificial pyres as Eleusis, and with the material deposited in the dromos of the Acharnai tholos tomb; see further Section 11.1) (Alexandridou 2017b: 285–6). We have no way of identifying the dead treated in this way at Vari, although Alexandridou has argued for a connection with the inhabitants of Lathouresa (see Section 4.1.1.3).

Further evidence of tomb-cult at Vari north cemetery comes from tumulus 1. Primary cremation continued to be dominant in the north cemetery until late in the fifth century, but this tumulus contained not a primary cremation but an adult inhumation burial, accompanied by an offering trench with three parallel ditches. The trenches contained pottery of early sixth-century date, including pots that can be ascribed to the Gorgon Painter and to Sophilos, but primarily from the hands of what appear to be local potters, who have been named the Anagyrous Painter and the Lotos Painter (Section 4.5.3). But pottery recovered from looters who had illegally excavated here is of late seventh-century date (including work ascribed to the Nessos Painter), and includes large kraters and louteria, lidded amphoras, and lekanai. An adjacent pyre, dating to after the erection of the tumulus, yielded an iron knife and pottery of the second quarter of the sixth century (including a lekane ascribed to the Polos Painter) (Papaspyridi-Karouzou 1963; Alexandridou 2011: 34–5; Alexandridou 2017b: 286–8). The use of a burial rite unusual for the cemetery, and the nature and high quality of the pottery, all point to an exceptional burial being marked in exceptional ways.

Equally, but very differently, exceptional is the seventh-century cemetery at Phaleron (Rönnberg 2021a: 350–1). The cemetery had been first used in the eighth century and went on being used until c. 400. Excavations in the early twentieth century uncovered a large number of child burials of seventh and early sixth-century date (Young 1942), along with a single pit containing 18 skeletons, shackled in iron around the neck, arms or legs, with no grave goods. When excavations were resumed in 2012, over 1,000 further burials were excavated, bringing the total close to 2,000, a high proportion of them of seventh-century date. Most of the burials recovered in recent excavations were carried out in simple pits, with 30 percent burials of children in pots and about 10 percent primary cremations.

These recent excavations have uncovered a great many more individuals who were shackled or tied up, some in individual graves and some in large pits, many of them face down or on their sides. These include one group of 16 and, most remarkably, another group of 79 in three rows, including 40 out of a single row of 47 carefully deposited one after the other, most of them shackled (the sequence between the rows cannot, unfortunately, be determined). This group has been dated to the second half of the seventh century by two associated oinochoai. The 79 were predominantly, if not exclusively, male, and of the 53 skeletons of which more can be said than that they were "adult," six were aged 12–19, 33 aged 20–34, 13 aged 35–49, and just one over 50. Some 14 to 25 cases of bone fractures that occurred around the time of death were observed, and these may have been from fatal blows to the head as a means of execution (Ingvarsson, Bäckstrom, Chryssoulaki et al. 2019; Prevedorou and Buikstra 2019). Although it is identification of the particular occasion for mass execution that has excited most speculation, the most remarkable feature is the ability of the city to carry out such mass killings, and clearly on more than one occasion. This cemetery offers a rare glimpse of early Athens manifesting its statehood in a demonstration of the state monopoly of legitimate violence (see Section 7.2).

4.4.4 The Later Seventh and Sixth Centuries

Toward the end of the seventh century Athenian burial practices change again. Offering trenches largely disappear (with the exception of their later use in connection with the fallen at the Battle of Marathon; Whitley 1994b) during the course of the first half of the sixth century, and use of primary cremation declines. By the end of the sixth century simple pit inhumations have become dominant once more. Cemeteries and plots appear to have gradually become larger. Although the building of burial mounds continues, particularly in the Kerameikos, some mud-brick, or in the Attic countryside sometimes stone-built, structures (conventionally known as "built tombs") are now constructed over individual burial pits, some of considerable size (I. Morris 1987: 86–7, 128–37).[28] The earliest burial plaques, showing scenes of mourning, date to the late seventh century; these seem to have been fixed to built tombs (Gaspari 2007–2008: 105–8). Burial mounds, and probably the built tombs, seem to have been marked, generally with a large pot and in particular with a krater. From the second quarter of the sixth century, at latest, both figurative decoration and more elaborate epigrams appear on the shafts of grave *stēlai*. The surviving figures are always men (although one youth is accompanied by a younger sister), and they are often explicitly identified as performing actions strongly associated with men, in particular athletics, gymnasial activities, and warfare (see further Section 12.1.3).[29] Similarly, from shortly before 600 *kouroi* and *korai* are found used as gravemarkers, as, very occasionally, were seated figures and horsemen (with notable examples from both Vari and the Kerameikos) (see further Section 12.1.2).[30] Among the earliest Athenian *kouroi* are one found near the Dipylon Gate, two found in the Kerameikos (see Figure 7), and a *kouros* in New York whose findspot is uncertain but which has been claimed for the Attic cemetery at Olymbos, north of Anavyssos, from which at least one later *kouros* came (Richter 1970: #1, 6, and 9 (cf. 7); D'Onofrio 1988: esp. 85–6; Niemeier 2002; Karakasi 2003: 165). The earliest funerary *korē* from Attica is perhaps that from Agios Ioannis Rentis, to be dated around the end of the first quarter of the sixth century; the so-called Berlin Standing Goddess from Keratea and a *korē* from Moschato date not much later (Karakasi 2003: 116, 61).

Although the *kouros* and *korē* offer non-specific images, not only do the surviving bases bear inscriptions identifying the deceased by name, and by implication identifying the figure in the sculpture with the deceased, but from the second quarter of the century onward there are more or less elaborate associated

---

28. For the possible lag between town and country over the changes at the end of the seventh century, see Alexandridou 2008: 68.

29. There are three *stēlē* bases, all from Athens itself, with epigrams for women; all appear to have been much wider than the standard bases, and Jeffery suggested that *stēlai* for women may have had a different appearance from those for men, much more like the rather squarer Classical *stēlai* (Jeffery 1962: 149–50).

30. Just two funerary statues of horsemen survive, one from the Kerameikos (Kerameikos Museum P6999; Eaverly 1995: #5 [which may go with a known base (*IG* I³.1218) that otherwise would belong to a second Kerameikos equestrian monument]), and the other from Vari (Athens NM 70; Eaverly 1995: #11). For the range of funerary sculpture including seated figures, see D'Onofrio 1995b: 192–9.

FIGURE 7 Naxian marble kouros (the (Sacred Gate Kouros); c. 600; height: 2.10 m; excavated in the Kerameikos in 2002. Kerameikos Archaeological Museum Inv. 1700.

epigrams. These frequently identify *korai* and *kouroi* as set up by a parent (i.e., the deceased as having died young), invite the viewer to mourn, and may say something about the virtues of the deceased ("a good and sensible man") and, exceptionally, reveal the circumstances of death—always death in war ("furious Ares slew him as he fought in the front rank").[31] Epigrams that related to *stēlai* had less work to do, since the *stēlē* itself said something about the activities of the deceased, but they similarly identify the deceased by name, often the kin who set up the monument, and perhaps the sculptor, and may add something about the qualities of the man.[32]

31. *IG* I³.1200 (Xenokles), 1211 (Xenophantos), 1214 (Nelonides), 1240 (Kroisos), 1251 (unknown woman), 1261 (Phrasikleia), 1269 ("a good and sensible man"). See for further discussion D'Onofrio 1988: 91–4.

32. *IG* I³.1194bis (Tettichos), 1196 (Chairedemos), 1204 (Thrason), 1206 (Aisimides), 1215 (Stesias), 1229 (Oinanthe), 1231 (Philoitios and Ktesias), 1234 (Alkimachos), 1241 (unknown), 1243 (Damasistratos), 1257 (Lyseas), 1258 (X[enophon?]), 1265 (Archias and his sister), 1273bis (Autokleides), 1277 (Kleioites), 1278 (Theosemos).

The custom of surmounting a *stēlē* with a sphinx seems to have died out in the third quarter of the sixth century, and with it the last indications of the otherworldliness of death. One *stēlē* of c. 560 has a running Gorgon in relief below the figure, but later examples have figures riding horses.[33] Death is turned into an opportunity to advertise the affective bonds within a family and to parade the qualities admired in men and, rather less frequently, women.

These monuments show clearly that sophisticated images and epigrams were by no means a feature merely of the town. Both in terms of artistic quality and in terms of literary sophistication, the *stēlai*, *kouroi*, and *korai* from Attica are quite as outstanding as those from Athens itself.[34] Whereas earlier burials must have created their maximum effect at the moment of burial, when the elaborate primary cremation and offering trench rituals will have impinged on sight, hearing, and smell, and have been hard to ignore, sixth-century burials left permanent markers that kept the dead in mind, and drew attention to the families that were locally dominant.

A number of ceramic funerary plaques survive: the earliest plaque, dating from the late seventh century, has relief decoration, but all subsequent plaques are painted (Boardman 1955; Shapiro 1991; Bournias 2017). Down to the last quarter of the sixth century the plaques were made to be part of a series; at the end of the sixth century single plaques were made, perhaps reflecting a reduction in the size of tombs. Many of the surviving plaques can be ascribed to the hands of well-known black-figure pot painters, including Sophilos, Lydos, Exekias, and the Sappho Painter, and their close links to painted pottery help their dating (see Figure 8). No plaques were painted in the red-figure technique, and the latest plaques date to 500 or shortly after. Several surviving plaques have writing on them, and in at least one case that certainly includes a name, suggesting that the plaques might be bespoke goods; but the plaque with the most writing on it simply identifies participants by their relationship (mother, father, brother, sister, grandmother: Paris Louvre MNB 905, ascribed to the Sappho Painter, c. 500, from Cape Kolias). The plaque series show mourners and processions as well as the laying out of the corpse; the single plaques show the laying out of the corpse. The corpse being laid out is most commonly female, but

---

33. For the Gorgon, see Athens NM 2687 (Richter 1961: #27). For charioteer and horsemen, see New York Metropolitan Museum 36.11.13 (Richter 1961: #45), Rome Barracco (Richter 1961: #64), Athens NM 30 (Richter 1961: #70), Athens NM 31 (Richter 1961: #71).

34. G. Anderson 2003: 24–6 (cf. D'Onofrio 1984) tries to draw a contrast between the use of *kouroi* in Athens and their use elsewhere in Attica, but the small number of data points makes his supposed pattern vanishingly insecure. To map distributions fully demands taking into account both fragmentary statues and bases on which statues once stood.

FIGURE 8 Athenian painted funerary plaque; c. 520–510; 26 x 36.2 x 0.9 cm. Metropolitan Museum New York 54.11.15.

there are some men, in particular young men. The visual emphasis, however, is with the mourners.

At the end of the sixth century, there is yet another marked change in burial at Athens. The most striking aspect of this change is the enormous growth in the number of archaeologically visible burials. The sixth century had seen a gradual increase in numbers of burials per annum (by a factor of about three over the course of the century), although this was less apparent among the very small numbers of child burials than in adult burials. But in the last decade or so of the sixth century the number of burials archaeologically recovered increases enormously (by a factor of four for adults, of eight for children), and the number of child burials comes close to matching the number of adult burials. There is a small increase in the size of burial plots (i.e., the size of a group that buries together) but a very significant increase in the size of the cemeteries. The whole appearance of the Kerameikos cemetery was transformed, and a number of new cemeteries come into existence (I. Morris 1987: 70–1, 87, 134). Grave *stēlai* vanish before the end of the sixth century, and of the certainly or probably funerary *kouroi* known from bases that have sometimes been thought to date to after 500, two of the four are for non-Athenians; the Athenians both come from Attica rather than Athens itself—Aristodikos from near Anavyssos and Nausistratos at Charvati.[35] Burial plaques cease just after 500. After 480, perhaps after 490, no grave received a stone grave marker of any sort until c. 430.

There is textual evidence for the regulation of burial practices, both at the beginning of the sixth century and at some uncertain point later, but exactly how those regulations relate to the archaeology is far from clear. A speech of Demosthenes (43.62–3) quotes a law, ascribed to Solon, prescribing that, when someone dies, they must be laid out in their house and then buried the next day before sunrise, with a funeral procession with men in front of the corpse and women behind, and with the women restricted to close relations and those over 60. Cicero in two passages of *On the Laws* (*Leg.* 2.59, 63–6) quotes Solonian funerary legislation restricting the mode of female mourning and what the corpse should be dressed in and imposing penalties for damaging a tomb or funerary monument; Cicero claims that this legislation was followed closely by the Roman authors of the Twelve Tables. Plutarch in the *Life of Solon* gives more detail of the regulation of women's behavior and reports a Solonian prohibition on sacrificing an ox to the deceased and on visiting the tombs of non-family members outside the context of the funeral (Blok 2006).[36] (For Solon's legislation more generally, see Section 6.2.)

Much of what Solon is said to have regulated could not be expected to leave archaeological trace—the clothing in which the corpse was dressed simply does not survive, and the only evidence for the dress of mourners comes from painted pots and plaques. Sacrificial pyres with animal bones are known from cemeteries both before and after Solon, but the animal bones identified are always from small animals, not oxen. We might see a reflection of the requirement that female mourners have a family connection in the funerary plaques where the participants are identified by their relationship to the deceased.

Cicero also records that "some time after Solon" (*post aliquanto, Leg.* 2.64) limits were imposed on how much labor (no more than three days' work for 10 men) could be put into a tomb, and that sculpted monuments and plaster work were banned. Scholars have variously connected this legislation with the

---

35. The non-Athenians are both Samians, Aischros (*IG* I³.1366) and Antistasis (*IG* I³.1368). For Aristodikos, see *IG* I³.1244, for Nausistratos, see *IG* I³.1253. *IG* dates these four bases to 520–490, 500–480, 500–490, and c. 500, respectively (always with question marks). For all these late funerary *kouroi*, see Karusos 1961.

36. Anderson's attempt (G. Anderson 2003: 26) to link the absence of funerary *kouroi* from Athens itself between c. 590 and c. 530 to Solon's "sumptuary legislation," which he regards as applying to Athens itself but not Attica, takes no account of the attested content of Solon's legislation.

disappearance of *stēlai* surmounted by sphinxes in the 530s, in favor of simpler *stēlai*; with the end of plaque series, in favor of individual plaques, at about the same date; and with the end of sculpted *stēlai* and *kouros/korē* grave markers altogether, in the years following 500. Of these changes the most dramatic is the disappearance of all stone tomb markers, a change that is so complete that it does appear to reflect some legislative action.

4.5 The History of Pottery
4.5.1 Athenian Pottery Before the Eighth Century

Athens had a continuous tradition of fine pottery production through the Late Bronze Age and into the Early Iron Age. Basic techniques of preparing clay, throwing a pot on a potter's wheel, and use of "black glaze," a slip that changes color from red to black when fired in an oxygen-free atmosphere, were never lost. Conventionally the point of maximum rupture is taken to be the replacement of what has become known as the Submycenaean style 1125–1050) by what has been termed Protogeometric style (c. 1050–900). Submycenaean encompasses a far smaller range of shapes than had been current at the height of the Late Bronze age, but it still featured such characteristic Mycenaean shapes as the stirrup-jar.

Protogeometric, a style marked by the introduction (perhaps from Cyprus?) of the multiple brush and the compass and their use together, substitutes jugs for stirrup-jars, begins to enlarge the repertoire of shapes again, and is dominated, as will be all Attic pottery production down to 700, by large pots, particularly kraters and amphoras (Desborough 1952: 3–4; Schweitzer 1971: 24–5; R. M. Cook 1997: 5–9; Boardman 1998a: 13–15). Attic Protogeometric (PG) pottery distinguished itself by the taut precision of its forms, achieved by use of a fast wheel; by the pure abstraction of its decoration, uninfluenced by naturalistic forms except in as far as one or two figures of horses appear; and by certain particular tendencies, not least giving pots high conical feet.

Another shift, to what is conventionally called the Geometric style, took place c. 900. Around that time the fashion for the high foot disappeared from open pots (skyphoi), and various closed pots change their shape. Black glaze now covers the whole pot, semicircles disappear from the decoration, and circles are more sparingly used, while meanders and chevrons became more common. The square decorative panels that had appeared in Protogeometric on skyphoi now appear also on amphoras. Scholars distinguish this style as Early Geometric (EG; 900–850) (Desborough 1952: 119–26; Schweitzer 1971: 24–5; R. M. Cook 1997: 18–19; Boardman 1998a: 24; Coldstream 2008: 9–15).

In the second half of the ninth century the amount of plain black surface is reduced, and by 800 some pots become entirely covered with patterned decoration. Panels of decoration grow to fill the available space (width of neck, space between handles, etc.), giving the decoration a closer relationship to the shape of the pot. Various new forms appear, including feet in the form of clay loops (a feature apparently taken over from Cyprus) and handles molded to give the impression that they are of twisted rope; various sub-types of the pyxis become important shapes, and the flat variety may be decorated on its round bottom surface. The earliest monumental grave-marker pots appear at the end of the ninth century (see Section 4.4 for further details), a krater (Kerameikos Inv. 1254; Kübler 1954: pl. 22) and a belly-handled amphora (see Figure 9; Kübler 1954: pl. 47) just over a meter in height from the Kerameikos (see Section 4.4.1) (R. M. Cook 1997: 19–20; Boardman 1998a: 25; Coldstream 2008: 16–21).[37] Scholars distinguish this style as Middle Geometric I (MG I; 850–800).

4.5.2 The Eighth Century

The monumental MG I krater from the Kerameikos has figures of a horse and a mourning woman close to the surviving handle, but the regular use of figurative decoration does not begin until the first half of the eighth century, as part of the style conventionally labeled Middle Geometric II (MG II; 800–760). Not only are there more figures, but the figures move from being subsidiary to being the center of attention. Both in terms of distribution and in terms of manufacture, figure scenes seem to have caught on across Attica. This applies not only to *prothēsis* scenes related directly to the use of the pot, but also to other scenes. To MG II belong, on a large krater now in New York (see Figure 10) and on a small skyphos from Eleusis (see Figure 11), the earliest scenes on Athenian pottery of what will become a popular iconographic choice: fighting on land and sea.[38] At the same time three-dimensional clay figures of horses come to be added to the lids of some flat pyxides, and miniature pots to the lids of some globular pyxides; the elaboration of some vessels suggests that they must have been comparatively luxury items (Schweitzer 1971: 32–7; R. M. Cook 1997: 20; Boardman 1998a: 25; Coldstream 2008: 21–8).[39]

The scenes of fighting on both the New York krater and the skyphos from Eleusis are remarkable for their elaboration. The New York krater (see Figure 10),

---

37. On the workshop to which both Kerameikos marker pots belong, see Kourou 1997. On monumental pots and graves more generally, see Vlachou 2017.

38. For the theme, see Ahlberg 1971a; Moore 2000.

39. For figure scenes on pots produced in Attica, see Vlachou 2011.

FIGURE 9 Athenian MGI belly-handled amphora; second half of ninth century; height: 1.07 m; from the Kerameikos cemetery.

which must have stood over a grave, has scenes of the laying out of the corpse (*prothēsis*) in panels on the center of both sides, although these are poorly preserved, and there is a mourning female figure beside one handle. Below this is a continuous band of figurative decoration, showing on each side a ship (running from the left handle to below the *prothēsis* scene) and a row of warriors. The soldiers, carrying what has become known, from their appearance on Late Geometric (LG) pottery (see below), as "Dipylon" shields, march in the direction that the ship is facing and fill the space in front of and behind the ship. Both ships have birds on their sterns and warriors fighting in single combat on the ship itself, along with an archer shooting from the ship and warriors carrying Dipylon

FIGURE 10 Athenian MGII krater; first quarter of eighth century; height: 99.1 cm; diameter: 94 cm; from the Kerameikos cemetery. Attributed to the Workshop of New York MMA 34.11.2.

shields. The centers of the two ships are not well preserved, but on at least one side some sort of sail is depicted, with a bare-headed figure sitting beneath (Marwitz 1961; Ahlberg 1971a: 27–9; Mertens 2010: 46–51).

On the Eleusis skyphos (see Figure 11), one side shows a ship with elaborate bow and stern, a figure managing a steering oar, and another figure, shown above the ship, with a bow shooting to the left. The ship is flanked by two figures with Dipylon shields, each with two spears carried diagonally on their left side and one spear carried horizontally. A bird sits on one end of the ship. The other side of the skyphos shows six figures. In the center are two figures floating more or less horizontally, their heads to the right and the right hand of the lower figure linking with the left hand of the upper figure. They are flanked by two archers drawing their bows, about to fire at each other. Behind these are two further standing figures; the figure on the right appears to be about to throw a spear with his left hand, while the figure on the left has a curious oblong implement across its waist. It is not entirely easy to judge the spatial contexts: the archer above the ship

FIGURE 11 Athenian MG II skyphos; c. 800; height: 6.4 cm; from Eleusis. Eleusis Archaeological Museum 910 (741).

might be intended to be standing on land beyond it; the two horizontal figures on the other side may be intended to be represented as in the sea. What is clear is that we are being reminded of a context of fighting that includes both archers and heavily armed warriors, and both fighting on land and fighting that involves ships and the sea (Ahlberg 1971a: 34–7).

The rather trivial nature of the Eleusis pot that bears this scene contributes to its significance. For this is very clearly not a scene painted by an artist unfamiliar with the conventions of figurative art. As Bernhard Schweitzer noted, this artist "sees the moving figure with the eye of a sculptor," shows a capacity to capture motion, and is far from rigid in the way he sets up his symmetries (Schweitzer 1971: 37). Like the New York krater, the Eleusis skyphos shows complete familiarity with the iconographic conventions that will be regular in Late Geometric figure scenes, but it also stands clearly in the tradition of figurative representation known from the Late Bronze Age. Here and elsewhere in later Geometric art the details of particular figures (e.g., the man throwing the spear) coincide so closely with representations in Mycenaean glyptic and painted pottery that some knowledge of that tradition must be postulated. The thin surviving thread of animal images on pottery from Protogeometric through to the eighth century does not itself give evidence for continuity, and the possibility of Mycenaean pottery being rediscovered and exerting its influence has been suggested (and there is indeed evidence for rediscovery of old tombs, see Section 11.1) (Benson 1970; Ahlberg 1971a; Coldstream 2006). But just as we know that the tradition of oral epic poetry persisted from the Bronze Age down to Homer in the seventh century, carrying with it various formulaic phrases that preserved the memory of lost Bronze Age objects, so this case gives grounds, not least in the high degree of competence shown by the Eleusis skyphos, for thinking that in some medium or another, and textiles are one possibility, the tradition of figurative representation survived in Athens, potentially carrying with it similar "fossils."

There is one further notable aspect of the scenes on the New York krater and the Eleusis skyphos. This is the very notion of fighting on a ship. Although fighting on ship appears on fragments of LH IIIC kraters from Kynos in Lokris (Dakoronia 2006), scenes of fighting on ships appear also in Near Eastern, and in particular Egyptian, art while a number of the other fighting motifs, including the single combat motif, are closely paralleled in North Syrian art. It looks as if there may be multiple influences combining to produce these scenes, and that remains true as these scenes of fighting on land and sea are repeated and elaborated on pottery from the second half of the eighth century, when additional motifs (warriors falling from chariots, chariots driving over corpses, piles of corpses) appear that have their closest parallels in Assyrian art (Benson 1970: 88–105; Ahlberg 1971a: 71–106, esp. 105–6). It seems that from the beginning of the eighth century, artists were able to draw upon both a tradition of figurative art inherited from the Bronze Age and on models from the Near East. But what is it that inspired them suddenly to do this?

Figurative decoration becomes a dominant element on pots in what is conventionally termed Late Geometric I (LG I; 760–735). That style showed a predilection for covering the whole pot, and the decoration itself becomes more complicated and more elaborate, with double and triple meanders and combinations of lozenges and zigzags that have caused scholars to talk of "tapestry" design. But different workshops seem to have put their energies into different aspects of design, with especially elaborate decorative motifs coming from the workshop of the so-called Dipylon Master (named after the findspot of its best known products, the Dipylon cemetery, on which see Section 4.4.2) (see Figure 12) (Coldstream

FIGURE 12 Athenian LGIa krater ascribed to the Dipylon Master; height: 0.58 m (in present form); c. 750; from the Diplyon cemetery. Paris Louvre A517.

2008: 29–53 ["Dipylon master" 29–41]; R. M. Cook 1997: 20–2; Boardman 1998a: 25–7; Mertens 2010: 52–7; Coulié 2015 [Dipylon workshop]; Vlachou 2015 ["Hirschfeld Painter"]).

The most famous pots of this period are the extremely large amphoras and kraters produced to mark graves, particularly in the Dipylon cemetery. These pots, which stand up to 1.8 m high in the case of some amphoras, 1.25 m for kraters, invariably bear in the handle zone an image of the laying out (*prothēsis*) or carrying out (*ekphora*) of the dead body on a bier, surrounded by mourners. Those images are often supplemented with further scenes lower on the body of the pot; belly-handled amphoras receive depictions of mourners, whereas kraters receive depictions of armed men and chariots in procession, or of fighting on land and/or at sea, in the tradition already discussed.[40] These scenes are highly legible, employing schematic figures with triangular upper bodies and arms comprising thin straight lines, and repeating identical forms for identical actions. Thus, mourners raise one

---

40. On *prothēsis* and *ekphora* scenes, see Ahlberg 1971b; Rombos 1988: 77–91; Cavanagh and Mee 1995; Kourou 2002: 38, 85–8; Hiller 2006; cf. also Benson 1970: 88–99. On chariot processions and processions of warriors, see Rombos 1988: 92–153. On fighting on land and sea, see Ahlberg 1971a.

or two arms to tear their hair, where the upper arm either represents a continuation of the outline of the triangular body or is vertical, and the lower arm turns horizontally to meet the top of the head. When warriors carry a Dipylon shield, its distinctive outline replaces their bodies and the upper parts of their legs. Male and female figures are distinguished by women being shown skirted, or with visible breasts, or by particular gestures: it has been disputed whether having two arms to the head marks the female mourner, whereas the male mourner has one arm to the head and the other raised or touching a sword, or whether female mourners must be skirted, but breast indications on some unskirted figures suggest that two arms to the head may be a gendered gesture. The clarity with which types of figures and actions are indicated enables quite complicated situations to be shown.

Much attention has been devoted to the ways in which warriors are shown on these pots. We have already had occasion to refer to the warrior with the Dipylon shield. Such warriors dominate the processions in LG I, sometimes alternating with archers, although spearmen without shields are also shown. The dominance of the Dipylon shield in LG I is despite the fact that already in MG warriors with round shields had been shown, and warriors with round shields become important in LG II. The Dipylon shield also appears represented on its own, and in LG II (and again, later, in Protoattic pottery) will be shown as a shield device on a round shield—notably on an amphora (Benaki Museum 7675) where the *prothēsis* scene on the neck shows weapons hanging behind the dead body (see Figure 13).[41]

All of this makes it clear that the Dipylon shield was a powerful signifier—but of what? Was it a product of painters' imagination, aesthetically preferable to the round shield that obscured so much and introduced too much black paint to the pot surface? Was its resonance "heroic," reminding viewers of the great exploits of which they learned in oral epic and associated with those who built the Bronze Age monumental tombs that they from time to time discovered? Was it a contemporary variant of a functional shield, favored by some particular group? The Dipylon shield is an exaggerated form of what becomes a standard form of shield (the so-called "Boeotian shield") whose continuous circumference is interrupted by two small cut-outs, and that exaggeration likely gave the shield its attraction for artists, making it readily legible and, for the strict artists of Late Geometric I, aesthetically preferable. But that does not prevent it from having further significance.

What further significance the Dipylon shield has depends on how we interpret the scenes on LG I pots. The representation of the laying out and carrying

---

41. For discussion, see Hurwit 1985a; S. Langdon 2008: 263–5.

FIGURE 13 Athenian LG II amphora; height: 59.5 cm; 720–700. Attributed to the Benaki Painter. Benaki Museum 7675.

out of the corpse on pots that were placed on graves, and the distinguishing of female corpses on pots placed on female graves and of male corpses on pots placed on male graves, indicates that the scenes shown relate in a quite specific way to contemporary life. On some pots the second band of decoration also relates directly to the funeral—so the largest of all belly-handled amphoras (Athens NM 803) shows a continuous string of mourners in its second frieze. It would be unsafe to conclude, however, that all the figure scenes in the second band of decoration conjure up some contemporary event. The very limited range of types of scenes in LG I, and the high degree of repetition of incidents in scenes of fighting on land and sea argue against any attempt here to represent some particular recent event, and in favor of viewers recognizing familiar story incidents, if not a single familiar story.

Developments in the last third of the eighth century (LG II, 735–700) provide much more data for understanding the significance of figure scenes. Significant innovations in form occur in this period. The giant pots made as grave markers are found no longer. Familiar shapes, such as the neck-handled amphora, become progressively narrower and acquire molded additions; molded snakes had first appeared on the handles late in LG I, but now they are found also on the rims and at the junction of neck and body. Some old shapes, notably the flat pyxis and the krater of the shape that had marked graves, disappear completely. A new spouted krater appears, and along with it a new shape of shallow skyphos or cup.

Along with changes in form come changes in style—although it is hard to talk of a "period style" when different workshops make distinctive stylistic choices. There are nevertheless some general trends. No significant new motifs are introduced into the pre-existing repertoire of linear decoration, but, when they are not avoided altogether, older motifs become debased and frequently executed carelessly, with multiple brushes used more for rapidity than for regularity. Meander decoration becomes relatively rare except on the neck of amphoras, and nonfigurative decoration on the body of amphoras is often limited to lozenge chains, four-limbed sigmas, checkerboard, and zigzags. Decoration ceases to relate sensitively to shape, and on some pots numerous narrow bands of decoration are used (Whitley 1991: 162–5; Kourou 2002: 38–62; Coldstream 2008: 53–90).[42]

Figurative decoration evolves in significant ways. The men, women, birds, and animals in figured scenes cease to be so starkly geometric: torsos are no longer pure triangles, as a straight-sided element is inserted to represent the waist; skirts acquire something of a swing; calf muscles bulge; some animal haunches and bodies begin to fill out. An air of animation is produced that is exploited by innovations in iconography. To the chariots of LG I are added riders; to the goats, deer, and horses of LG I are added cows, bulls, and running dogs. More exotic creatures are also introduced: sphinxes, centaurs, winged goats, and lions fighting men or other animals. Alongside the funeral scenes, processions of warriors and chariots, and warfare of LG I we now have scenes of athletics (boxing), dancing (see Figure 14) (male, female, and armed), hunting, and cult. Fighting on land or sea and ships effectively disappear from the repertoire, found only on a small number of oinochoai and one krater. Some new themes seem to have been the specialty of a single workshop (cult scenes the specialty of the so-called "rattle group"), others are widely adopted (e.g. dancers and riders) (Rombos 1988: 372).

---

42. On the shallow skyphos, see Borell 1978.

FIGURE 14 Athenian LG II skyphos; c. 735–720; diameter: 16 cm; from the Kerameikos cemetery. Attributed to the Burly workshop. Athens National Archaeological Museum 874. Photo by Giannis Patrikianos.

Two contrasting features of these iconographic innovations are significant. The first is that in adding athletics, dancing, cult, and hunting to the selection of human activities shown, artists are adding subjects that would have been familiar to them from daily life. They are also adding subjects where the interest is more generic than particular. This is obviously especially true of scenes of cult and of dancing (itself plausibly in a cultic context), where the whole aim of a ritual performance is to carry out again exactly the actions that have been carried out on other occasions. But in the case of hunting and athletics there is also a strong focus on taking part in an activity with clear rules and conventions, and showing that one can carry through those rules effectively—capturing or killing an animal using recognized techniques, or competing with set equipment and set limits on the means that may be used. The second feature of the iconographic innovations is the introduction of creatures that can never have been witnessed, and while winged goats and sphinxes seem to have been a peculiarity of a single workshop (the Workshop of Athens 894), centaurs are painted in three different workshops (although again most popular with the prolific Workshop of Athens 894) and on four different shapes.

To understand what lies behind these iconographic changes, it is important to consider the uses to which the pots in question were put. The ending of the practice of putting very large pots on graves as markers was also the ending of pots being used as ways of advertising certain sorts of activities to a general public. The decorated pottery used in funerary contexts of the late eighth century was concealed in, rather than exposed on, graves, and, with the development of the practice of offering trenches, pots were deposited there, frequently after having been subjected to fire (see Section 4.4.2) (Whitley 1991: 178–9). In the late eighth century engagement with images on pots therefore became much more closely tied to particular occasions, as they were viewed with the heightened emotions of the funeral, or the excitement of the drinking party.

In the discussion of funerary practices (Section 4.4.2), attention was drawn to the distinctive grave goods that seem to have marked graves of young women at Athens in the eighth century. Life stages, and the transitions from one life stage to another, seem more generally to have been a subject to which images on pottery drew attention. The monsters that arrive in Athenian LG II pottery—the winged goats, centaurs, and sphinxes, to be joined in the seventh century by Gorgons—drew attention to the distinctiveness of men, animals, and birds precisely by exploring what happened if one blurred the distinctions. It is notable in this context that the earliest images of centaurs seem to focus on the centaur as a friendly rather than a hostile figure, gesturing toward the story of the centaur Cheiron as teacher of Achilles. Arguably images of fighting between men and lions, and even images of the encounter between men and the elemental sea in shipwreck scenes, achieve a similar effect by slightly different means.

But the new scenes that appear are not all scenes that pit humans against nature—many of them explore associations between humans. The association of men and women in mourning, or of men in forming an army, is now joined by the association of men and women—and perhaps specifically young women—in the dance and more generally in ritual. These scenes of dancing are notably absent from amphoras but frequent on "tankards" (despite the name, best seen as a form of jug) and on hydriai. Although both those vessels are found in graves, their primary function seems likely to have been in some of the rituals of life. Dance iconography is found in the Late Geometric material from the Sanctuary of Artemis Mounychia (Section 11.2), and in the seventh century it will be found too on the Athenian Acropolis (S. Langdon 2008: 56–125 [for monsters], 26–96 [for maidens]).

Even images that appear at first glance to focus on a particular incident turn out, on closer examination, to be less concerned with some particular story than with the challenges of life. An especially interesting example of this is provided by a LG II kantharos, dating to around 720, now in Copenhagen but probably from a grave in the Dipylon cemetery (see Figure 15). The central scene here shows a man in the jaws of two lions. This scene is flanked on one side by two men fighting with swords (but without armor), on the other by a man with a lyre and two women (one with visible breasts) with trailing garlands and jugs on their heads (an activity paralleled in a number of Geometric figurines). Beyond the sword fight are two further figures, a woman, again with visible breasts, holding a trailing garland and a man who holds her hands.

On the other side of the kantharos the center is occupied by a pair of boxers, flanked on one side by armed dancers performing before a judge and on the other by acrobats performing before a man playing a lyre. How do these scenes fit together? What we seem to have is a rehearsal of the qualities expected in the ideal young man—the ability to fight with sword, to box, to dance in armor, to perform acrobatics, to play the lyre for festival dancing, and to win a bride. The scene of the man in the jaws of two lions has been seen as, by contrast to the other scenes, symbolic, acting like a Homeric simile, and making reference to a heroic death. But for all that the man's predicament is severe, it is not clear that we should regard him as doomed: our ideal young man will get himself out of this encounter, too.[43]

The more closely the images on later eighth-century Athenian pottery are considered, the less clear it is that any of them pick up particular stories. They reveal rather just how rich a repertoire of physical activities was available to the eighth-century imagination, and that wealth of imagery seems best explained by the deployment of such a repertoire of activities in eighth-century Athenian life. The scenes on Late Geometric pots are clearly not snapshots of daily life in eighth-century Athens, but they suggest a community whose ways of thinking about the world are primarily shaped through the structure of challenges posed

---

43. For other readings, see S. Langdon 2008: 197–200 and Giuliani 2013: 37–41 (written in ignorance of each other) with references. For symbolic readings of the lions, see Rombos 1988: 314–5.

FIGURE 15 Athenian LG II kantharos; c. 720; height: 17 cm (including handles); from the Dipylon cemetery. Attributed to the Burly workshop. National Museum of Denmark, Copenhagen NM 727. Photo by Nora Petersen.

by contemporary social life. We look in vain for any artist having recourse to established stories of any kind involving particular characters.[44] All the evidence points to their depicting eighth-century Athenians living in the present.

4.5.3 The Seventh Century

The picture presented by seventh-century Athenian pottery is quite different. In its repertoire of shapes, in its iconographic choices, and in its color palette the Athenian pottery of the seventh century, which is known as Protoattic, presents an appearance very different from that of the eighth. But the transition is gradual, with the nature of the figure-drawing changing first, then the types and organization of the non-figurative decoration and, finally, shapes and iconography.

Already, perhaps shortly after 720, some Athenian artists had begun to paint animals in a style that was far less analytic, made no attempt to reduce bodies and limbs to simple shapes and straight lines, and began to fill the figures with organic life. This is seen in the pots produced in what has become known as the Workshop of Athens 897, not least in the amphora Athens NM 897 itself, with its two friezes of running dogs, whose highly stylized bodies nevertheless capture something of the muscular strength in the fore- and hindquarters of hunting dogs, as well as something of the way dogs run. Then, in the products of the Workshop of Athens 894, we find pots where the picture area is enlarged, outline drawing is applied to the skirts of women and even to the legs of a bier, the parallel lines that represent the manes of horses are drawn longer and human hair is similarly represented (Agora P4990, NM 810). Adventurous experimentation with poses leads in the most striking case to a rearing horse with a massively elongated neck (Athens NM 810). In parallel with these figurative developments, spirals and hooked triangles appear in the decorative zone.[45] There had been marked

---

44. Ahlberg-Cornell (1992: 132–40) argued that three scenes on Geometric objects "with certainty" refer to the mythic/epic sphere. Two of these occur only in non-Athenian glyptic/relief sculpture—Aias carrying the dead body of Achilles and Herakles and the Lernaean hydra— and of these nothing precludes the former from being a generic scene of the carrying off of a dead soldier, and nothing identifies the latter as more than two figures and a snake. The third scene occurs several times on Athenian pottery in LG I and LG II and shows what appears to be a single body with two heads and four arms and legs. This has been widely identified as a scene of the twin brothers known as the Molione or Aktorione, but the occurrence of this double figure twice in a single scene on a krater in New York (Metropolitan Museum 14.130.15) guarantees that it is simply a graphic convention to show a pair of people working closely together. See Boardman 1983: 25–6; Dahm 2007; Giuliani 2013: 35–7.

45. The development of Protoattic pottery is discussed by J. M. Cook 1934–1935; Brann 1962; Rocco 2008; Strasser 2010; the whole Protoattic phenomenon has now been reassessed by Arrington 2021. On Protoattic ornament, see Arrington 2021: 170–80, 92–6.

differences within the Attic Late Geometric style from the very start of LG, but at the end of the century the variety becomes magnified, and for a while there are effectively separate traditions—a rather debased form of Geometric painting, that will come to be called Subgeometric, and a more adventurous style that will come to be called Protoattic.

The leading experimentalist in the late eighth century is one of the great distinctive Athenian pot-painters, the Analatos Painter (see Figure 16) (named after a hydria found in that suburb of Athens, probably from a grave [Athens NM 313]). To the developments already mentioned, the Analatos Painter, making good use of outline drawing, added a repertoire of winged sphinxes, of elegantly wavy or even exuberantly curly hair in horses' manes, and of lions showing off their impressive muzzles and women their elaborate garments. Above all he introduced an array of curvilinear decoration both on a large and small scale, with great panels on the neck of and friezes on the body of vases featuring stylized plant motifs. The proportions of the amphoras, hydriai, and loutrophoroi that the Analatos Painter decorates are distinctly more elongated than their LG II

FIGURE 16 Early Protoattic krater; c. 690; height: 39 cm; found on Aegina. Attributed to the Analatos Painter. Munich, Staatliche Antikensammlungen und Glyptothek 6077.

predecessors, proportions that seem to have required the filling in of the space between neck-handles and neck.[46] The hand of the Analatos Painter has been found largely in Athens itself, in the Agora and Kerameikos, but also in the cemetery at Merenda, at Eleusis, and in the sanctuaries of Artemis Mounychia in the Peiraieus and of Apollo on Aegina.

One of the Analatos' Painter's contemporaries has been given the name the Mesogeia Painter because his pots have been found at Spata, at Kalyvia Kouvara, Keratea, and Anavyssos—all in or just south of the Mesogeia; they have also been found in Athens, in the Sanctuary of Artemis Mounychia, and on Aegina. This distinctive, if overlapping distribution suggests that different workshops had distinct connections, or perhaps that different communities had different stylistic preferences. For although the work of the Mesogeia Painter has much in common with that of the Analatos Painter, the friezes in the works found in and around the Mesogeia are dominated by lions and winged sphinxes and centaurs; humans and horses enjoy rather less favor (Rocco 2008: 31–40).

These early Protoattic painters, active from just before 700 to perhaps 680, although introducing further exotic creatures to the iconography, are quite as keen as Geometric painters to fill every space between figures with ornament and to show equally little interest in portraying mythology. This situation quite changes in the next generation (Middle Protoattic, 675–650) with what has become known as the Black and White style. Painters now make a lot of use of white paint to point up details and contrasts—a wonderful example is the alternating black and white horses, and gleaming white helmets contrasting with their black crests, on the lid of a pyxis or lekanis from the Kerameikos (Kerameikos #75; Rocco 2008: 164 # 11 [and compare Rocco 2008: 142 #1, a krater stand in Berlin (A40) from Aegina]). Figures come to dominate the surface of the pot completely, with slim bands of decoration dividing them or framing the pot. The earliest instances of incision occur in this period, both for ornament and for figures, and some painters seem to have gradually moved from painted lines to incised lines. Whereas the figures of the Analatos Painter or Mesogeia Painter took part in *prothēsis* scenes or formed friezes of dancers or warriors, in the Black and White style continuing representation of marching warriors is joined not only by processing dignitaries in fancy clothing, but also by figures who engage in activities so individual that they can be identified as particular mythological episodes. Although the total corpus is not large, the range of myths that can be recognized is impressive (see further discussion to follow). Writing appears on a krater stand attributed to the Polyphemos Painter, now in Berlin (see Figure 17), problematically identifying one of a series of

---

46. On the Analatos Painter see Arrington 2021: 54–5, 157–9, in addition to Denoyelle 1996.

FIGURE 17 Middle Protoattic krater stand; c. 650; height: 68 cm; found on Aigna. Attributed to the Polyphemos Painter. Formerly Antikensammlung, Staatliche Museen zu Berlin A42 (destroyed in World War II). Eilmann and Gebauer 1938: 31.

well-dressed, bearded, standing dignitaries with spears, of a sort quite frequently shown at this period, as Menelaos, but otherwise identification of scenes does not require writing, since the episodes chosen are normally highly distinctive (J. M. Cook 1934–1935: 187–94; S. P. Morris 1984; Rocco 2008: 95–168).

The name of Menelaos is written on the stand in its Doric form and using a shape of lambda rare in Attic writing, and this has led to the suggestions that the painter of the stand, which was found on Aegina, was Aeginetan, and even that this style of pot production was an Aeginetan rather than an Attic style. But despite the marked turn to myth for subject matter and the "change in personality" that the style shows, by comparison with early Protoattic, the style fits neatly into the development of Athenian pottery, and although well represented on Aegina, the majority of pots of this style have been found in Athens.[47]

In the middle of the seventh century the Black and White style went out of fashion, and new techniques and decorative motifs came in, under the influence of contemporary Corinthian and Cycladic practice. The new techniques include greater use of incision and polychromy. The amount of pottery known from this period is rather small, and it is hard to follow iconographic trends as far as figurative scenes are concerned. The most impressive product of the period is the Kynosarges amphora (Athens NM 14497), once standing some 1.4 m high, recovered from the Athenian Kynosarges cemetery, southeast of the Acropolis, beyond the Ilissos river (see Section 4.3). Now fragmentary, this showed a pair of wrestlers on its neck and on the body two figures in a chariot pulled by winged horses, behind whom is a larger figure, elaborately dressed. Although scholars have suggested possible myths that might be shown here, precise identification remains uncertain, just as it is uncertain whether the wrestlers should be related to myth or to life (J. M. Cook 1934–1935: 195–200; Rocco 2008: 169–96).

Protoattic pottery has been recovered from many different contexts, including the Agora well deposits, which give evidence of use outside sanctuary and funerary contexts. There is no doubt, however, that the finest Protoattic pots come from cemeteries, and that a significant proportion of Protoattic pottery was made for cemetery use. This is clear in the distribution of those Protoattic pots with figurative decoration, but it is especially clear in the range of elaborate shapes recovered from offering-trench deposits (on which see Section 4.4.2) in the Kerameikos and elsewhere, including vessels with elaborate snake and mourning-women attachments or griffin protomes (Whitley 1994b). Although amphoras continue to be important throughout Protoattic production, the range of Protoattic shapes comes to be quite distinct from the range of Late Geometric shapes, with new shapes of (lidded) krater standing on a high foot and narrowing toward the mouth, high-footed krateriskoi and cup-kraters, high-footed cups with up-turned handles, elaborate krater stands, a distinctive shape of narrow jug with a tapering neck that has come to be known as a Phaleron jug (because it has been found in several Phaleron burials), a broad-bellied squat jug famous from the name-work of the Ram Jug Painter, high-footed lebetes or cauldrons with flower or animal-head protomes, and incense burners. Although some of the tendencies are on display from early in the seventh century (and may, as in the case of

---

47. On the Menelaos inscription, see H. R. Immerwahr 1990: 9; Wachter 2001: 26–7. On the Aeginetan origin of the stand, see S. P. Morris 1984: 5–7, 16–17, 41–6. On the "change from one personality to another," see J. M. Cook 1934–1935: 189 and generally Arrington 2021: 156–82.

the high foot, be a development of a feature found already in some shapes earlier), the range of shapes becomes increasingly innovative in the course of the seventh century (Rocco 2008: 204–6). A significant proportion of the vessels of exceptional shape must have been made to order, a process that seems confirmed by the occurrence of painted dedicatory inscriptions on a small number of Protoattic sherds (H. R. Immerwahr 1990: 9–10; Rocco 2008: 213–14).

The turn in Protoattic pottery to scenes referencing episodes in myth is closely paralleled to what is happening elsewhere in the Greek world. Identifiable scenes of myth, sometimes confirmed by painted inscriptions naming the figures, occur on Protocorinthian and on pottery from the Cyclades (Ahlberg-Cornell 1992). In particular, the repertoire of Archaic terracotta relief pithoi from the Cyclades is dominated by scenes of myth. Athenian painters were certainly aware of what was going on in Corinth and in the Cyclades; scholars have sometimes indeed wondered whether some of the painters of Protoattic may have been trained outside Athens, but a great deal of Corinthian pottery is found in seventh-century Attica, and, although Protoattic pottery is not widely exported it is found in the Cyclades, so that close contact is probably sufficient to explain shared traits.[48] What makes what happens in Attica different, and remarkable, is the strength of the preceding tradition of representation of scenes that relate to life as observed and experienced. The shift in the world of reference occurs even while the main occasions for engaging with the imagery—at feasts and drinking parties and at funerals—remain the same.

Two features of the scenes on Protoattic pottery that reference myths are notable. One is the range of myths referenced—Herakles and the centaur Nessos, Perseus pursued by the sisters of the Gorgon Medusa whom he has just decapitated, Peleus bringing Achilles to the centaur Cheiron, the sacrifice of Iphigeneia, the murder of Agamemnon or Aigisthos, Odysseus and his men blinding Polyphemos, and Odysseus and his men escaping from the Cyclops' cave. The regular appearance here of scenes that do not form part of the Homeric poems indicates that images on pottery did not begin to reference myths because the arrival of some widely performed text made Athenians familiar for the first time with a particular set of stories. There is no reason to suppose that the stories themselves were new to Athenians.

The second notable feature of mythological scenes on Protoattic pottery is the ingenuity of the representations. If the stories were not new, all the signs are that pictorial representation of the stories was new. This is most obvious with the problems that seventh-century artists have with the Gorgon. The earliest extant representation of the Gorgon is probably that on a relief amphora from Thebes

---

48. Compare Rocco 2008: 149 (cf. 145, 148), discussing the Ram Jug Painter in response to Papadopoulos and Smithson 2002; Koutsoumpou 2017.

FIGURE 18 Middle Protoattic amphora; third quarter of seventh century; height: 1.42 m; found in a tomb in Eleusis. Attributed to the Polyphemos Painter. Eleusis Archaeological Museum 2630. Photo by Sarah Murray.

(Louvre CA 795) on which the Gorgon is represented as a female centaur (essentially a woman with the body of a horse attached to her own clothed body). On a famous amphora found at Eleusis (see Figure 18), the Protoattic Polyphemos painter chose to represent her sisters as like human women (albeit women showing one bare leg), but with faces that were more like metal cauldrons or pots with attachments than like a human face (Eleusis 2630).[49] Only in the third quarter of

49. Despite the claim by S. P. Morris 1984: 44 that these Gorgons are of Peloponnesian type, rather than being "an imaginary conflation of Oriental vessels and monsters by the artist," the ivories from the Argive Heraion that she cites do not seem to me significant parallels.

the century did representations on ivory reliefs initiate what becomes the classic frontal face with grinning mouth and lolling tongue.

The visual ingenuity of the painters is striking. Thus on a krater attributed to the Ram Jug Painter (once Berlin A32) we find a scene that scholars have variously identified as showing the murder of Agamemnon by Aigisthos or of Aigisthos by Orestes; the painter chooses to convey the slyness of the killing by placing the murderer behind his victim, while conveying the contrast between killer and victim by showing the one in black silhouette and the other in outline drawing. Although at this period outline drawing does not equate to female gender or femininity (Odysseus is shown in outline drawing both when blinding Polyphemos and when escaping under a ram), the use of outline drawing both for the victim and for the woman in front of him, unites them as a pair, something highly appropriate if the victim is Aigisthos and the woman Klytemnestra.

Much the same can be said about the scene of Odysseus and his men escaping the Cyclops' cave on the jug (Aegina Archaeological Museum 566) that gives the Ram Jug Painter his name. The decision to show Odysseus with legs crossing over each other, a face with two eyes rather than simply in profile, and on one side of, rather than between the legs of the ram, emphasizes his substantiality and his visibility, encouraging the viewer to think about the Cyclops' blindness and the importance of Odysseus being out of touch rather than out of sight. The placing of the scene on a jug of very unusual shape massively contributes here, for the upper surface of the body of the jug forms the upper surface of the body of the ram, and we easily see how a Polyphemos who passes his hand over the back of the ram, to ensure that he is not being ridden, fails to locate the all-too-visible man who lies below.

In ways like this, Protoattic painters did not simply remind those who looked upon their pots of stories that they knew; they made them revisit and engage with the dynamics of those stories. In some cases that engagement is made to interlock with engagement with other scenes evoking contemporary activity or the animal world. This is something on which the Polyphemos Painter seems to be especially keen. Both the Menelaos stand (Figure 17), discussed above, and a second stand, also found on Aegina, have scenes of processing dignitaries. On the Menelaos stand those dignitaries are juxtaposed to men mounted on fine horses, to sphinxes, and to lions attacking a deer; on the other stand they are juxtaposed to warriors on the verge of a hostile confrontation (some of them marching in from the right and others, their spears leveled and their shields thrust forward, attacking from the left), to a series of cocks, and to a procession of women carrying bowls on their heads. It is tempting here to see these stands as variously offering excuses for linking the contemporary elite to the kings of heroic stories and for talking about their civic, military, and religious contributions to a world in which, as the aggression of various animals shows, violence is endemic.

The pot that has given the Polyphemos Painter his name (see Figure 18) is arguably more ambitious still, juxtaposing as it does not different scenes with contemporary resonance, but exotic myths that draw attention to fundamental human abilities. The body of this amphora shows a decapitated Gorgon and her two sisters pursuing the hero responsible, Perseus, next to whom stands his protector, Athena. The shoulder has a lion confronting a boar, and the neck Odysseus and companions thrusting a long thin object into the eye of a seated Polyphemos, who has a cup in his hands. The economy with which the image alludes to the story of Odysseus getting the Cyclops drunk so that he may put out his eye is one notable feature here, but even more notable is the shared interest of the two scenes in sensory deprivation. It is not simply that the killing of the Gorgon and the blinding of Polyphemos deprive them of their senses, but that the issue of the senses and of sensory deprivation is at the heart of the story of the Gorgon turning those who look upon her to stone. Whether this amphora was made for funerary use is disputed, but the decision to use this vessel for a child burial seems unlikely to have been innocent (Osborne 1988a; but see Whitley 1994b). (For discussion of SOS amphoras, see Section 8.1.)

4.5.4 The Late Seventh and Sixth Centuries

Already in the middle of the seventh century some Protoattic artists, and in particular the painter of the New York Nessos amphora, had come close to abandoning the brush for the incisor, supplying much of the detailed drawing by incision upon a black silhouette. Athenian painters were thus moving toward adopting the black-figure style, in which incisions are made into silhouetted figures painted in black slip, with further detail added in purple or white. Although Corinthian artists were pioneers in developing black-figure technique, their Athenian counterparts became, in the space of a couple of generations, its leading practitioners.

From around 625 incision takes over completely, and the quantity of filling ornament is drastically reduced. Initially this distinct change in the appearance of Attic pottery is not matched by changing shapes or context of use. In the cemeteries of the Kerameikos and at Vari, for example, early black-figure pots are found in the context of offering trenches in ways exactly parallel to earlier Protoattic pottery. Amphoras, skyphos-kraters, egg-shaped kraters, and louteria continue to dominate the earliest black-figure. The painters whose work Beazley placed at the head of Attic black-figure as the first painters listed in *Attic Black-Figure Vase-Painters* (1956) depicted processions of women, sphinxes, lions, chariots, felines attacking calves, and among myths Herakles and Nessos, Perseus and the Gorgons, and Bellerophon and the Chimaera. Although Bellerophon does not appear on extant Protoattic pottery (he does appear on Protocorinthian pottery), these scenes are all very much in the Protoattic tradition (Boardman 1974: 14–20; Beazley 1986: 1–11). One of the earliest black-figure painters, the Anagyrous Painter, seems to have worked at Vari (ancient Anagyrous) using local clay resources, as did a second painter, whose work extends slightly later, the Lotos Painter (see Section 4.4.3). A further group of painters can be identified from their clay and the findspots of their products as working in eastern Attica (their work is found up and down the east coast from Sounion to Rhamnous—but also elsewhere in the Mediterranean, from Berezan to Ragusa [Boardman 1998b; Alexandridou 2011: 44–5]).

Changes in the repertoire of shapes and of images quickly followed the changing style of painting. In particular at the end of the seventh century the skyphos, at least partly under the influence of Corinthian pottery, acquires a spreading ring foot; in the early sixth century this turns into the conical foot of the so-called Komast cup and the taller flaring foot and more emphatically out-turned rim of the Siana cup (see the discussion later in the text) (Brijder 1983: 44–8 [for origins]; Brijder 1991; Brijder 1997; Brijder 2000; Alexandridou 2011: 16–17). Neck-handled amphoras continue, but alongside them the so-called one-piece amphora, whose foot, body, and neck offer a continuous curving profile. This shape had first appeared in Late Geometric, but it had not been produced in significant numbers in the seventh century; now it becomes distinctly more popular and will be particularly popular in the middle of the sixth century. The skyphos-krater disappears, shortly followed by the egg-shaped krater (although this shape reappears, repurposed, as the lebes gamikos, which is strongly associated with marriage), to be replaced by the rounded bowl of the dinos or lebes, supported on an elaborately turned stand, and then shortly afterward by the column krater, a shape strongly associated with Corinth. The hydria, which had not been significantly in evidence since the early seventh century reappears in the early sixth century, first with a round body but then becoming popular in a form with the shoulder sharply offset (Moore and Pease Philippides 1986: 4–7, 22–38; Alexandridou 2011: 7–11). The shapes that appear to have been made specifically for deposit in offering trenches disappear, and the repertoire of shapes seems to be more closely tied to domestic use, particularly at drinking parties. It is a marked feature of the various developments in shape that they take their cues either from pots produced elsewhere—in Corinth or in the east Aegean—or from bronze or wooden items (so the round dinos imitates a bronze shape; its stand imitates a wooden item turned on a lathe).

In the first half of the sixth century the iconographic choices of Athenian painters show distinct change. Although Perseus and the Gorgons remain popular, Herakles and Nessos attract only relatively slight attention and Odysseus and Polyphemos disappear.[50] In general, "man and monster" scenes become less fashionable, and scenes where men engage with other men are introduced. So, the hunt for the Kalydonian boar appears, with the focus not on a single hero's struggle with a beast but on how a group of heroes work together. Similarly, the marriage of Peleus and Thetis gives an opportunity to show a great procession of all the gods coming to celebrate, and painters grapple with various parts of the story of the Seven against Thebes. Such scenes are best shown on large vases, and the most spectacular examples of Athenian black-figure painting in the early sixth century are to be found on dinoi and kraters (Shapiro 1990).

For the first time, these outstanding examples of painting can be ascribed to artists who are not merely named by scholars on the basis of observed similarity between scenes on different pots (i.e., attribution), but on the basis of the artist's own signature, for a number of early sixth-century pots are signed by their potter and/or their painter. Two of these self-identified artists stand out, Sophilos and Kleitias. Sophilos was clearly an ambitious painter in various ways, decorating large pots and trying out ambitious mythological scenes (Bakir 1981; Williams 1983).[51] A famous fragment, found at Pharsalos in Thessaly, shows (and labels) the funeral games of Patroklos, a dinos in Paris attempts to show a four-horse chariot head on, and a nuptial lebes from Smyrna shows the wedding of Menelaos and Helen.

The most impressive scenes, however, are of the marriage of Peleus and Thetis, which Sophilos painted twice on dinoi, one of them dedicated on the Athenian Acropolis (British Museum 1971, 1101.1; Acropolis Museum 587; see Figure 19).[52] On the better preserved example in the British Museum, Peleus stands outside his house, which has a recognizable Doric colonnade, receiving the gods coming singly or in pairs, on foot—except for Okeanos whose sea-creature body has no feet—or in chariots, with the female goddesses dressed in extremely elaborate chitons decorated, like Sophilos' pots, with friezes of animals. Generally, the chitons emerge from under himatia (cloaks), but Hebe is shown simply in a sleeveless

---

50. For a general discussion of the change in mythological scenes on Athenian black-figure and red-figure pottery over time, see Osborne 2021a.

51. Beazley (1956: 37) thought that because Attic script does not distinguish long and short "o," we cannot know whether the first "o" in this name is properly short or long, but we have more than 40 individuals named Σώφιλος from Classical and Hellenistic Athens, and only one, the father of the tragedian Sophocles, named Σόφιλλος, so almost certainly we should treat the first "o" as long. Kleitias, by contrast, is a rare name, not attested in Athens for more than 200 years after the painter's death.

52. On the scene of the funeral games of Patroklos, see Moore 2016.

FIGURE 19 Athenian black-figure dinos and stand signed by Sophilos; 580–570; height: 71 cm. British Museum 1971, 1101.1.[53]

chiton, presumably because she is still young. Depictions of the marriage of Peleus and Thetis allowed painters to show off their full color palette and compositional originality. They also constitute the first appearance of Dionysos in Athenian art (Carpenter 1986: 1–12). Like the scene of Patroklos' funeral games, this is a celebratory scene—quite unlike the man-and-monster scenes preferred in Protoattic.

---

53. The British Museum acquired this vase from a private collector; additional fragments were acquired from the Getty Museum and from the New York art market (Williams 1983: 9). There does not seem to be any published information about its provenance, but it is likely that it was found in Italy.

Not that Sophilos is uninterested in animals—under the influence of Corinthian pottery his pots are loaded with friezes of animals and birds of all sorts—but human–animal confrontation is rare: his extant repertoire includes just one image of Herakles engaging with a centaur (presumably Nessos) and one of Herakles engaging with the sea-creature-bodied Nereus. If the images of Nessos and Nereus look back, one other fragment, from Lindos on the island of Rhodes, certainly looks forward. This is a fragment showing a young woman in a short but highly decorated chiton running off to the right and looking back over her shoulder at a hairy but otherwise human creature who grasps her elbow and displays an

FIGURE 20 Athenian black-figure volute krater signed by Kleitias and Ergotimos (the François vase); c. 570–560; height: 66 cm; found at Chiusi. Florence Archaeological Museum 4209. Photo by Serge Domingie.

erect penis. This is the first of thousands of satyrs (sometimes referred to as silens) on Athenian pots, and also the first of hundreds of scenes of sexual pursuit.

Sophilos' world of imagery is very much also that of Kleitias, not least on Kleitias' most famous pot, the François vase (see Figure 20; Torelli 2007; Hirayama 2010; Shapiro, Iozzo, and Lezzi-Hafter 2013). This volute krater (a rare shape and another that is borrowed from bronzework, where, unlike in clay, its handles make structural sense[54]), which declares itself made by the potter Ergotimos, has not one figural frieze and several animal friezes, as Sophilos' dinoi have, but five figural friezes—one on the rim, one on the neck, two on the body, and one on the foot, and just one animal frieze on the lower part of the body. The marriage of Peleus and Thetis and the funeral games of Patroklos reappear here, along with the hunting of the Kalydonian boar, but there are new arrivals too. We have our earliest scenes on pottery of Theseus (here arriving on Crete with seven youths and seven maidens), of the return of Hephaistos to Olympus, and of pygmies fighting cranes. We also plausibly can recognize the earliest scenes of Achilles pursuing Troilos (a theme taken up on Siana cups), and (on both the handles) of Aias carrying from the battlefield the dead body of Achilles; both these scenes had appeared in the seventh century on terracotta reliefs and, in the case of Aias and Achilles, on a bronze shield band, but to our knowledge this is their debut on Athenian pottery.[55] Kleitias is notable for the amount of imagery and the number of motifs that he borrows or adapts from elsewhere, and for his unusual interest in the Phrygians and costume elements associated with peoples on the northern borders of the Greek world. He is also notable for his enthusiasm for writing, labeling virtually everything on the pot, including inanimate objects; he was clearly highly literate and closely engaged with the poetic traditions of his time, but some of the oddities of his spelling have suggested that his father may have come to Athens from Thrace (Wachter 1991: 103).

The inclusion of so many figured friezes raises a question that Sophilos' pots do not: what are the grounds for juxtaposing these particular scenes? Many of the scenes are linked to Achilles, and those that are not can be read as commentary on the Achilles scenes. The *Iliad* had made Achilles the hero par excellence for embodying the tensions between individualism and corporate responsibility, and those tensions are repeatedly explored here. That in itself is not surprising—like

---

54. The handles of the François vase were in fact repaired, using lead, in antiquity, possibly even, given the use of lead, before the pot left Athens. See Iozzo 2013: 58–61.

55. Troilos appears on terracotta reliefs from eastern Crete (Boardman 1981–1999: s.v. Troilos 7a and b); Aias and Achilles appear on a terracotta relief from Lemnos (Boardman 1981–1999: s.v. Achilleus 860; and cf. the reliefs decorating a female figure from Tarentum, Boardman 1981–1999: s.v. Achilleus 861) and on a bronze shield band from Olympia (Boardman 1981–1999: s.v. Achilleus 862).

nature vs. culture, individual vs. community is a grid so coarse that almost anything can be fitted in to it—but the range of individual and communal challenges here is exceptional. Exceptional, too, is the way in which the scenes combine tragedy and joy—Theseus' arrival with the young people of Athens reminds of past sorrow as well as of future joy (and sorrow, given Theseus' father's death); the Kalydonian boar will be defeated, but both a hunter and a hunting dog have been already killed; the excitement of the chariot races is tempered by the fact that these are funeral games.

Mixed emotions are roused also by the decision to confront the viewer with a frontal Dionysos carrying an amphora among the gods attending the marriage of Peleus and Thetis, so bringing the users of this krater up against the out-of-body experiences promised by its contents. This is a message further reinforced by the decision to make Aphrodite the goddess who, standing in front of seated Zeus and Hera, greets Dionysos as he brings Hephaistos back to Olympus, and to have Hephaistos followed by a baggage train of sexually excited satyrs (Silenoi). By these means Kleitias calls to mind Hephaistos' past history of marriage to Aphrodite, his cunning in catching Aphrodite and Ares making adulterous love, and his entrapment of Hera on a carefully wrought throne from which he is being brought back to Olympus to release her, having been tricked by Dionysos making him drunk. Fragments of contemporary lyric poetry (Alkaios 349 Lobel-Page) show poets exploring just these themes, and this krater offers cues to a whole range of poetic performances (Stewart 1983).

Although Kleitias is extreme in his use of writing, there is generally an explosion of writing on Athenian pots in the half-century after 580. Writing had the advantage not simply of enabling painter and potter to identify themselves and of identifying the characters shown, and therefore the story being alluded to, but also of enabling the artist to say something about the figures shown. For beyond its main characters, the figures required by the action of the story are often not named when a story is told in words but can be labeled when shown on a pot. So Kleitias names the dogs in the hunting of the Kalydonian boar, not only giving them what may have been names typically given to dogs (Labros [boisterous], Korax [raven], Egertes [Waker]). but also using the names to heighten the pathos: so the dog who is leaping up and sinking its teeth into the hindquarters of the boar is called Marpsos (snatcher), but the dog lying dead in front of the boar, never to jump up again, is called Hormenos (leaper). Other artists use names in similar ways, and women's names offer particular opportunities. The painter of Tyrrhenian amphoras, discussed below, known as the Timiades Painter, gives his Amazons names like Pantariste (best of all women) and Andromache (man-fighter), while the Prometheus Painter gives the female spectators who watch Theseus battling with the minotaur names like Timodike (honoring justice) or Demodike (popular justice), names suggestive of a particular political ideology.[56]

Alongside the transformation in the representation of myth on large pots, there was also, again in the years following 580, a revolution in imagery that had no mythological reference. The Komast cups mentioned above get their name from their imagery—representations of dancing revelers, who are either naked or represented wearing a sort of leotard. These figures had first appeared on Corinthian pots, and it is clear that the Athenian artists borrowed the type from Corinth (Seeberg 1971; Smith 2007; Smith 2010). Generally, they represent only male dancers, some bearded, some beardless youths; however, in some images we see white-fleshed women wearing short tight dresses dancing with a man. Scholars have taken a great deal of interest in these dancers, largely because of their costume. In Corinthian representations the dancers' costume so exaggerates their buttocks that they have become known as "padded dancers," and this has encouraged linking them to the padded costumes of actors in later Athenian comedy, and so finding a place for them in the prehistory of drama. However, the way in which they quickly shed any padding, and the costume itself, in Attic representations, along with the obvious humorous aspects of these scenes (whose strong sexual content, most explicitly in the Corinthian examples, drawing attention to the erotic attractions of the buttocks, has too often been ignored) make a connection with drama or indeed with ritual of any sort unnecessary. These are lewd scenes of drunken dancing shown on pots themselves used at drinking parties. The painter challenges the drinkers to exercise, or abandon, their self-control by scenes that need bear no close relationship to any aspect of Athenian life (Brijder 1983; Green 2007; Isler-Kerényi 2007; Wannagat 2015).[57]

Reveling was the most common scene on the so-called Tyrrhenian amphoras, made in Athens from the late 570s to the 540s. These are a set of ovoid neck amphoras (and other shapes painted by the same painters) decorated with a series of three or four friezes on the body, of which the top depicted a figural scene, and the other friezes either animals or lotus/palmette decoration. Forty-six of the 72 examples with known provenance have been found in either Vulci or Cerveteri, and most of the rest have been found in Etruria, although isolated examples have been found in Klazomenai, Tharros in Sardinia, Naukratis, Phokaia, Megara

---

56. For the François vase, see Wachter 1991. For the Timiades Painter, see H. R. Immerwahr 1990: 41 (cf. Henderson 1994). For the Prometheus Painter (Leiden PC 47), see Kreuzer 2013: 111–2. On writing on early Greek pottery more generally, see Osborne and Pappas 2006.

57. Note Green 2007: 98: "The presumption should be that in drawing a padded dancer, the vase painter is probably not drawing a figure of everyday life or genre."

Hyblaia, and Athens itself. Nevertheless, it is clear that the clay used is Athenian, and there are strong links in terms both of decorative scheme and of the themes depicted with Athenian pottery. The favored mythological scenes concern either Herakles or the Trojan cycle, and some of the scenes shown are unusually violent—most strikingly the sacrifice of Polyxena at the tomb of Achilles, the killing of Troilos shown with his head cut off, and the murder of Eriphyle. Alongside the *komos* scenes are a number of sexually explicit scenes showing sexually excited men, some of whom penetrate women from the rear and one of whom ejaculates; some women are shown exposing their buttocks. One of only two scenes of sodomy in the Athenian black-figure corpus appears on a Tyrrhenian amphora that shows a man having anal intercourse with another man whom he has forced to his knees. One of the Tyrrhenian amphora painters mixes satyrs with men in these erotic scenes. These are the earliest sexually explicit scenes on Athenian pottery, but soon sexually explicit scenes appear on Band cups (see the discussion later in the text) (Kluiver 2003, who is conclusive against Carpenter 1984 on the origins of Tyrrhenian amphoras).

Around 570 the Siana cup (the known examples of which, like the Komast cups, are neither signed nor feature any other writing) was invented (see Figure 21). These cups feature a broad rim, with painted scenes often carried uninterruptedly across the division between body and rim, and they use the interior as well as the exterior of the cup as a space for painted scenes. On these cups dancers (mostly male, but in one case including a naked woman) are joined by a whole series of further scenes referencing everyday life. We see drinkers reclining at symposia; warriors fighting and going to war; cavalcades of horsemen and later horse races; youths racing; men wrestling, boxing, and throwing the discus and javelin; meetings between men, including the earliest scene in Attic pottery of a man courting a youth; youths and women; and bulls being led to sacrifice (Brijder 1983; Brijder 1991; Brijder 2000).[58] But myth scenes, rarely shown on Komast cups, are also well represented on Siana cups: in addition to Gorgons (with or without Perseus), sphinxes, and various sea monsters, we get Bellerophon and the Chimaera, various pursuit scenes (including Peleus pursuing Thetis and her Nereid sisters and Achilles pursuing Troilos); the Kalydonian boar-hunt; an increasing variety of scenes of Herakles, not only in combat with various parties, but also being received on Olympus; and Dionysos with a female figure or with satyrs or nymphs/maenads.

Alongside and eventually replacing the Siana cups, another cup-making tradition developed around 560, namely producing cups with taller stems and exterior

---

58. For homoerotic courtship, see Brijder 2000: 583 discussing Taranto 20253 by the Red-Black Painter (c. 550).

FIGURE 21 Athenian black-figure Siana cup; c. 560; diameter: 26 cm; said to be from Taranto. Attributed to the Taras Painter. Allard Pierson Museum, University of Amsterdam, APM13.367.

decoration placed either just on a band between the handles, with the rest of the cup being black, or only on the lip, with writing in the handle zone. These cups have become known as Little Master cups, and sub-classed into Gordion cups, Lip cups, and Band cups, depending on the location of the figured decoration (Beazley 1932; Beazley 1986: 48–52; Heesen 2011). The great majority of Band cups are between 0.19 and 0.22 m in diameter, whereas Lip cups come in a wider range of sizes, with just under a third having a diameter of 0.14–0.17 m, just under a third 0.17–0.21 m, and just under a third 0.21–0.25 m. Perhaps the most distinctive feature differentiating Little Master cups from Siana cups is abundant use of writing—artists' signatures, apostrophes to the drinker, identities of figures, and, on later examples, nonsense.

About 40 percent of Little Master cups with figured decoration show genre scenes (agriculture, hunting, dancing, sex, etc.) on the exterior, with animals the second most popular subject and mythology constituting less than 20 percent, but mythological scenes are more popular than genre scenes or animals on the interior (Heesen 2011: 241–6). This is partly about the limited space on the exterior, but we should be aware of the difference between the view of the drinker, who is faced with the scene on the tondo, and the view of the rest of the drinking party, which is of the exterior. That said, although several scenes of courtship between bearded men and youths—in one case with manifest sexual excitement—appear on cup interiors, numerous scenes of youths and of satyrs masturbating and of men and women in sexual intercourse occur predominantly on cup exteriors. There is normally some link between the scenes on the two sides of the exterior, although spreading a single scene over both sides of the cup is relatively rare. Few of the themes shown are innovative, and over time a small number of themes come to dominate, in particular satyrs and maenads and Herakles and the Nemean lion. Perseus makes no appearance, and Peleus just once pursues Thetis, though Herakles' combat with Nessos is popular. The effect of the narrow band of decoration is to make even simple motifs very striking. Single animals, whether realistic (fighting cocks facing off, a swan or other single bird, a ram or goat or deer) or fantastic (siren birds or winged sphinxes), when given careful miniaturist attention arguably produce a greater impact on the viewer than do complex multi-figure scenes, although these too are executed in impressive detail and with effective use of added color. Some artists even attempt to show frontal four-horse chariots within the narrow band but later painters, particularly the prolific Centaur Painter, saw that running figures were particularly suitable, and painted many pursuit scenes.

Some painters seem to have produced solely or mainly Little Master cups, but other painters, including Kleitias and the Amasis Painter (see the discussion later in the text), produced some Little Master cups while working over a much wider range. Their work is sometimes clearly influenced by the Little Master tradition.

FIGURE 22 Athenian black-figure globular aryballos signed by Nearchos; c. 570; height: 7.8 cm. Metropolitan Museum New York 26.49.

A notable instance of this is Nearchos, whose son is a major Little Master potter. Nearchos was responsible for a very striking aryballos (Osborne 2007c; Mertens 2010: 62–5). The aryballos, although massively popular earlier at Corinth, was not a common shape in Athens. On the example now in New York (see Figure 22), Nearchos decorates the body of the aryballos with stripes that emphasize its shape and encourage the viewer to hold it, and then paints tiny figures on the rim and the handle plate to depict figures of Hermes and Perseus, three masturbating satyrs, and a battle between pygmies and cranes. Hermes and Perseus are named, and the three satyrs are given names suitable to their action—Terpekelos, Dophios, and Phsolas, the first referring to pleasure (τέρψις), the second to masturbation (δέφομαι), and the third to the erect penis (ψωλός)—while among the pygmies various short nonsense inscriptions are found. The mixture of sense and nonsense among these inscriptions is important, since sometimes nonsense inscriptions have been thought to be written by illiterate artists and/or for illiterate viewers. But Nearchos is clearly literate, writing in a beautifully clear miniature hand, and any reader who is to enjoy his jokey satyr names must be literate, or in literate company, too. There is probably no single explanation for nonsense inscriptions, which in any case vary from combinations of letters that simply do not make Greek words to series of dots where one would expect letters; some may have been primarily decorative, but some at least seem to have been cues to the viewer to talk about the scene in front of them, identifying the figures and their action, and perhaps vocalizing the noises those figures make (as here perhaps with the cranes) (H. R. Immerwahr 1990: 26–7; Heesen 2011: vol. 1: 233–41; Heesen 2016; Yatromanolakis 2016; Chiarini 2018) (see further Section 9.3).

Nearchos demands our attention for two further reasons (see also Section 11.4). From the Athenian Acropolis survives a fragment of an oversize kantharos (a cup with high handles that comes to be particularly associated with the god Dionysos, a shape found in Athens mainly in sanctuary contexts, although found in graves in some other areas of Greece), signed by Nearchos as painter and potter (Athens National Museum Acropolis Collection 1.611) (Mommsen 2009). This fragment, showing the harnessing of the chariot of Achilles, is exquisitely painted, and is one of several examples on the Athenian Acropolis of unusually fine pots being used as (and surely made as) dedications. The head of Achilles, the dress of the woman holding his armor, the heads and manes of the horses, all are intricately detailed. The choice of scene is novel, both in itself and because of its clear relation to a particular passage of the *Iliad* (19.353–93). Although Nearchos has named his horses Chaitos and Eutheias rather than the *Iliad*'s Xanthos and Balios, scholars have surely been correct to see this as the moment when Achilles has his chariot harnessed so that he can go into battle to avenge Patroklos by killing Hektor—the moment at which in the *Iliad* one of the horses addresses Achilles to remind him of his own mortality. Although the chariot race on the François vase has a similar relation to the *Iliad*, here what is remarkable is the moment chosen—not a moment of action but a moment between actions. Such a choice of moment will mark some of the great black-figure pots of the mid-sixth century. Nearchos' aryballos and this kantharos fragment between them foreshadow the two very different styles of the painters whose output dominates mid-sixth century Athenian pot-painting—the jokey and impertinent Amasis Painter and the deeply serious Exekias.

The second reason that Nearchos deserves our attention is a dedication from the Acropolis dating perhaps some 30 or more years later than this pot. A base for a *korē*, and almost certainly for a *korē* that can be identified, records a dedication made by one Nearchos the potter as the first fruits of his works (*erga*; *IG* I³.628). Although only the last two letters of the Greek word for potter have been preserved, the strict spacing of the letters, and the rarity of the name in Athens, make the restoration plausible. This is one of a number of dedications by craftsmen, including the potters Andocides, Euphronios, and Onesimos, made on the

Athenian Acropolis in the half century before 480.[59] Nearchos' dedication is particularly striking since the *korē* involved, by the sculptor Antenor whose signature is on the base, is the largest (2 m tall) and most imposing of all the *korai* (Athens Acropolis Museum 681 with *IG* I³.628) from the late Archaic Acropolis.[60] Both our understanding of the nature of the Athenian economy and our understanding of the social status of craftsmen in Athens must take these dedications into account.

All the earliest painters and potters who sign their names on Athenian pots have Greek names—although in some cases Greek names unexampled later.[61] We cannot know what their social status was, since in the Classical period it was common for slaves to have names indistinguishable from the names of Greeks, and a number of the names might well be considered "speaking names" relevant to their profession—as with Ergotimos and his son Eucheiros and Nearchos's son Ergoteles.[62] What we can say is that none of those who sign advertises a non-Greek origin. But in the middle of the sixth century two major figures in Athenian black-figure pottery advertise non-Greek names: Lydos ("the Lydian") and the potter Amasis (who only ever signs pots as their maker, but who may have been also the person who decorated the pots in question, a person whom scholars call the Amasis Painter). Lydos and the Amasis Painter, like Nearchos and another great mid-sixth century potter and painter, Exekias (a man possessed of a good Attic name), painted a wide range of shapes from Little Master cups to monumental pots, but in character their products are quite different from one another.

Lydos' finest surviving pot is a fragmentary dinos from the Athenian Acropolis showing a Gigantomachy—a scene that first appears to us in Athenian painted pottery on this and another Acropolis dedication, a kantharos painted by Nearchos (Athens National Museum Acropolis Collection 607, 614, respectively) (Beazley 1986: 38–40; Shapiro 1990: 129). The extant fragments make clear the extraordinary skill and detail in Lydos' drawing, and his feel for the use of color, which is lavished on shield devices, including a wasp on the shield of the giant fighting Aphrodite. A separate scene of animals being led to sacrifice shows

---

59. Keesling 2003: 50–9, 69–74; Keesling 2005: 401–3; but see Keesling 2005: 415–21 for skepticism about other dedications identified by Raubitschek as having been made by potters or pot painters. See also Sections 8.3 and 11.4.

60. See Section 11.3 for discussion of *korai* from the Acropolis.

61. On the status of potters and painters generally, see Laurens 1995; Williams 1995; Williams 2009; and Section 8.3.

62. On slave names, see Vlassopoulos 2010. Ergotimos might mean "who values labor"; Ergoteles, "who perfects labor"; and Eucheiros, "good at handicrafts."

further sharp observation of animal anatomy and posture. Lydos' scenes elsewhere are less complex than the Gigantomachy, with a preference for scenes that involve processions or groups of standing figures surround a central encounter. Most of Lydos' scenes are mythological, but not all, and he is responsible for a set of funerary plaques found at Spata (Boardman 1955: 59 #7; Boardman 1974: 52–4; Tiverios 1976).

Exekias, too, painted funerary plaques (Boardman 1955: 59–60 #10, cf. #11–13), and he shared Lydos' preference for scenes of myth, but his choice of myth and his compositional preferences were quite different. Exekias generally avoided frieze-type scenes and the pot shapes, such as column kraters, that lent themselves to such compositions. He preferred encounter, and in general not cluttering the field with spectators. His compositions have a strong focus— often enough not on a particular figure but on the object that is effecting their interaction—in his most famous scene, the gaming board on which Achilles and Aias play (Vatican 344/16757). Exekias was primarily a painter of amphoras, taking advantage of the field offered by the broad-shouldered, short-necked amphora that had become popular among Attic potters in the second quarter of the century. All his work is deeply serious: for instance, on an amphora in Munich he juxtaposes a scene of a warrior carrying the dead body of another, in the traditional pose of Aias carrying off the dead Achilles, on one side, with the same again on the other, as if war had only one outcome, corpses (Munich 1470). When he made and painted one of the first Type A cups (see Figure 23), with lipless shallow bowl and short stout foot, he showed at each handle two opposed armies fighting over a dead body—the body face down and still armed on one side, naked and face up on another. But Exekias was not without humor: the inside of the cup, decorated in a novel technique using coral red (see the discussion later in the text), shows Dionysos sailing in the boat in which, according to the *Homeric Hymn to Dionysos*, pirates had kidnapped him. Dionysos fills the boat—around whose mast a vine twists, laden with grapes—and the pirates, now dolphins, swim around it. Exekias evidently liked the analogy between wine and the wine-dark sea: he painted ships sailing round the inner rim of his only fully preserved dinos (Villa Giulia 50599) (MacKay 2010: 1–10, 31–40, 215–42, 327–52, 73–86, with references).

No such seriousness, and a very different sort of humor, is found in the works of the Amasis Painter (Karouzou 1956; von Bothmer 1985; True and Belloli 1987). His compositional preferences for strong vertical lines and symmetrical compositions, and even some of his stylistic details (e.g., a red hair circle around male nipples) are shared with Lydos. But the Amasis Painter has a distinct interest in scenes that relate to life rather than myth, and, unusually among such scenes, to domestic life. Outstanding in this respect are a pair of lekythoi of unusual shape,

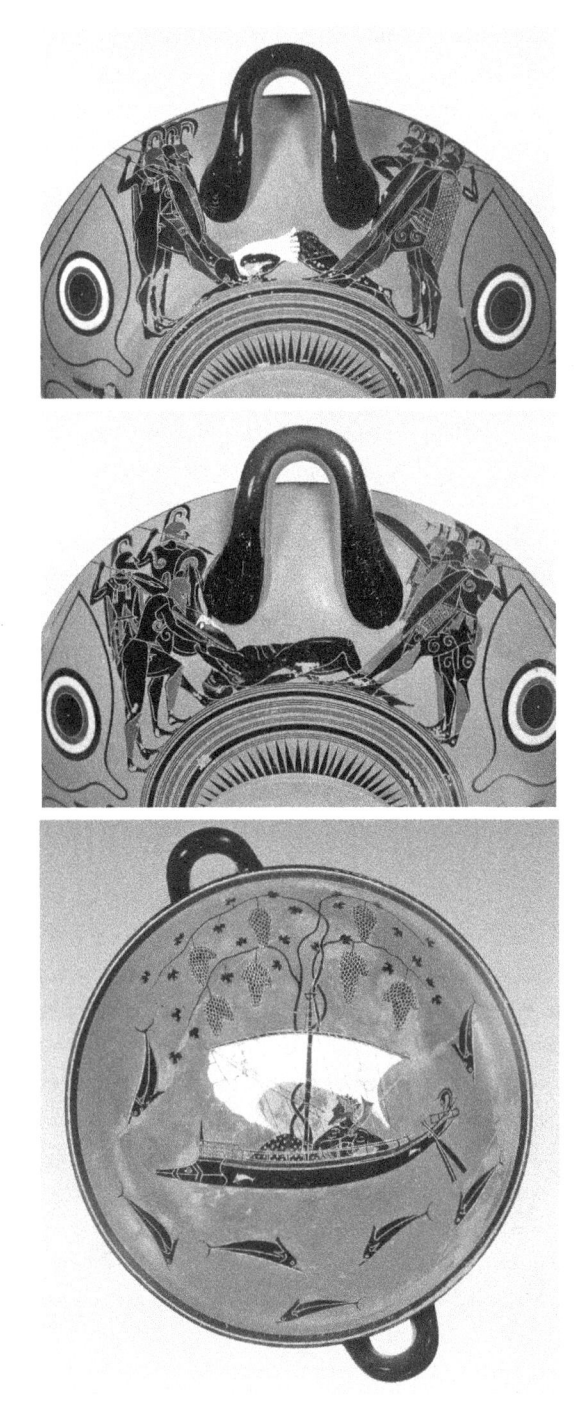

FIGURE 23 Athenian black-figure eye cup potted and painted by Exekias; c. 540–530; diameter: 30.5 cm; from Vulci. Munich, Staatliche Antikensammlungen und Glyptothek 8729 (formerly 2044).

one showing a wedding procession (but with a cart rather than a chariot), and one showing women working wool, including weaving at a loom (New York Metropolitan Museum 56.11.1 and 31.11.10, respectively). Neither of these are remotely "snap shots" of life—note the immensely elaborate clothing of the women working wool, shown in miniaturist detail—but both are concerned to suggest common experiences (look, for example, at the pose of the figure on the back of the cart or the straining necks of the donkeys).

Most striking of all about the Amasis Painter is his range. This is evident from a comparison of three of his cups. A kylix in New York shows on one side a stable scene (see Figure 24). The stable is indicated by a series of very thin columns with Doric capitals, marked out in red and white, supporting a frieze of alternate black and red squares, with every other red square, except at the very right-hand end, carrying the image of a bird or an animal. We think of triglyphs and metopes, except that we suddenly find in the last metope on the right not an animal but an archer. In the next metope we find a male figure falling out of the metope, as if shot! In the stable are four horses, attended by four stable hands, with, on the right, a clothed bearded figure with a staff. But on the backs of two of the horses

FIGURE 24 Athenian black-figure kylix; c. 540; height: 12.4 cm. Attributed to the Amasis Painter. Metropolitan Museum New York 1989.281.62.

are two smaller figures, one clinging onto one of the capitals, the other an archer in Scythian costume about to shoot. On the other side of the cup is a much more conventional scene of warriors gathering around the god Poseidon, identified by his trident. Here again there are two Scythian archer figures as well as heavily armed infantrymen with impressive shield devices. Put together these scenes provide an imaginative take on the *Iliad*'s description at the beginning of Book 13 of Poseidon getting his horses from his stable at the bottom of the sea and harnessing his chariot to go and join the fighting at Troy.

A drinking vessel of slightly different, unusual shape (see Figure 25), part way between cup and skyphos, now in the Louvre shows a single scene on its broad band of decoration (Louvre A 479). This is a scene of naked courting couples exchanging love-gifts; four pairs of bearded men face beardless youths and extend toward them some bird or animal, while under each handle a bearded man sits or crouches with bird or beast in hand, apparently waiting for a lover. However, in the middle of each side we have not man and youth, but man and naked woman, with the woman picked out in added white; one woman is offered a bird, the other a flower. The boundary between fantasy and reality is constantly challenged here—both by imagining gifts of a panther as well as a hare and by the assimilation of young women to the naked youths.

FIGURE 25 Athenian black-figure cup-skyphos; c. 550–540; height: 11.5 cm; from Camirus on Rhodes. Attributed to the Amasis Painter. Paris, Louvre A479 (MNB 1746). Photo by Les frères Chuzeville.

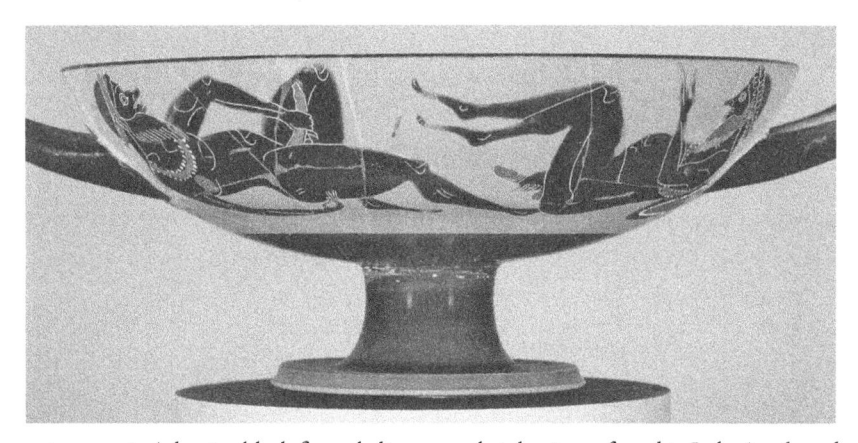

FIGURE 26 Athenian black-figure kylix; c. 520; height: 8 cm; found in Italy. Attributed to the Amasis Painter. Museum of Fine Arts, Boston 10.651. Gift of Edward Perry Warren. Photograph

The third cup, now in Boston, is quite different (see Figure 26). Exekias seems to have invented, with his cup showing on its interior Dionysos sailing, the "eye-cup," whose exterior is painted as a form of mask, with a pair of eyes. On other cups the Amasis Painter replicated this, with standing figures between the eyes. But the cup in Boston has on one side a siren whose body is made into a single eye (a trope that later painters will copy). Under its handles, instead of the battle scene over a corpse, we have defecating dogs, and on the other side we have two very large, bearded figures lying on their backs masturbating. There is a rumbustious humor here that pokes fun at the solemnity of Exekias' pious cup.

No other painters of black-figure pottery can quite match the characterful products of Exekias and the Amasis Painter, but much was done under their influence. This is seen both in the adoption of scenes that they pioneered—as in the large number of scenes of Achilles and Aias playing dice that follow Exekias' amphora—and in the way they compose scenes or the types of scenes that they choose for representation. One good example of the latter is the amphora with Eos mourning Memnon that gives his name to the Painter of the Vatican Mourner (Vatican 350/16589). Here the central standing figure of Eos with the dead Memnon lying before her, and his armor arrayed behind her, feeds upon Exekias' scene of the suicide of Aias (Boulogne 558), learning pictorial lessons that are applied in a distinct mythological context (Beazley 1956: 140.1, 686; Beazley 1971: 58; MacKay 2010: 243–53).

The range of myths shown on these later sixth-century black-figure pots widens significantly. This is evident in the variety of scenes related to the *Iliad*, but also in the range of scenes of Apollo, of Dionysos, of Athena, and of Herakles and Theseus. Amphoras attract some non-mythological scenes, particularly of warfare, but also, in one famous case, of the olive harvest (British Museum 1837.0609.42, attributed to the Antimenes Painter). Other shapes receive decoration that reaches more frequently toward the real world. Pelikai, for instance (a special shape of amphora that seems to have been variously used for oil and water, but not normally at the symposion), offer scenes of sale of oil, of drawing water, of butchery, of fishermen, of athletics and music-making, and of a cobbler at work (Shapiro 1997).

Notable are a number of scenes, on a variety of shapes, of what have sometimes been termed "pre-dramatic choruses." These scenes show a series of men dressed up in the same unusual fashion and maintaining the same pose, as if all choreographed, usually facing an aulos-player. In several cases men manifestly dressed up as animals are involved. Were the images from a century later, scholars would undoubtedly have identified these groups as choruses in comedy, but it was only in the fifth century that comedy became formalized as part of the City Dionysia festival at Athens. Those for whom these scenes must reflect something from life are obliged to imagine that there were comedy-like dramatic events before the invention of comedy, or that we have here illustrations of choruses performing the dithyramb, but arguably this is to neglect the way in which all images invent a performance, and to remove these scenes from the wider context of what gets represented on pottery, which is not the particular but the generalizable (Trendall and Webster 1971; Green 1991; Csapo 2003; Osborne 2008; Hedreen 2013).

As we have seen, Athenian pottery had long taken inspiration for pot shapes from other pottery traditions within the Greek mainland and from traditions of metalwork. But from the middle of the sixth century we meet a new development: the borrowing of shapes from a non-local tradition in order to target products to that non-local market. The earliest clear example of that comes with what have become known as Cypriot jugs—vases with a globular body and narrow tapering neck that closely imitate the shape of bichrome jugs of Cypro-Archaic II, while maintaining Attic painting traditions. A number of different Attic workshops seem to have made such jugs, which are only found on Cyprus (Fletcher 2008; Fletcher 2011).

One late sixth-century Attic workshop applied much more extensively this model of producing pots in shapes that were not common in Greece but were popular in a specific, non-Greek market. Some 139 black-figure pots, diverse in both form and style, and another 10 in red-figure, are signed, in a number of different hands, "Nikosthenes made [this]"—a signature that seems to signal the workshop, not the individual potter involved. This workshop specialized in shapes borrowed from elsewhere, primarily from Etruria, shapes that in many cases were only ever attempted in Athens by this workshop. Most particularly the workshop produced what have become known as Nikosthenic amphoras—amphoras with a carinated body and flat handles that borrow an Etruscan bucchero shape. With the exception of one found in Athens, all 86 Nikosthenic amphoras for which a general or particular provenance is known come from Italy, and the 40 for which a specific provenance is known all come from Cerveteri. It is notable that although 18 pots from Nikosthenes' workshop have been found at Vulci, none was a Nikosthenic amphora. Very precise marketing seems certain (Tosto 1999: 237–40).

Nikosthenes' workshop was generally highly innovative in terms of shapes, producing not merely amphoras of particular shape, but also kyathoi (ladels), cups, and pyxides. Other potters too were experimenting. The wine-cooler known as the psykter first appears about 530 (we have one from the Nikosthenic workshop). Experimentation went beyond shape, however, extending most importantly to technique. Various experimental techniques can be found in late sixth-century Attic pottery. Exekias had pioneered, on the interior of the eye-cup in Munich showing Dionysos sailing, a technique known as "coral red" (used to depict the "wine-dark sea"), which involved producing a particularly lustrous red that was darker than the red of the clay itself by applying a slip that did not turn black in the firing process (exactly how this was achieved remains unclear) (Cohen 2006: 43–70; Maish 2008; Walton, Doehne, Trentelman et al. 2008). Within a decade or so of that cup, the Nikosthenic workshop had experimented with several other new techniques. These certainly include the technique of polychrome painting on a black ground that has come to be known as Six's technique (Cohen 2006: 71–104; Brijder 2008), and the use of white ground (Mertens 2006; Neils 2008). White-ground painting continued to be practiced straight through the Classical period, becoming particularly important as a technique for lekythoi destined for burial in graves.

The most important development, however, was the invention of red-figure (Williams 1991; Robertson 1992: 7–14). This involved the reversal of black-figure so that instead of the figures being painted in black on the red clay background, the figures were reserved in red clay and the background filled in with black. Whether the honor for the invention of this technique also belongs to the Nikosthenic workshop is disputed—very early red-figure pots were also produced in the workshop of the potter Andocides (Williams 1996).

The earliest red-figure pottery is quite closely parallel to black-figure in its preferred pot shapes, iconography, and composition.[63] Indeed there has been a great deal of scholarly dispute as to whether the black-figure artist to whom Beazley

---

63. For the early history of Athenian red-figure pottery, see Boardman 1975: 11–88; Robertson 1992: 7–19.

gave the name the Lysippides Painter, who worked with the potter Andocides, is or is not identical to the red-figure artist known as the Andocides Painter, who also worked with him. Shortly after the invention of the new technique a number of amphoras and cups were produced that were decorated partly using black-figure technique and partly using red-figure technique. The interior of one particularly adventurous cup (see Figure 27) offers a red-figure scene of a youth handling an amphora, surrounded by a black-figure scene of ships sailing round the cup (British Museum 1843.11-3.29, attributed to the Painter of London E 2).

But as the so-called "bi-lingual" pots themselves make clear, black- and red-figure techniques worked so differently in their relationship to space, with black-figure offering flat silhouettes set in undefined spaces, red-figure potentially three-dimensional bodies spatially defined only in relationship to each other, that different subject-choice and different picture fields were appropriate (Cohen 1978; Cohen 2006: 18–42). Already the Andocides Painter tries showing figures who are twisting and occupying space, and another early exponent of the new technique, Psiax, who also worked with the potter Andocides, tries a variety of figures shown moving in one direction but looking back, or, in one case, a warrior looking out to face the viewer. Such poses were as useful in showing scenes

FIGURE 27 Athenian black-figure kylix; c. 510–5100; diameter: 15.24 cm; from Vulci. Attributed to the Painter of London E 2. British Museum 1843.1103.29.

of myth as scenes of life, but they did enable a wider range of scenes of life to be undertaken, and it is in scenes that relate to life—scenes of the gymnasium, of anonymous warfare, of the symposion itself, of reveling—that red-figure artists increasingly indulge.

The invention of the red-figure technique did not mean the end of black-figure painting. It was easier in black-figure to make clear the actions of smaller figures, and so possible to fit more figures into the same space. Complex mythological scenes or battle scenes continued to be better served by black-figure, and at the end of the sixth century a number of new scenes are introduced that are shown only in black-figure, including Achilles dragging Hector, Herakles and Helios, the maritime adventures of Dionysos, and Theseus at the labyrinth, as well as women at the fountain house and visits to the tomb (Hatzivassiliou 2010: 95–7). The use of added color, which had been undertaken to particularly impressive effect in the years before the invention of red-figure by the Swing Painter, who uses bold blocks of color to distinguish figures and make them stand out, continued to be a highly effective resource. A fine example of this comes on a hydria of the so-called Leagros group (named for its prominent use of the acclamation *Leagros kalos*— "Leagros is handsome") where the standard scene of Aias carrying off the corpse of Achilles from the battlefield is redeployed to show a male warrior carrying off a dead Amazon (Achilles carrying off Penthesileia?), with other warriors and a slumped Amazon corpse in the background (British Museum 1836.0224.128). Added white here picks out the bodies of the Amazons in a very striking way.

Increasingly, however, the use of the black-figure technique came to be limited to a narrow range of pot shapes, with smaller shapes (jugs, small cups of various sorts, small oil vessels) produced in black-figure, whereas larger symposion vases and large containers were produced mainly or entirely in red-figure (Hatzivassiliou 2010: 7). Use of black-figure is notable on two particular shapes. The first of these is the Panathenaic amphora (see Figure 48). From the reorganization of the Panathenaic games in the 560s (see Section 11.3), Athenian potters had been manufacturing neck amphoras of a particular narrow-necked shape that were awarded, full of oil, as prizes to victors. These amphoras uniformly had on one side a striding Athena, her shield advanced before her and her spear poised to strike, shown between columns, and on the other side an image related to a Panathenaic event. These amphoras turn up all round the Mediterranean, and it is clear that they became a coveted symbol of athletic prowess (see Section 13.1). Their format reflected and championed Athenian identity at home and abroad, and they go on being produced in this form through the fifth and fourth centuries (Bentz 1998).

The second pot shape decorated largely in black-figure was the lekythos (see Figure 28). The lekythos was an oil flask, and it became customary at Athens to deposit these, sometimes in some numbers, in graves. Often, they are small and,

FIGURE 28 Athenian black-figure lekythos; early fifth century; height: 14.6 cm. Attributed to the Marathon Painter. Metropolitan Museum New York 75.2.21.

increasingly, their decoration is hasty and sketchy, but they were evidently cheap to produce, and since they served their minimal purpose of evoking some sort of impression of the world of the person being buried, they continued to be made as they had long been. Indeed, the peak of production of black-figure lekythoi came only in the very late sixth and early fifth centuries. Despite the relatively low quality of many images, these lekythoi also continued to be exported widely, with black-figure lekythoi particularly popular in Sicily, and indeed black-figure pottery was more widely distributed than red-figure (Hatzivassiliou 2010: 8–10).

Black- and red-figure pots of the end of the sixth and beginning of the fifth century come to purvey two rather distinct views of the world. This is partly because of the continued dominance of myth in black-figure pots, whereas scenes of life are more prominent in red-figure, but that is far from a complete explanation. Scenes of life are quite notable in black-figure too, just as red-figure is far from uninterested in myth. Rather the distinction is between a focus on action in black-figure, and a focus on the individuals involved in action in red-figure pottery.

The focus on individuals in action can be illustrated by various late sixth-century and early fifth-century red-figure pots. Some of the finest pots of the end of the sixth century have been ascribed to a group of artists who have been given the name "Pioneers" (Robertson 1992: 20–42; Neer 2002: 87–134). This is a group of red-figure painters who, unusually, refer to each other explicitly in their work. It is also a group of artists all of whom offer themselves to us as distinct personalities by signing their pottery, although the question of whether the signatures all correspond to distinct persons has recently been questioned (Hedreen 2014; Hedreen 2016: 22–48). Their qualities are well exemplified in a belly amphora signed by Euthymides, (see Figure 29). On one side a soldier is shown fastening on his breastplate. To his proper left stands a handsome woman who holds his spear and raises his helmet aloft, as if about to put it on his head when he turns her way. On the other side of the soldier stands a bearded, balding man, well mantled in a cloak, a knobbly stick in his extended left hand, and staring intently at what the warrior is doing. A shield with a satyr-head motif stands of its own accord between warrior and woman, and above it the woman's name is written vertically: Hekabe. Elsewhere on the pot the warrior and the old man are also named: Hector and Priam.

The absence of any historicizing—the woman could almost be an Acropolis *korē*, the satyr at home in the tondo of a cup—adds to the pathos. We know from the *Iliad* about Hector departing for battle, and we know he will not come back alive. Showing soldiers arming was already a well-established tradition in late sixth-century black-figure pottery, where the preferred image showed the putting on of the greaves (Lissarrague 1989; Lissarrague 1990). The combination of a composition that makes the warrior's concentration on what he is doing patent with the identification of this as the tragic warrior par excellence completely transforms a routine image into one that focuses upon the individual life.

On the other side of this amphora we see three bearded revelers, one with a kantharos, one with a stick, all three with cloaks over their shoulders or across their arms in such a way as to do nothing to conceal their nakedness. The three dance, the central figure seen from the back, twisting round. Again, there is writing between and above the figures. This time it gives not only three names—Komarchos ("leader of the revel"), Eudemus, and Teles—but also "as never Euphronios." Euthymides, who proudly records also his father's name when he signs on the other side of this pot, boasts of his graphic prowess by naming another of the Pioneers—a painter

FIGURE 29 Athenian red-figure neck-amphora signed by Euthymides; c. 510; height: 60 cm; from Vulci. Munich, Staatliche Antikensammlungen und Glyptothek 2307.

himself responsible for some extraordinary feats of drawing.[64] Once more here the words interact with and change the viewer's engagement with the picture, turning a carefree drunken romp into a character-defining performance.

4.5.5 The Early Fifth Century

The concentration on the individual is much more obvious in the works of the great painters of amphoras and other large pots in the succeeding generation, the first decades of the fifth century. Two painters dominate this output, neither of them signs his own name—the Kleophrades Painter and the Berlin Painter.[65] The Kleophrades Painter has sometimes been identified with Euthymides, and there is no doubt that some of the Kleophrades Painter's work is particularly closely related to that of Euthymides.[66] But what the Kleophrades Painter shares with, and plausibly learned from the Berlin Painter is the use of just a single figure to dominate the side of an amphora or krater. These figures may be truly isolated, or they may be linked to another single figure on the other side of the pot (Herakles on one side of an amphora linked to Athena on the other; Ganymede on one side of a krater linked to Zeus on the other). But the isolation of a figure against the black background, coupled in some cases with some extremely elaborate painting sometimes involving special techniques such as added clay for Herakles' curly hair and beard, place massive emphasis on the individual figure, effectively slowing down any action and drawing attention to the mental disposition involved, not simply the physical manifestations.

One example usefully illustrates not just this way of focusing on the individual, but also the return of the satyr as a figure good to think with on pots. As we have already seen, satyrs entered Athenian imagery in the early sixth century as figures strongly associated with Dionysos and drunkenness and its effects as well as figures liable to sexual excitement and keen to obtain sexual pleasure (Carpenter 1986; Hedreen 1992; cf. Lissarrague 2013). Although plenty of satyrs are to be found on early red-figure vessels, particularly cups, the satyr had not been a central figure. With the Kleophrades and Berlin Painters the satyr comes back into the limelight, but in something of a new guise. For both painters realize that if one puts the satyr under the spotlight, then the question of what divides satyr from man (or god) becomes central.

So, on a neck amphora in Harrow (see Figure 30), the Kleophrades Painter depicts on one side a satyr in profile, moving to the right, naked but carrying

---

64. For the writing, see H. R. Immerwahr 1990: 65. On Euphronios, see Goemann, Giuliani, and Heilmeyer 1991; Neer 1995; Neer 2002: 44–65.

65. These painters were subject to classic studies by Beazley. See Beazley 1910; Beazley 1911; Beazley 1930; Beazley 1933. For recent studies, see Kunze-Götte 1992; Padgett 2017.

66. For the identity of Euthymides and the Kleophrades Painter, see Ohly-Dumm 1984, against Robertson 1992: 57.

FIGURE 30 Athenian red-figure neck-amphora; first quarter of fifth century; height: 46.6 cm. Attributed to the Kleophrades Painter. Harrow School Museum 55 (formerly 1864.55).

a shield (of which we see the inside) and spear. On the other side is another, younger, satyr, standing and holding out a helmet in his left hand, a pair of greaves in his right, and displaying characteristic sexual excitement. The amphora sets up a puzzle: between the two sides we have all the elements of a hoplite's arms and armor except the breastplate. But why are these elements divided between the two satyrs? Do these satyrs know what to do with these pieces of martial equipment or not? Just how like men are satyrs? And just how like satyrs are men? If drinking and fighting are the characteristics that mark out men (from children or from women), how exactly do they relate? This satyr anticipates many revisits to these questions as fifth-century painters repeatedly explore the "citizen satyr" (Lissarrague 2013).

Alongside the large pot tradition represented by the Pioneers and by the Kleophrades and Berlin painters, there was a tradition of cup painting that ranged even more widely in its imagery. From Exekias' eye-cup onward, painting had broken away from the narrow limits imposed by Band- and Lip-cups, to cover the whole exterior of cups and a smaller or larger part of the interior. The exterior of cups came to be the ideal space for using many-figured compositions to explore complicated myths or complex social situations—often with considerable humor. The inside of cups gave scope to focus on a single figure or the interactions of a pair of figures.

Among a large number of different painters of cups, three are particularly distinguished by their large output and by the quality of their work, two who sign as painters, Douris and Makron, and one who does not but is known by the name of the potter with whom he worked, the Brygos Painter (Boardman 1975: 132–78; Robertson 1992: 84–106).[67] Two cups by Douris will illustrate something of the range and the structure of these images.

A cup now in Vienna (see Figure 31) has on one side of its exterior seven bearded men arrayed into two groups that face each other (Buitron-Oliver 1995: #42). The group on the left consists of a figure wearing armor and carrying a sword, behind whom stand two unarmed men in himatia. The group on the right consists of an unarmed man in himation and chiton behind whom stand three men in himatia, at least two of whom are carrying swords (that part of the vase has suffered extensive damage). The figure wearing armor and carrying a sword is being restrained by the two men behind him from using his weapon against the figure in himation and chiton, while the man behind the figure in himation and chiton draws his sword as he prepares to intervene.

---

67. For Douris, see Buitron-Oliver 1995. For Makron, see Kunisch 1997.

FIGURE 31 Athenian red-figure kylix signed by Douris as painter and Python as potter; c. 480: diameter 33.8 cm; from Cerveteri. Vienna Kunsthistorisches Museum 3695.

On the other side of the exterior six bearded figures appear, three on either side of the goddess Athena. By Athena's feet is a block on top of which are two piles of pebbles, to which the figures nearest Athena are adding their pebbles. The figure on the far left is raising his hands in positive reaction to the large pile of pebbles on his end of the block. The figure on the far right has turned his back on the block in despair at the small pile of pebbles at his end. In the interior of the cup a bearded and a beardless figure pick up the helmet, breastplate, shield, and spear; the greaves on the ground wait to be collected.

What we have here is the dispute among the Greek heroes as to which of them should have the arms of Achilles after his death. Aias and Odysseus almost come to blows over this, a vote presided over by Athena is set up to decide the issue, and Odysseus ends up receiving the armor. Douris names none of the figures, but the clarity of gesture and the clear distinction between the figures—in particular, between the chiton-wearing Odysseus and the armed Aias, with the latter needing to be restrained from attacking the former—makes clear the roles and the narrative. Scholars have wondered whether we should not see here a nod toward Athens' new and distinctively democratic manner of taking decisions, and there is a clear parallel with the later judicial scene in Aeschylus' *Eumenides* (Spivey 1994). Certainly, the question of how to achieve proper dispute settlement is flagged up here—but so too, in the despairing Aias, is the tragic consequence of Aias' suicide. This is no straightforward celebration of law-court votes as an easy way to settle everything.

A second cup by Douris (see Figure 32) offers a somewhat similar relationship between the two exterior sides and the interior, but it has to do with life rather than myth (Getty Museum 86.AE.290). Diana Buitron-Oliver identifies the scene in the interior of the cup as a music lesson: a well-mantled boy holding a lyre stands in front of a man wearing a himation and leaning on a stick; behind the man is a stool (Buitron-Oliver 1995: 78 #93). On each side of the exterior of the cup we find three standing bearded men and two seated boys. Above the heads of each boy is a lyre and in the middle of the scene a net bag also hangs. A bearded man interacts with each seated boy and in one case the man proffers a hare to the boy and in another boy has a hare on his lap. The bearded figure on the far right is in both cases a spectator to the scene. On one side he reacts visibly by raising his right hand, in the other he stares intently, his right hand on his hip. Should we see this as a scene of education, like the famous scene on another of Douris' cups (Berlin Antikensammlung F2285), where the words on a scroll that a seated bearded man hold out, apparently for the boy in front of him to read, are legible? (Beazley 1948a: 337–8; H. R. Immerwahr 1964: 18). Or should we reckon this a scene of courtship? Can we draw a line between the erotics of courtship and the erotics of pedagogy?

These cups were made for use at drinking parties, and it is likely that the amphoras, as well as the kraters of the Kleophrades and Berlin Painters, were also made for drinking parties. Scholars have sometimes been concerned that the predominantly Etruscan find-spots of the best-preserved Athenian pots of this period, as of the sixth century, might indicate that the scenes painted were themselves aimed specifically at the Etruscan market (the economic aspects

FIGURE 32 Athenian red-figure kylix signed by Douris as painter, and Python as potter; c. 480; diameter 31.2 cm; acquired from private collector. Malibu, Getty Museum 86.AE.290.

of this question are explored further in Section 8.3; see also Section 12). But although the Nikosthenic workshop shows that it was certainly conceivable that Athenian pot-producers should style their pots for a specific Etruscan market, and although there are a small number of scenes (e.g. athletes shown in loincloths rather than naked, Shapiro 2000) that do indeed look as if adapted to Etruscan tastes (McDonnell 1991), the distribution of the same scenes in Etruria and in Athens, and the way in which the type of scene represented changes in a coordinated way across a whole range of broad subject areas, both point to Athenian painters' choices being primarily dictated by local Athenian cultural factors and the Etruscans voraciously consuming whatever was produced.[68] The quality of pottery found in Etruria suggests that the Etruscan market was discriminating as to quality, but that does not require that it was also discriminating as to subject matter.

However, 480 is far from constituting a marked break in Athenian pottery production. Indeed, it is extremely doubtful whether, if we did not otherwise know of the Persian Wars, we would be able to predict them from any features of Athenian pottery. Nevertheless, although the painters of the next generation are in a variety of ways deeply indebted to the painters whose work we have just looked at, there are distinct changes both in prevailing pot shapes—in particular the distinct decline of the amphora—and in both the content and the nature of the iconography (cf. the use of the title "mannerist" to refer to the most influential painters of larger pots in that generation) (Boardman 1975: 179–207; Robertson 1992: 133–59). White-ground lekythoi become a significant part of the Athenian funerary assemblage in the next generation, and with them comes a change in the iconography associated with funerary vessels (Oakley 2004). By the middle of the century the whole iconography of Athenian painted pottery has been transformed (Osborne 2018c).

For further discussion of the cultural place of Athenan pottery, see Section 12. For the, in some ways parallel, history of Athenian sculpture, see Section 12.1.

---

68. I make this argument more extensively in Osborne 2018c: esp. 46–8.

5

Political History

5.1 Introduction

We can write no history of Athens' political institutions before the seventh century. Mythology handed down the names of various kings of Athens, including Theseus, but although later tradition ascribed to those kings various political actions (a census to Kekrops [Philochoros *FGrH* 328 F95], *synoikismos* to Theseus [see Sections 4.1.1.1 and 4.1.1.3]), such claims were at best highly inferential. The continued existence into the Classical period of laws of Drako from the late seventh century and of laws of Solon from the start of the sixth century put historical deduction on a more secure basis, and in the case of Solon there was his explicitly political poetry to exploit also. For the political reforms of Kleisthenes at the end of the sixth century, we can derive evidence from the on-going practice of the fifth and fourth centuries, both as revealed by the epigraphic record and as described in the second half of the Aristotelian *Constitution of the Athenians*. For political history as for other aspects of Archaic Athenian history, the Persian Wars form an appropriate terminus.

When we turn from the history of the constitution to the history of political events we are rather less well served. For Athens, as for other cities, memory of past political events depended upon their continuing relevance to on-going political debates. It is because tyranny remained a significant threat in Classical Greek cities, and because families involved in resisting tyranny in the Archaic period had a continued role in Classical politics, that stories of Kylon's attempted coup and of the Peisistratids continued to be told.

The major issue that lies behind all aspects of Athenian political history in the Archaic period is the issue of how the community divided (for a discussion of this issue in terms of settlement pattern, see Section 4.1). The traditions handed down highlight both divisions caused by the gap between the rich and the poor and divisions consequent upon regional differences. Any understanding of Athenian

The Oxford History of the Archaic Greek World. Robin Osborne, Oxford University Press. © Oxford University Press 2023. DOI: 10.1093/oso/9780197644423.003.0005

politics in the Archaic period depends on discerning where the fault lines within Athenian society lay, and how these changed over time, but since understanding those fault lines is important also for our understanding of the subdivisions of the citizen body and our understanding of Athenian law, there is further relevant discussion in Sections 5.3 and 6. (For physical aspects of politics in Athens, see Section 4.3.)

5.2 Structure of the Political System and Change over Time

5.2.1 The Athenian Political System in the Seventh Century

The Hellenistic "Parian Marble" (*FGrH* 239), a chronology of Greek history that was compiled in or close to 264/3, begins with the reign of Kekrops, whom it identifies as the first king of Athens and dates to 1581/0. It then dates the judgment at Athens of a dispute between Ares and Poseidon, the founding event of the Areopagus as a law court, to 50 years later, the first Panathenaia to 76 years later, and Demeter's bringing agriculture to Athens and establishing the Proerosia (a festival to Demeter held in the autumn) to 172 years later. (Triptolemos is said to reap the first harvest the next year and the Eleusinian Mysteries to start a couple of decades or so later.) The Parian Marble, whose early events are dominated by Athens, and which was presumably based on the works of the Atthidographers, dates the first archon to 683/2, but then skips over Drako and Solon to record Peisistratos becoming tyrant in 561/0. Later chronographers offer a fuller political history, according to which from 1069/8 Athens was governed by archons for life chosen from the royal house, from 753/2 by archons elected for 10 years, and from 683/2 by annual archons.[1]

There is little to be gained from these traditions for our understanding of Athenian history except that there was never a time in Athens when anyone could remember there not having been an archon; no credence should be placed in the dates given or the claims about how the arrangements had developed. In the Classical period there was certainly an inscribed archon list, fragments of which survive, but we do not know when the Athenians began the practice of inscribing archons' names, or to what extent later historians of Athens projected the list backwards to support the story that they told.[2]

---

1. The material is conveniently collected in Harding 2008: 82–7.

2. For an optimistic account of both archon lists and the survival of Archaic Athenian inscribed texts more generally, see Stroud 1978; for a recent assessment, in the context of a discussion of such lists more generally, see Christesen 2007: 100–4.

The story of the developments of the main Athenian magistracies that is told by the Aristotelian *Constitution of the Athenians* is one that could simply have been deduced from the fact that in the Classical period there were nine archons: the eponymous archon, who gave his name to the year; the *basileus* archon, who oversaw Athens' official religious activities; the polemarch, who originally had played a leading role in the Athenian military; and six *thesmothetai*, who oversaw much of Athens' legal system. That there were three specific archons no doubt suggested that they were prior to the *thesmothetai*. That one archon was called the *basileus* suggested a prior history of kingship—something that stories of Theseus et al. independently supported.

The *Constitution of the Athenians* (3.2–3) offers a version that is transparently rationalizing: the first archonship was that of *basileus*, because that was traditional (*patrios*); the second was that of polemarch, because some *basileis* proved cowardly; and the last was the eponymous archon, as shown by the fact that all the really old festivals are looked after by either the *basileus* or the polemarch (Rhodes 1981: ad. loc.). The author of the *Constitution of the Athenians* takes the establishment of the *thesmothetai* and perhaps also the Areopagus Council (3.4–6), which was filled by ex-archons, to have happened after the appointment of the first archons and before the time of Drako; other ancient scholars debated whether the presence of the Council of the Areopagus in Solon's laws did or did not establish that that Council preceded Solon (Plut. *Sol.* 19.3–5), and both ancient and modern scholars have made guesses as to what the original roles of the Areopagus Council and *thesmothetai* were, but such guesses cannot give us history (Hignett 1952: 76–80; Rhodes 1981: 102–3; Wallace 1989: 3–7).

Modern discussions frequently simply substitute modern for ancient rationalizing—as in arguments that the archon must have preceded the polemarch since otherwise he would have been given a more specific title than simply "archon" (Hignett 1952: 43). We simply cannot know what led to the establishment of the eponymous archonship, or precisely when that office was created. If it is indeed the case that some form of political unity was new (or some earlier Bronze-Age unity recreated) in the eighth century (see Section 4.1.1.1), then all stories of how kingship turned into "aristocracy" are likely to be at best vast oversimplifications.[3] But before we simply dismiss the Aristotelian story completely it deserves some closer scrutiny, in the light of what may well be the very words of a seventh-century text—Drako's homicide law.

---

3. For the tendency even of archaeologists to prefer theoretical speculations based on the traditions about kings and presumptions about an aristocracy to analysis of archaeological data, see Hölscher 1991: 356–62.

At the end of the fifth century, as part of a more general republication of the laws, the Athenians republished Drako's homicide law (Osborne and Rhodes 2017: #183A). This law, discussed further below and in Section 6.1 (where the text of the law is given), presupposes the existence of various conventions pertaining to the settlement of disputes, including a role for phatries and for a public body with 51 members, the Ephetai. Ancient sources placed Drako's legislation in the late 620s, and although the basis on which they did so is uncertain, this is certainly the right sort of date (Rhodes 1981: 109). We can therefore have some confidence that by the last quarter of the seventh century the Athenians had set up dispute settlement mechanisms that drew upon, and served, a large population within which phatries and families were significant sub-groupings.

The Aristotelian *Constitution* twice (3.1, 3.6; cf. also 1.1 on choice of jurors) remarks that the magistrates were originally chosen "according to excellence and wealth" (ἀριστίνδην καὶ πλουτίνδην). This is a phrase Aristotle uses twice in *Politics* (1273a23–4, 1293b10), but the phrase "according to excellence" is also found in the republication in 409/8 of Drako's homicide law, in the text of which there is no reason to suppose that Drako's own wording is not being reproduced (see Section 6.1 for further discussion). That law makes provision for 10 members of a homicide victim's phratry to be chosen "according to excellence" (ἀριστίνδεν ḥαιρέσθον, l. 19) if the deceased has no living relatives to decide on the treatment of the perpetrator.

This phrase in Drako's law has been the basis of much speculation about the nature of the Athenian *politeia* in the seventh century and caused a great deal of confusion, but its historical significance has excited too little attention. The confusion has come from the fact that someone in antiquity read Drako's law hastily and took the "according to excellence" phrase to apply not to the 10 members of the phratry chosen, but to the Ephetai themselves.[4] In consequence Pollux (8.125) claims that Drako established the Ephetai "chosen according to excellence." Later lexicographers interpreted this as meaning that the Ephetai were men who "had the reputation for having lived best" (Photius and Suda s.v. ἐφέται). MacDowell recognized what the lexicographers had done to Pollux, but not that Pollux had himself derived his statement from a misunderstanding of Drako's law (MacDowell 1963: 50).[5] All this has diverted attention from how remarkable a word ἀριστίνδην really is.

---

4. This error is repeated in Figueira 2015b: 314, in what is otherwise the best and fullest discussion of the word ἀριστίνδην.

5. MacDowell himself understands the law rightly (1963: 124); cf. Rhodes 1981: 647.

The important thing about ἀριστίνδην is that it does not commit itself to specifying the source of excellence. English translators have regularly translated it as "according to rank," restricting the excellence to excellence formally recognized by society.[6] Others, pointing to the regular use of "good" and "best" to refer to those of good family, translate as "on the basis of good birth" (Rhodes 1981: 97–8; Osborne and Rhodes 2017: 507, 11). But the adjective "best" was never restricted in its use to birth—as the lexicographers who misunderstood the phrase show clearly by wanting it to refer to moral excellence.[7] The value of the term surely resides in its very openness: had Drako wished to make birth the criterion, there were straightforward ways of doing so. What is more, since the choice is between members of a phratry, all of whom were linked by kinship, birth is hardly a good discriminator to apply in this case.

The significance of Drako's use of a term that insists on discrimination, while not spelling out the grounds of that discrimination, is the very availability of that term. Athenians in the seventh century had decided that there were occasions, including presumably the selection of archons, when it was important to select the best people for the job in hand, but they had also decided that the criteria of excellence could not be predetermined. Selection on grounds of birth was not definitively ruled out, but it was not assumed. Unsurprisingly, for a society likely to have been familiar with Homeric epic and the poetry of Hesiod, the question of excellence was one open to debate, and with it the question of who appropriately should take on the responsibilities that needed to be distributed within the community. Despite the persistence of the idea in modern scholarship, the idea of a dominant aristocracy of birth in Archaic Athens has no support from ancient sources.[8]

But the term "according to excellence" is also important because it is a competitive term. The decision not to default to a choice made solely on grounds of birth or age is a decision that expects and encourages elite competition. Such competition is repeatedly implied both by the archaeology of the seventh century (see Section 4.4.3) and by such narrative history as can be safely reconstructed (not much more than the attempted coup by Kylon, as discussed in this chapter). We must envisage a community that comes together periodically and decides

---

6. So MacDowell 1963: 124; Stroud 1968: 6. Hignett 1952: 78 n.6 takes the phrase obviously and straightforwardly to refer to birth.

7. Well stressed by Figueira 1984: 455.

8. For the "eupatridai," see Section 5.3. On aristocracy in the Archaic period more generally, see Duplouy 2006; Fisher and van Wees 2015. The idea of aristocracy is particularly persistent within German scholarship (see, for example, Stein-Hölkeskamp 1989: esp. 139–204; Kienast 2005a), but remains widely assumed (cf. Flament 2011).

who is to take on responsibility for the coming year. As the community became more active, being among those given that responsibility became a more compelling ambition. Controlling that ambition and the consequent competition was to be the political priority of the sixth century.

One further feature of Drako's surviving homicide law deserves attention: the very existence of 51 Ephetai. The importance lies in both the process and the number. The number is significant in two ways. First, 51 is a large number, both absolutely and in relation to the size of seventh-century Athens. Large numbers may be good for finding the right answer in difficult cases, but they are good above all for ensuring that decisions are owned by the whole community. Second, 51 is an odd number. The implication is that decisions will be reached by voting, and that consensus is not required. This is not a body that is acting as a council, deliberating until it decides what is best; it is a body where individuals are being asked to choose options according to their individual judgments. Between them, these two principles tell us quite a lot about politics in seventh-century Athens.

The law on involuntary homicide is the only law of Drako to survive, and it does so because Solon kept this law when he himself created new laws. In the fourth century Athenian orators treat all homicide laws as laws of Drako. What Athenians in the Classical period knew of Drako's other laws was effectively nothing. The claim that all Drako's laws had death as a penalty (Plut. *Sol.* 17.2) is manifestly false, but the tradition that Drako's activity was not limited to homicide regulations is plausible, even if the particular claims made in antiquity are questionable. Since Solon replaced all except the homicide laws, it is not surprising that nothing further could be known about Drako's laws, even in antiquity.

The one political incident from the seventh century about which Athenians continued to talk in the fifth century was the failed attempt by Kylon to seize the Acropolis in a political coup (Osborne 2009: 202–3). The murder of his supporters, when they had made themselves suppliants, led to a curse on the family of those responsible, the Alkmaionidai, and the repeated reference back to this curse even in the fifth century kept the story alive (while no doubt guaranteeing that the truth of what happened was well out of sight). We have accounts both in Herodotos (5.71) and Thucydides (1.126.2–10) that give us a great deal of detail— and an account from Plutarch that gives even more (*Sol.* 12). The incident is dated only by Kylon's having been an Olympic victor, where he appears in the victor lists for 640 (Moretti 1957: 65 #56). Those lists may be mistaken, but we have no firm grounds for amending them.[9]

---

9. For an unconvincing attempt to date the incident to the 590s, see Lévy 1978.

As presented in the fifth century Kylon attempted to use his charisma as an Olympic victor, together with the high status he gained from having married the daughter of Theagenes, tyrant of neighboring Megara, to seize power in Athens. After consulting with the Delphic oracle (an act mentioned by Thucydides but not, curiously, by Herodotos) and being told to take control of the Acropolis during the "greatest festival of Zeus," Kylon and his age-mate supporters seized control of the Acropolis during the Olympic festival, but then found themselves besieged there. Thucydides claims that Kylon himself and his brother managed to escape and that his supporters took refuge in a temple or at an altar, but they were torn away and killed. Other sources imply that Kylon was among those killed. Responsibility for this act rested on the magistrates—the nine archons, according to Thucydides, the "prytanies ("presidents") of the naukraries" according to Herodotos. The ultimate consequence was that, during Kleomenes' intervention in Athens in the late sixth century, 700 families were expelled on the grounds that they were accursed due to their descent from the individuals responsible for the death of Kylon (Hdt. 5.72.1). In the Classical period what was remembered was that the curse included the family of the Alkmaionidai.

Herodotos' mention of the "presidents of the naukraries" is the earliest mention of the institution of the naukrary. Naukraries had ceased to exist by the Classical period, but there was sufficiently frequent mention of them, and of officials named *naukraroi*, in Solon's laws to excite explanation from the Aristotelian *Constitution of the Athenians* and from the Atthidographers, whose work is variously reflected in later lexicographers. The *Constitution of the Athenians* 8.3 suggests that naukraries were subdivisions of tribes (see Section 5.3), with 12 in each of the four tribes, and that they were expected to collect and disburse funds (at this stage funds consisting of something other than coinage). A plausibly Solonian law (Solon *Laws* F79b Leão and Rhodes, from Androtion) indicates that not only *naukraroi*, but also officials known as *kolakretai* ("ham-collectors") had access to naukraric funds.

What exactly was a naukrary?[10] The *Constitution of the Athenians* 21.5 thinks of them as being predecessors of demes, with the demarchs taking over the responsibilities of the *naukraroi*.[11] Pollux (8.108) repeats this information but

---

10. On naukraries, see Rhodes 1981: 151–2; Lambert 1993: 252–6; Kienast 2005a: 78-81; van Wees 2013: 44–61.

11. The *Constitution of the Athenians* states that demes replaced naukraries, but Kleidemos (*FGrH* 323 F8) claimed that Kleisthenes simply increased the number of naukraries from 48 (4 x 12, [Arist.] *Constitution of the Athenians*. 8.3) to 50: "when Kleisthenes had made 10 tribes instead of 4, it happened that they were divided into 50 parts, which they called naukraries, just as now they call symmories the groups formed by the division into 100 parts." Naukraries leave

then goes on to claim, presumably drawing on the same source on which the Aristotelian researcher drew, that each naukrary provided two horses and one ship. Since naukrary derives from the word for a ship-captain, it is both plausible that there is a naval connection and inevitable that tradition would find such a connection. What is not inevitable is the suggestion that naukraries were responsible for providing the cavalry. If we ask what seventh-century Athens needed public funding for, the main possibilities are religious activities, on the one hand, and military activities on the other. We know from Androtion (Solon *Laws* F79b Leão and Rhodes) that the naukraric fund paid the expenses of sacred ambassadors (*theoroi*) to Delphi, so they had some responsibilities related to religion, but this does not mean that they did not also have a military role (on the Athenian armed forces in the Archaic period, see Section 5.3).

The tradition that naukraries had "presidents" seems to go back beyond Herodotos, to judge from an *ostrakon* cast against Xanthippos (the Alkmaionid father of Perikles) in 488–485, referring to him as "one of the accursed prytaneis" (van Wees 2013: 49–50). Even if true, however, this tells us little since we never subsequently hear of them, and our only knowledge of them in action would be in the context of Kylon's failed coup. However, if we accept that naukraries were responsible for the cavalry and navy, it would be unsurprising if the *naukraroi* as a body might be called upon to take responsibility in what was effectively a moment of military crisis, whether supporting or supplanting the archons to whom Thucydides ascribes authority.

The story of Kylon's failed coup was clearly good to think with. It drew attention to the potential political danger that can be posed by those who become popular for non-political activities. It drew attention to the danger that those who have married into powerful families abroad might use that power for political purposes at home. It helped to explain on-going hostility between Athens and its neighbor Megara (see Section 7.1.1), and it accounted for the ancestral curse on the Alkmaionidai, which was repeatedly used as a weapon within Athenian politics. Because the story floated, not fixed to a particular date, other characters could be brought into it, including Solon (Plut. *Sol.* 12.2, 12.4) and Epimenides of Crete, who is supposed to have effected a purification ([Arist.] *Constitution of the Athenians.* 1; Plut. *Solon* 12.4–6)—despite the fact that those found guilty had been tried and banished. Because the attempted coup failed, this also became a story for thinking about how, in a world where individuals and cities consulted oracles of the gods before embarking on major enterprises, Kylon could have

---

no trace in our Classical sources, but it is not impossible that they retained some responsibility for the navy, as Kleidemos seems to imply.

consulted Delphi and still failed (a question answered by making Delphi refer ambiguously to "the greatest festival of Zeus;" Thuc. 1.126.6).

When a story is so good to think with, it is hard to know what can be reclaimed for history. Perhaps little more than that there was an episode of violent civil strife in the generation or so before Solon, and that the question of legitimate and illegitimate use of violence was a pressing one. Whether or not they are to be associated with Kylon (and the execution of shackled prisoners at Phaleron is completely inconsistent with the story of the execution of suppliants in Athens), the burials at Phaleron of groups of shackled young men who have been executed (see Section 4.4.3) further confirm this situation.[12] State power was sufficiently firmly established to enable a command to execute a non-trivial proportion of the young men of Athens to be given and carried out. Conflicts that led to this degree of (counter-)violence would provide a background for Drako's homicide law, the most important element of which was arguably the recognition that there needed to be a way of dealing with unintentional homicide, and that there needed to be a limit also to who could prosecute a homicide. Drako's law is as much concerned with giving a guarantee that there is a limit to what the friends of someone who is killed can do as with enabling them to act. What is to be noted is that Drako's law is very much about killing among equals; there is no trace of concern here for how one deals with the killing of slaves, or indeed of foreigners, but there is a concern for Athenians continuing a feud even when one party has, as the law requires of even the unintentional homicide, withdrawn from Attica.[13]

5.2.2 Solon's Reforms

If the political problem in the last quarter of the seventh century came from competition among the elite, the political problem of the first decade of the sixth century was distinctly different. So, too, is our evidence quite different. The survival through their later quotation of both a substantial quantity of Solon's poetry and several of what are more or less certainly Solon's laws enables us to see Archaic Athens through the eyes of a central actor.

---

12. The suggestion that a specific mass grave of shackled young men excavated at Phaleron might be related to Kylon's coup is based solely on this being the only incident of the right sort of date recorded in our textual sources (see Ingvarsson, Bäckstrom, Chryssoulaki et al. 2019).

13. *Constitution of the Athenians* 4 preserves what it claims to be a "constitution" designed by Drako. There are reasons for thinking that this was added late in the composition of the text of this work (including its clumsy mention in *Constitution of the Athenians* 41.2, where it appears between the second change to the Athenian constitution under Theseus and the third under Solon), and its particular concerns suggest that it had origins in the debate about the constitution in 411. See Rhodes 1981: 84–7, 113–7. I simply pass over this constitution here.

Much that antiquity reported about Solon was as speculative and imaginative as what they reported about other aspects of Archaic Athenian history.[14] It is telling that Herodotos, although he knows Solon as a law-giver, presents Solon simply as a stock "wise man" and in a historically unlikely engagement with the Lydian ruler Kroisos (1.29–43). The stories that enabled Plutarch eventually to write a whole biography of Solon were very largely the creation of the fourth century and later. This does not mean that those who invented them did not make some attempt to get access to solid facts about him from his poetry, his laws, and from looking at Archaic inscribed material. But it does mean that, where such evidence is not explicitly deployed, we have no reason to trust what we are told. Like Kylon, although for quite different reasons, Solon proved massively good to think with. Many of the aspects of Athenian life illuminated by Solon's poetry and laws will be explored in subsequent sections. The focus here is on Solon and politics, and these emerge most clearly from his poetry, rather than from what we know of the laws (which are further discussed in Section 6.2).[15]

To understand Solon's politics properly we need to know his dates—although given the difficulty of dating other figures and events, this is less important than we might expect. Ancient chronographers claim that Solon was archon in 594/3, and Solon's laws are generally thought to date to his archonship (so explicitly [Arist.] *Constitution of the Athenians* 5.2; Plut. *Sol.* 14.3, 16.5). The Aristotelian *Constitution* itself seems to date Solon's archonship to 592/1, and the problems that this creates have caused some modern scholars to think we should rather date Solon as lawgiver, if not also as archon, to the 570s (Rhodes 1981: 120–2; cf. de Ste. Croix 2004: 75–80). A date in the 570s eases some ancient claims about Solon's relations with various other historical figures, including Peisistratos and Philokypros, king of Cyprus, but it compresses the period of political turmoil between Solon and Peisistratos implausibly. 594/3 may not be correct, but the 590s remain the most plausible decade for Solon's main political activity.

Solon's poetry flags up a number of political issues. We have no independent evidence for when each of the poems was written, and therefore it is not easy to construct from the poetry itself how Solon's political views developed. The conventional ordering of fragments groups poems by meter, rather than attempting any chronological reconstruction. The best we can do is to note recurrent interests. Some of these had to do with Athens' relations with the rest of the world,

---

14. On the early reception of Solon, see Nagy and Noussia-Fantuzzi 2015. Rönnberg 2021a: 40–56 is skeptical about ascribing anything firmly to Solon, but much of the argument for doubt ends up being a matter of *petitio principii* based on preconceived views of what would or would not be plausible.

15. On Solon generally, see Osborne 2009: 204–13.

and in particular it is clear that Solon maintained that Salamis was part of Attica (F1–3 West; see Section 7.1.1). But the most prominent issues relate to internal politics. Solon sees Athens as in danger of being torn apart by citizens motivated by material gain. In more than one poem he lays out the problem as being one that brings about enslavement and the selling of poor citizens into slavery abroad (F4, 9, 11, 36 West); currently, Solon claims, Athens has bad constitutional arrangements and needs to replace these with a good set of laws that will ensure straight justice (F4).

That there was a political crisis around 600 brought about by extreme economic and social inequality is confirmed by fourth-century sources. Solon seems to have been firmly associated with two problematic terms that no ancient scholar managed to find mentioned in his poems: *hektemoroi* and *seisachtheia*. The term *hektemoroi* was obsolete by the fourth century, and ancient scholars fought to understand its import; clearly it meant "those of the sixth part," but did it mean those who paid a sixth part (in rent), or those who retained a sixth part (paying the remaining five parts in rent)?[16] *Seisachtheia* is a term meaning "shaking off of burdens," and Plutarch (*Sol.* 15.3) claims that Solon used the term of what he had achieved—but to what did it actually refer? Around the uncertainty over the reference of these terms lies the central debate about what the crisis was that Solon faced and what his solution was.

The term *hektemoros* is first used in *Constitution of the Athenians* 2.2 when [Aristotle] says that the poor, their wives, and their children were enslaved to the rich and were called *pelatai* and *hektemoroi*. The whole land, [Aristotle] goes on, was in the hands of a few, and those who did not pay their rent were led off as slaves. Given that Solon identified Athens' problems as caused by greed and, given how implausible it is (see Section 8.1) that the agricultural land of Attica was fully exploited in 600, questions of land tenure, how there came to be a large group of tenant farmers, and why they had so much trouble paying their rent, would appear to be crucial. Scholars have sometimes convinced themselves that the problem was over-exploitation of the land and declining fertility and therefore declining agricultural production, but this seems to import an inappropriate agricultural model from the modern world.[17]

The best guide to what the problem was lies in the solution that Solon effected through his laws. Solon became associated both with some "shaking

---

16. That five-sixths was retained is spelt out by Plutarch *Solon* 13.4 (and implicit in [Arist.] *Constitution of the Athenians* 2.2); that only one-sixth was retained is claimed by Eustathius 1854.31 on *Odyssey* 19.28. For more recent views, see Gallant 1982: 123–4.

17. French 1956, cf. Rhodes 1981: 93–4; *contra* Gallant 1982. See also I. Morris 2002: 32–41.

off of burdens" and with actions that meant that *hektemoroi* are never again heard of in Attica. In his poetry, Solon certainly claims to have brought back to Athens, and presumably restored to freedom, men who had been sold—those who had been sold justly as well as those sold unjustly (F36.8–13 West)—and to have freed men in Attica who had been held in "shameful slavery, trembling at the habits of their masters" (F36.13–15). Part of what Solon did to achieve this was to abolish enslavement for debt—a man could no longer offer his own body as security for a loan ([Arist.] *Constitution of the Athenians* 2.2, 4.4, 6.1, 9.1; Plut. *Sol.* 13.4, 15.2). Remarkably, to have secured the results to which Solon lays claim, this must have been done retroactively, and it is a measure of the strength of feeling in the community that this could be achieved, presumably involving compensatory payments to those who had bought the now-freed slaves. Even if we take the reference to the slavery of those who trembled at the habits of their masters to be metaphorical, the return of those sold abroad must involve actual slaves somehow bought back. The magnitude of this achievement must not be underestimated.

Abolishing enslavement for debt by itself, however, effected rather minimal change in economic and social relations, particularly since debt bondage (that is, pledging one's services to a creditor until a debt was paid off) remained legal (Harris 2002). To count as "shaking off of burdens" and to account for the disappearance of the *hektemoroi*, something more must have been involved than ruling out selling oneself, as opposed to selling one's services. Solon's poetry contains both a claim to what he did and a denial: Solon denies that he gave equal shares of the land to the "good" and the "bad" (F34.8–9 West), and claims to have given the people (*dēmos*) as much honor or reward (*geras*) as was sufficient for them, not adding to, but also not detracting from, their honor, while claiming to have devised nothing that was unseemly (F5.1–4 West). Part of this is political posturing: Solon is keen to present himself as the moderate man in the middle, talking of himself as a boundary-stone that is fought over (F37.9–10 West), as a wolf surrounded by dogs (F36.27 West), or as extending a strong shield over both sides and preventing either side gaining victory (F5.5–6 West). But this political claim is one that Solon must make because not everyone saw it that way. Something that he did seemed, to his critics, to have given the people more reward than they deserved and to have shown insufficient respect for the elite. What was this?

In Fragment 36, Solon claims to have done what he got the people together to do, and that "the greatest and best mother of the Olympian gods, black earth" could join him in bearing testimony that he abolished the boundary stones once fixed everywhere, so that the earth that was once enslaved was now free (F36.1–7 West). In the Classical period notices were inscribed on stones put up on the boundaries of property when that property had been used as security for a loan, and so the Aristotelian *Constitution of the Athenians* (12.1) thinks that this amounts to cancellation of debts. But the earliest such mortgage marker dates to the late fifth century, and there is no evidence at all that the practice of using boundary markers in this way went back earlier.[18] We should take these boundary stones to be just that, not records of loans secured by the land in question but stones that laid claim to land, and their removal to be a challenge to that claim (Rihll 1991).[19]

So, what did Solon do? The contrast between the settlement pattern of Attica in the seventh century and that prevailing at the end of the sixth century lies primarily in the development of communities in areas of sub-prime land (see Section 4.1.2.2). It is attractive, therefore, to think that Solon's removal of boundary stones freed up land for settlement. One attractive possibility is that by challenging the wealthy who had more or less literally staked out claims to extensive tracts of Attica, and who allowed others to work that land only on the stringent condition of receiving only one-sixth of the land's product, Solon put the land of Attica into the hands of the majority, rather than the few (thus reversing the situation described in [Arist.] *Constitution of the Athenians* 2.2). The enslavement of the land and the enslavement of the poor had been done away with at a single stroke.[20] Later tradition denied that Solon had redistributed land (*Constitution of the Athenians* 11.2; but contrast Arist. *Pol.* 1266b15–16 on Solon realizing the political power of leveling out property) both because of the way it understood the reference to boundary stones and because of a reluctance to see the "moderate" Solon as espousing redistribution of land, which was in the Classical period a radical rallying cry.[21]

To understand how Solon achieved this, we need to understand the whole of what Solon did as a package. As we will see in Section 6.2, Solon's laws carefully establish property rights: the *quid pro quo* for land redistribution was future security of property holding. Solon offered a future in which legal protection

18. Finley 1951 is the classic study of these mortgage markers. Although acknowledging that there were no extant boundary stones recording loans until c. 400, Finley himself considered the stones removed by Solon to be of this sort (Finley 1981: 63).

19. This is to argue for a position diametrically opposite to that of de Ste. Croix 2004: 109–28, who thinks that Solon's actions were entirely about debt.

20. For this reconstruction, see Faraguna 2012; cf. Leão and Rhodes 2015: 112. I amend here slightly the view I offered in Osborne 2009: 211.

21. In a similar way there was a dispute in antiquity as to whether Solon had abolished debt; the *Constitution of the Athenians* (12.1; cf. Plut. *Sol.* 15.5) takes Solon F36 West to show this, but Androtion denied it (*FGrH* 324 F34; Plut. *Sol.* 15.4).

extended beyond the person, as in Drako's homicide laws, to a person's property. The mutual suspicion among the élite, manifest already both in Kylon's attempted coup and in the scapegoating of the Alkmaionidai in the aftermath of that coup, seems to have been deployed by Solon to persuade them to accept the denial of their claim to largely uncultivated land in return for legal protection of their core property, which now became formally the basis of their standing in society through the new division of political rights according to census classes (see Section 5.3).

Such legal protection, however, demanded more than simply a code of laws. It demanded that those laws could be effectively enforced—and enforced in a non-partisan way (cf. Section 5.2.1). As far as we can see, in the seventh century Athens was run by a small group of magistrates, the nine archons centrally, those in charge of the naukraries locally. The ex-archons may have had considerable influence, but what formal powers belonged to the Council of the Areopagus (which consisted of all living ex-archons) is less clear. Homicide cases were handled by the 51 Ephetai. The Solonian amnesty law (which may indeed be the law by which he reinstated enslaved Athenians to their freedom), cited by Plutarch (*Sol.* 19.4) as the eighth law on the 13th *axōn*, a reference so precise as surely to be genuine, has Solon restore rights to all who had been deprived of them, except for those condemned by the Areopagus, the Ephetai, or the *prytaneion* presided over by the *basileus.* Those may indeed have been the only judicial institutions, and their concern primarily murder and insurrection. Solon's property laws, and his extension of the lawcode more generally, demanded additional institutional support, and he supplied it with new law-courts. Later tradition is unanimous in making Solon the founder of popular courts, and the right to judge a right that he extended to all Athenian men, however poor ([Arist.] *Constitution of the Athenians* 9.1; Plut. *Sol.* 18.2–3; see further Section 6.2).

The question of whether Solon introduced further constitutional innovations is debated. Even before Solon, as we have seen, some form of community gathering will have been necessary to produce annual magistrates. Such a gathering may have been closer to the sort of assembly found in the Homeric poems—more an occasion when those gathered are told what is happening than one where they decide what is happening—than to the democratic assembly of the fifth century. But the difference between telling people that it is opportune or necessary to go to war and asking them whether or not a war should be undertaken may be moot, and it may depend primarily on the authority carried by the magistrates of the moment. Accounts of the sixth century tend to assume that after Solon major decisions, such as granting Peisistratos a bodyguard (Hdt. 1.59.4, cf. [Arist.] *Constitution of the Athenians* 14.2, Plut. *Sol.* 30–1, Diog. Laert. 1.49–54), rested with the assembly of all Athenian men, but that may be simply retrojection of fifth-century expectations.[22] Routine matters were presumably dealt with by magistrates, and they will have decided whether to summon the people.

In Classical Athens, formulating policy and summoning the assembly were in the hands of the Council of 500, and later tradition credits Solon with creating a Council of 400, consisting of 100 men drawn from each of the four Ionian tribes. Although the presence of this council in the historical record is shadowy (at best it perhaps appears at Herodotos 5.72.1–2),[23] its existence is plausible. Unfortunately, we have no evidence for how its members were chosen, and the particular political significance of the creation of this Council therefore escapes us.

We are equally in the dark about whether Solon gave any status to the communities of Attica that would become Kleisthenic demes (see Section 4.1.2.2). Demetrios of Phaleron, no mean authority, for all his late fourth-century date, claimed that demarchs were instituted by "the men around Solon," to administer local justice (F145 Wehrli). How this relates to the tradition that Peisistratos initiated "judges throughout the demes" ([Arist.] *Constitution of the Athenians* 16.5; see Section 6.3) is unclear, but Demetrios may have been correcting the Aristotelian tradition (Kienast 2005a: 73–7). Given the pre-existence of demes as communities and given that whatever naukraries were they were not communities, it is hard to fathom how the officers of naukraries can have raised funds from the area for which they were responsible without local knowledge about those communities. But if they needed to tap into local knowledge, they needed someone made responsible for passing on that knowledge. A demarch might have performed that function.

It is a measure of Solon's political success that overt strife between mass and elite is completely absent from subsequent Athenian politics in the Archaic period. But such strife had not been the only issue in the seventh century; strife within the elite had been a problem too, seen most obviously in Kylon's attempted coup. Whether Solon attempted to do something about that depends on whether we side with Aristotle in *Politics* (1273b35–1274a3, 1274a16–17, 1281b25–34) or with his researcher in *Constitution of the Athenians* (8.1) as to whether election was the way of selecting archons even before Solon, and Solon left the selection procedure unchanged or whether he introduced change. According to the *Constitution*

---

22. Unless the law discussed in Section 5.2.4, in connection with Kleisthenes, really belongs in this context, as Ryan 1994 has suggested.

23. Plutarch (*Sol.* 19.2), in discussing the Solonian Council of the 400, implies that in his poetry Solon compared the Council of the Areopagus and the Council of the 400 to two anchors (δυσὶ ... ἀγκύραις). For discussion of whether the metaphor is in fact genuinely Solonian, see de Ste. Croix 2004: 84–5 with n.40.

of the Athenians Solon invented a system whereby each of the four tribes chose 10 candidates, and the nine archons then being drawn by lot from those 40 (Rhodes 1981: 146–9).[24] It is perhaps good evidence that Solon did introduce such a procedure, that strife over the archonship dominates our accounts of Athenian politics in the wake of his reforms (see Section 5.2.3): the introduction of the lot would seriously impede the chances of particular individuals from gaining office, and from gaining the particular office they wanted in the year they wanted it, and frustration with this may have been behind violating the rules and resorting to violence.

5.2.3 The Peisistratids

No other sixth-century Athenian attracted the interest of later writers in the way that Solon did (chronologically the next Athenians to have a *Life* written by Plutarch are Themistokles and Aristeides). The elements of the Peisistratid period that drew the attention of Herodotos and Thucydides concerned the accession to power of Peisistratos and the removal from power of his sons, and the Atthidographers seem to have been able to fill in very little else. The only significant addition that they made, perhaps on the basis of the archon lists, was an account of the breakdown of regular Athenian government in the years after the passing of Solon's laws ([Arist.] *Constitution of the Athenians* 13.2–3). According to this tradition there were two years in which the Athenians chose no archon (we are not told how this came about—because the elite boycotted the procedure? because they refused to accept what the lot produced? because the successful candidate was bullied into standing down?), and then one Damasias refused to give up the office of archon and stayed in power for two years and two months before being expelled. The *Constitution of the Athenians* (13.2) claims that after Damasias' expulsion from office the Athenians elected 10 archons, five from the "eupatrids," three from the "rustics" or "countryfolk" (*agroikoi*), and two from the craftsmen (*demiourgoi*). Whether any genuine history lies behind this is doubtful, but if it does it perhaps reflects a dispute over whether birth should play any part in securing election to the archonship (on the eupatrids, see Section 5.3).

We can be more confident that genuine history lies behind the accounts given of how Peisistratos gained power (Lavelle 2005). Herodotos (1.59–64) and later sources agree that Peisistratos seized power three times. The first time he used

---

24. The case against use of the lot in the choice of archons is most powerfully articulated by de Ste. Croix 2004: 89–104.

self-inflicted wounds to persuade the Athenian to grant him a group of body-guards, which he then used to seize the Acropolis. The second time he made an alliance with Megakles (on whom, see below) and then returned to Athens in a chariot, accompanied by a strapping young woman whom at least some Athenians evidently took to be Athena herself. The third time he fought his way to power by securing support from friendly elites in Argos, Eretria, and Naxos; recruiting a mercenary army; and defeating the Athenians in battle at Pallene. Herodotos gives no indication of chronology, but the *Constitution of the Athenians* (14–15) adds dates that are best interpreted as equating to 561/0 for the first coup, 556/5 for the first expulsion, 552/1 for the second coup, 546/5 for the second expulsion, 536/5 for the third coup, and 528/7 for Peisistratos' death. The first and the last of these dates is plausible, but scholars have worried about many of the inter-mediate dates, not least because Herodotos seems to imply a much earlier date (around 545) for the third coup (Rhodes 1981: 191–9). The dates do matter, not least because they affect what else can plausibly be attributed to Peisistratos (see Section 11.3), but the nature of the political struggle does not hang on the pre-cise dates.

Herodotos (1.59) already sees the coup that brought Peisistratos to power as consequent upon factional divisions that had a basis in part in family politics and in part in regionalism, and the *Constitution of the Athenians* (13.4) elaborates this into a dispute between parties of more conservative and more populist per-suasion (Sealey 1960; Hopper 1961; Holladay 1977). According to both sources, the three main factions were the "Men from Over the Hill" (northeast Attica), under the leadership of Peisistratos; the men from the coast, under the leadership of Megakles; and the men from the plain, under the leadership of Lycurgus. To what extent these groups were essentially factions formed around a charismatic leader from a prominent family, who happened to have a local following, and to what extent the leaders were themselves products of strong and distinctive local interests is impossible to assess.

However, Peisistratos' success, first in persuading the Athenians to give him bodyguards with whom he installed himself in power, and second in persuading the Athenians that Athena herself had brought him back to take charge, indi-cates that he could command support well beyond the "Men from Beyond the Hills." Ironically, what propelled Peisistratos to power most effectively seems to have concern about the very elite competition of which he was himself a product—both concern at the violence into which it might descend and con-cern that the constitutional means of regulating the competition might come up with the wrong answers (and a divine "overrule" be appropriate). But if backing Peisistratos was a route to avoiding civil strife, it took some time to achieve that effect.

The Peisistratos whose story is told by Herodotos (1.59–64) is something of a text-book tyrant.[25] He can claim to have his future success predicted by the Delphic oracle; he first gains power by capitalizing on his fame as a general by political sleight of hand; he then uses religious aura to gain power a second time; and, finally, he gets support from other nearby states to establish himself militarily. All the basic means of gaining political power are rolled into a single cautionary tale that has the Athenians repeatedly deceived. By contrast the *Constitution of the Athenians* presents the positive side of the story. In its account (15.4–5) Peisistratos puts a stop to civil strife, something symbolized by his depriving the Athenians of their arms and telling them to go about their daily affairs without them, and that he will look after public affairs. He proves humane and fair, encouraging agricultural production and taxing it for public benefit, and generally making life easier for those outside the city. He is said to have instituted traveling judges to try minor cases ([Arist.] *Constitution of the Athenians* 26.3, 53.1; Section 6.3). He obeys the laws, and he comes to be favored by rich and poor alike. His rule is like the mythical "age of Kronos" (*Constitution of the Athenians* 16). Whatever one thought about tyranny, Peisistratos' story could provide support for one's view (Osborne 2009: 267–9; more generally McGlew 1993).

We may get closer to historical reality with the accounts of how Athenian politics unfolded under Peisistratos' sons. Not only were these events considerably closer in time to the fifth-century informants of Herodotos and Thucydides, but also, whereas fifth-century Athenians generally wanted to forget any connections they had with Peisistratos, they were keen to memorialize any part their family played a role in the downfall of the tyranny. This does not, of course, mean that the stories they told were true: Thucydides himself emphasized how much wishful thinking there was in the story of tyrannicide that most Athenians told (6.54–9). Nevertheless, just as the story of Harmodios and Aristogeiton murdering Hipparchos remains true, even if Hipparchos was not strictly "the tyrant" and the murderers' motives were not political, accounts of events such as the murder by the Peisistratids of Kimon son of Stesagoras (Hdt. 6.103.3) likely record actual occurrences with some degree of accuracy, although perhaps not the underlying motivations or larger context (in the case of Kimon, a sudden death in suspicious circumstances, whether or not it was his Olympic victories that precipitated it).

One striking feature of the accounts of the rule of Peisistratos' sons, Hippias and Hipparchos, at Athens is that, for all the sophisticated cultural and local politics reflected in the regulation of Homeric performances at the Panathenaia and the institution of Herms marking the halfway point between Athens and each of

---

25. On the so-called "despotic template," see Dewald 2003; cf. Osborne 2009: 180–5.

the demes (see Section 11.3), what remains at the center of traditions about sixth-century politics is rivalry between elite families (Stahl 1987). Kimon's family, the Philaidai, establish themselves as rulers of Athens' settlement in the Thracian Chersonese (Hdt. 6.34–41; see Section 7.1.1). The Alkmaionidai move in and out of exile, storing up goodwill at Delphi by spending money on the restoration of the temple of Apollo there (Hdt. 5.62; cf. 1.64.3, 6.121.1, 123.1 for their exile), but also putting in an appearance in the archon list for 525/4 (Meiggs and Lewis 1988, 6.6). The Gephyraioi stand, somewhat mysteriously, behind the actions of Harmodios and Aristogeiton (Hdt. 5.55). Isagoras, who emerges as the chief rival political leader to Kleisthenes, is reported by Herodotos to have been from a distinguished family (5.66) and was certainly distinguished enough to seek to establish formal friendship with the Spartan king Kleomenes (5.70.1—although it is Isagoras' wife in whom Kleomenes is said to have been particularly interested).

One intriguing possibility is that the importance of different élite families is reflected in the earliest Athenian coinage, minted perhaps in the 520s. These earliest coins have been termed *Wappenmünzen* because their different symbols have been taken to stand for different families (Section 8.4). If this is correct (and it is a big *if*), then we would have a centralized recognition and management of the separate families' interest.

Central recognition and management of the elite families seem to be what emerges from a fragment of a late fifth-century inscribed archon list that preserves the names of the archons from 527–526 to 522–521 (Meiggs and Lewis 1988: #6, *IG* I³.1031). In successive years we meet [On]eto[rides], [H]ippia[s], [K]leisthen[es], [M]iltiades, [Ka]lliades, and perhaps [Peisi]stratos. That is, we have in succession Onetorides, the son of a rich but otherwise not very politically active Athenian family; Hippias, the son of Peisistratos himself just as he took over power; Kleisthenes, the most politically ambitious of the Alkmaionidai; Miltiades, the most prominent member of the Philaidai; Kalliades, a man whose name is too common for us to be sure of his family; and the homonymous grandson of the tyrant (cf. Thuc. 6.54.6–7). The *Constitution of the Athenians* 22.5 suggests that Peisistratos had returned to direct election of archons, but it would be surprising for them to want to encourage electoral competition in this way, and if there were elections this pattern of appointments as eponymous archon in the 520s looks to have been stage-managed from above. Manage it they might, but events show that elite ambition was something the tyranny could never satisfy. Equally, what the elite could not do, as long as the tyranny kept popular support at home and remained popular with neighboring states, was to topple the tyrants.

This fragment of an archon list is as close as we come to understanding how the governance of Athens worked under the tyranny. *Constitution of the Athenians* 16.8 claims that Peisistratos administered everything according to the laws, and it comes up with various anecdotes in which Peisistratos puts on a show of legal compliance, but in a subsequent chapter (22.1). Solon's laws are said to have been done away with as a result of not being used under the tyranny. The truth is that, while we can be reasonably certain that Athens was not micromanaged by the Peisistratids in these years (it had to be worthwhile for ambitious members of other families to hold office), we have little idea of what precisely the tyrants thought they must intervene in, and what not.

The strength of the tyranny, and the political fatuousness of elite ambition, emerge strongly from the story of the killing of Hipparchos by Harmodios and Aristogeiton (Hdt. 5.55, 6.123; Thuc. 6.53–9; [Arist.] *Constitution of the Athenians* 18; M. W. Taylor 1981; Azoulay 2017). Whatever their motives, and the reduction of their motives to a personal matter by Thucydides is itself politically motivated, the tyranny survived the murder, and the tyrannicides themselves were killed. Despite the claims made in Athenian drinking songs (quoted at Ath. 695a) that Harmodios and Aristogeiton had killed the tyrant and made the Athenians *isonomoi* (equal before the law), the killing of Hipparchos had, if anything, only the effect of making Hippias more suspicious and violent. Nor did Alkmaionid occupation of a fort at Leipsydrion, probably in the foothills of Parnes (Hdt. 5.62.2, [Arist.] *Constitution of the Athenians* 19.2–3), have any effect on Hippias' grip on power. What did for the tyranny in the end was clever exploitation of Spartan political and military ambitions.

Whatever the truth of the story that the Alkmaionidai bribed the Delphic oracle to instruct the Spartans to free Athens from tyranny (Hdt. 5.63.1), there can be little doubt that the reason why the Spartans were persuaded to intervene in Athens was political—as is apparent from the fact that they were willing to make several attempts to do so, and they did not cease intervention when Hippias departed (see further Section 7.1.2).

It took Sparta two attempts to remove the Peisistratids from Athens, and the story Herodotos retails has their success contingent on a lucky capture of Hippias' children (5.65.1; cf. [Arist.] *Constitution of the Athenians* 19.6). When newly freed Athens fell immediately into political turmoil with Isagoras and Kleisthenes competing for power, the Spartan king intervened again but departed after the Council (which Council, the Solonian Council of 400 or the Areopagus Council, is being referred to is unclear) led resistance that turned into a full popular rising (5.72).[26] Whatever the details of the events, which undoubtedly got embellished in the telling, the core of the story is that Kleisthenes had embraced the people and made promises of reforms that had captured the popular imagination (5.66.2,

---

26. The classic discussion is Ober 1993.

69)—popular imagination that was most plausibly responsible for the drinking songs that reclaimed the initiative and the credit for removing tyranny for two heroic Athenians.

5.2.4 The Kleisthenic Reforms

Herodotos (5.69) gives a minimal account of Kleisthenes' reforms: Kleisthenes created 10 tribes instead of four.[27] The Aristotelian *Constitution of the Athenians* (21.2–5) is rather fuller: Kleisthenes replaced the Council of 400 with a Council of 500, 50 from each tribe; he grouped the demes into 30 *trittyes*, 10 of the urban, 10 coastal, and 10 inland, and then distributed the *trittyes* into the tribes by lot in such a way that each tribe had one city, one coastal, and one inland *trittys*; he made their deme name part of citizens' official nomenclature and put a demarch in charge of each deme, giving the demarchs the responsibilities that had previously rested with the *naukraroi*. Whereas Herodotos locates Kleisthenes' motivation for the tribal reform in hatred of the Ionians (hence rejection of the four Ionian tribes) and imitation of his maternal grandfather, Kleisthenes of Sikyon, who had renamed the tribes at Sikyon, the *Constitution of the Athenians* suggests that Kleisthenes desired to mix up the people, disguising the presence of those who had no Athenian family history to which to appeal (cf. Arist. *Pol.* 1275b34–7), and to ensure that his new political units did not coincide with any old political units.

The important historical question is not what motivated Kleisthenes, but how his proposals attracted general support. It is not obvious that enlarging the Council by 25 percent or replacing the traditional tribes (which in fact seem to have continued to exist for religious purposes) would in themselves be popular measures. Nor is it obvious that making the local units demes, of which there came to be 139, rather than naukraries, of which there had been 48, was in itself

---

27. At 5.69.2 our texts of Herodotos add that he created 10 phylarchs instead of four, and he distributed 10 demes to the tribes. Scholars have amended the text to say that he distributed the demes to the tribes "by tens" (δέκαχα), for which there is a good epigraphic parallel in Osborne and Rhodes 2017: #191.34. For whether δέκαχα can mean this, see de Ste. Croix 2004: 179. We know that there were more than 100 demes (but we also know that the total number of demes in the tribe Aiantis was fewer than 10, de Ste. Croix 2004: 172). An alternative approach is to athetize the whole sentence (since phylarchs in Classical Athens were rather minor military officials). Kienast 2005b attempts to defend Herodotos' text and explain how Aiantis lost four demes through military casualties and the plague! If one needed to explain the loss of four demes one might do better to suppose that what had originally been separate demes were absorbed into Aphidna, where the existence of a number of communities later treated as demes is known (Traill 1975: 87–91). For the general case for post-Kleisthenic changes in demes, see Osborne 2009: 285–7.

necessarily particularly attractive, though the possibility of local government being entirely based on individual local communities (most demes seem to have been nucleated settlements[28]) may have had some appeal.

The crucial feature seems to be the very one that is least obviously functional— the distribution of demes into *trittyes*.[29] We know that the way in which tribal representation in the Council of 500 worked was that each deme had a given quota of members of the Council, that it had to meet annually (whether the rule that one could only serve twice on the Council, and not in successive years was applied from the start we cannot tell, but the requirement to be aged thirty was surely original). But the fact that it was deme quotas that produced the Council only makes the *trittyes* seem more otiose. Where *trittyes* were important were in people's perceptions. Although *trittyes* may have served some military purposes (there are muster-posts from the Peiraieus, as well as from the assembly-place on the Pnyx, which group men by *trittys* [*IG* I³.1117–31]), they were primarily, as [Aristotle] indicates, a way of ensuring that each tribe's representatives in the Council were drawn from each of the three geographical regions of Attica ([Arist.] *Constitution of the Athenians* 21.4). *Trittyes* ensured that the regional basis that Peisistratos had advertised in calling his supporters the "Over-the-Hill-Men," and was perceived to be displayed in Megakles' coastal and Lycurgus' inland support, was in future to be neutralized by recognizing that these regional differences existed and by ensuring that the body that prepared all the business for the Assembly was seen to have all three regions of Attica equally represented. At the same time, that every tribe included people from all three regions meant that all tribally based activities, whether military or religious, mixed up Athenians whose families came from all over Attica.

Athenian support for Kleisthenes' reforms was a vote for inclusiveness, not exclusiveness, and it was a vote for putting power into the hands of relatively ordinary men. Although we cannot be sure what the membership rules for the Council were originally, the very number of demes and the size of the Council were bound to distribute power widely. Scholars have sometimes suggested that Kleisthenes manipulated which deme was in which tribe to break up existing links by putting religiously linked demes into different tribes and strategically placing demes in which his own family were involved into the same tribe.[30] The

---

28. This is the position I argued for in Osborne 1985: 15–42, and although exceptions can be cited, particularly in marginal areas and where special factors were in play (cf. Osborne 1997b; Lohmann 1993), the evidence seems to me still to support this claim.

29. On the *trittyes*, see Siewert 1982; Traill 1986; and especially Stanton 1994.

30. The classic statement of the case is Lewis 1997; see also Stanton 1984.

negative side of this may have some force: combining men in different units for politics than for religion militated against political exploitation of religious ties. The positive side of the argument is much harder to see as effective. There were simply not enough tribal activities in which demes worked together to make having one family's weight all in one tribe prove an effective weapon—even when for one-tenth of the year one tribe acted as a standing committee (*prytaneis*) to the Council, an innovation that may have been introduced only in 462 (Rhodes 1972: 17–19).

Kleisthenes' reforms were certainly conceptually complex, even by the standards of quite complex political organizations elsewhere (N. F. Jones 1987, 28–71; O. Murray 1990; Lévêque and Vidal-Naquet 1996; cf. Osborne and Rhodes 2017: #24). Scholars have sometimes thought that they were also extremely hard to put into practice, involving a lot of work on the ground (Eliot 1962: 136–47). However, it seems more plausible that Kleisthenes adopted a relatively "light touch" organization, asking Athenians to register in whatever they took to be their local community and then on the basis of the lists collected distributing demes into *trittyes* and tribes. From that point on demes were probably left to organize themselves, provided that they appointed an annual demarch (in the Classical period, at least, by lot), and saw to an annual process for allotting whatever quota of councilors (*bouleutai*) was given to them. There would certainly have been a few months of work needed to set up this system, but not years of work.[31]

Herodotos famously connected Athens' increasing prominence and her military success to freedom from tyranny and the institution of equality of public political speech (*isēgoriē*) (5.66.1, 78), explaining that, once they were free, every individual was keen to work for the advantage of the city. The story of Athens' military turn-around is almost certainly more complicated than this (see Sections 7.1.2 and 7.2), and Kleisthenes' tribal reform seems from the beginning to have had a military dimension. But Herodotos' stress on equality of speech is important. One consequence of Kleisthenes' reforms is that we begin to see a new sort of evidence—public decisions inscribed on stone.

What is conventionally regarded as the earliest of these, dated to between Kleisthenes' reforms and 500, is a decree about settlers on Salamis (*IG* I³.1, Meiggs and Lewis 1988: #14), headed simply "the people decided" (ἔδοχσεν τõι δέμοι); what becomes the regular heading "the Council and people decided" ([ἔδοχσε]ν [: τῖι βολῖι] : καὶ [τ]õι δέμοι :) first appears on regulations about Eleusis (*IG* I³.5)

---

31. Andrewes 1977; Fachard 2016: 194–5. I am unpersuaded by Badian 2000.

around 500.[32] The interest of the Salamis decree lies in its concern to regulate the "tax payment at Athens and military service" (Ἀθέ]νε|σι τελε̃ν καὶ στρατ[εύεσθ]αι) of "the klerouchs in Salamis" (τ[ὸς ἐ Σ]αλαμ[ῖνι κλερόχ]ος) and the responsibility of the archon (here most plausibly interpreted as the "archon of Salamis" attested later, [Arist.] *Constitution of the Athenians* 54.8, 62.2) to "exact these or else be held responsible at his final examination" (ἐσπράτεν δὲ τὸν ἄ]|ρχο[ν]τα, ἐὰν [δὲ μέ, εὐθ]ύ[νεσθαι) and "to pass judgment on the arms of the armed men" (ho[πλισμένο]|ν δὲ [τ]ὸν ἄρχοντ[α τὰ hόπλα κρίν]|εν). Some responsibility of the Council appears to be described just as the text breaks off. It is attractive to think that the question of the duties of those on Salamis, which was outside the deme system, arose from discussion of the duties of regular citizens resident in the demes to which political recognition had just been given.

Army organization seems to have been one of the topics that remained on the agenda after Kleisthenes' initial reforms. *Constitution of the Athenians* 22.2 has the generalship, with one general from each tribe, instituted in 501/0. This was an important decision because the generals were directly elected, whereas the polemarch (who until the battle of Marathon maintained overall, or at least titular, control of the army and was stationed on its right wing [Hdt. 6.111.1]), was simply one of the archons. The *Constitution of the Athenians* 22.5 and Herodotos 6.109.2 disagree on whether the archons were at this period directly elected or chosen by lot—the story of the competition between Isagoras and Kleisthenes for the archonship (Hdt. 5.66) strongly implies that election of the archon was the procedure used directly after the fall of the tyrants. However, the decision to have 10 elected generals strongly suggests that the office of polemarch was not itself directly elected but allotted (perhaps simply in an allotment among elected archons of who did what office). The co-existence of the polemarch and 10 generals made for an awkward command structure, as Herodotos' account of the deliberations before Marathon indicates (6.103–10).

The other topic on the agenda immediately after the Kleisthenic reforms was the powers of the new Council of 500. The *Constitution of the Athenians* (22.2) says that in 501/0 the Council oath was initiated. Although some scholars think that the oath was introduced at this point because it was only at this point that the Council itself was properly up and running, this seems implausible (see previous discussion in this chapter). One of the laws re-inscribed at the end of the fifth century (see Section 6) that survives on stone, places limits on the powers of the Council (*IG* I[3].105, Osborne and Rhodes 2017: #183B); that law starts with the text of an oath. Although other contexts are possible, it is attractive to see this as

---

32. On Salamis, see Lambert 1997: 94–103; M. C. Taylor 1997 on this inscription pp. 11–21).

part and parcel of the introduction of the oath for the Council of 500. If this is correct, this text provides evidence that the oath was part of a concern to define what the new Council could and could not do; in particular, decisions involving war and peace and capital punishment are reserved for the assembly.

If the *Constitution of the Athenians* (22) supplies a reliable account of the course of events, the influence of particular individuals was also on the political agenda, with Kleisthenes introducing a law on ostracism. Ostracism was an institution whereby the Athenians allowed themselves to vote an individual into exile for 10 years, with no loss of property or formal citizenship status, as long as at least 6,000 Athenians voted, writing down on a piece of broken pottery (*ostrakon*) the name of the person they wished to see expelled (Brenne 1994; Brenne 2001; Siewert 2002; Forsdyke 2005: 133–65; Brenne 2019). The role of expulsion in the events that surrounded the overthrow of tyranny and the setting up of democracy, along with the insistence on a large number of people voting, which is in harmony with the spirit of the law limiting the powers of the Council, make this new law fit comfortably into the last years of the sixth century.

What is puzzling is that, even on the account given in the *Constitution of the Athenians*, the law was not used until 488/7, and then was used repeatedly during the rest of the 480s. It might have been thought important from the start of democracy to put into the hands of the people, but with strict controls, the power of exile that had been so prominent in the immediately previous years, but no occasion arose on which to use those powers for almost two decades. Alternatively, it was only in the fraught atmosphere of the 480s, when Athenians seem to have been seriously divided over foreign policy decisions, that a way of removing individuals temporarily from the Athenian political scene was thought necessary.[33]

In the two decades after 500 the most important Athenian political debates were about foreign policy—about whether to support the revolt of Ionian cities from Persia, about war with Aegina, about how best to resist the Persian invasion that ended with the Battle of Marathon, and about what subsequent measures were necessary to resist any further Persian hostilities (see Section 7.1.2). But there were clearly on-going internal political debates too. The most important of these was about the selection and powers of the archons. There is no sign that the archons had played a significant role in politics since Isagoras, archon in 508/7, but in 487/6 full allotment from preselected candidates was introduced ([Arist. *Constitution of the Athenians* 22.5, but there were more plausibly 100 than 500 preselected candidates). Committed as the Athenians were to the democratic

---

33. For a powerful case for the Kleisthenic date, see de Ste. Croix 2004: 180–9.

importance of allotment, they knew that military leadership could not be allotted simply to anyone. Having all archons allotted solved the problematic relationship between polemarch and generals by making it not only appropriate but necessary to remove war entirely from the polemarch's responsibilities, but more importantly the use of allotment in the selection of archons made it extremely difficult to use that magistracy as part of a bid for personal power (leaving the generalship as the one directly elected office that could be so used) (Badian 1971; de Ste. Croix 2004: 215–32). Along with the first use of ostracism, this further suggests that anxieties over the role played by particular individuals were considerable in the wake of Marathon. Those anxieties might be plausibly linked to the various foreign policy strains. It was, and would continue to be, a problem for democracy that relations with other cities had to be conducted through individuals, and that those relations were best conducted if the individuals involved stayed the same. Certain families, indeed, seem to have become specialists in relations with particular cities, and they might acquire a semi-official status as *proxenoi* (for further discussion, see Section 7.1.2). All of this will have felt rather uncomfortable in a city where everything else was being decided by the popular assembly.

5.3 Subdivisions of the Citizen Body

The Athenian citizen body divided itself in a variety of different ways (Ismard 2010; Humphreys 2018). As far back as we can trace, the Athenians were divided into (the four Ionian) tribes and into phratries, and some Athenians, at least, identified themselves as belonging to *genē* (family lines with particular religious responsibilities, see below for further discussion). Solon created divisions into different classes dependent on wealth, and Kleisthenes brought in a new tribal structure consisting of 10 tribes with eponyms taken from local heroes. In every case, what an Athenian could and could not do was affected by which of the groups he belonged to.

The four tribes common to cities that claimed to be Ionian and subdivisions of those tribes in the form of *trittyes* make their primary appearance in Athens in the surviving fragments of the re-inscription of the Athenian sacred calendar in the last decade of the fifth century (on which see Section 11.3), and are likely to have been part of the formal division of Athenians from at least the time of Solon.[34] There we meet the tribe Geleontes and a *trittys* named the Leukotainiai ("white-ribboned ones") but also tribe-kings (*phylobasileis*) with religious responsibilities (Lambert 2002: 362–7, 92–5). The wording of Drako's law on homicide (see

––––––––––––

34. See Section 11.3. On the Ionian tribes, see Grote 2016.

Section 6.1) implies that the tribe-kings played a role in judging cases of homicide by the late seventh century. What functions the four Ionian tribes had before the creation of the 10 Kleisthenic tribes is unknown, but a military role is likely (it has been speculated that the "white-ribboned ones" had white ribbons on their spears), particularly given the responsibilities carried by their sub-divisions, the naukraries (on which see Section 5.2.1). Even after the Kleisthenic reforms, the tribe-kings continued to serve with the *basileus* archon in judging cases of homicide ([Arist.] *Constitution of the Athenians* 57.4).

We have no idea at what stage or in what circumstances the Athenians organized themselves into the Ionian tribes, nor do we know when the *trittyes* of those tribes were invented. Both tribes and phratries figure as units into which men, and specifically soldiers, might be organized in *Iliad* 2.362–3, and we should probably think that Athens had organized itself in tribes for as long as it had organized an army—so certainly from the eighth century. But the sharing of tribal organization across the Ionian cities and, even more, the shared Greek use of the Indo-European word for "brother" to mean "fellow member of a descent group" suggest an early origin for these units (Lambert 1993: 268–71). It is significant for the antiquity of the tribe and the phratry that although both were descent groups, the relationship between them is not clear: phratries are not themselves sub-divisions of tribes. This suggests that they have separate origins and were probably initially created for separate purposes and in separate circumstances (Lambert 1993: 14–17, 271, 371–80 [arguing against the view that the statements in F3 of the *Constitution of the Athenians* are speculative schematization]).

Phratries make their first appearance in Athenian texts in Drako's homicide law (see Sections 5.2.2 and 6.1), where, if the Ephetai decide that a man guilty of homicide killed unintentionally, then in the absence of any close relative it is for 10 members of the dead man's phratry to agree that the perpetrator of the homicide need not go into exile. It is simply assumed that every Athenian is a member of a phratry. The phratry is treated as a wider kin unit, close enough to the dead man to have his particular interests at heart—a role familiar from phratries in the Classical period (Lambert 1993: 248–9). Phratries appear to be descent groups independent of the descent groups that were the Ionian tribes, and the relationship between the two remains obscure, but one possibility is that tribes were a top-down imposition for the purposes of organizing the state, phratries a bottom-up creation securing family interests and the transmission of property (Ismard 2010: 50, 75–6, 81, 102–3).

The only other appearance that phratries make in what may be an Archaic text is in a passage that the Roman legal *Digest* of Justinian quotes from, it alleges, Solon's laws (*Digest* 47.22.4, Solon *Laws* F76a Leão and Rhodes). The quotation is certainly corrupt, but the point of the law is that Solon recognized agreements made between members of a group as valid, provided that they did not contravene the law. The law lists groups of various sorts, including "those who go off for booty or trade," but also members of a phratry (Lambert 1993: 250; Ismard 2018: 146–8). Given that part of the point of the law would seem to be to confirm that agreements among members of a group had legal validity even if that group was informal, this law tells us nothing about the phratry as such.

Kleisthenes' reforms left the phratries unchanged.[35] All those who were granted Athenian citizenship in the Classical period were expected to join a phratry, with the exception of those admitted in large groups.[36] Our best evidence for the working of the Classical phratry comes from a phratry inscription (a decree passed in 396/5) which is entirely devoted to the process of admission to phratry membership (Rhodes and Osborne 2003: #5), and the phratry is most frequently mentioned in court when it is a question of affirming someone's legitimate birth, family membership, and citizenship (Dem. 57 24). Mentions of phratry membership in comic texts and speeches indicate that phratries continued to be a social group important in Athenian lives (though this aspect is better illustrated elsewhere, see Rhodes and Osborne 2003: #1).

There is no reason to think that phratries were any less important in Athenians' social lives in the Archaic period, but were phratries the gateway to Athenian citizenship prior to the Kleisthenic reforms? Answering this question depends in part on whether we consider "citizenship" to be a category appropriate to Athens before Kleisthenes. Plutarch claims that Solon's law about naturalized citizens grants the right to become citizens only to those in perpetual exile from their own land or who move with their whole household to Athens to practice a trade (Solon *Laws* F75 Leão and Rhodes; Plut. *Sol.* 24.4). But it is unclear that Solon in fact did more than *allow* that these two groups might "become Athenians;" whether that involved a requirement that they be accepted by phratries is quite unclear. Scholars have attempted to see in ancient accounts of such groups as the Gephyraioi signs that groups might be given only partial citizenship rights in the Archaic period (Hdt. 5.57.2 is the main evidence), but on Herodotos' own chronology the Gephyraioi came to Attica at the end of the Bronze Age, and the idea that there were precise citizen rights at that stage is preposterous.

Certainly, there were later traditions that after the fall of the tyrants there was a review (*diapsēphismos*) of the citizen body "because many were sharing Athenian

---

35. Aristotle *Politics* 1319b19–27 can be read to imply that Kleisthenes increased the number of phratries, but Aristotle seems to have grouped Kleisthenes' increase in the number of tribes with a phratry reform at Cyrene. See Kearns 1985.

36. Lambert 1993: 51–2, for the exceptions (the Plataians, the Samians, those enfranchised in the course of restoration of democracy in 403) and 31–57, 237–9, more generally.

political life when not entitled to do so" ([Arist.] *Constitution of the Athenians* 13.5). In the same vein, Kleisthenes is said to have introduced the practice of referring to an Athenian by their deme name (demotic) rather than their father's name (patronymic) to make "new citizens" invisible ([Arist.] *Constitution of the Athenians* 21.4), and in *Politics*, too, Aristotle refers to Kleisthenes enfranchising foreigners (1275b34–9; but how to understand this passage in detail is much debated). These traditions indubitably show later concern with the question of citizenship, and there were certainly later citizen reviews in both fifth and fourth centuries.[37] But a citizen review shortly after 510 is implausible—particularly in the face of the tradition that the Athenians allowed friends of the Peisistratids to remain in Athens ([Arist.] *Constitution of the Athenians* 22.4). To be practical, a review of citizen membership would require records of admission to citizenship to exist, but such records are implausible prior to the creation of deme registers.

It is worth asking what Athens might need a notion of citizenship for. Some scholars have suggested that it was needed to oblige military service, and in noting that Solon introduced a law of slander that included alleging that someone had thrown away their shield as an example of slander (along with suggestions that they were a father-beater or mother-beater, or murderer), have claimed that this presupposes that throwing away one's shield was itself a legal offence. But this is hardly entailed: the problem is not that to allege this is to allege that someone has broken the law, it is to allege that they have engaged in socially reprehensible behavior (we know of no specific law against beating one's parents—arguably precisely because this was universally acknowledged as unacceptable) (van Wees 2018: 116). Already in the *Iliad* (14.235–9; cf. 12.248–50, 18.300–302) and *Odyssey* (13.256–66), the peer pressure to fight for one's community is noted as near-irresistible. Military activity in Archaic Athens seems frequently to be undertaken by the whole community (Thuc. 1.126.7 for action against Kylon; Hdt. 1.62.3 for resisting Peisistratos at Pallene), and while military activities can either be undertaken in that way by general levy, or by recruiting volunteers, no prior definition of who might be eligible is required.

Arguably, no restrictive notion of who was and who was not Athenian was required since there was no reason to exclude anyone, and in consequence there was no need for a defined gateway to being Athenian, whether through a phratry or otherwise. Indeed, arguably Solon's introduction of census classes (see further below), distributing obligations as well as rights across the citizen body, made policing who was and who was not Athenian less rather than more necessary. As

---

37. For the citizen review held in 445/4, see Philochoros *FGrH* 328 F119; Plut. *Per.* 37.4. For the citizen review held in 346/5, see Dem. 57.26; Aeschin. 1.77.

long as a man could not evade the main taxation units, the naukraries (on which see Section 5.2.1), concern with his origin was in no one's interests.

In the Classical period those seeking to demonstrate that they were, or that someone else was not, a member of a particular family, as well as referring to the phratry, also refer to the *genos* (Isae. 7.15–17; [Dem.] 59.59–61). The nature of the *genos* (pl. *genē*) has been much debated, partly because *genos* is a word that has both a general meaning ("race," "type") and a particular Athenian use.[38] Athenian *genē* were, as their name implies, descent groups (i.e., one could only be a member of *genos* by birth).[39] In this they were like phratries, and indeed seem in at least some cases to have been nested within phratries (cf. esp. Andoc. 1.125–7). They commonly bore names that identified them as descendants of a particular individual, although it was already noted in antiquity that some of these individuals were certainly fictitious; but, in some cases, their names referred rather to a location (as with the Kolieis, the Kephisieis and, most famously, the Salaminioi).

What distinguished *genē* was that they provided priests for public cults (something explicitly known for about half the 50 or so *genē* whose names we know) and were responsible for the organization of certain festivals. What the origins of this arrangement were is quite unclear, but for the *genē*, as not for the phratries, an origin in historic time (i.e. within the period after 800 being discussed here) seems certain in at least some cases. At what date it ceased to be possible for a family to found a cult open to all Athenians and claim status as a *genos*, or alternatively for the Athenian people to vest responsibility for a new cult in a particular family (for we should probably think of the initiative as running in both directions) is unclear (Parker 1996: 56–66).[40] It seems most plausible that at all stages of Athenian history some Athenians did and some did not belong to a descent group that administered a cult.

The question of whether the *genē* exercised political power and constituted some sort of aristocracy has been the subject of considerable debate. Were there political or social roles in Archaic Athens for which one had to be a member of a *genos*? This has become closely bound up with the nature of the so-called Eupatridai, the "well-fathered ones," of which ancient sources make mention. The term eupatrid first occurs in the late sixth century when it appears in the epitaph found at Eretria of one Chairion, "an Athenian of the eupatrids" (*IG*

38. The fundamental reassessment is Bourriot 1976. See further Lambert 1999.

39. Establishing the nature of the *genos* is difficult in part because *genos* had a non-technical sense of "family," and it is impossible to be sure, unless the word is used in an explicitly religious context, whether a writer is using the term *genos* in its technical Athenian sense or not.

40. For the ways in which new cults were supported in the fifth century, see Osborne and Rhodes 2017: #37 (Athena Nike); *IG* I³ 136.29–31 (Bendis); Parker 1996: 125–7.

XII.9.296), and in a drinking song, quoted by the *Constitution of the Athenians* (19.3), about the vain attempts to dislodge tyranny by launching attacks from Leispydrion: "Alas Leipsydrion, what men you destroyed, good at fighting and eupatrids who showed at that moment from what sort of fathers they descended." The term has been taken in the past to refer to a particular set of noble families, but there is nothing about these early uses that requires anything more than that individuals are laying claim to good birth.

Such claims as we have that being a eupatrid was a qualification for certain offices (i.e., that there were a defined number of families, membership of which was required for serving in particular roles) come from late sources offering rationalizing accounts of early Athenian history.[41] We do know that every candidate for a magistracy in Classical Athens was asked at their *dokimasia* not only about their parentage and deme, but also whether they had cults of Apollo Patroos and Zeus Herkeios ([Arist.] *Constitution of the Athenians* 55.3), but although it has been suggested that the *genē* alone originally honored Apollo Patroos, there is no evidence that this was the case.[42]

There is no reason to deny that families responsible for major priesthoods made as much political and social capital out of that as they could. But equally, families responsible for priesthoods of obscure cults were probably not in a good position to use that fact to great advantage. Some extremely prominent families, indeed the most prominent families of all in late Archaic Athens, the Alkmaionidai and the Philaidai, are not known to have had responsibility for any priesthood.

All the groups examined so far were descent groups, but inevitably, as soon as there was any notion of hereditary property ownership, descent groups tended to have a local focus. A number of phratries seem to have been associated with a particular locality, and the *genos* about which we know most, the *genos* of the Salaminioi, not only has a name with geographical reference, but also divided itself into two groups, the Salaminioi from Sounion and the Salaminioi from the seven tribes.[43] Whether the naukraries were defined by place of residence or by

---

41. See Plutarch *Theseus* 25.2 (probably derived from the lost beginning of the *Constitution of the Athenians*) and note the claim by Pollux 8.111 that the *phylobasileis* were drawn from the eupatrids. See further, Figueira 1984: 454–9; *contra* Pierrot 2015.

42. The suggestion goes back to Andrewes 1961: 7–8, and relies on a particular understanding of Demosthenes 57.67. That passage only implies that cults of Apollo Patroos and Zeus Herkeios were looked after by *genē*. That "these deities are unlikely to be the distinctive gods of any *genos*" (Andrewes 1961: 7) does not prevent it being *genē* who provided the cult personnel for the sacrifices to these gods that Euxitheos attended.

43. On the Salaminioi, see Ferguson 1938; Parker 1996: 308–16; Osborne and Rhodes 2017: #37.

family, we do not know, but the comparison with the later demes suggests that they certainly had a strong local flavor. Not the least importance of exposing the idea of a "caste" of Eupatridai as false is that it leaves seventh-century Athens without any groups that are geographically cross-cutting. But Solon created groups that were based neither on heredity nor on locality.

The Solonian census classes have been another subject of extensive scholarly debate. Even in antiquity there was a difference of view as to whether the groups into which Solon divided Athenians according to wealth were pre-existing or whether he created them. The latter is the view given by Plutarch (*Sol.* 18.1–2), the former that of the *Constitution of the Athenians* (7.3), in which we find the awkwardly put claim that Solon "divided them into four census groups, just as it had been divided previously, into 500-bushel man (*pentakosiomedimnos*), and horseman, and *zeugitēs*, and thete."[44] That in some sense there were horsemen, yoke-men, and poor laborers previously is certain, and to that extent *Constitution of the Athenians* must be correct. But whether these divisions were formalized in any way is much harder to know, and the existence of the 500-bushel men as a recognizable group before Solon extremely unlikely.[45]

Already in antiquity too there was a dispute over how the Solonian classes were assessed. The *Constitution of the Athenians* (7.4) claims that the horseman and yoke-man classes, like the 500-bushel men, were defined in terms of bushels (*medimnoi*) of dry (grain) and liquid (wine and oil) goods taken together, with 300 bushels being the boundary for horsemen and 200 bushels for yoke-men. However, the author goes on to say that some people think that one qualified as a *hippeus* simply by being able to maintain a horse.

Solon's census classes remained, in some sense, current in Classical Athens ([Arist.] *Constitution of the Athenians* 26.2, 47.1), but nevertheless the *Constitution of the Athenians* seems likely to be wrong both in general and in detail. Its statement that the census was defined in bushels of dry and wet goods taken together can be shown to be false: there is good evidence that Solon employed a "barley standard" in which other goods were assessed in terms of bushels of barley (de

---

44. The meaning of *zeugitēs* has been extensively debated, between "hoplite" (a man "yoked" to his fellow heavily armed soldiers in the battle-line, cf. *Il.* 13.701–8), and "yoke-man," i.e., owner of a pair of oxen. The latter possibility finds support in the existence, according to Pollux, of a *zeugēsion* tax on those who kept a yoke of oxen (Pollux 8.132 with van Wees 2006: 352–3; van Wees 2013: 86 and n.13).

45. The supposed "Constitution of Drako" (on which see n.13 in Section 5.2.2) at *Constitution of the Athenians* 4.2–4 ties eligibility for particular offices to the monetary value of estates, but it also presupposes the Solonian census classes, using them to determine the level of fines for non-attendance at its Council of 401. The presence of the Solonian classes here may indeed account for the claim that they pre-existed Solon made in 7.3 (*pace* Rhodes 1981: 137).

Ste. Croix 2004: 33–40). There is no other support for the idea that the *hippeus* and *zeugitēs* were defined in terms of agricultural production, a claim that occurs only in passages about Solon's census classes that evidently derive from a single source.[46] The definition of the super-elite in terms of a barley standard does not demand that all other groups were so assessed, and the bureaucracy necessary if other groups were to be rigorously assessed in that way is simply unthinkable. At some point after the census classes had ceased to have any actual significance, the other classes were "rationalized" in terms of the 500-bushel men.[47]

The beauty of the Solonian system was its simplicity. The restriction of the most important positions in the city to the 500-bushel men meant that anyone who could demonstrate that level of wealth would be keen to do so—thereby opening themselves up to appropriate taxation. Horsemen and yoke-men were easy to identify simply through the presence of horses or yokes of oxen. Nothing at all complex was required: self-reporting and neighborly observation were sufficient to make this class system work.

Why did Solon invent these classes? Solonian classes had three advantages. First, they made financially discriminatory treatment of citizens possible, most obviously for purposes of taxation, but also for purposes of imposing fines, and probably for purposes of army organization (see Section 7.2). Second, they drew attention to the common interests of men who lived in different parts of Attica, encouraging a sense of solidarity that was not merely local. At the level of those who were wealthy, competition was in some circumstances a more likely consequence than solidarity, but at the lower levels, Solon recognized and made more straightforward the articulation of "class interests." Third, they offered possibilities of social mobility that were not on offer from divisions that based themselves on descent groups. Politically, the move was masterful, since at the same time that it opened up possibilities of social advancement, it also formally entrenched the exclusive access of the rich to the highest office in a way unlikely to have applied previously.

---

46. In addition to [Arist.] *Constitution of the Athenians* 7.3–4 and Plut. *Sol.* 18.1–2, see Pollux 8.130.

47. The position adopted here is broadly that of de Ste. Croix 2004: 5–72 (cf. Duplouy 2014); the best statement of the contrary position is van Wees 2006 (cf. van Wees 2013: 82–91; van Wees 2018: 134–9). Attempts to establish that horsemen and yoke-men were defined in the terms claimed by the tradition lead to impossibly distorted views of Archaic Athens: when a family needed perhaps as little as one-eighth of 200 bushels of barley a year to live off, the thetic class would embrace an extremely wide range of Athenians, including those who were very comfortably off (and could certainly afford a yoke of oxen). Van Wees (2006: 365–6; cf. Foxhall 1997: 129–32) sees this consequence and has to argue for a yawning gap with no farmers of the middling sort; the argument from differential dowry rates (Dem. 43.54) fails to see that there is a punitive element in these rates (van Wees 2006: 362–3).

The *Constitution of the Athenians* (7.4; also Pollux 8.131) offers what it regards as an example of the social mobility that these new classes enabled: a dedication of a statue of a horse on the Athenian Acropolis by one Anthemion son of Diphilos celebrating his having exchanged his thetic status for that of *hippeus*. How Anthemion, whose dedication raises various difficulties (Rhodes 1981: 144–5), achieved his new wealth is not apparent, but the possibility of visible social advancement was arguably particularly important at a time when the Athenian economy was becoming more diverse (see Section 8). The keenness of certain craftsmen to advertise their success by making striking dedications on the Acropolis is worth noting in this context (see Sections 4.5.4 and 8.3).

It is hard to gauge the effect of Solon's census classes, although clearly some of the debates about access to political office are played out in terms of these classes in the fifth century (as with the formal extension in 458/7 to the *zeugitai* of the possibility of serving as archon, [Arist.] *Constitution of the Athenians* 26.2). When Kleisthenes introduced radical new subdivisions of the Athenian citizen body he left the Solonian classes untouched. His reforms (see Section 5.2.4) focused on the tribes and *trittyes* and on the demes.

Kleisthenes' reform have something in common with Solon's census classes, for in this case, too, political reform made use of a pre-existing unit, the deme, and what Kleisthenes did was to give that pre-existing unit new, formal powers (Raubitschek and Jeffery 1949: 467–78). Empowering the demes—the villages of Attica and separate communities within the town of Athens itself—was at the heart of Kleisthenes' reforms. It was in giving every village and community representation on his new Council of 500 that Kleisthenes guaranteed that that Council would represent the whole of Attica, and by so doing he sought to put an end to the pattern of regional and family-focused politics that preceded and followed the Peisistratid tyranny. Demes were now obliged to have an annual deme magistrate, the demarch, who was expected to oversee what was required of the deme—the selection of members of the Council but also the payment of taxes (*eisphora*, property tax), the pursuit of state debtors, the burial of abandoned corpses, and some sorts of religious participation (Osborne 1985: 74–7; Whitehead 1986: 130–9). In return for formalizing their say in central politics, Kleisthenes had ensured that no community in Athens could slip under the radar, and that the city had a mechanism for ensuring local compliance with and enforcement of central demands.

As a result, the list of their members that demes now had to keep took on considerable significance. Classical sources mention something that they call the *lexiarchikon grammateion*, which ought to mean "register of the *lexiarchos*," but which in the Classical period was kept by the demarch. This register recorded deme members—something necessary for financial purposes, for the enlistment of soldiers and perhaps sailors, and plausibly for the selection by lot of the Councilors. Although we know nothing of any earlier *lexiarchoi*, it is a plausible speculation that Solon had established such officials to keep a record, for both financial and military reasons, of who belonged to each of the top three census classes (van Wees 2018: 139–40).[48] Whether the deme also noted census class we do not know, but the deme registers collectively now constituted a list of citizens. What they do not seem to have constituted is a land registry, although the amount and value of property owned by the rich was something demarchs had to know in order to raise the *enktetikon* (tax on property owned by non-deme members) and *eisphora* (J. K. Davies 1981: 143–7; Whitehead 1986: 132–3; Fachard 2016: 194). With Kleisthenes it became important, for the first time, to be able to assign not simply the wealthy but everyone to a deme, since local self-government depended on keeping local decisions in the hands of local people. Arguably, it was this need for local exclusiveness, at least initially, and not any need or desire for exclusiveness at the level of the Athenians as a whole, that led to a distinct sense of citizenship.[49]

Kleisthenes' formalization of the deme impacted strongly on Athenian identity. The *Constitution of the Athenians* (21.4) claims that Kleisthenes empowered the demes in part so that Athenians would stop identifying themselves by their patronymics, thereby drawing attention to their family lines, and would instead start identifying themselves by the name of the deme. By the time the *Constitution* was written, Athenian decrees record citizens' names with both patronymic and demotic, but the history of the adoption of the demotic is complex. On the one hand, the complete absence of any evidence for the use of demotics prior to the Kleisthenic reforms strongly suggests that those reforms created the demotic when they created the formalized deme—this was not another case where what had been casual practice now got formally recognized, but a new practice. On the other hand, Athenian decrees and other official documents in the first half of the fifth century regularly use simply the name, without demotic or patronymic, and it is striking that when the listing of war-dead in inscriptions begins they are listed by tribe but without demotic or patronymic (e.g., *IG* I³.1477).

Extant post-Kleisthenic dedications from the Athenian Acropolis, presumably reflecting dedicants' own preferred naming practice, are varied. Down to 475

---

48. The information in Pollux 8.104 is hard to make sense of, despite van Effenterre 1976: 13–14.

49. This is essentially the argument presented in Manville 1990, and I am not convinced that it has been overturned by recent attempts, for which see Duplouy and Brock 2018, to turn citizenship into an Archaic notion (as previously discussed). For the continued permeability of the citizen body in fact, see C. B. Patterson 1981: 40–81; Watson 2010: 260–4 as well as the discussion in Section 10 .

there are more or less the same number (42 and 38) with name alone and with name and patronymic, and only a third as many (14) with name and demotic (three have name, patronymic, and demotic). Subsequently during the fifth century use of the full name (name, patronymic, demotic) increases, but more or less equal numbers of inscriptions continue to use name alone, or name and patronymic (Winters 1993).

Ostraka, which presumably reflect how others think of a person, use name and patronymic five times as often as they use name and demotic in the years down to 460, and very rarely use both patronymic and demotic. But a closer look at how the individuals against whom *ostraka* are written reveals that patronymics are much more common than demotics in all but two instances. *Ostraka* cast against Themistokles in the 480s use the demotic more or less as often as they use the patronymic; *ostraka* cast against Themistokles in the ostracism of the 470s (471 [?]) use the demotic half as often as they use the patronymic. But of the 585 *ostraka* cast against Menon son of Menekleides of Gargettos in 471 (?), 490 use the demotic, 76 the patronymic, and 19 both patronymic and demotic (Winters 1993; Brenne 2001: 76–86).

All of this suggests that the invention of the demotic was indeed embraced by some to express their own identity and by some to identify particular individuals and distinguish them from possible homonyms; usage seems to have depended on particular circumstances and how a man was thought of could vary over his lifetime, but there was no official policy about naming, and patronymics went on being widely used. So, although Kleisthenes made it possible for men to signal their local identity rather than their family, the numbers choosing to prioritize their local identity in this way was not large.

Once Kleisthenes had decided to empower the villages of Attica in this way, it is not clear that he really needed the tribes and *trittyes* for any political purpose— although no doubt the *trittys* arrangement was useful in making obvious the cross-regional nature of the new tribes. If Kleisthenes needed new tribes at all— beyond simply signaling that radical change had occurred—it was because, for some particular purposes, bodies comprising one-quarter of the population (assuming that the four old tribes were more or less equal in population terms) were too large (on Athenian demography, see Section 9.1). The primary candidate for what such a purpose might be is the army, although the widespread use of the new tribes as the basis for religious competition (see Section 11.4) might indicate that Kleisthenes also envisaged such a role from the beginning. Indeed, military use of tribal divisions was traditional, and Kleisthenes' new tribes were immediately put to military use. This is manifested not simply in the tribal basis for the election of generals ([Arist.] *Constitution of the Athenians* 22.2), but also by the listing of Athenian dead on Lemnos under the heading of the tribe Hippothontis shortly after 500 (*IG* I^3.1477).

Kleisthenes seems not to have abolished any of the earlier civic units. The only case where there is a question is the naukrary. Certainly, naukraries are not evident in Classical Athens, but the Atthidographer Kleidemos (*FGrH* 323 F8) claimed that Kleisthenes had simply increased their number from 48 to 50, and we know too little of the nature of the naukrary to maintain that this is impossible. In other cases, we are sure of the continued existence of the earlier units. Phratries and *genē* were certainly affected in as far as the recognition of Athenians as citizens now primarily happened not in the phratry but in the deme. *Genē* may have found themselves with a reduced role in some respects, as the deme took responsibility for overseeing, and sometimes funding, numerous local sacrifices and festivals, many of which had presumably earlier fallen to *genē*, but those *genē* that supported the cults of the heroes who were chosen as the eponyms of the new Kleisthenic tribes will have found their duties significantly enhanced (Kearns 1985).

Much has been made by modern scholars of the fact that some old religious associations that involved more than one community now found the communities of which they were composed placed in different tribes, but although tribes were a way of organizing major civic festivals, there seems to have been relatively little religious activity at the tribal level, and so the extent to which different tribal affiliation disassociated those previously associated is uncertain; notably our best evidence for one of those old religious associations whose members now belonged to more than one tribe, the Tetrapolis, comes from the fourth century (Lambert 2000; Lambert 2018).

Significantly more dramatic was the effect on the old Ionian tribes, and plausibly *trittyes*. Although we cannot be sure of their roles, other than the religious roles that they retained in the Classical period, it is highly likely that they were the basis of the Archaic Athenian army organization and of the organization of the old Solonian Council. The very roles that had put them most in the public eye were now removed. Somehow, they continued to operate and tribe-kings to be chosen (see previous discussion and Section 11.3), but their absence from Athenian literature is a measure of their disappearance from Athenian consciousness.

6

Legal History

6.1 Drako

For most Archaic cities, what we know about their law derives primarily from epigraphic remains. Athens is different. Although Drako's law survives republished on stone at the end of the fifth century, its content was effectively known through a quotation in a Demosthenic speech prior to the discovery of the inscription. And our knowledge of Solon's laws is derived entirely from literary texts. This has two effects. The first is that we are rarely confident that the laws that are ascribed to Solon have come down to us in an unedited form, and, in some cases, we can have little confidence that the law was Solonian at all. The second, however, is that for Solon and Athens, as for nowhere else before the fifth-century Gortyn code, we have a chance to understand not simply an isolated enactment, but also something of the concerns and structure of the body of laws as a whole.[1]

Drako (see also Section 5.2.1) was held in later antiquity to have produced a number of laws, and to have in every case made the penalty death (Plut. *Sol.* 17). We know the latter to be false (Plut. *Sol.* 19; cf. Pollux 9.61), but there is no reason to doubt that his legislative activity covered a number of topics, even if we are in no position to comment on how his laws were organized or in what sense, if any, they constituted a "code" (Stroud 1968, 75–83). The only Drakonian law of which we know the content is the law of accidental or justifiable homicide, retained by Solon and republished in the late fifth century.

The *stēlē* with the inscribed version of the republished law survives, and since the law was also quoted in the aforementioned Demosthenic speech ([Dem.] 43.57), the wording of the law can be relatively safely restored (Osborne and

---

1. On the first issue, see Scafuro 2006; Rhodes 2006. On the latter, see Osborne 1997a against Hölkeskamp 1992a; Hölkeskamp 1992b; Hölkeskamp 1999; Hölkeskamp 2005.

The Oxford History of the Archaic Greek World. Robin Osborne, Oxford University Press. © Oxford University Press 2023.
DOI: 10.1093/oso/9780197644423.003.0006

Rhodes 2017: #183A). The surviving parts of the law set out how the case of some-one who commits an act of involuntary homicide is to be handled:

First *axōn*.

> And if anybody kills anybody not from forethought, he shall be exiled. The *basileis* shall pronounce responsible for homicide [? the one who him-self killed or the one] who planned it; the Ephetai shall decide it.
>
> There shall be reconciliation, if there are a father or brother or sons, to be granted by all, or the person who objects shall prevail. If these do not exist, then as far as cousinhood and cousin, if they are all willing to grant recon-ciliation, or the person who objects shall prevail. If none of these exists but he killed unwillingly and the fifty-one Ephetai decide that he killed unwill-ingly, let ten members of the phratry allow him to enter [Attica] if they are willing: let these be chosen by the fifty-one according to excellence.
>
> And those who killed previously shall be liable to this ordinance.
>
> There shall be a proclamation against the killer in the agora by those as far as cousinhood and cousin; there shall join in the prosecution cous-ins and cousins' sons and brothers-in-law and fathers-in-law and phratry members
>
> ... is responsible for homicide ... the fifty-one ... convict of homicide ...
>
> If anybody kills a killer, or is responsible for his being killed, when he is keeping away from a frontier market and Amphictyonic contests and rites, he shall be liable to the same things as for killing; the Ephetai shall decide
>
> ... he is a freeman. And if he kills a man by defending immediately when the man is forcibly and unjustly taking and removing, that man shall have been killed without penalty ... (trans. R. Osborne and P. J. Rhodes)

The homicide law reveals the existence of a judicial structure presided over by magistrates (in this case the *basileus archon* and the heads [*phylobasileis*] of Athens' four Ionic tribes, who collectively make up the *basileis* mentioned in the text of the law) and involving a body, the Ephetai, a jury of 51, possibly chosen from the mem-bers of the Areopagus, who decided a particular homicide case (see further Section 5.2.1). The title Ephetai is cognate with *ephesis*, the term used by the *Constitution of the Athenians* 9.1 for referral to a court, and it indicates that they were primarily a judicial body. But how complex was the judicial structure? Plutarch (*Sol.* 19.2) claims that Drako's homicide laws never mentioned the Areopagus, but always talked of the Ephetai. On the other hand, Plutarch himself already notes (*Sol.* 19.3–4) that Solon's own laws, and in particularly the amnesty law (Solon *Laws* F22/1 Leão and Rhodes), imply a pre-existing court of the Areopagus passing sentences of *atimia*. So it looks as if the structure of homicide courts became more complex after the time of Drako (presumably as the result of Solon's own reforms), but that, although we cannot recover the principles upon which differentiation was made, there was already a division of different cases between different courts before Solon (Gagarin 1981, 125–32; Rhodes 1981: 647–8).

One striking feature of Drako's homicide law is its elegant formulation. The essential points about the legal treatment of homicide are set out at the start: first we have the basic penalty, then we have how the trial is going to be conducted, then we have the possibility of pardon. This is followed by a description of the steps to be taken by the killer and by the victim's relatives: there is to be a proclamation against the killer, the individuals who can prosecute are specified, then, after the loss of some clauses that probably covered the safe passage of the killer into exile, we have a clause about protecting the killer when in exile. The word order within the clauses seems specially chosen to make it easy to distinguish one clause from another, and the separate clauses are all self-contained (Gagarin 1981: 145–62; Carawan 1998; Gagarin 2008: 93–109). All of this seems to be a product of a lawgiver who has a very clear grasp of what needs to be done and a strong sense of what it is that people need to be told. It encourages us to expect Athenian law-giving to be systematic.

Drako's law both requires and limits the use of self-help by victims of offenses (the relatives of the person killed, in this case). But exactly what back-story we should tell to get us to this point has been disputed. Had self-help long been limited and intervention by some form of court or arbitration panel required (as we might deduce from the trial scene on the shield of Achilles in *Iliad* 18), or was the extent of civic control over individual self-help limited to an advisory role? Certainly, the prominence of the relatives, not simply in securing the prosecution in the first place but in the decisions that are taken (about pardon, but also about the killer breaching the conditions of his exile), is striking. The procedure seeks to establish a way forward that the relatives of the man killed can buy into. But the essential decisions are taken by the court, and we should see the role played by the relatives as more the product of the tiny administrative superstructure of the Athenian state at this point than a reflection of the power of families (as opposed to the state). This becomes clearer when we examine the legislation of Solon.

6.2 Solon

Our knowledge of Solon's laws derives from excerpts preserved in later authors who refer to them or claim to quote them. Many of these excerpts are brief and do not put us in a position to understand the nature of the law involved. But the number and range of references does allow us to form an idea of the overall shape of his legislation, both in terms of its scope and in terms of the court organization.[2]

The *Constitution of the Athenians* (9.1) picks out as two of the three most "demotic" (democratic?) features of Solon's constitutional arrangements (in addition to banning loans on security of the body), the possibility for a third party to prosecute wrongs and the possibility of referring all cases to a lawcourt. There is no doubt that Solon was an important innovator when it came to procedural law (Gagarin 2006). The basic structure of Athenian law in the Classical period certainly went back to Solon, and that structure depended upon the division of legal cases into those that could only be brought by the injured party (*dikai*), and those which could be brought by anyone (*graphai*). Homicide continued to be a *dikē*, with the relatives of the person killed treated as the injured party. *Graphai* seem to have been offenses where the victim was either not a person or not in a position to bring a prosecution (e.g., crimes against the state, or against the gods), or was disabled by the offense itself from bringing a prosecution (e.g., the *graphē* for being wrongly shut up as an adulterer, or the *graphē* for *hybris*, "insolent/aggravated violence," where part of what made *hybris* different from battery [*aikeia*], which was prosecuted in a *dikē*, was that the bullying involved in *hybris* itself was likely to prevent the victim being free to prosecute). We should assume that whatever else Drako's laws covered, prosecution was in all cases limited to a victim (the family was treated as a victim in homicide cases). Solon's contribution was to recognize that in some circumstances someone other than the victim needed to act, albeit within certain constraints (for instance, those prosecuting in a *graphē* who did not win one-fifth of the votes of the jurors were fined [Dem. 22.26–7]).

The significance of Solon's insistence that all cases could be referred to a court is in the existence of popular courts. In Drako's homicide law the verdict is decided by the Ephetai, who were probably drawn from the Areopagus. Solon created a popular court, the *eliaia*. The *eliaia* seems to have reviewed magistrates' decisions, confirmed or modified serious penalties, dealt with cases where earlier decisions had been ignored (best illustrated in the laws quoted in Dem. 24.105; cf. also Lys. 10.16) and heard appeals (Plut. *Sol.* 18.3). There was now the possibility of a popular check on magistrates' decisions, a procedure that became in time the automatic referral of many cases to a popular court (although magistrates continued to play a part in initial hearings and the preparation of the case for the court); when exactly referral to a court became standard is not clear, but

---

2. For a recent edition of Solon's laws, with translations and commentary, see Leão and Rhodes 2015.

plausibly this would be in the 450s, after Ephialtes' reforms and when jury-pay was introduced.[3]

Solon's laws certainly included quite detailed consideration of court procedure (Solon *Laws* F39–F46 Leão and Rhodes). We know, for instance, that he specified voting with ballots (*psēphoi* [pebbles], as opposed to voting by raising a hand) (F45), that he imposed a time-limit (three days) within which fines had to be paid (F46), and that he made some specification about witnesses (using a word for witnesses, *idyoi*, obsolete in Classical Attic Greek) (F41). But in this, as in other matters, we have little idea of how full or systematic the regulations that he laid down were.

The re-inscription of Drako's homicide law is headed "first *axōn*," with a second heading "second *axōn*" later in the inscription, and ancient sources reference Solon's laws by referring to them by *axōn*. What exactly an *axōn* was has been disputed, but Stroud in the fullest study concluded that they were four-sided pieces of wood, mounted in an oblong frame that could be rotated to be read (Stroud 1979; cf. esp. *Etym. Mag.* s.v. ἄξωνες.). We are told that they were brought down from the Acropolis to the *bouleuterion* by Ephialtes (Anaximenes *FGrH* 72 F13). We hear about 21 Solonian *axōnes* and, although the number of references to laws by *axōn* is small, the references offer a glimpse of the organization of the laws. We are told that a law forbidding agricultural exports other than of olive oil was on the first *axōn*, a law on obstructing access to property for those who have won that property in a lawsuit on the fifth, a law offering amnesty to *atimoi* on the 13th, a law on the price of sacrificial beasts on the 16th, and a law on adopted sons being free to return to their natural family only if they left legitimate children in their adopted family in the 21st.

Since these laws deal with widely different matters, it is unsurprising that they are found on widely separated *axōnes*. That the law on agricultural exports is reported from the first *axōn*, when we know Drako's homicide law to have been on the first *axōn*, may only indicate that Drako's *axōnes* and Solon's *axōnes* were separate, and that it is literally true that Solon did not disturb Drako's homicide laws. The idea that what determined the order was organization according to the magistrate in charge in each case has been much debated. The law on agricultural exports (Solon *Laws* F65 Leão and Rhodes), from the first *axōn*, includes an instruction to the archon to pronounce curses on anyone exporting, or else himself face a fine of 100 *drachmai*, and this supports the idea that the laws started with the responsibilities of the archon. The amnesty law, from the 13th *axōn*, explicitly excludes those condemned by the *basileis* (Solon *Laws* F70 Leão

---

3. MacDowell 1978: 29–35 remains the best discussion of these issues.

and Rhodes). But the evidence is in the end insufficient to determine an answer (Ruschenbusch 1966: 11–12, 25–31).

Solon's laws certainly seem to have covered offenses against the state. A Solonian law depriving of their civic rights anyone who attempted to overthrow the constitution (Solon *Laws* F37 Leão and Rhodes), is both independently attested and cross-referenced in the amnesty law (Solon *Laws* F22/1 Leão and Rhodes), which restores rights to some *atimoi*, depending upon the circumstances in which they had lost their rights. Much more debated is whether the law ascribed to Solon (Solon *Laws* F38 Leão and Rhodes) that required a man, on pain of loss of civic rights, to take one side or the other in time of *stasis* should be regarded as genuine. The law was very widely alluded to in antiquity, largely because of its paradoxical character, but that does not guarantee that it is genuine.[4] Its interest, if genuine, comes in the way in which it does not simply make involvement in politics by all Athenians possible, it makes it necessary. In the same class of public offenses would be the so-called "entrenchment clause" (i.e., a clause attempting to prevent a decision being overturned) whereby anyone who tried to overturn the laws is accursed (Solon *Laws* F93 Leão and Rhodes); this law is too closely linked to the tradition that after enacting his laws Solon went abroad for 10 years (Hdt. 1.29.1; cf. [Arist]. *Constitution of the Athenians* 11.1, Plut. *Sol.* 25.6), during which time the Athenians were not to change them, to be believed.

A great many of the other laws ascribed to Solon concern property, either directly or indirectly, and regardless of the questionable authenticity of some, property was surely a major Solonian concern. So we have Solonian laws on marriage, dowries, legitimacy, and inheritance (including the circumstances in which a will could be questioned); on adoption (the point of which in Athens was not to provide a child with parents but to provide parents with a child and heir); on care for parents; on what can be done at and spent on burials; on how close to the boundaries of someone else's land one can plant trees or dig a well; and perhaps on idleness.

One law that has evoked much scholarly discussion is that which, ostensibly, changed Athenians' official weights, measures, and coins (Kraay 1968; Rhodes 1975). Athens had no coins at this period (see Section 8.4), and this law is therefore not genuine in that respect. However, a number of laws ascribed to Solon make mention of fines or prices in *drachmai*, and there is no reason to deny that weighed silver was used as a standard means of payment in Athens by the start

---

4. The debate is well summarized in Leão and Rhodes 2015 ad loc.

of the sixth century (Kroll 1998; Kroll 2008b: 14–17).[5] But did Solon change Athenian measures and weight standards? It is certainly true that in the late Archaic and Classical period Athens used the same weight standard as Euboia; that standard differed from the so-called Pheidonian standard that was used on Aegina (Lang and Crosby 1964). We might wonder whether prior to Solon Athens used any particular weight standard. We know SOS amphoras (see Section 8.1) to have varied in their capacity and so at best offered a rather approximate measure of liquid measure, and until a state required payments in weights of silver there was nothing that had to be produced to a uniform standard. If fines and payments in weights of silver were new with Solon, his role may have been simply to specify for the first time the standards that were to be used in Attica.[6]

The great majority of legislation ascribed to Solon can be seen to attempt to prevent disputes or make it easier to settle them. The laws bearing on property, for example, served to reduce the possibility of conflict either between generations or between neighbors, and they prevented the use of wealth to make an exceptional display. The sixth-century religious calendar ascribed to Solon (see Section 11.3) itself should be thought of both as making sure that sacrifices that should happen did happen and as preventing religious festivals from becoming sites of conspicuous and competitive display. Although modern scholars list his laws about rape, adultery, and other sexual offences as "moral offenses," laws that impose fixed fines on those who have intercourse with a free woman by force or who oblige a free woman to provide services as a prostitute are better seen as setting the penalty that the woman's relatives can exact than as establishing a regime of sexual surveillance.[7] The provisions about adultery are particularly significant here, since all the surviving allusions to the treatment of adultery that are ascribed to Solon seem in fact to relate to the definition of adultery given in the context of making the killing of an adulterer caught in the act, "genitals in genitals" (Solon *Laws* F28c Leão and Rhodes), a case of justifiable homicide.

The law on justifiable (or involuntary) homicide, whether unchanged from Drako or developed by Solon, displays a structure that we can see in other laws ascribed to Solon, in that it tries to specify precisely the various circumstances in which homicide can be justified—because it happens accidentally in games; or on the road; or in war; or the victim was committing adultery with a wife,

---

5. Fines in *drachmai* appear in Solon *Laws* F65, 32–3, 26, 30 (cf. 36) Leão and Rhodes; payments in *drachmai* in 77, 81, 92, [143a] (cf. 79).

6. On how weighing and measuring operated practically, see S. Johnstone 2011: 35–61.

7. "Moral offenses": Solon *Laws* F26–31 Leão and Rhodes, cf. Ruschenbusch 1966: 77–9; Ruschenbusch 2010: 57–63 where they are labeled "Sittlichkeitsdelikte."

mother, sister, daughter, or concubine kept for the purpose of begetting free children (Solon *Laws* F20 Leão and Rhodes; [Dem. 23.53]; cf. F19 [Osborne and Rhodes 2017: #183A, 37–8; Dem. 23.60] for a further clause). The provision that it does not count as adultery if the woman sits in a brothel or is a street-walker ("promenades manifestly") must also belong to this law (Solon *Laws* F29 Leão and Rhodes). The same concern to cover the possibilities exhaustively is found in the law allowing those without male offspring to bequeath their property as they wish, provided that they are not "mad, senile, under the influence of drugs or sickness or the persuasion of a woman, forced by necessity, or in chains" (Solon *Laws* F49a Leão and Rhodes [Dem. 46.14]). Similarly, the law that required sons to support their parents exempted from that duty both sons to whom no craft had been taught and those born of a prostitute or who had been hired out for prostitution, only also to specify that those hired out for prostitution had nevertheless the duty to bury their father when he died (Solon *Laws* F55–7 Leão and Rhodes).[8] The desire to specify sometimes leads to rather surprising stipulations: so Plutarch (*Sol.* 20 2–6) notes that in the law on heiresses Solon not only specified that the next of kin who married an heiress must have sex with her three times a month, but also that "a bride should be shut up in a room with the bridegroom eating a quince."

The point of the high degree of specificity of the laws was presumably to simplify the administration of justice by defining in advance what did or did not count as an offense. The effect, however, was eventually rather the reverse: the various qualifications in the laws became an agenda for prosecution, so that, for instance, the validity of a will could be challenged by alleging madness, senility, the influence of a woman, etc. Equally the question arose of exactly what the terms of the law meant, and whether one should follow only the letter or also the spirit of the law, allowing argument over broader and narrower interpretations (cf. Lys. 10). This should not obscure the care with which Solon's laws attempt to pick their way through the situations that are likely to give rise to disputes, distinguishing between circumstances that make a dispute justifiable, and justiciable, and those that do not.

Much remains obscure about Solon's laws because so much of what we are told about them takes clauses out of context. It is very hard, for instance, to know what to make of claims that "Solon prevented men selling perfume" (Solon *Laws* F73

---

8. Another example would be the Solonian law on associations (Solon *Laws* F76 Leão and Rhodes), discussed in Section 5.3. To object that this law omitted some associations and therefore is evidence against codification (Ismard 2018: 147), misses the point that all lists of this type necessarily omit some relevant circumstances. As the *Constitution of the Athenians* (9.2) saw, one cannot judge the intentions of the lawgiver from the results.

Leão and Rhodes) we have no idea of the context in which that might have been stated. Similarly, we have no idea of the legal context of the law, of which Aeschines makes much in his prosecution of Timarchos, that "a slave is not to make love to a free boy or pursue him on pain of being struck 50 blows with the public lash" (Solon *Laws* F73 Leão and Rhodes; Aeschin. 1.138–9). That Aeschines quotes this along with a law forbidding slaves from exercising or rubbing themselves down with oil in the gymnasium might suggest that both provisions were part of a statute on what slaves could or could not do, but they could equally both belong to a law on what the limits were to acceptable behavior in the gymnasium.[9]

Solon did not mark the end of law-making in Athens, but the framework within which Athenians were to settle their disputes throughout the Classical period, and hence a whole way of seeing the world, was essentially established by him.

6.3 The Peisistratids

Tyranny was in general held by the Greeks to be extra-constitutional, and it was part of the story of Peisistratos' tyranny that Peisistratos did not change the laws. This is repeated by all our ancient sources in slightly different forms (e.g., Hdt. 1.59.6; Thuc. 6.54.6), and both *Constitution of the Athenians* 16.8 and Plutarch *Solon* 31.3 also tell stories of Peisistratos himself being willing to stand trial. *Constitution of the Athenians* 22.1 does suggest that some Solonian laws were simply forgotten, but it is clear that the Solonian legal framework continued.

There can be no doubt that laws, in the sense of permanent rules, were made under the Peisistratids, not least because the establishment of or changes to any recurrent religious festival was a matter of law, but we know neither exactly how they were made (by the assembly? by tyrant's fiat?) or what their substance was. The one legal innovation that is specifically claimed for Peisistratos concerns the administration of justice.

According to *Constitution of the Athenians* 16.5, Peisistratos established "jurors across the demes" to deal with justice locally and prevent loss of working time through country residents having to come into the town to settle their disputes. Beyond telling us also that Peisistratos himself went out settling disputes across the territory, the Aristotelian author gives no further detail. Later in his text he will tell us of the institution of 30 "jurors across the demes" in 453/2 (26.3) and of the increase of these to 40 early in the fourth century, and the limit of their competence to fines up to 10 *drachmai* (53.1). Some scholars have taken the

---

9. For discussion of these laws, see Fisher 2001: 283–4.

Peisistratid institution to be a retrojection, but it is of a piece with the concern with Attica displayed by other Peisistratid actions (see Section 11.3).

6.4 Kleisthenes and After

Kleisthenes' constitutional reforms clearly demanded a great deal of new legislation, and so too, in a less dramatic way, the various revisions to religious festivals, partly as a result of the new institutions Kleisthenes had established, will have involved new laws (Sections 5.2.4 and 11.4). But we know of no interventions in how people lived their lives or what behavior was or was not regarded as acceptable in the early years of democracy, and Kleisthenes does not figure in later discussions of lawmakers.

By the latter part of the fifth century, Solon's single *eliaia* with oversight of and right to review magistrates' decisions had been replaced by automatic reference to a popular court. Although magistrates retained competence to administer small fines, the norm was for cases to go to a magistrate for initial registration and then be considered by a jury (varying in size according to the severity of the case) over which that magistrate presided. The jurors were drawn from a panel of 6,000 enlisted annually from those over 30 years of age and made to swear an oath to vote according to the laws, or where there is no law "by the most just understanding," to consider only what is relevant to the law in question, and to listen to both sides (Mirhady 2007; Sommerstein and Bayliss 2013: 69–80).

We do not know at what point the juror's oath was introduced; in the form in which it is referred to by Classical writers it must be post-Kleisthenic, but that does not preclude there having been an earlier form sworn by the *eliaia*. Similarly, we do not know at what point reference to a court became standard, although this must surely have occurred before payment for jurors was introduced in the 450s ([Arist.] *Constitution of the Athenians* 27.3). Some scholars have favored the view that the agent of change was Ephialtes and that curtailing magisterial powers and the creation of the popular court system went along with his restrictions on the power of the Areopagus (cf. Wade-Gery 1958: 180–200; Osborne and Rhodes 2017: #120, commentary on 113), but others have associated the juror's oath with the Council oath of 501/0 and have favored the view that the practice of magistrates referring disputes directly to a court emerged gradually. But if such normal practice might develop over time, the institution of the juror's oath must have occurred at a particular moment, and as a consequence of thought being devoted to the judicial system. If the reforms that placed new limits on the judicial powers of the Council of 500 (Section 5.2.4) belong shortly after the Kleisthenic reforms, it is good evidence for such thought occurring then, but current evidence does not allow a definitive story to be told.

7

Diplomatic History and External Relations

7.1 Relationships with Other Polities

7.1.1 The Sixth Century to the Fall of the Peisistratids

We cannot write a history of Athens' relations with other cities before 600. There is no doubt that Athens was variously engaged with other cities, as indicated by the tradition that Kylon, who attempted a coup in Athens around 630 (see Section 5.2.1), was the son-in-law of Theagenes, tyrant of Megara. Archaeologically, we can trace close material connections of various sorts at different periods between Athens and a variety of neighboring places (cf. the close links between Athens and Salamis in the Submycenaean period [Sections 4.1.1.2 and 4.4.1], or between Athens and Aegina in the seventh century, on which see Section 4.5.3), but we have no way of using those material connections to write any form of history of foreign relations.

Essentially, any history of Athenian relations with other powers that we write starts with the evidence of two poets. We owe to the involvement of Alkaios of Mytilene in the fighting about it our knowledge that the Athenians captured Sigeion, just south of the entrance to the Hellespont, in the late seventh century (Alkaios F167, 306, 428 Lobel-Page; Hdt. 5.84.2–95.1; Strabo 13.1.38–9). Strabo, citing Alkaios as his source, states that the initial Athenian commander was the Olympic victor Phrynon, that Pittakos led the Lesbian opposition to Athenian occupation, and that Alkaios both lost his weapons (which were dedicated by the Athenians in a temple of Athena Glaukopis) and killed Phrynon in single combat by capturing him in a net.

The Oxford History of the Archaic Greek World. Robin Osborne, Oxford University Press. © Oxford University Press 2023.
DOI: 10.1093/oso/9780197644423.003.0007

The details of the narrative that Strabo wove out of the verses of Alkaios are suspect, but Alkaios' evidence establishes a general date for the Athenian capture of Sigeion, an undertaking that must have been meant to capitalize upon the movement of shipping in and out of the Hellespont.[1] Athenian presence in the Sigeion area in the sixth century (discussed further below) is confirmed by two epigraphic texts (Cirio 1980, summarized at *SEG* 30.1038): a graffito in Attic script on a middle Corinthian krater found at Ophryneion in the Troad and dated to the first quarter of the sixth century (Jeffery 1990: 373 #75), and the tombstone of Phanodikos. Phanodikos' tombstone, from Sigeion itself and dated to the second quarter of the sixth century, is inscribed first with 11 lines of eastern Ionic script (as used in Phanodikos' native Prokonnesos) and then with a further 11 lines in Attic script, repeating the same information but substituting a different word for the krater stand and adding two further clauses. The Attic inscription reads as follows:

> I belong to Phanodikos, son of Hermokrates, Prokonnesian. I gave a krater, a stand, and a strainer for their *prytaneion*, a memorial for the Sigeieis. If I suffer any damage, take care about me, Sigeieis. Haisopos and his brothers made me. (*IG* I³.1508; Jeffery 1990: 371 #43–4; Threatte 2015)[2]

The importance of this text lies not simply in its confirmation of Athenian presence through the use of Attic script, but the indication it gives that the settlement had a *prytaneion* and that settlers from elsewhere than Attica, in this case Prokonnesos, were part of the early community and centrally involved in its civic institutions.

Much closer to home, Solon F1–3 West are the basis of our knowledge of Athenian action in relation to Salamis. Plutarch and Diogenes Laertios in their lives of Solon tell of his having flaunted a ban on raising the topic of Salamis in the Assembly by feigning madness and producing a poem, from which various lines are quoted that both shame the Athenians as the people who gave up Salamis (in part by means of what was likely a neologism, the term *Salaminapheteis* [Σαλαμιναφετεῖς, "those who yielded Salamis"]) and that urge the Athenians to fight for the desirable island (Plut. *Sol.* 8; Diog. Laert. 1.46–8; M. C. Taylor 1997: 21–47). What sort of prehistory to this moment we should reconstruct (beyond the minimum that something had happened that Solon

---

1. For the site of Sigeion, see D. Müller 1997: 932–5.

2. See also https://research.britishmuseum.org/research/collection_online/collection_obj ect_details.aspx?objectId=459473&partId=1.

could claim constituted the Athenians "giving up" Salamis) is unclear. The Submycenaean archaeological evidence suggests that Salamis and Athens were very closely linked, and our best evidence for Salamis' independence is its separateness from Athens in the *Iliad*, an independence that in antiquity already the Athenians may have attempted to do something about by an insertion in the Catalog of Ships.[3] Whether the fact that the places said to have been raided by Aias in Hesiod's *Catalog of Women* (F204.44–51 Merkelbach-West) do not include Athens has any significance in this regard is doubtful. Those who contextualized Solon's Salamis poem later, by reference to some earlier long war with Megara, may simply have been guessing on the basis of the verses in front of them.

By the end of the sixth century, Athenians certainly occupied Salamis, as is apparent from the earliest extant Athenian decree, which concerns Athenians living on Salamis (*IG* I³.1.1; Meiggs and Lewis 1988: #14; see also Section 5.2.4). But exactly what had happened, and when, in the sixth century is unclear. Pausanias (1.40.5) tells of the Athenians taking control of Salamis in the time of Solon, noting that the Megarians claim that this happened through the treachery of some Megarian exiles. Plutarch tells what he calls the "popular version," in which Solon tricks the Megarians into sailing from Salamis to Cape Kolias in Attica to attack Athenian women celebrating Demeter there, only to substitute disguised and armed young Athenian men for the Athenian women, kill the Megarian invaders, and take advantage of the absence of Megarians on Salamis to seize the island (Plut. *Sol.* 8.4–6; cf. Polyaenus *Strat.* 1.20.2). Aineias Tacticus, writing in the fourth century, had already given a version of the story of men at a festival of Demeter turning out to be women, but situates the festival at Eleusis, ascribes the idea of substituting men for women to Peisistratos, and has a raid on Megara as the consequence, with no mention of Salamis (Aen. Tact. 4.8–12; cf. Just. *Epit.* 2.8.1–5; Frontinus *Strategemata* 2.9.9).

Little that is historical can be gleaned from these stories, or from Plutarch's alternative version (Plut. *Sol.* 9, perhaps reflected in Ael. *VH* 7.19), which involves a Delphic oracle and a night raid, again with capture of a Megarian ship and trickery employed by the Athenians that eventuated in the capture of the island. Plutarch claims a later ritual and a temple of Enyalios at Salamis as evidence in favor of this version, but the ritual and temple have left no other textual or material trace. Not only is it not possible to tell any story of how the Athenians captured Salamis, but it is also not even possible to date the event, or say whether Solon or Peisistratos was involved, although already Herodotos alleges that Peisistratos'

---

3. Arist. *Rh.* 1375b30; Strabo 9.1.10. See Kirk 1985: 207–9 on *Il.* 2.558.

first coup was facilitated by the fame he had achieved as the man responsible for the capture of the Megarian port of Nisaia (Hdt. 1.59.4).[4]

It is notable that in none of the stories does the *genos* of the Salaminioi (see Section 5.3) play any part. This is probably good reason to think that the connection of *genos* with the island of Salamis was early, since had it been historical it would surely have figured in "ownership" claim), although some have thought that inventing a body of people given the name "Salaminioi" was a way in which the Athenians created a claim to the island c. 600 (so Ferguson 1938: 42; see also Osborne 1994a: 154–9; M. C. Taylor 1997: 47–63).

As early as the fourth century, there was a tradition that what eventually settled Athens' dispute with Megara over Salamis was Spartan arbitration (Arist. *Rh.* 1375b29–30; Strabo 9.1.10; Plut. *Sol.* 10.1, 4; Diog. Laert. 1.48), something which, if plausible at all, is plausible only late in the sixth century.[5] An arbitration shortly before the date (last decade of the sixth century) of the Athenian decree about the rights and obligation of settlers on Salamis would be convenient, but that does not mean it is true (and were it true then the failure of Herodotos or Thucydides to mention it is surprising). Two things should be stressed. One is that at the time of Kleisthenes' reforms Salamis was not firmly enough part of Attica for it to be treated as one or more "deme" in Kleisthenes' new constitutional arrangements (on which see Section 5.2.4). This may imply that Athenian control over the island was recent in 508. The second notable thing, however, is that Salamis does not seem to have been a bone of contention in the fifth century. Athens and Megara engaged in border disputes in the fifth and fourth centuries, but Salamis was not what the quarreling was about. Whatever happened in the sixth century, and whenever precisely it happened, the settlement of Salamis as Athenian was decisively achieved.

The confusion of stories about Athens and Salamis should not obscure the broader framework. We have stories too of "ancient" hostility between Athens and Aegina, with an elaborate tale, that also brings Epidaurus into the picture, told by Herodotos (5.81.1, 82–89.1). That story has much elaboration, but its existence reflects tensions caused by the growing power imbalance between Athens and the other polities in and around the Saronic Gulf. Exactly what incidents happened, and when, is unclear, but the stories remind us that there

---

4. It is a measure of the way similar items are recycled in different combinations that Plutarch has the Athenians lose Nisaia and Salamis in the disturbances following Kylon's attempted coup (*Sol.* 12.3).

5. One of the arbitrators named by Plutarch (*Sol.* 10.4) is called Kleomenes, and he has sometimes been thought to be the king of that name, and his arbitration to belong to his presence in the area in 519. See M. C. Taylor 1997 42–7.

were more parties interested in events on Salamis than simply Athens and Megara.[6]

Athens' relations with the world beyond the Saronic Gulf in the sixth century are equally hard to reconstruct in any detail. The traditions about Solon have him interacting with individuals and cities over a wide geographical area. The traditions about Peisistratos suggest that he had influential contacts in a wide range of Greek cities. He is said to have married an Argive wife, Timonassa, in addition to an Athenian wife (the latter of whom was the mother of Hippias and Hipparchos) (J. K. Davies 1971: 445–50). That the Argive wife is said by the *Constitution of the Athenians* (17.4) to have been previously married to Archinos the Ambraciot, whom it identifies as a Kypselid, is strongly suggestive of the inter-connections of elite families around the Greek world. Peisistratos is further said to have gained resources for his third attempt to get power at Athens from the mines at Mt. Pangaion in Macedonia, having settled at Raikelos in the Thermaic Gulf, and to have had the Thebans and Lygdamis of Naxos, as well as a thousand Argive troops, backing him as he set out from Eretria, where he presumably also had support, to face the Athenians in battle at Pallene ([Arist.] *Constitution of the Athenians* 15.2, 17.4; cf. Hdt. 1.62–3; J. K. Davies 2013: 46–7). Peisistratos is then said to have installed Lygdamis in power at Naxos (and Lygdamis is subsequently said to have helped Polykrates gain power in Samos [Polyaenus *Strat.* 1.23.2]).

At some point in the first half of the sixth century the Athenians seem to have been removed from Sigeion, so that Peisistratos had to launch a military campaign to wrest back control from the Mytileneans. Peisistratos' son Hegesistratus took power there, and when Hippias was expelled from Athens it was to Sigeion that he chose to go (Hdt. 5.94)—an indication that this "Athenian" settlement was something of a personal fiefdom, recognized as "Athenian" but open to someone in exile from Athens. Herodotos also records that Hippias was offered Anthemous to settle in by Amyntas king of Macedon and Iolkos by the Thessalians (who had been involved in resisting the first attacks on Athens by the Spartans attempting to unseat Hippias)—further indications of the strength of Peisistratid links across the north Aegean (Hdt. 5.63, 94, with Hornblower 2013 ad loc). Athens seems to have preserved at least some of those links following the downfall of the Peisistratids, for according to Herodotos (8.136.1) Alexander of Macedon was an Athenian *proxenos* before 480.

But Athenian presence in the north Aegean was by no means all tied to the Peisistratids. In the mid-sixth century, and presumably with the encouragement of the Peisistratos, Miltiades established Athenian control over

---

6. For some speculation, see Figueira 1993: 41, 51, 56, 85–6; Hornblower 2013: 232–3.

the Thracian Chersonese, the land on the European side of the Hellespont (J. K. Davies 2013: 45–6). The story that Herodotos tells is of the Dolonkoi, who then inhabited the Thracian Chersonese, being oppressed by their local rivals, the Apsinthians, and consulting the Delphic oracle, which gives them advice to recruit as leader the first person who offers them hospitality. This turns out to be Miltiades (the Elder), whose father Kypselos was archon in 597/6 (Develin 1989, 34), and Miltiades himself consults the Delphic oracle before agreeing (Hdt. 56.34–6). Nepos has a very different version of this story in which the initiative belongs with the Athenians (*Milt.* 1.1–3). Neither version is plausible, since the Delphic oracle reacted to precise questions rather than giving spontaneous advice about general situations. However, that the Dolonkoi might have chosen to go to Athens in search of help is not implausible, given the Athenian presence at nearby Sigeion, and that Peisistratos might have thought that sending off Miltiades to the Chersonese was a good idea is equally plausible.

Herodotos records that Miltiades' first act was to wall off the Thracian Chersonese to protect it from invasion (6.36.2–37.1). Miltiades seems also to have established, on an acropolis just west of the probable line of his wall, a settlement named Agora (which later became Lysimacheia).[7] Herodotos proceeds to tell how Miltiades made war on, and was captured by, the people of Lampsakos, but was freed on the intervention of Kroisos. If this intervention is to be believed, then it provides the best dating for the whole episode, since it would have to occur before the fall of Kroisos in the 540s. Miltiades seems to have been born in the 580s, and Miltiades' departure from Athens would likely have occurred during Peisistratos' first or second period of tyranny (c. 561/0—c. 556/5) or more or less immediately after Peisistratos' victory at Pallene (probably c. 552/1) (J. K. Davies 1971: 299–300; Rhodes 1976; Rhodes 1981: 191–9). Kroisos' intervention would also be good evidence for the close links between Lydia and the Greek cities of the mainland that are reflected by the stories (most notably Hdt. 1.46–56) of his involvement with the Delphic oracle and dedications at Delphi and Thebes.

Herodotos proceeds to tell us that at Miltiades' death, sometime after 528 (Hdt. 6.103.4), he was given the full honors of an *oikistēs*, including equestrian and athletic competitions staged in his honor and that, since he was childless, he was succeeded by his half-brother Stesagoras, who was, however, killed by trickery in on-going hostilities with Lampsakos (6.38). We can date Stesagoras' death to 516/5, because of the sequence of events that follows (see Hdt. 6.40.1).

At this point, Herodotos records the Peisistratids sending Stesagoras' brother, also named Miltiades (the Younger), who had been archon in 524/3 (Develin

---

7. For discussion, see D. Müller 1997: 766–70.

1989: 47), to govern the Chersonese. Miltiades took drastic action to assert authority over the leaders of neighboring communities and linked himself with the Thracians by marrying the daughter of the Thracian king Oloros (Hdt. 6.39.2). But Darius' decision to invade Scythia in 513 destabilized things. Miltiades became famous for advising the Greek rulers of cities in Ionia and the Hellespont, whom Darius had left to guard the bridge over the Ister, to abandon their station and so abandon Darius to his fate in Scythia (Hdt. 4.136–7). However, he failed to persuade his fellow Greek rulers, who perceived that it is was Persian favor that enabled them to sustain their positions, and, in the aftermath, Miltiades had to abandon temporarily the Chersonese because of Scythian attacks (Hdt. 6.40).

The passage of Herodotos in which the events that follow are recounted poses notorious chronological difficulties, and we cannot be sure how long Miltiades was absent from the Chersonese. At some point, dated by some to before 507 but more plausibly the 490s, he led the Athenian capture of Lemnos (Hdt. 6.137–40) and probably also Imbros (cf. Hdt. 6.41.2).[8] He was certainly in the Chersonese in 493, in which year his deteriorating relations with the Persians came to a head. Part of the Phoenician fleet seems to have been sent against him, and Miltiades decided to take his wealth and flee to Athens (Hdt. 6.41). It is tempting to think that the Phoenician fleet was present only because of the recent Athenian capture of Lemnos and Imbros, a capture that both the Athenians and Miltiades himself seem to have advertised widely. We have helmets inscribed "Athenians, from the spoils from Lemnos" surviving from Olympia and (probably) the Athenian Acropolis, and a helmet dedicated by Miltiades (occasion not certain) from Olympia.[9] But by this time the world of Athenian foreign policy had been completely transformed.

7.1.2 From the Fall of the Tyranny to 480

The tyranny of Peisistratos and his sons was notable for the absence of foreign policy initiatives, beyond assistance to Lygdamis. But the fall of the tyranny both involved the formation of relations and extensive engagement with other cities (above all Sparta, see Section 5.2.3). This was partly a matter of chance—the

8. For the earlier date, see Hornblower and Pelling 2017: 294–5; they seem to me to be too confident that Lemnos was in fact taken without fighting.

9. *IG* I³.1466 (Olympia), 518bis (Acropolis, inscription only partially preserved), 1472 (Miltiades at Olympia, cf. Pausanias 6.19.6 where is it unclear whether the horn dedicated by Miltiades to celebrate the capture of Teichos Aratou was dedicated by the older or the younger Miltiades). The dedication by "Rhamnousians from Lemnos" found at Rhamnous (*IG* I³.522bis) seems to relate to post-Persian Wars Athenian occupation.

establishment of democracy at Athens happened to come at the time when the Persians were exploring the possibility of tightening their grip on the western fringe of their empire and of extending their power—but it was partly a consequence of the rather different outlooks of tyrants and of a sovereign people. For tyrants, unless they were actually under attack, the possible gains of foreign adventures were unlikely to be matched by the downside risks of failure, of putting arms into the hands of a resentful people, and of provoking revolt by asking too much of their population. By contrast, for a sovereign people, generals were expendable, and wars good at bringing unity.

If the Peisistratids themselves wanted to avoid hostile engagement with other cities, those Athenians who sought to dislodge them were faced with a dilemma as to how they might overthrow the well-entrenched family of tyrants. The Athenians needed outside help to end the tyranny, but, in the aftermath, they sought to portray the overthrow of the Peisistratids as the result of the Athenians' own actions. To Thucydides' disgust, one version that they told claimed, as we have seen (Section 5.2.3), that a bold assassination had freed Athens from tyranny and enabled democracy. In another version the emphasis was on the Alkmaionidai bribing the Delphic oracle so that whenever the Spartans consulted the Pythia they were told to free the Athenians. That story suited both the Alkmaionidai and the Spartans, for whom it facilitated a policy reversal, but, even if oracles did play a part, they will hardly have constituted sufficient reason to persuade either the Spartans themselves or their allies that attacking Attica was appropriate.

For the Spartans, the evidence suggests that they saw internal opposition to the Peisistratids at Athens as offering an opportunity. This is seen in the determination with which, after a failed naval expedition led by an otherwise unknown Spartan, they had their king, Kleomenes, lead a land campaign that succeeded largely in consequence of the fortuitous capture of Hippias' sons (Hdt. 5.63–5). And when their favored leader, Isagoras, began to lose out to his political rival Kleisthenes, the Spartans attempted to support Isagoras by demanding Kleisthenes' expulsion, and by having Kleomenes invade again—only to meet concerted popular resistance that left Isagoras, Kleomenes, and their supporters besieged on the Acropolis and having to agree to a truce (Hdt. 5.72.1–2).

What exactly was Sparta trying to achieve? On one reading, what Sparta wanted was to bring Athens within the Peloponnesian League (Wolff 2010). Sparta had extended her web of alliances as far as Megara more than a decade before this but had refused to ally with Plataia, driving her into alliance with Athens (Hdt. 6.108, Thuc. 3.68.5). So, was Athens simply next on the list of candidates for Peloponnesian League membership? It looks as if the story is a little more complicated. Herodotos has Kleomenes claim to Plataia that she was simply too far away from Sparta for Sparta to be able to protect her, but Sparta had its eyes on a more powerful friend than Plataia—Thebes, with whom Plataia's relations were hostile. With Sparta's further invasion attempt in 506, the Boiotian interest becomes clear. Herodotos says that Kleomenes' arrival with a large army at Eleusis was coordinated with Boiotian attacks on two towns at the western end of Athens' Parnes border, Oinoe and Hysiai, and with attacks by Chalkis on the eastern end of that border (Hdt. 5.74; the Boiotian military successes in this campaign are confirmed by a dedication from Thebes, *SEG* 56.521; for further discussion, see H. Beck 2023, sec. 7.4). Unfortunately for Kleomenes, at Eleusis he met with resistance within his Peloponnesian League army: first the Corinthians withdrew their support, we may suspect worried by the Boiotian dimension, and then Kleomenes' fellow king Demaratos followed suit (Hdt. 5.75.1). The Peloponnesian League army at Eleusis disintegrated and departed, and the Athenians took immediate advantage and defeated both the Boiotians and the people of Chalkis—on a single day, as they claimed (Hdt. 5.77).

The Athenians exploited their military success to the full. Herodotos (5.77.2) records that they sent 4,000 settlers to occupy the land that they had confiscated from the *hippobotai* of Chalkis—a number remarkable both absolutely (that 4,000 Athenians could be found who were in a position to take up land grants in Chalkis, particularly when at more or less this time the Athenians were also able to find settlers to send to Salamis) and in terms of the extent of land-holding by the *hippobotai* that is implied. That the klerouchs remained, and did not simply become absentee landlords, is implied by the way in which they were subsequently detailed to help Eretria against Persian invasion in 490 (Hdt. 6.100.1; for further discussion, see Fachard and Verdan 2023, sec. 7.4).

The Athenians also showed off their success on the Acropolis, with what must have been the most spectacular dedication that had up to that time been made there: from the ransom paid by the Boiotian and Chalkidian prisoners, the Athenians dedicated a victory monument in the form of a bronze four-horse chariot, placed to be the first thing that those entering the Acropolis saw. That dedication was accompanied by an inscription (re-carved in the middle of the fifth century after the original was damaged in the Persian sack) (Hdt. 5.77.4; Meiggs and Lewis 1988, #15; *IG* I³.501). The original version seems to have read:

> The sons of the Athenians, in deeds of war, quenched *hybris* with a hard iron chain, when they subdued the peoples of Boiotia and Chalkis. They dedicated to Pallas a tithe from which these horses.

Spartan embarrassment was severe, and the effects of these events would be felt long afterward as the tense relationships between Athens and Sparta and between the two Spartan kings played themselves out.

The Athenians seem to have realized that the rejection of Kleomenes, and with it, presumably, the rejection of becoming one of Sparta's allies in the Peloponnesian League, meant that they needed friends elsewhere. Herodotos (5.73) records the Athenians sending an embassy to Persia, or rather to the Persian satrap at Sardis. This is, in itself, perfectly plausible, given Miltiades' earlier involvement with Darius' Scythian campaign. How much of the further detail can be trusted is less certain. Artaphrenes' supposed question about who the Athenians were and where they lived fits with an Herodotean theme of Greeks' insignificance in the eyes of the empires of the east, but it is manifestly implausible. Nor is the notion, put about by the Greeks, that there were no relations with the Persians except by totally surrendering one's territory and claim to independence, a plausible one.[10] We can certainly imagine the Athenian envoys indicating to Persia that Athens would be willing to ally on terms that later the Athenians regarded as unacceptable, but we should not think that the ambassadors promised to subordinate Athens to Persia or that Herodotos is here hiding anything. But whatever the details of what happened, Athens entered no formal diplomatic relationship with Persia.

Thebes did not take lightly their defeat along with the rest of the Boiotians by Athens. Herodotos recounts a story that the Thebans, after having been told by the Delphic oracle to seek help from those that are closest, worked out the meaning of that oracle in mythological terms: Thebe and Aegina were both daughters of Asopos, and hence the Thebans secured the assistance of Aegina, at least to the extent of the Aeginetans lending their gods in support of a Theban campaign against Athens (Hdt. 5.79–81). Thebes made aggressive but not very successful moves against Athens in, probably, both 505 and 504, and in the latter year Aegina took advantage of Theban engagement with Athens to raid Phaleron and the demes on the coast of Attica (Hdt. 5.81.3, 89.1). Herodotos explains the absence of reprisals from Athens by a Delphic oracle ordering them to cultivate the hero Aiakos and not attack Aegina for 30 years (Hdt. 5.89.2–3), but there may have been more directly military concerns that

---

10. Scholars have noted the difficulty of finding any Achaemenid evidence for giving of earth and water (Kuhrt 1988; Rung 2015). The motif occurs repeatedly in Herodotos (5.17–18, 73.2–3; 6.48–9; 7.138.2, 163.2, 233; 8.46.4; cf. 7.32, 131, 133.1, which have earth alone), but there is no independent evidence. Although, for example, S. West 2011 (cf. Hornblower 2013: 110) sees here a Darian adaptation of Greek practice (cf. Gottesman 2010) for use in Europe, her observation that, since the practice stopped with Plataia, "It is unlikely that [Herodotos] could get reliable information about the ceremonies involved" is important. Much, in my view, has been altered in the telling.

Kleomenes was planning to assemble an army to forcibly restore Hippias to power in Athens.[11]

According to Herodotos, the Spartans' decision to attempt to restore Hippias followed their discovery that the original intervention to get rid of Hippias had been brought about by Alkmaionid bribery of the Delphic oracle. In fact, Boiotian encouragement likely played a part in that original intervention. But when Kleomenes sought to get together a Peloponnesian League army for a new invasion of Attica in 503, he was stymied by his allies' opposition to making Hippias tyrant once again (Hdt. 5.90–3). On Herodotos' account the opposition was led by a Corinthian, and we should probably see here fears on the part of Corinth that the absence of a powerful state outside the Peloponnesian League would make its own position within the League weaker.

Upon this tense situation outside events now impinged. By the same token that Greek tyrants in Ionia supported Darius because they depended upon him, so those who wished to overthrow their rulers at home realized that to do so demanded also revolting from Persia. The year 499 saw an "Ionian spring" as tyrants in Ionia tumbled, and the Ionian cities sought to co-ordinate their revolt from Persia. This was not an event without planning—or without the participation of some rulers who had been sustained to this point by Persia but had come to feel unduly constrained. Herodotos tells a colorful story of Aristagoras of Miletos coming to Sparta and Athens to seek help, being rejected by Sparta but being promised help by the Athenians (Hdt. 5.97). Herodotos observes that it was easier to deceive and impose upon 30,000 Athenians than upon Kleomenes of Sparta, but he also observes that Athens was predisposed to hostility toward Persia because, by now, the ex-tyrant Hippias was in Persia, working to get the Persians to restore him. Whatever the arguments that persuaded the Athenians— they would certainly come to employ the politics of Ionian kinship in succeeding years and that may have been a factor on this occasion—a naval force of 20 Athenian ships was dispatched (although these may not have been triremes, since Herodotos 5.99.1 appears to contrast Athenian ships to Eretrian triremes) to assist the Ionians' revolt.

Although the number of ships sent by Athens in 499 to Ionia is small by comparison to her later fleets, this is the largest number of ships we have evidence for the Athenians putting into action up to this time. Although in theory the Athenian naukrary system would yield a navy of 48 ships (see Section 5.2.1), nothing that we know of Athenian history in the sixth century demands more than

---

11. The chronology of the Athenian conflict with Aegina is much disputed. For the chronology adopted here, see Hornblower 2013: 232; Hornblower and Pelling 2017: 209. For alternatives, see Figueira 1993: 133–46.

a handful of ships. The Athenians' prior engagements in Asia Minor, at Sigeion and the Thracian Chersonese, along with Hippias having chosen to take refuge in the Persian empire (Hdt. 5.96), more than adequately explains the substantial commitment the Athenians made to the Ionians.

In the end Athenian participation in the Ionian revolt was short-lived. The Ionians marched against, captured, and burned Sardis, and the Persians responded by pursuing them to Ephesos and defeating them there in a battle. At this point, the Athenians withdrew, although the revolt spread north to the Hellespont and Thrace and south and east to Cyprus, and action continued for another four years until the Ionians were defeated at the Battle of Lade in 494 and Miletos was sacked. (The latter event produced a powerful reaction in Athens, where the tragedian Phrynichos was fined after putting on a tragedy *The Capture of Miletos*, on the grounds that he reminded the Athenians of their ills [Hdt. 6.21.2]). Herodotos (5.103.1) claims that many appeals were made to the Athenians to continue their involvement, but he offers no reason for the Athenians' withdrawal. One possible reason is continued tension in the Saronic Gulf. Although the chronology of Herodotos' own account is very hard to resolve, Athens and Aegina were certainly in conflict again between 500 and 480, and what happens makes best sense if it happened before the Battle of Marathon.

As Herodotos tells the story (6.87–93), the Aeginetans ambushed a ship carrying Athenian sacred officials to a quadrennial festival at Sounion and put the distinguished Athenians on board in chains. Athens then encouraged an Aeginetan dissident named Nikodromos, who captured the Old City of Aegina, but by the time the Athenians had borrowed 20 ships from Corinth so as to be able to face the Aeginetans at sea Nikodromos had been forced to flee. The Athenians won the battle at sea, driving the Aeginetans to seek help from Argos. The Athenians settled Nikodromos and his fellow dissidents at Sounion, which they used as a base for raiding Aegina. The Aeginetans managed to inflict a minor defeat on the Athenians at sea.

The most important consequence of these hostilities was a change in the Athenian relationship to the sea. In his archonship in 493/2, Themistokles persuaded the Athenians, according to Thucydides (1.93.3–8) to fortify the Peiraieus.[12] This was an extraordinarily radical move. There is no sign up to this point that the Peiraieus, rather than Phaleron, was any sort of center for Athenian shipping. Access to what would become the Great Harbor seems to have been difficult because of marshy conditions (see Section 8.3 for further discussion). What

---

12. For the issues with this passage, see Hornblower 1991–2008: vol. 1: 138–9. On the fortification of the Peiraieus, see Section 8.3. For the geological history, see Goiran, Pavlopoulos, Fouache et al. 2011.

Themistokles seems to have seen is that, if Athens were to form a large naval fleet, the Great Harbor would be the only place where it could be safely sheltered. The development of the Peiraieus therefore went hand in hand with the development of the fleet. This decision must therefore have been closely linked with the second great initiative of Themistokles.

That second initiative was to persuade the Athenians to invest the profits of a windfall from the Laurion silver mines (see Section 8.2) in strengthening their navy. According to Herodotos (7.144), the Athenians had intended to distribute the income from the silver mines to the population so that everyone received 10 *drachmai*, but Themistokles persuaded them instead, in the light of the war with Aegina, to expend the money on building a navy of 200 ships. Thucydides repeats the claim that the war with Aegina was the crucial motivation for this act of shipbuilding, although the *Constitution of the Athenians* (22.7) has a different version in which Themistokles simply has the money entrusted to 100 rich individuals to use for the public benefit, and each of these men then builds one trireme. The *Constitution of the Athenians* dates this to 483/2, giving the name of the archon, but it has never been credible that shipbuilding on this scale (particularly if Herodotos is right to talk of 200 ships and not 100) could be completed in the three years between then and the sea battle at Salamis in which they proved crucial. The Aristotelian author must have become confused, and we should date this initiative too to Themistokles' archonship. The two initiatives together show the continued force that magisterial office gave to an individual's voice in the years prior to the decision in 487/6 to appoint archons by lot (Section 5.2.4).

But Athens' naval supremacy lay in the future. The Persian invasion of Attica in 490 was not defeated at sea but on land, in what must remain one of the most extraordinary battles in history.[13] Darius had followed up his defeat of the Ionians at the Battle of Lade in 494 by moving against the Greeks of the mainland. Mardonios, the general responsible for settling affairs in Ionia after the revolt by removing tyrants and allowing some form of local popular sovereignty (Hdt. 6.43), went on an offensive against the Greek cities of Thrace. Herodotos treats this expedition as if its object was the invasion of Greece, but its aims may have been more limited and neither the stories of a great fleet being destroyed in a storm, nor the claims of significant casualties being inflicted upon the Persian army, are to be trusted (Hdt. 6.44–5). Greek cities in Thrace certainly became subject to Persia at this point (some of them would remain under Persian control long after 480), and Thasos was apparently made to tear down part of its walls and surrender its ships

---

13. The story of the Persian invasion and the Battle of Marathon has been told many times over. For a straightforward account, see Lazenby 1993. For discussion of the history of the scholarship on Marathon, see Fink 2014.

(Hdt. 6.46–8). A diplomatic campaign was also launched. Athens and Sparta later claimed to have given the Persian heralds short shrift, but Aegina and apparently other islands indicated a willingness to join themselves to Persia (Hdt. 6.49, 7.133).

In 490 Darius launched a new offensive, directly aimed at Eretria and Athens, under the command of Datis (a Mede) and Artaphernes (Darius' brother). Herodotos claims an expedition of 600 ships, but this appears to be a conventional number. The fleet landed at Naxos, setting fire to city and sanctuaries after the Naxians had fled to the interior. It landed also at Rheneia, next to Delos, after the Delians too had fled (to Tenos), and on Delos Datis is said to have made a massive offering of incense. Herodotos claims that when the fleet moved on to Eretria, the Eretrians were split over what to do and that after a week of siege, the city was betrayed to the Persians, who took the city and burnt its sanctuaries. The Persians then moved on to Attica and landed at Marathon, as Hippias' father had done when he staged his third and successful bid for power (Section 5.2.3). But rather than land and march toward Athens, the Persians waited to engage the Athenians at Marathon itself (Hdt. 6.103).

Whatever the numbers of Persians involved, and the figures offered by ancient authors are unbelievable, there is little doubt that the 11,000 or so Greeks (10,000 Athenians and 1,000 Plataians) were heavily outnumbered. An Athenian attempt to recruit the Spartans (and presumably Sparta's allies, too) failed (though it is hard to see how any Spartan army could have been mobilized in time, unless the appeal had been sent as soon as news of a Persian fleet bound for Greece had arrived). The battle (on which see Section 7.2) left, according to Herodotos, 6,400 Persians and 192 Athenians dead (along with an unknown number of Plataians). The Persian expedition against Greece was abandoned.

Who did what in the Battle of Marathon became so important that little that was reported afterward can be trusted. Herodotos becomes very exercised by a story that the Alkmaionidai had attempted to betray the Athenians by using a shield to flash messages to the Persians, a story that he attempts to refute at length (Hdt. 6.121–31). There is not much doubt that tensions over the appropriate attitude to Persia going forward were one of the factors in the ostracisms of the 480s (on which practice see Section 5.2.4): we have one wonderful *ostrakon* that has the name of Kallias son of Kratios of Alopeke, who was linked to the Alkmaionidai, on one side, and a nicely drawn Persian archer on the other (see Figure 33). Other *ostraka* call Kallias "one of the Medes" or accuse Habronichos of medizing and Leagros of treason. One *ostrakon* accuses one Arist–, perhaps Aristeides, of being the brother of Datis.[14]

---

14. Brenne 2002: 56, T1/46–61 for Kallias, T1/41 for Habronichos, T1/71 for Leagros, T1/37 for Arist–. See also Brenne 1992.

FIGURE 33 Two sides of an *ostrakon* cast against Kallias, possibly in 471; found in the Kerameikos. Kerameikos Museum 849; Brenne 2002: T 1/46 and T 1/156.

It is worth observing that these allegations of particular foreign sympathies, aimed largely at members of wealthy families, were in a sense inevitable. Wealthy visitors to Athens would regularly enjoy hospitality from wealthy Athenians, and by that means wealthy Athenians acquired both knowledge about the affairs of other cities and developed connections that could be drawn upon in times of need. This meant that those Athenians were in the best position to find out about the affairs of other cities and could expect a more ready reception there than those who had no prior ties. We simply do not know enough during the Archaic period to tell stories of particular close relationships in detail (our best data concerns the Peisistratids, a slightly special case). There can, however, be no doubt that were our information better we would find in the Archaic period the pattern familiar in the Classical period, where we have signs of hereditary connections with particular cities running in a family for generations, as well as indications that other cities often had more than one wealthy Athenian (acting as their *proxenos*) helping with their interests. The considerable body of relevant evidence from Classical Athens shows that acting as an ambassador was regularly the job of wealthy and well-born individuals (Mosley 1973; Sato 2015).

Part of the debate in Athens did not simply concern Persia—it concerned how Athens should react to the cities that had supported Persia. Herodotos claims that Miltiades exploited the fame that he gained as the general responsible for the victory at Marathon by persuading the Athenians to give him 70 ships and a body of troops without revealing what he was going to do with them. He then sailed against Paros, on the grounds that it had given a trireme in support of Persia (but also, Herodotos says, because of a personal grudge), laid siege to the city, and demanded 100 talents to lift the siege. The siege failed, Miltiades injured himself—the Parians claimed he did so trying to commit sacrilege—and when he returned to Athens he was prosecuted by Xanthippos, fined 50 talents, and died of his injuries (Hdt. 6.132–7; another version at Ephoros *FGrH* 70 F163). Whatever the truth of this story—and the claim that the Athenians gave Miltiades a fleet and troops without some idea of the aim is hard to believe— it is a measure of the tensions of these years that Xanthippos was subsequently ostracized.

7.1.3 The Second Persian Invasion

Attitudes to Persia and attitudes to other Greeks were closely bound up together at this point, since at least in the second half of the 480s, it became clear that the Persians would not take their defeat at Marathon as the end of their interest in the Greek mainland. The question of how best to resist the Persians came to the top of the political agenda, and the Persians on one hand and the Athenians and the Spartans (sometimes separately, sometimes jointly) on the other embarked on active diplomatic initiatives.

Once more, what happened was so consequential that no faith can be put in any of the details of the stories that were later told. Herodotos himself illustrates this with the variety of stories later told to explain why Argos stayed neutral and did not support the Greek resistance (Hdt. 7.148–52). Spartan and Athenian overtures in search of allies seem to have met with little success. Herodotos tells of the rejection of appeals by Gelon of Syracuse and the Cretans (Hdt. 7.145, 153–67, 169–71), and the failure of the Corcyraeans to act on their promise to help (7.168). In the end few Greeks from outside the southern mainland supported resistance to Persia, and when the names of those who had joined the resistance were carved on the Serpent Column at Delphi after the war, a mere 31 cities or peoples were listed. Outside Sparta's Peloponnesian allies we find only Athens, Plataia, Thespiai, three cities from Euboia, a group of Cycladic islands (Keos, Melos, Tenos, Naxos, Kythnos, Siphnos), the people of Poteidaia and, from northwest Greece Leukas, the Anactorians, and the Ambraciots (Meiggs and Lewis 1988: #27). Those from northwest Greece and the Poteidaians can be reckoned to have been brought into the war by Corinth; Athens' part is likely to have been bringing in the Euboian cities and some of the Cycladic islands (note the absence of Paros), though presumably the presence of Melos is due to its relationship to Sparta. We do not know exactly what Athenian actions during the 480s brought Keos, Kythnos and Siphnos into the conflict on the Athenian side; information about the 480s is too sparse to be confident that there were no Athenian overtures to the islanders during that decade.[15]

As the Athenians later represented it, part of the preparations for war included their consulting the Delphic Oracle (Hdt. 7.140–3). The developed story that we have from Herodotos has an initial consultation met by advice to flee, the Athenian delegates refusing to accept this and asking for a better oracle, and Delphi then delivering the advice that Zeus has given them a wall of wood that will not be ravaged, and that "divine" Salamis will see many dead. Themistokles then persuades the Athenians that the "wood wall" refers to their ships.

There are numerous features of this story that conflict with what we know of consultations of the Delphic oracle, and there can be no doubt that the story has been improved in the telling.[16] That Athens consulted Delphi is not itself implausible, however, and the nature of the consultation may itself have brought about oracular mention of the wooden wall. The important point is that at some point Themistokles persuaded the Athenians that they should be willing to abandon Attica itself and trust in the fleet. As Herodotos saw, in his famous verdict on the key role played by Athens in Greek victory (Hdt. 7.139), had the Athenians

---

15. *Contra* Brunt 1953: 146–8 (= Brunt 1993: 61–3). Tenos and Naxos got on to the Serpent Column by virtue of their forces deserting in the course of the war (Hdt. 8.46.3, 82; we cannot exclude the possibility that that was true also of some others).

16. I discuss the Delphic oracle at Osborne 2009: 192–4; see also Kindt (2016) on Delphic oracle stories.

not been prepared to withdraw from their territory, or had they not opposed the Persians by sea, the outcome of the Persian invasion would have been quite different.

All the Greeks suffered from the difficulty of getting accurate information about the Persian forces. Herodotos explains Thessalian medizing by the decision of Greek forces not to take a stand in the vale of Tempe after the Greeks get news from Alexander of Macedon about the size of the Persian army and realize the strategic weakness of their position in Tempe (Hdt. 7.172–4). The initial Greek move seems indeed to have been to fall back before the Persian advance, looking for a strong position from which to resist.

Herodotos has a similar story of the Greek fleet, when it realized the size of the navy that the Persians had gathered, wanting to fall back too, and only being prevented by Themistokles' bribing the Spartan commander Eurybiades, using a small part of a much larger bribe that he had been given by the Euboians, who were anxious not to be left exposed (Hdt. 8.4–5). That story, which also features Corinthian resistance, overcome by more bribery, is part of a larger story element that is about who was formally and who was really in charge of the Greek navy, and about the gracious way in which the Athenians conceded leadership despite providing by far the largest naval contingent. Many features of the story betray modification in the interest of Athens. When a storm at sea wrecked a large part of the Persian fleet off the coast of Thessaly, the Athenians proceeded to claim that they had successfully prayed for the help of the north wind, Boreas. When the Greeks set three ships to watch for the advance of the Persian fleet, it is only the crew of the Athenian ship who escape capture (Hdt. 7.179–82). Xerxes offers special rewards for the capture of Athenian ships (Hdt. 8.10). The Greek fleet in a minor action had managed to capture some stragglers from the Persian fleet (Hdt. 7.188–96), but in the first major naval encounter of Artemision it was an Athenian who was the first to capture an enemy ship and win the prize for valor (Hdt. 8.11). In the second full-scale clash, though the result is indecisive, it is once more an Athenian who performs best (Hdt. 8.15–17). We cannot know the truth of any of these details.

The Greek army found the strong position it wanted in the pass at Thermopylai, where the narrow defile meant that a smaller Greek force had a chance of resisting the larger Persian army—until the Persians found a way around the pass. The Greek defeat at Thermopylai (August 480) made naval withdrawal from Artemision unavoidable. In the event, the Greek fleet withdrew all the way to Salamis, where it helped with the evacuation of Attica, ferrying Athenians to Salamis, to Aegina, and to Troizen, where a further fleet had been gathered. The Persian army proceeded to invade Attica and sack Athens, as richly attested in the archaeological record (Shear Jr. 1994; Camp II 2022).

Herodotos tells us that Athens contributed 180 out of a total of 378 ships to the Greek fleet (Hdt. 8.43–8), and that the Athenians, and in particular Themistokles, showed the most acute understanding of the strategic issues and took a crucial role in securing—in the end, so the claim goes, not without some trickery—that the Greek fleet took a stand at Salamis (Hdt. 8.49, 56–63, 75–6, 79–83). When battle was joined, in September of 480, Herodotos again records various Athenian claims to primacy (the first ship to ram) but admits rival Aeginetan claims and allows the Aeginetans praise for the greatest courage (with the Athenians second), although Aristeides is also picked out for special mention (Hdt. 8.84, 93, 95). Herodotos also has an Athenian version that claims that the Corinthians attempted to run from the battle altogether, but he acknowledges that this version was contradicted by the Corinthians, and the Corinthians in fact saw to the erection on Salamis of a monument commemorating their particular contribution (Meiggs and Lewis 1988: #24; Plut. *On the Malice of Herodotos* 39).

There is no reason to doubt that Athenian leadership, ship numbers, and naval skill did play an enormous part in securing a defeat of the Persian fleet that was sufficiently decisive to end effectively the naval part of the campaign. But the account is best evidence not for the details of what happened but for the importance of these events as the basis on which the Athenians claimed leadership in the years following. The naval battles of the Persian wars are properly seen not as terminal to Persian ambitions to take control of the Aegean but as setting up future Athenian control there. The whole story offers a fascinating episode in oral history, not least in the way that Themistokles acquires a role that celebrates him both as the man whose ingenuity (and willingness to use deceit) secured the crucial strategic moves, and as the man whose interests in his own future, regardless of long-term political events, led him to squander opportunities and made his own eventual repudiation by the Athenians inevitable (Hdt. 8.109–12). Once more, as with Miltiades in 490, Themistokles' abusive actions include turning on Athens' Cycladic neighbors, in this case Andros, Paros, and Karystos (Hdt. 8.111–12). We may suspect that Themistokles has here at least in part been used to cover up an abuse of power for which the Athenians more generally were responsible.

The battle at Salamis was enough to secure the return of the Persian king Xerxes himself to Susa, but it did not end Persian presence in Greece. The Persian infantry retreated from Attica to Thessaly, but there regrouped (Hdt. 8.133). Herodotos has a story of the Persian commander Mardonios—in the interval between the battles at Salamis and Plataia—using Alexander of Macedon as a messenger to the Athenians to try to persuade them to make peace on favorable terms, of Sparta sending a counter-embassy, and of the Athenians declaring their commitment to freedom and to the Greeks as a people united by blood, language, and gods.[17] This claim is juxtaposed to Theban advice to Mardonios that he should simply bribe selected individuals so as to break up the anti-Persian coalition (Hdt. 9.2), and to the story that, when Mardonios occupied Athens for a second time and sent another messenger to the Athenians on Salamis, an Athenian who advised that it might be sensible to agree to the Persian proposal was stoned to death (9.4–5). As recorded, this all looks like an elaborate rehearsal of Athenian virtues (with a particularly stark contrast drawn between Spartan concerns that the Athenians might succumb to Persian blandishments and Sparta's failure to come to Athenian aid in time to stop their having to evacuate their homeland for the second time [Hdt. 9.6]), but that there were diplomatic initiatives, and fears of diplomatic initiatives and of bribery, from the Persians is not in itself incredible.

When in the summer of 479 Peloponnesian troops began assembling en masse, Mardonios transferred his forces from Attica into Boiotia, presumably in part to avoid getting trapped in Attica and in part to have the largest possible plain available for fighting in. Herodotos records a debate among the Greek army, mustered at Plataia and camped near the Persian army, that was occasioned by a claim by the Tegeans to take the left wing of the army, the second most responsible position after the right wing, taken by the Spartans themselves. The Athenians are awarded the left wing of the army by acclamation (Hdt. 9.26–8). In the battle the Spartans and Tegeans, ostensibly as the result of dissension among the Spartan troops about the Greek army's plan to shift positions, find themselves opposing, and after some hard fighting, defeating the Persian soldiers and driving them from the field. The Athenians find themselves facing the Greek allies of the Persians. Herodotos' story is that most of those allies fought in a cowardly way, but not the Thebans, 300 of whom were killed (the Boiotian cavalry also play an important part in protecting the Persian flight and inflicting massive casualties on the Megarians and Phleiasians) (Hdt. 9.67–9). When the fleeing Persians take refuge in the wooden fort that they have constructed, it is the arrival and courage of the Athenians that lead to the tearing down of the defenses (Hdt. 9.70). Herodotos judges the Spartans to have been the most distinguished in the actual fighting, although the Athenians and Tegeans fought bravely, but it is the Athenian Sophanes who gets the longest write-up of all those singled out for personal valor (Hdt. 9.71–5).[18] Herodotos does not record it, but later authors claim that the Athenian casualties in the battle numbered

---

17. For a discussion of Herodotos' treatment of Alexander of Macedon, see Badian 1994.

18. For an argument that Herodotos performed his account of Plataia at Athens, see Oliver 2017: 40–86. (I owe this reference to Paul Christesen.)

just 52, all of them from the tribe Aiantis (Plut. *Arist.* 19.6, quoting Kleidemos *FGrH* 323 F22).

Already, early in 479, the Greeks had been persuaded by the Ionians to send their fleet, under the command of the Spartan king Leotychidas, across the Aegean—initially to Delos but then on to Samos (Hdt. 8.130–2, 9.90–6). Supposedly on the very same day as the Battle of Plataia, they engaged the Persians at Mycale. Herodotos' account gives the Athenians a key role. It is the Athenian half of the army that engages the Persians first, and more or less defeats the Persians before the Spartans arrive to clean up (Hdt. 9.102–3). It is the Athenians who are said to have proved the best in the battle, with two Athenians particularly singled out (Hdt. 9.105). Immediately, a crucial discussion follows between the Greek army and the Ionian Greeks, who have again revolted against the Persians. Whereas the Peloponnesians want to transfer the Ionian population to mainland Greece, giving them the land of those who had medized, the Athenians determine to continue fighting for and in Ionia and win the debate. All the Greeks sail for the Hellespont, but, when the Peloponnesians decide to sail home from there, the Athenian commander, Xanthippos, and the Athenian contingent in the fleet carry on the fighting. In terms of Athenian interests in the area (Sigeion, the Thracian Chersonese) this was an entirely predictable decision in line with long-standing Athenian policy. But in the new context of an Ionia with a serious chance of gaining freedom from Persia, this gesture looked different. This became the crucial turning point, setting in train a sequence of events that led directly to the founding of the Delian League and to the Athenian Empire (Hdt. 9.106–7, 114–21).

It is not surprising that the story that Herodotos tells is the story that serves to explain the situation that prevailed in his own day. However partial his account, with its repeated emphasis on Athenian priority, that was the account that was required to explain the imposition of Athenian control over the Greek world, and indeed the splitting of Greek cities between those sympathetic to Sparta and those sympathetic to Athens that is so marked a feature in Thucydides' account of the Greek world in 432. As to the details of what did happen in the Persian Wars, we have no way of telling—except that there must be limits to how far from the truth Herodotos' account can be, given the results that followed.[19] In the end what is at issue is not the particular actions of individuals or the degree of trickery that a Themistokles or cruelty that a Xanthippos (Hdt. 9.120.4) displayed, it is the determination of the Athenians to resist Persia, emphasized by Herodotos

---

19. For comparison of Herodotos with Diodoros, and stress on the way in which Diodoros' account is structured by moralizing exempla see de Bakker 2019; Van Wees 2019.

(most explicitly at 7.139), and their willingness to resume and expand their earlier involvement in the northeastern Aegean.[20]

7.2 Military Organization and Military Conflicts

We do not have the material with which to explore in detail any of the military conflicts in which Athens was involved down to the Persian Wars. We have no fine-grained knowledge of either the army or the navy, and we cannot even begin to reconstruct the course of specific military conflicts.

There can be no doubt that Athens had an organized army and navy already in the seventh, if not in fact the eighth, century, despite a persistent tradition in scholarship denying that Athens had a formally organized army until Kleisthenes.[21] Armed soldiers are represented on a great many Late Geometric pots made in Athens, and the familiarity of Athenians with warfare, whether from stories or from experience, is clear (see Section 4.5.2). What is more, the ability of the Athenians in the later seventh century to arrest and execute a group of 79 young men, as revealed in the Phaleron cemetery (see Section 4.4.3), must have depended on the ability to muster and deploy an armed force. Whereas expeditions against Salamis or Sigeion might be based on a fighting force recruited specially and solely for the purpose, only a pre-existing force can be summoned to face a sudden threat to state security.

Any sort of armed warfare demands considerable organization, since it requires that men have military equipment, that they know how to use that equipment, that they have some shared understanding of what the immediate short-term tactical and long-term strategic goals are, and that there is provision to supply them with food and drink, while they live, and to remove and bury their bodies, if they die. As soon as a community plans for its self-defense it needs to be able to deliver all this. Equally, communities that choose not to defend themselves, but to pay others to defend them, need to be able to raise the required funds.

As we have seen, organization of Attica into naukraries dates to before Solon (see Section 5.2.1). Shadowy though the naukrary is, there is no doubt that one of the things that naukraries did was raise money, and, according to Pollux 8.108, each of the 48 naukraries provided two horses and one ship (i.e., a total

---

20. Herodotos' attitude to the Athenians has been variously discussed, see especially Moles 2002.

21. For what follows, see especially van Wees 2013. The claim that the Athenians had no army is most clearly expressed by Frost 1984, that it had no navy by Gabrielsen 1985; Haas 1985; Gabrielsen 1994: 19–24.

of 96 horses and 48 ships). We have evidence of naukraric funds being used to pay the expenses of envoys to Delphi (probably from a Solonian law), and this further strengthens the argument that already before Solon naukraries were paying the costs of communal military undertakings (Androtion *FGrH* 324 F36). The role given by Herodotos (5.71.2) to the "*prytanies of the naukraroi*" in the Kylonian affair further confirms the central involvement of naukraries in military organization.

Nothing tells us the size of army that Athens could deploy in the sixth century, but, if we take the provision of one ship (presumably a pentekonter) per naukrary seriously, then a body that could provide (and man) one ship could presumably be reckoned to put at least 50 infantry into the field. An Athenian army of between 2,500 and 5,000 men organized in four tribal units and 48 sub-units is likely to be what we should be envisaging. The possibility of raising an army of that size and a fleet of 50 ships explains the way in which the Athenians throughout the sixth century find no apparent problem in launching major military campaigns that depended on ship-borne transport of troops, whether in the context of their action on Salamis, their establishment of a settlement at Sigeion, or their intervention first in the Thracian Chersonese and then on Lemnos and Imbros. Our meager sources are not interested in the logistics behind these campaigns, but this absence of evidence cannot be taken as evidence of absence.

Even when we are supplied with rather more detail by our ancient sources for the reforms of Kleisthenes, the nature of Athenian army and navy organization remains obscure. By the fourth century there were not only 10 generals, but also two elected hipparchs for the cavalry, 10 elected phylarchs commanding tribal cavalry units, and 10 elected taxiarchs in charge of tribal infantry ([Arist.] *Constitution of the Athenians* 49.2, 61.4–5). Under the taxiarchs, and appointed by them, were *lochagoi* and possibly *trittyarchoi*.[22] How far back this arrangement dates is unclear (neither taxiarchs nor phylarchs appear until the casualty lists of the latter part of the Peloponnesian War). Similarly, although we know that by the late fifth century Athens had a system which ascribed responsibility for individual triremes to trierarchs, we know neither when trierarchs were first selected nor whether initially trierarchs had financial responsibility for a trireme, as they did in the fourth century, or were merely trireme commanders (Gabrielsen 1994: 26–39).

Our ignorance also extends to recruitment and training. In the late fifth century, the tribal officers drew up a list—the so-called hoplite *katalogos*, naming

---

22. The best brief description of Athenian army organization is found in Gomme, Andrewes, and Dover 1945–1981: vol. 1: 22–4 as part of a discussion of what Thucydides assumes and never explains.

who was to fight, taking into account both ability and past service (Thuc. 6.31.3, Lys. 9.15). Presumably a similar process of selection was employed from the very beginning of democracy, except in cases when there was a universal levy, at which point everyone able to serve up to the age of 59 was expected to turn out (Thuc. 2.31). Although neither the deme nor the trittys formed a military unit as such, we know that men from the same deme served together (Whitehead 1986, 224–6, citing Lys. 16.14, 20.23; Isae. 2.42; Theophr. *Char.* 25.3). The naukrary was not a community in the way that the deme was, but it would seem to have been the only sub-*polis* institution that could have served the same sort of purpose in the Archaic period, and we should expect its officers to have had some role in military levies.

Issues of training impinge upon our source material even less. The line that Thucydides has Perikles adopt in the Funeral Oration (2.39), that the Athenians by their courage can match the Spartans without needing to train, may have been good for boosting morale among infantry who were repeatedly belittled (cf. [Xen.] *Constitution of the Athenians* 2.1), often by contrast to their naval counterparts, but it can have had little truth. Hoplite warfare demanded training, and although the nature of the training given in Athens prior to the reorganization of the *ephebeia* in the 330s is obscure, some form of training, albeit unsystematic, of young men when they first became of an age to fight, will have gone back to the Archaic period, perhaps accompanied by some form of ephebic oath.[23]

Training was equally important for ship's crews. We do not know what proportion of Athenians would acquire some experience at sea during the Archaic period, but the advent of the trireme guaranteed that no one in the ordinary course of moving themselves or goods around the Mediterranean acquired experience in a ship of that kind. Xenophon provides a long description of how the fourth-century general Iphikrates turned a voyage around the Peloponnese to Corcyra into a training session (Xen. *Hell.* 6.2.27–30, 32). Athenians came, indeed, to pride themselves on their skill with triremes, but that demanded constant training of new recruits. No doubt this was achieved in part through mixing new recruits with those with long experience, but the very mixed composition of some Athenian triremes, drawing on sailors from various places and also drawing on slaves (Osborne and Rhodes 2017: #190), suggests that explicit training exercises will often have been necessary. The trireme races that we know to have been part of at least one festival will have contributed to this training (Lys. 21.5).

---

23. On the need for training, see Crowley 2012: 22–6; Konijnendijk 2018. On the archaism of the ephebic oath (Rhodes and Osborne 2003: #88), see Siewert 1977.

But perhaps the most important area of military organization is the financial. The financial responsibilities of the naukraries more generally show that Athens had early devised a mechanism for dealing with the considerable expenses of military engagement. Exactly what form those expenses took is less clear. We have epigraphic evidence that Eretria was paying its sailors by the last quarter of the sixth century, and any naval campaign that kept sailors away from home for any substantial period must, at the least, have required funds for feeding those sailors.[24] Greeks were selling their services as soldiers as early as we have records, and modern prejudices against mercenaries should not obscure the role that military pay played in forming Archaic armies: any army that sought to maximize the quality of its troops would need to make service financially viable for the physically strong but financially weak. Rather than seeing the evidence for Peisistratos and his sons using paid non-Athenian troops as evidence for their disbanding any Athenian army, we should see paid troops as a necessary supplement to a citizen militia, a way of acquiring troops who could perform specialist services, or serve in conditions (i.e., over a long period) in which citizen militias could not (van Wees 2013: 69–75). Although stories of Peisistratos and his sons disarming the Athenians appear in the *Constitution of the Athenians* (15.3–5) and Thucydides (6.58), except as merely fleeting measures they cannot be squared with the evident availability of Athenian troops when needed (including to resist Kleomenes).[25]

The development of naval warfare, and in particular the replacement of the pentekonter by the trireme (more or less trebling the manpower demand for the same number of ships, as is seen when Polykrates replaces a fleet of 100 pentekonters with one of 40 triremes, Hdt. 3.39–44), had a significant impact on military expense. Triremes had such superior qualities, above all of speed, that once one city deployed them then any city with pretensions to naval self-defense had to go over to using them.[26] What is more, the ability of Persia to put fleets of 200 triremes into commission (cf. Hdt. 5.33.2) meant that trireme fleets had to be large. It is in this context that Themistokles' naval law (see Section 7.1.2), arranging for the direct application of silver from Laurion to naval expenditure, has so transformative an effect. Athens could not only make the change from pentekonters to triremes, but it could also equip itself with a significant fleet of

24. For Eretria, see *IG* XII.9.1273–4, with van Wees 2013: 26–7 and Fachard and Verdan 2023: sec. 6.

25. *Contra* van Wees 2013: 72 it seems to me incredible that one should take *only* Thessalian cavalry to have been available to Hippias to resist the initial Spartan invasion.

26. On the evolution of the trireme and some of its consequences, see Morrison, Coates, and Rankov 2000 and Figueira 2015a; see also J. K. Davies 2013: 49–53.

triremes, all without markedly increasing the burden on individuals. That they could not do the same, along with the difficulties of acquiring the skilled labor required to build triremes, lay at the root of Athens' allies' decisions after 479 to contribute to the Delian League in money rather than ships.

As to the tactics employed by Athenian sailors and soldiers, we cannot begin to give an account until the Persian wars. As regards the battles of Marathon, Salamis, and Plataia, it is tempting to think that the very length of Herodotos' accounts means that we can trace how the battles were fought in detail. Far from it. The problem is not that Herodotos is unreliable, or a poor military historian. Rather the problem is that Greek battles were such that no one, during the battle, had any good idea of what was happening overall—all they knew was about their own actions and what was done to them. No doubt some battles were simple— one side broke through the line of the enemy and forced them into retreat. But as soon as some success was found on both sides, the complexities of what happened, together with the interest of all parties in playing down their own failures and playing up their successes, meant that recovering a bird's eye view of the battle was impossible. And in the case of the Persian wars, the very fact that the enemy were Persian further militated against getting enough accounts of what had happened to overcome the deficiencies of any single account. Add to that the fact that both Marathon, where the Persians had the sea to their rear, and Salamis, fought within very confined waters, were far from typical of land or sea-battles, and the possibilities of learning anything from attempting to reconstruct the battles on the evidence that we have in Herodotos are essentially nil.[27]

7.3   *Colonies*

Athens laid claim to have been a great colonizer, but at a point far back in history. Taking advantage of the common dialect used by Greeks on the east coast of the Aegean and in the Aegean islands and themselves, the Athenians claimed that they were the mother city of the cities of Ionia. There is no doubt that Athens and the cities of the eastern Aegean had much in common, both in terms of shared elements of material culture at the end of the Bronze Age and in the Early Iron Age and in terms of common Ionian institutions (notably the four Ionian tribes and the festival of the Apatouria). The amount of movement across the Aegean throughout the period from the twelfth to the eighth century should not be underestimated. But equally the political need, in the sixth through fourth centuries in particular, to tell stories that established links has to be stressed. It is no

---

27. The classic discussion, delivered in 1920 but published only in 1964, is Whatley 1964.

accident that the city of Miletos told a whole range of stories of its foundation—that it was founded by Cretans led by Sarpedon, Athenians led by Neileus, or established by an autochthonous, or alternatively a Cretan, man named Miletos. Nor is it by chance that as the Spartans and the cities of the Peloponnese came to identify themselves as founded by the children of Herakles returning home so cities outside the Peloponnese came to identify themselves with populations displaced by the returning Heraklids. There is no reason to think that in any strong sense the cities of the eastern Aegean were Athenian foundations.[28]

Within the Archaic period, when so many other cities were participating in one fashion or another in the foundation of settlements outside the Greek mainland, in Italy, Sicily, North Africa, the Black Sea, and beyond, Athens seems to have mostly sat on the sidelines. The settlements established by Athens were not opportunistic settlements in parts of the world as yet unfamiliar to Greeks, but settlements established by military actions against other Greeks, in the case of Sigeion and then of Salamis and Chalkis, or settlements established by invitation of existing residents, in the case of the Thracian Chersonese (at least if we accept the story told).[29] As we have seen (Section 7.1), in the cases of both Sigeion and the Thracian Chersonese the settlements became strongly attached to a single Athenian family, while at the same time serving general Athenian interests (and in the case of the Thracian Chersonese forming the launching point for further Athenian settlement on Lemnos and Imbros).[30]

How are we to explain this pattern?[31] Athenian activity clearly focuses in two areas, locally, and around the entrance to the Hellespont. Locally, possession of Salamis was clearly essential for Athenian security. If an independent Aegina was the "eyesore of the Peiraieus," as Perikles is supposed to have called it (Plut. *Per.* 8.5), an independent Salamis would have been much more so. Athenian hostility to, and later replacement of the population of, Aegina fits into the same pattern. But such regional consolidation will not really explain Chalkis. Euboia was indeed not far distant, but the sole part of Attica with which the Euboians seem to have had any history of close interaction and rivalry was the territory of Oropos, which was only intermittently part of the Athenian state. That said, it is worth

---

28. For further discussion, see Osborne 2009: 47–51; Mac Sweeney 2013; Mac Sweeney 2015: 3–7.

29. Here as elsewhere I ignore the possible evidence in Ps-Skymnos that Elaious was also an Athenian foundation. See Igelbrink 2015: 111–13.

30. Figueira 1991: 136 n.13: "the personality of powerful individuals is a modality through which the *polis* may implement a grand policy."

31. For discussion of the pattern, see Figueira 1991: 131–60.

noting that Thucydides claims that the loss of Euboia was a major problem for Athens in the Peloponnesian War, since, once the Spartans occupied Dekeleia, it was more use to them than Attica (Thuc. 8.96.2, cf. 95.1, 7.28.1, 2.14.1); all of this was because of central Euboia's agricultural wealth and natural resources.

Sigeion, the Thracian Chersonese and, at the end of the Archaic period, Lemnos and Imbros were rather differently motivated. Their relationship to the Hellespont is what is crucial, and had Athens had no interest in what was coming from the Black Sea it is hard to think that she would have put emphasis there. What is surprising, however, is the early date at which Athens becomes interested in the area. There is no way in which Athens was regularly consuming more grain than it could produce before 600;[32] the Athenian economic crisis at the end of the seventh century was about land distribution, not about absolute land shortage (see Sections 5.2.2 and 8.1). But Attica most securely produced barley; Athenians came to prefer to eat the bread wheat of which the Black Sea was a major source. That Athens found itself in conflict with Mytilene over Sigeion, and then with Lampsakos over the Thracian Chersonese, strongly suggests that in both places the central interest was ensuring that other Greeks were not in a position to determine control. The control of the two settlements by family dynasties further shows the degree to which these were independent settlements and not merely agents of Athens. Seizing Lemnos and Imbros was similarly unlikely to be about their own agricultural capacity, although in the case of Lemnos, at least, this was considerable, but about removing a potential base from which Athenian interests in the area might be disrupted.

Consolidation of local interests is common enough across the Archaic Greek world, although not all cities were in a position to achieve their aims in this respect. But Athens' settlements in the northeastern Aegean are exceptional. The closest parallel for the strong ties with a group of settlements in the same region like this, and with direct rule in the way that Sigeion and the Thracian Chersonese were ruled, is to be found in Corinth's interests in northwest Greece and the Ionian sea and her interest in controlling Corcyra (on which, see Gehrke and Sapirstein 2023: sec. 7; C. A. Morgan 2021: sec. 7).

---

32. This is accepted even by Moreno 2007: 312–3. Garnsey argued that Athens did not need imported grain before the middle of the fifth century (Garnsey 1988: 107–19).

8

Economic History

8.1 Agriculture and Animal Husbandry

Ancient sources are divided about the qualities of the Attic landscape as far as agricultural productivity is concerned. Thucydides (1.2.5) makes the thin soil of Attica the reason why it enjoyed a history free from civil strife: rich soils, he claims, lead to inequalities between rich and poor, and therefore it led to political strife and encouraged invasion. Attica had, in Thucydides' view, been free from strife and invasion because its soil was poor. The picture of Attica as denuded of soil is further promoted by the claims in Plato's *Critias* (110e–111e) that many years of downpours had washed away the soils from Attica's mountains, leaving them sticking out like bones in a sick body. By contrast, Xenophon (*Vect.* 1.3) praises the fertility of Attica, claiming that many crops that would not even sprout in other places bear fruit in Attica because of the gentle climate. The truth is that the diversity of its landscape means that Attica is rich in different ecological niches, and that although some areas do suffer thin soil, other areas have quite fertile soils. Traces of terracing on hill slopes that have not been exploited for arable agriculture since antiquity indicate that even poor soils were turned to agricultural use in the Classical period.[1]

What puts most pressure on agriculture in Attica today and most probably in antiquity, given the likely similarity in climate (see Section 3.2), is interannual variability in the timing and amount of rainfall. Although on average Attica receives enough rain suitably distributed across the autumn, winter, and spring to sustain cereals, there are significant annual, seasonal, and regional variations. What matters most is seasonal shortfall; insufficient rain during the

---

1. For ancient terracing in areas long abandoned by farming, see Bradford 1956; Bradford 1957; Lohmann 1993. For problems of dating terracing, see Price and Nixon 2005; Foxhall 2007: 61–9.

The Oxford History of the Archaic Greek World. Robin Osborne, Oxford University Press. © Oxford University Press 2023. DOI: 10.1093/oso/9780197644423.003.0008

growing season is not uncommon, causing crop reduction in something like one year in seven. There is, in addition, spatial variation in that some parts of Attica can suffer severe drought when other parts receive sufficient rain. Data about the twentieth-century climate in Attica suggest that extensive cultivation of legumes in Attica is highly risky (rainfall being sufficient only about half the time), wheat yield is likely to be reduced by insufficient rain once or twice a decade, and barley yield is likely to be endangered perhaps once in 20 years on average (Osborne 1987: 31–4). The cereal harvest in Attica is regularly the earliest in Greece.

Although Classical sources make occasional reference to the landscape, and rather more reference to agriculture, their descriptions are not such as to allow us to form any clear idea of the extent of agricultural exploitation or the relative distribution of cereals, olives, and vines in Attica. The fame of Attic honey, specifically that from Hymettos, and the fact that the placing of beehives is already at issue in Solon's laws (Solon *Laws* F62 Leão and Rhodes), reflect the exploitation of the garrigue at the borders of agricultural land (Pl. *Crit.* 111c), and are a reminder that the productive landscape was significantly larger than the area given over to arable farming.[2] Since the first identification of ceramic beehives at the Vari house, numerous such beehive fragments have been found all over Attica (J. E. Jones, Graham, and Sackett 1973: 397–414; Crane and Graham 1985; Osborne 1985: 193). The marginal landscape was exploited also by hunters and was the testing ground for manly valor (cf. Section 10, and, on the dedications at the Sanctuary of Zeus on Parnes, Section 11.1).

Modern scholars agree neither about the proportion of Attica in agricultural use in the Classical period nor about the agricultural productivity rates that could be achieved in antiquity.[3] For the Archaic period it is even harder to estimate either of these. It is very likely that, as the population grew, the proportion of Attica exploited agriculturally expanded. That is implied both by the archaeological record of settlement patterns (see Section 4.1.2) and by the reconstruction of what happened under Solon (see Section 5.2.2). It is also likely that agricultural productivity increased, if for no other reason than that increasing population pressure is likely to have increased the number of person-hours per unit area, and therefore to have led to something of a shift to more intensive agriculture.

---

2. Maquis and garrigue are similar kinds of vegetation, but the former is denser, with more closely spaced shrubs.

3. Optimistic views are to be found in Garnsey 1985; Garnsey 1988: 89–106; Osborne 1987: 27–52; Garnsey 1992; Osborne 1992; Osborne Forthcoming. For pessimistic views, see Sallares 1991; Stroud 1998; Moreno 2007. The case against optimism depends, in my view, too much on extrapolation from very different agricultural practices.

In economic terms, the consequences of these changes will have been a marked increase in the aggregate agricultural output of Attica and an increase, but less marked, in the agricultural output per unit area farmed, but perhaps no change or little change in the output per person.

But did the nature of the agricultural economy change? There is, as outlined in Section 5.2.2, reason to believe that Solon altered the distribution of land ownership. The Solonian reforms had no necessary consequences for the nature of the agricultural economy, but some change is made plausible by the Solonian law limiting export of agricultural produce to olive oil (Solon *Laws* F65 Leão and Rhodes [= Plut, *Sol.* 24.1])—the genuineness of which is argued for by the precise *axōn* reference given. The background to this law may well lie with those who, before the Solonian reforms, controlled large tracts of land and chose to sell barley abroad in order to buy wheat, and, in consequence, left part of the Athenian population short of the staples on which to live.[4] Given the financial demands made of the rich, banning export of produce other than olive oil might be expected to have brought a move to increase production and export of olive oil, rather than simply a change in the consumers to whom grain was sold.

Athenian olive oil exports can, to at least some extent, be traced on the basis of a particular type of pottery—the so-called SOS amphora. Named "SOS" after its distinctive neck decoration consisting of two concentric circles flanked by two pairs of parallel zigzags with at least five bars, this is an ovoid neck-handled vessel used to transport oil, which was made in very similar form in both Athens and Euboia. The amphora varies in height from 0.58 to 0.75 m, and in diameter from 0.43 to 0.49 m, and therefore varies in volume, but approximates to 1 Attic *metretēs*. The form may have been influenced by earlier North Aegean amphora types, but the earliest Athenian SOS amphoras date to the middle of the eighth century, and the latest to the first half of the sixth century. They are found from Essaouira (Mogador) on the Atlantic coast of Morocco and Huelva on the Atlantic coast of Spain to Beirut and Tell Defenneh on the eastern shores of the Mediterranean and Taganrog and Gorgippia in the Black Sea. The highest concentrations are in Sicily, where Megara Hyblaia has produced 159 imported Athenian SOS amphoras down to 580, with only seven amphoras from other places during the same period (most of those were imported during the second half of the seventh century). There is some reason to suspect that many of the earliest SOS amphoras may have been transported by Phoenicians—they seem to

---

4. For claims that the political crisis of c. 600 was a result of the population of Attica exceeding its carrying capacity, see Moreno 2007: 312–13.

travel not with Athenian fine pottery but with Phoenician "torpedo" amphoras and Corinthian aryballoi (Johnston and Jones 1978; Pratt 2015).

The chronology of this distribution is not sufficiently precise to indicate whether levels of oil production in Attica were affected by Solon's law. However, after around 580 we cease to find SOS amphoras, with the exception of a small number in later sixth-century contexts in the Troad, and from that point on there is no distinctive Attic transport amphora form. There is some evidence that Attic oil ceased to be exported except in the form of prize amphoras for victors at the Panathenaia (on which see Section 11.3) (scholion on Pind. *Nem.* 10.35–6; Bresson 2016: 403–5).

8.2 Natural Resources

There can be no doubt that the non-agricultural economy of Attica grew over the course of the Archaic period but establishing the extent or rate of that growth is difficult. Classical Athens was economically significantly dependent upon the products of the Athenian silver mines in the very southern part of the peninsula of Attica at Laurion. Here silver is trapped in a geological sandwich between layers of schist and of marble. Some of the silver could be mined by direct access from the hillsides, but gaining access to the richer ores demanded tunneling, and so more or less extensive infrastructure (Conophagos 1980: 155–212; Rosenthal, Morin, Herbach et al. 2013). The earliest evidence for exploitation of the silver (and lead) dates to the Early Bronze Age. There are signs of some exploitation in the ninth century with evidence of metalworking from Thorikos, which was one of the great mining centers. Ingots and scraps of Laurion silver have been found in seventh- and sixth-century contexts as far east as Israel and as far west as Sicily. The earliest Athenian coinage (so-called *Wappenmünzen*, see Section 8.4), which dates to the third quarter of the sixth century, includes silver that had not been mined at Laurion (the silver in question probably came from Macedonia), but later *Wappenmünzen*, and the Owl coinage introduced in the last quarter of that century, are of Laurion silver.

But if there was significant silver production from Laurion already before 500, production seems to have further increased in the early fifth century. The ancient sources (see Section 7.1.2) talk of a major silver strike in the early fifth century, used to fund 100 or 200 triremes, and this strike has been associated with the discovery of a new, rich layer of silver (the so-called "third contact" between marble and schist) (Picard 2001). There is little doubt that the scale of income coming to Athens from the silver mines increased very markedly at the end of the Archaic period. We have no knowledge of how the silver mines were run in the sixth century, and indeed little knowledge of how they were run in the fifth, but the default assumption must be that the workforce consisted primarily of slaves.

Some private individuals may have been significantly enriched by their mining activities already in the sixth century.[5]

8.3 Craft Production and Trade

Did any other craft activity make a significant contribution to the Athenian economy? The most promising candidate is production of pottery, both because of the quantity of pottery produced and because of dedications on the Athenian Acropolis of substantial statues by men certainly or probably identifying themselves as potters (Nearchos, Andocides, Mnesiades, Euphronios, Peikon, and Onesimos) in the half-century before 480 (Laurens 1995: 168–70, Keesling 2003: 50–9, 69–74; Franssen 2011: 205–42).[6] Estimates for the number of potters and painters working at any one time in Athens have been getting smaller, as it appears that Beazley may have identified too many, rather than too few, painters' hands. The total workforce in the Kerameikos at any point in the sixth century may have been no more than 100, 0.5 percent of the free adult population (but some may not have been free adults) (Sapirstein 2014: 184).

Two things emerge from the size of the workforce making pottery. One is that, although the number of dedications by potters is not large, it is notably large by comparison to that by members of any other profession. (Raubitschek and Jeffery 1949: 465 lists only two fullers, one tanner, one architect, one shipbuilder, one scribe, and one washerwoman.). The second is that other craft activities that we know little about may have employed similar numbers. The largest known Classical Athenian workshop, employing possibly as many as 120 slaves to make shields (Lys. 12.19), may have been swollen by the demands of a long war, but the workshops inherited by Demosthenes, with 20 slaves making furniture and more than 30 making knives (Dem. 27.9), and one owned by Timarchos, with nine slaves and their overseer making shoes (Aeschin. 1.97), may not have been unusual in size, and one should imagine a number of such workshops existing back into the Archaic period.

How many such workshops we imagine in the Archaic period, and from what date the numbers of such workshops in Athens had been significant, depends on what we take the structure of the economy to have been. Here again

---

5. On the operation of the Laurion mines, with a particular focus on Thorikos, see the articles collected in Morin 2020.

6. Raubitschek and Jeffery 1949: 465 reaches a total of 29 potter/painter dedications, but only by dint of treating all dedicants who have names known to be painters' names as potters/painters and all dedications that mention *erga* as dedications made by potters/painters. See also Sections 4.5.4 and 11.4.

the best evidence we have is pottery. Pottery has two advantages: the first being that it survives, and the second that fine pottery can be dated to within a quarter of a century and often traced back to a particular workshop. We can show from the distribution of pottery that Athens was in direct or indirect contact with markets all over the Mediterranean, and from different period-specific distribution maps that the number of markets with which Athens was in contact grew over time (cf. Section 8.1 on SOS amphoras). By looking closely at exactly what neighboring markets received we can further show that we are not always, and probably not generally, dealing with "down the line" trade, but with direct links from Athens to particular markets (Lynch and Matter 2014). But we can also show that markets were discriminating. Particular markets took goods from one pottery workshop rather than another, and in some cases they took only certain shapes of pottery from particular workshops (see Section 4.5.4 on Nikosthenes' workshop). We can also show that shape is a more important discriminator than iconography—unsurprisingly, perhaps, since shape determines function—and that market discrimination according to workshop is already occurring by c. 600.[7]

The importance of these extrapolations from pottery production, distribution, and consumption lies in what they imply about the scale and nature of exchange. No doubt merchants were always trying to interest customers in items that they had not bought before, but the patterns revealed by pottery strongly suggest that they had excellent knowledge of what *had* been bought before. Such knowledge implies a high frequency of contact, and a concern to minimize wastage. However small a proportion of any cargo pottery may have been, it was important enough for merchants to make sure they were carrying the sorts of pots that they could sell at the places they intended to visit. Merchants earned their mark-up by the specialist knowledge they came to possess, and not simply by taking the significant risks that will always have accompanied ship-borne trade, particularly in an era when no city was powerful enough to rid the sea of pirates, as the Athenians would rid the Aegean of pirates in the fifth century.

For Classical Athens it is clear that both citizens and non-citizens were involved in trade, and that of the non-citizens involved, some were men who had settled at Athens, while others stayed in Attica only long enough to sell or acquire a cargo. For the Archaic Athenian world, we have no good evidence. Non-Greeks feature strongly in exchange in Homer, but that exchange is largely opportunistic

---

7. See Osborne 2001 on Etruscan demand (cf. Reusser 2002; Paleothodoros 2009). See Osborne 1996; Sørensen 2001; Alexandridou 2012a on market discrimination.

and very different from the pattern we can see prevailing from at least 600.[8] The complementary distribution of Phoenician and Greek settlements in the central and western Mediterranean, along with the distinct distribution of seventh-century Phoenician metal vessels, suggests that Greek and Phoenician networks became increasingly separated over the course of the eighth and seventh centuries (Osborne 2009: 158–61). We should therefore probably think of most Athenian goods being carried by Greeks, but certainly not necessarily by Athenians.

Merchants, both Athenian and non-Athenian, engaged in sea-borne commerce had access to excellent harbors in Attica. Although archaeological evidence of ancient harbor facilities is not in every case forthcoming, textual evidence makes clear that in the Archaic period there were well-used ports at Rhamnous, Prasiai/Steiria (modern Porto Raphti), and Thorikos on the east coast of Attica; Sounion on the southern tip of the peninsula; and Phaleron and Eleusis on the east coast. (Eleusis had the advantage of being sheltered by Salamis, but also the disadvantage of insecurity as long as Salamis was not in Athenian hands.) There were also many other places where it was possible to beach a ship, or even, as at Marathon, a fleet.

Down to 490 the main port for the town of Athens was Phaleron (Hdt. 5.81, 85, and explicitly 6.116: "the sea-port of the Athenians at that time," τοῦτο γὰρ ἦν ἐπίνειον τότε τῶν Ἀθηναίων). The *Constitution of the Athenians* (19.2) claims that Hippias, at the very end of his reign, tried to fortify Mounychia, the small harbor on the south side of Peiraieus, whose earlier use is attested by the presence there of the Sanctuary of Artemis Mounychia (D'Onofrio 1995a: 83; Garland 2001: 7–14, 113–14; see Section 11.2). But as we have seen in Section 7.1.2, it seems to have been the insight of Themistokles that led to the development of the great harbor at Peiraieus, in the first place as a safe haven for the massive fleet of triremes that he persuaded the Athenians to build (figure 34). Known from its shape as the Kantharos ("beetle," but also a name given to a particular shape of drinking vessel with high handles), the main Peiraieus harbor lay on the north side of a peninsula, with the Mounychia and Zea harbors to the south. The advantage of the great harbor was not only its size, but also that it was protected at its western end by a small tongue of land known as Eetioneia.[9] The Themistoklean project presumably included port facilities, shipyards, and fortifications, but the destruction

---

8. I have argued elsewhere that a pattern of opportunistic trade will not explain how Greeks could risk settling in such large numbers at Pithekoussai that, by the late eighth century, they required imported foodstuffs; already at that point regular exchange links must have been possible and reliable (Osborne 2009: 110).

9. On Peiraieus in general, see von Eickstedt 1991; Garland 2001. For its geological history, see Goiran, Pavlopoulos, Fouache et al. 2011.

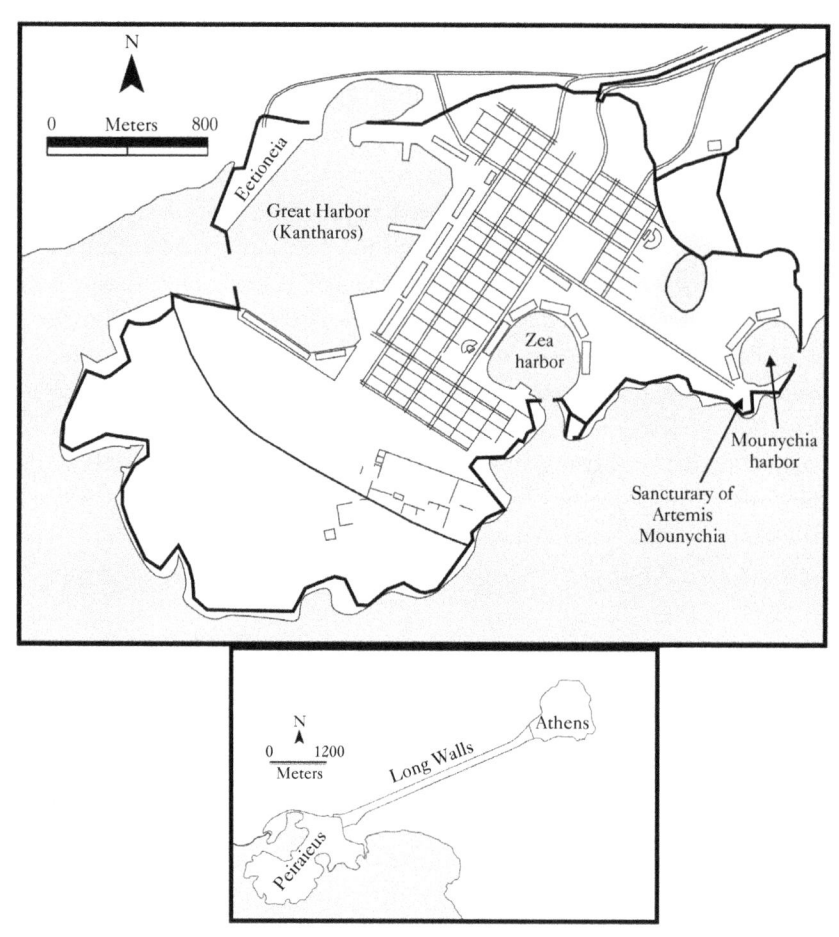

FIGURE 34 Plans of the Peiraieus and the Long Walls. Plan of the Peiraeus based on plan by Tomisti.

wrought by the Persians in 480, and successive rebuilding, have left behind only minimal traces of the Themistoklean Peiraieus (Garland 2001: 163–5).

Whatever settlement, if any, existed at Peiraieus prior to the Themistoklean initiative, it seems to have been sufficiently insignificant that a grid plan could be imposed in the fifth century. That act turned Peiraieus into a place unlike any other in Attica—although the degree to which it was occupied by rows of identical or near-identical houses has perhaps been overdone (Hoepfner and Schwandner 1986: 12–20). Aristotle (*Pol.* 1267b22–1268a14; cf. scholiast to Ar. *Knights* 327) ascribes its planning to Hippodamos of Miletos, but the ancient (and modern) tendency to ascribe any grid-planned city to him makes this questionable.

Peiraieus became not merely Athens' main military and commercial harbor, the linking of which to Athens itself by long walls transformed Athenian military strategy, but also a highly distinctive urban community marked by the more or less transient presence of large number of Greeks from elsewhere and of non-Greeks, and of a distinctively radical group of Athenian residents (von Reden 1995; Roy 1998). Its importance was such that the arrangements for appointing its demarch were handled centrally (although we do not know from what date this arrangement began) and that a separate set of officials came to be appointed to oversee its agora ([Arist.] *Constitution of the Athenians* 50.2, 51.3, 54.8; *IG* II².380, 1176, 1214, 1177, 2498). But, in 480, the commercial importance of Peiraieus remained in the future; even when, in the middle of the fifth century, the Athenians built the Long Walls, linking Athens itself to the sea, the southern wall was built so as to bring Phaleron within the walls—a measure of its continued use for shipping.

8.4 Coinage

The Greek world was a world without coinage until well into the sixth century. Then, from the middle of the century onward, Greek cities rapidly adopted the idea (Osborne 2009: 237–46, with a table of cities and their dates of earliest minting). However, there is good evidence for the use of weighed silver before coinage (Kroll 2008a), and we should probably imagine a wide range of possible pre-coinage exchange arrangements. Coinage made it possible to count, rather than to weigh, and the advent of small change made everyday retail transactions much more straightforward. However, the impact of coinage on trade between cities is hard to judge. Some coinages, notably Aeginetan, seem rapidly to have become widely recognized currencies, others remained essentially local.[10]

The earliest coins in the Greek world were made from electrum, a naturally occurring alloy of gold and silver, and date to the end of the seventh or beginning of the sixth century; the earliest silver coins to the second quarter of the sixth century. Both the earliest electrum and the earliest silver coins seem to have been minted in Lydia, but coinage was then adopted in Greek Asia Minor (Kroll 2012; Melitz 2018). In the area of the Greek mainland, Aegina was the first to mint silver coins, despite having no silver sources of her own, and did so before 550.

Athens followed perhaps a whole generation later, with a series of coins known as *Wappenmünzen* (heraldic coins), of which we know 13 *didrachmē* issues with a variety of devices and then two *didrachmē* and two *tetradrachmon* issues

---

10. For small change, see Kim 2001. For widespread use of Aeginetan coins, see Psoma 2016: 96. For the effect of coinage on structures of thought, see Seaford 2003.

with *gorgoneia* (heads of Medusa, an allusion to the *gorgoneion* on the aegis of Athena), as well as issues of single *drachmai*, *oboloi*, and half *oboloi* (Kroll 1981; Dawson 1999; Flament 2007: 9–23; van Alfen 2012: 89–91; van Wees 2013: 126–8). The initial 13 issues feature an unadorned incuse reverse but different obverse types including an amphora, astragal, bull, bull's head, horse, horse head, horse hindquarters, owl, scarab, and triskeles. Although the different types, which can be compared with the range of shield devices that appear on Athenian painted pottery, have been associated with different families (hence the name *Wappenmünzen*), there is no evidence for this; the coins are clearly a series, not independently produced. Most plausibly, the different types represent different annual issues, and if there is a personal link it is with the magistrate responsible for the issue. The issues are not large (35 dies) (there is also a very small electrum issue, in two denominations, of similar type), and the coins are not often found outside Attica. The silver used for the earliest issues is not primarily from Laurion and includes silver from Macedonia, but the proportion of Laurion silver increases over time (Davis, Gore, Sheedy et al. 2020). What is more surprising is that Laurion silver *is* one of the major sources of silver for Aeginetan coins from the very beginning of minting there (Flament 2011: 76).

The adoption of the unchanging type may indicate a change in the aim of the issues; an unchanging type enables easy, widespread recognition and may indicate that the Athenians began to think of their coinage as something that might travel. What is more, the change is accompanied by the innovative replacement of the incuse square with a reverse type, so as to incorporate an element of change alongside the constant *gorgoneion*. The addition at this time of the larger *tetradrachmon* denomination supports the idea that this coinage might be aimed abroad, and this may correlate with a desire to export Laurion silver.

After a few years of *gorgoneia*, and possibly around or shortly after 520, but perhaps as late as after the expulsion of Hippias,[11] the Athenians decided that even the *gorgoneia* coins were not sufficiently self-referential as Athenian products, and they changed to a coinage with Athena on one side, her owl on the other, and the letters AΘE next to the owl—a design that was then unchanged down to the end of Athenian *tetradrachmon* issues in the first century (Kraay 1956; Flament 2007: 25–443; van Alfen 2012: 91–2; van Wees 2013: 124–6).

---

11. The one relevant, fixed date is the use of an early owl to seal a document at Persepolis in 499 (Root 1988: 8–12). A unique owl has the letters AΘE replaced by the letters HIΠ (Seltman 1924: 76 pl. XXII π), plausibly standing for Hippias, but the circumstances in which this was minted are quite unclear (it might, for example, have been minted by Hippias while in exile in Sigeion).

Athenian owls seem to have been issued in quantity, with 29 dies for the two earliest types of owls, but 183 dies for the next three types. A decline in quality in the two types that appear to date to immediately before or during the Persian Wars offers further evidence for an increase in rate of minting at that point. The large issues would seem to reflect not only the discovery of the rich "third contact" in the Laurion mines, but also the Athenian use of that resource to fund substantial building of triremes (see Section 7.1.2). The presence of early owls in hoards indicates how widely they spread across the Mediterranean, since they feature in hoards from Motya, Gela, Messina, and Taranto in the west, through Chios in the Aegean, to southern Anatolia, Syria, and Egypt (Kraay 1976: 63).

8.5 Taxation

One aspect of life that coinage made easier was taxation. The laws attributed to Solon include a provision that a sheep and a *drachmē* were equivalent to a *medimnos* (of barley) for the valuation of sacrifices (Solon *Laws* F80/2 Leão and Rhodes; Plut. *Solon* 23.3). Although the sense of this has been much debated, it is best understood in terms of how obligations to provide animals for sacrifice could be converted into weighed silver or anything else measured on the "barley-standard." From as early as any cult was recognized as a cult for all Athenians, there must have been ways of covering cult expenditure. One way of doing this was to assign land to the cult or to the body responsible for the cult, so that expenses could be paid from the rental of that land (presumably initially in a fixed quantity or fixed proportion of the produce). In Classical Athens we have evidence for land owned by cults/*genē*, phratries, demes, and other associations (Papazarkadas 2011). But such sources of funding were, in the Classical period, supplemented, at least for major festivals, both at the deme level and at the *polis* level, by liturgies, obligations to provide funding that were imposed upon the wealthiest members of society.

The positive evidence for liturgies in Archaic Athens is small: the Aristotelian *Oikonomika* (1347a11–14) ascribes to Hippias the practice of encouraging performance of the liturgical roles of trierarch, phylarch, or *chorēgos* by making it possible to commute their performance into the payment of a modest sum of money. As it stands, this is problematic (there were too few triremes in Hippias' time to require development of trierarchs to fund them; we have no other evidence for the phylarchy as a liturgical position). Moreover, it is unlikely that any historical evidence was available, or required, to attach a clever financial ploy to a famous tyrant. No more credible is the claim in Demosthenes 42.1 that the law on *antidosis* (which enabled someone selected for a liturgy to challenge someone else whom they could demonstrate to be richer to engage in a mutual exchange of all of their property or take the liturgy instead) was Solonian.[12] But the existence of Archaic *chorēgoi* is itself entirely plausible (van Wees 2013: 97–100; Domingo Gygax 2016: 79–82). Certainly, the conversion of the Panathenaia into a festival with a massive competitive element (see Section 11.3) required that there was a financial scheme to support this, beyond merely using the oil from trees sacred to Athena for prizes. In the decades immediately after the Kleisthenic reforms a large number of new or newly enhanced competitive festivals were founded, and these, too, will have relied on some mechanism for funding (Osborne 1993; Fisher 2011; see also Section 11.4).

Rather than suppose that Hippias invented liturgies (and in fact the Aristotelian passage implies that he made them easier to bear, not that he invented them), we should accept that obliging individuals to shoulder expenses, particularly expenses related to festivals, was traditional—perhaps as old as civic expenditure itself. The distinction between voluntary and obliged expenditure was arguably itself hard to make in a small community, particularly where festivals involved feasting and where the religious context of the feasting would do little to mask the responsibility of local "big men" (van den Eijnde 2018). The calendar of sacrifices (see Section 11.5) established by Solon's laws would have made clearer than ever exactly what was needed on the financial front (and clarity over funding is one of the functions of Classical sacrificial calendars, whether of demes or of the *genos* Salaminioi).

That said, there is no reason to believe that Archaic Athens did not exact a range of taxes. Our best evidence comes from outside Athens, where the late sixth-century award of exemption from taxes at Kyzikos to a man named Manes names taxes on sale of horses, sale of slaves, something to do with ships, perhaps a tax on sales generally, and a tax of uncertain nature named the "quarter" tax (Dittenberger 1917–1920: #4; van Wees 2013: 28–9).[13] We should not imagine that these precise taxes were replicated at Athens, where the *zeugēsion* tax mentioned by Pollux (8.132) is perhaps our best parallel, but the focus of the Kyzikene taxes on sales is telling. Aristotle thought that Periander was already extracting harbor and market taxes in the early sixth century, and we meet tax on exports in Knossos in the middle of the fifth century. A two percent tax on imports and

---

12. We first meet *antidosis* in the second half of the fifth century in a deme decree, *IG* I³.254, see Osborne 2020b: 103–4.

13. For taxes showing up in our epigraphic sources only incidentally, see Lalonde, Langdon, and Walbank 1991: P26.460–98 (a record of sales made by Athens' *pōlētai* in the mid-fourth century).

exports seems to have been widespread, if not universal, across the Classical Greek world.[14] Such import, export, and sales taxes were almost certainly part of the Athenian tax portfolio at least from the time of Solon (that he can think of banning exports of agricultural goods other than olive oil is evidence for the possibility of oversight of what is being exported).

We have already met the financial responsibilities of the naukraries (Section 5.2.1). Whether the Athenian government in the Archaic period had other means of extracting money beyond liturgies and naukraries is not clear. The same Aristotelian passage that claims a role for Hippias in easing liturgy payments also claims that he imposed birth and death duties and some sort of tax on properties that transgressed onto public space, and there is a strong tradition of Peisistratos and Hippias imposing taxes of a tenth or a twentieth on produce. Obligations to sacrifice on the occasion of a birth (and a number of other occasions) are attested in the ancient phratry regulations of the Labyadai at Delphi (Rhodes and Osborne 2003: #1) and may well have been general. The evidence of a number of lexicographers pointing to an obligation to sacrifice on the Acropolis on the occasion of marriage (*proteleia*) is now reinforced by epigraphic evidence of one *drachma* payments to Aphrodite Ourania in the fourth century, apparently in lieu of sacrifice (*SEG* 41.182; Pollux 3.38; *Etym. Magn.* 220.54–7; Suda s.v. προτέλεια; Parker 2005: 440–2). In the Classical period Athenians were obliged to pay 1/60th of their barley crop and 1/120th of their wheat to Demeter and Kore at Eleusis, and more generally, many dedications on the Archaic Athenian Acropolis and elsewhere declare themselves to be "tithes" (literally "tenths") of what someone has produced. The traditions pertaining to the taxes levied by the Peisistratids are therefore traditions of tyrants claiming for the state what had traditionally been claimed for the gods—it is a mistake, in my view, to turn the stories into an Athenian proto-*eisphora*.[15]

One general point needs to be made. Linking the income of the city to the activity of its residents necessarily ties politics and the economy together. It has been popular in the past to insist that "trade and politics" were separate in ancient Greece, and more generally that Greek cities concerned themselves with economic transactions only when those were to do with food or military supplies.[16]

---

14. Periander: Arist. F611.20 Rose. Knossos: Osborne and Rhodes 2017: #B13–14.

15. As does van Wees 2013: 83–97. In Athens we have no evidence for the *eisphora* other than as a tax on the capital value of estates (Thuc. 3.19.1). Using the evidence of Plato *Laws* (955de) to conjure up a quite different sort of Archaic *eisphora* seems to me very dangerous. For another recent treatment of Peisistratos' land tax, see Kienast 2005a: 81–4.

16. The classic texts are Hasebroek 1933 and Finley 1973.

The way in which the finances of the Archaic city are tied not simply to all aspects of agriculture but to all imports and exports and to whatever other activities a city chooses to tax (and, through the liturgy system, to every activity by which a citizen makes money) straightforwardly contradicts this. The whole economy was politicized.

9

Familial and Demographic History (Including Education)

9.1 Demography

We are probably better placed to guess the size, and indeed the changing size, of the population of Athens than of any other Archaic Greek *polis*. Although, as we have seen (Section 4.4.2), there are reasons to doubt that there is a direct correlation between changing numbers of archaeologically known burials and changing numbers of those living in Athens, it is plausible that the increase in settlement numbers in and after the eighth century does offer some proxy for the expanding population (Section 4.1.3). But judging the rate of growth is not at all easy. If we want actual numbers of residents, we must find them based on working back from the Classical period.

Population estimates for the fifth century start from Thucydides (2.13), who provides us with detailed numbers of Athenian troops in 431. On the basis of these—along with assumptions drawn from actual or hypothetical age distributions of modern (pre-industrial) populations—scholars have estimated the number of Athenian adult male citizens in 431 at between 47,000 (Gomme 1933) and 60,000 (M. H. Hansen 1988). Mogens Hansen's arguments for an Athenian adult male citizen population at least close to 60,000 are hard to resist; however, working back from that number to the number in 480 is not straightforward. In 451 Perikles had moved a citizenship law restricting citizenship in the future to those who had both an Athenian mother and an Athenian father, and our ancient sources explicitly describe that measure as a response to the large size of the citizen body ([Arist.] *Constitution of the Athenians* 26.3). Scholars have argued, plausibly, that the population of Attica is likely to have been growing by more than just natural increase, and if this is true then we cannot calculate back from the 431

The Oxford History of the Archaic Greek World. Robin Osborne, Oxford University Press. © Oxford University Press 2023.
DOI: 10.1093/oso/9780197644423.003.0009

figure simply by allowing for generous natural increase at 0.5 percent per annum or even above (C. B. Patterson 1981: 40–81; Watson 2010: 260–4).

Herodotos (9.28) does give us a figure for the number of Athenian hoplites at Plataia in 480: 8,000 (compare the figure of 9,000 given by Nepos *Miltiades* 5.1 and Suda s.v. Ἱππίας for the Athenian hoplites at Marathon). Given the circumstances, this is likely to be close to the maximum number of Athenian hoplites. Herodotos also tells us that the Athenians had 180 triremes at Salamis, with a further 20 lent to the Chalkidians. But the number of men on each trireme is uncertain, as is what proportion of rowers were non-Athenian. All we can be certain of, given the lending of the 20 triremes, is that Athens could not conceivably man more than 180 ships (i.e., her manpower did not exceed 36,000 [180 x 200—the full complement of a trireme]). A number of scholars have circled around the idea that the Athenian adult male citizen population in 480 was about 30,000, and a number of this magnitude (implying a free Athenian population, men, women and children of around 120,000) is hard to avoid.[1]

Further calculation of the size of the Archaic population depends on back-projecting from this figure on the basis of a small natural growth rate. We do not know the growth rate of the population during the 300 years before 500 but it is likely to have been between 0.2 percent per annum and 0.4 percent per annum, implying that in 800 the total population of Attica will have been between 40,000 and 70,000.[2] Keeping numbers round, an estimate that there were 10,000–20,000 adult males residing in Attica in the early years of the eighth century is probably the right order of magnitude.

How did this population break down into classes? This depends on what we make of the Solonian census classes, over which a major debate has arisen. On standard assumptions about the ancient agricultural regime and productivity per unit area (see Section 8.1), those in the highest census class would have to farm 40 ha of arable land (with half of that fallow) to produce their 500 *medimnoi* (about 16 tons) of grain. If the census of *hippeis* required 300 *medimnoi* and that of *zeugitai* 200, then they needed around 24 ha and around 16 ha, respectively (with half of it fallow in each case).[3] This would mean that the *zeugitai* were essentially very well-off farmers, far above mere subsistence farming level. Even those who are the most optimistic about the agricultural capacity of Attica do

---

1. So C. B. Patterson 1981: 58, but the discussion on p. 59 of that work implies a figure of 25,000 (total free Athenian population of 100,000).

2. On the long-term population dynamics of Greek cities, see Scheidel 2003: 122–3.

3. These figures are calculated on the basis of the discussion of *pentakosiomedimnoi* found at van Wees 2006: 359; cf. Foxhall 1997: 130.

not believe that more than 40 percent of the 2,400 sq km of Attica was farmed.[4] The maximum number of *zeugitai* who could be supported by 96,000 ha would be 6,000 (this with no *pentakosiomedimnoi* or *hippeis*),[5] and once one allows for perhaps 200 *pentakosiomedimnoi* and 800 *hippeis*, who would need 8,000 and 19,200 ha, respectively, the maximum number of possible *zeugitai* would drop to 4,300, or just over 20 percent of the possible Solonian population of 20,000. More pessimistic views of how much of Attica could be cultivated (30 percent) would cut this figure to 2,800—still allowing no land to anyone poorer than a *zeugitēs*. On this view, Solon's census classes merely discriminated among the wealthiest Athenians, and there was a "yawning gap" between *zeugitai* and the mass of Athenians (van Wees 2006, 365–6).

I have argued (Section 5.3) that it is better to regard the supposed qualification levels in *medimnoi* for *hippeis* and *zeugitai* as a late invention and to take the possession of a horse or a yoke of oxen as the operative Solonian qualification. Those with very small plots would not have had sufficient use to justify keeping a yoke of oxen and the *zeugitai* would still be those in possession of a significant amount of land (perhaps 5 ha), but this would allow for 50 percent of the Solonian free male population to be of *zeugitēs* status and above—and still allow for public land and for a proportion of thetes with land.[6] Not the least advantage of this is that it makes it possible for the *zeugitēs* to be not merely a tax category, but also a useful military category—hoplites.[7] At the same time, it becomes clear that, as the Athenian population grew beyond the putative 20,000 Solonian citizens, there would come to be significant pressure on land—a pressure increased by the high degree of interannual variability of rainfall (and therefore crop yield) in Attica (Section 8.1).

Numbers of metics and slaves are extremely hard to calculate at any period, even for 431, and both figures can only be posited on the basis of assumptions made

---

4. For optimistic figures, see Osborne 1987: 43–7. For pessimistic figures, see Moreno 2007: 61. Fachard 2016: 207 calculates that 35 percent of Attica (88,000 ha) has less than a seven percent slope.

5. 2,400 sq km x 100 ha per sq km = 240,000 ha; 40 percent of 240,000 ha = 96,000 ha.

6. For the amount of land needed to justify keeping oxen, see van Wees 2006: 382–5. For hoplites and above constituting just over 50 percent of the Athenian male citizen population in 431, see Gomme 1933 table 1. M. H. Hansen 1988: 24–5 points out that allowance needs to be made for those unfit to serve, but this has little overall effect on the proportions of those qualified by their property to serve as hoplites.

7. van Wees 2013: 89 wants to combine his high wealth threshold for *zeugitēs* with their role as hoplites by suggesting that only *zeugitai had* to serve as hoplites, but in fact others, not so qualified by wealth, also served. But if no viable army can be formed from those who had to serve, the point of obliging them is lost (in my view van Wees 2013: 173 n.23 misrepresents Arist. *Pol.* 1297a29–b15).

about the attractiveness of Athens at different periods to non-Athenians, and about its (changing) reliance on slaves. Here we have very few ingredients to mix. Slave names among Athenian potters and painters indicate the presence of some slaves in the Athenian workforce—but equally the presence of clearly non-slave names (e.g., Exekias) argues for a mixed labor force (Williams 1995; Williams 2009). Solon's abolition of enslavement for debt is thought to have created a new demand for chattel slaves, but the extent of employment of slaves in agriculture is subject to much debate even for the Classical period.[8] We can be sure that slaves in Athens in 480 were numbered in their thousands, but it is hard to be more precise than that.

In the case of metics, precision is harder still. It is plausible that metic status did not exist during the Archaic period. There is plenty of evidence for the Athenian elite marrying non-Athenians—already Kylon is related by marriage to Theagenes tyrant of Megara (Thuc. 1.1.26.3); the Athenians Megakles and Hippokleides are the leading contenders in the contest for marrying Agariste, daughter of Kleisthenes of Sikyon (Hdt. 6.126–30); Peisistratos forms various marriage alliances outside Attica (J. K. Davies 1971: 445–50); the Philaidai, too, reinforce their links in the Thraceward region via marriage (Hdt. 6.39.2). We should imagine similar marriage links between Athenian women and non-Athenians. Plutarch ascribes to Solon a law giving the right to become citizens to those permanently expelled from their own city and to those bringing their whole household to Athens to practice a craft (Plut. *Sol.* 24.4, Solon *Laws* F75 Leão and Rhodes). This law implies a certain amount of economic migration, but otherwise only that those who had good reason to do so were free to come and live as Athenians.

As well as the distribution across status groups, within and beyond the citizen body, we can also say something about the distribution of Athenians across Attica. For assessing this we have a unique dataset, the quotas for how many members each Athenian deme returned to the Council every year (Sections 4.1.2.2–4.1.2.3 and 5.2.4). We have enough inscriptional evidence for membership of the Council of 500 in the fourth century both to show that each deme had a fixed quota and to show what that quota was (Traill 1975). Although the case for there having been some revision of quotas after Kleisthenes (to cope, for instance, with the creation

---

8. For scholarship arguing for the existence of widespread agricultural slavery in Greece, see, for example, Jameson 1977; Jameson 1992; Burford 1993: 208-22; Jameson 2002; Kyrtatas 2011: 96–7. For the contrary view, see Wood 1988: 42–79; Gallant 1991: 30–3; Osborne 1995: 32–4; Rihll 2011. Cartledge 2002: 163 is agnostic. For a bibliographic survey, see Bellen, Heinen, Schäfer et al. 2003: vol. 1: 450–64). Even if one assumes that agricultural slavery was widespread, it seems improbable that most households, which would have owned at most 5 ha of land, could afford to support more than one or two slaves. Rosivach 1993 offers comparative evidence from the northern British colonies in the present-day United States to argue that relatively few Athenian households owned more than one slave.

of the Peiraieus) is strong, there is reason to suspect that that revision was limited. The quotas had to have some relationship to actual populations since the rule came to be (we cannot be sure that this was Kleisthenes' doing) that one could not serve as a member of the Council unless one had reached the age of 30, had not served in the previous year, and had not served more than once previously.

What do the deme quotas reveal? In the Classical period the five demes within the Themistoklean wall returned 27 or 28 members to the Council of 500. About the same number again were returned by demes more or less immediately outside the walls. That is, Athenians within the city constituted around 5.5 percent of the Council, and Athenians from immediately around the city another 5.5 percent. This is a remarkably small figure—particularly when the largest single deme, Acharnai, returned 22 to the Council. The reason for this is presumably because many who were resident in the town for much of the year owned property outside the city, and they registered themselves there. Nevertheless, this figure warns us against over-inflating the demographic dominance of Athens. It is likely to have constituted between 10–20 percent of the total Athenian population during the period covered by this book. In the eighth century that probably means that the town population was of the order of 2,000.[9]

9.2 Familial History

Birth mattered in Archaic Athens. Although the claim to be "well-born" (one of the *eupatridai*) should, I have argued (Section 5.3), be seen as an informal claim and not something that qualified one for any particular set of duties or privileges, there is no doubt that which family a man or woman was born into mattered (Humphreys 2018). This was something encouraged by the practice of handing the priestly duties in particular cults down the family line (*genos*) (see Section 5.3), which seems to have been universal until the fifth century (when new cultic positions might be open to all Athenian men or all Athenian women and chosen by lot, as with the priestess of Athena Nike [Osborne and Rhodes 2017: #137]). It is also seen in the way in which curses also travel down the family line, as with the curse on the Alkmaionidai as a result of the Kylonian affair (Section 5.2.1), and in which the family is responsible for prosecution of homicides and recognition of cases where the homicide was accidental (Sections 5.2.1 and 6.1). But the emphasis on family extended well beyond religious matters: the way in which Herodotos gives details of the family background of rival politicians in

---

9. For a different way of calculating the population of eighth-century Athens, see I. Morris 1987: 99–101.

sixth-century Athens (Hdt. 1.59–60, 5.66, cf. 6.103) and of the "tyrannicides," Harmodios and Aristogeiton (Hdt. 5.55, 57), certainly reflects the lens of fifth-century storytelling, but it likely also reflects sixth-century categorizations.

Legally, the basis for the strength of family lines lay in Athenian inheritance law as formalized by Solon (whose main innovation in that regard seems to have been the introduction of the possibility of bequeathing property by will). If a man had legitimate male children, his property passed to those children. If he had no legitimate male children but legitimate female children, the property could pass indirectly to the daughter(s) as residual heiress(es), or he could make a will in which he bequeathed property to those he adopted as son(s), who had to marry the daughter(s). If he did not have legitimate children, male or female, he could either adopt a male child or bequeath his property by will.[10] Illegitimate children seem to have had no inheritance rights, and equally no obligation to look after their parents. Those who were adopted could not, even if childless, bequeath their property—it presumably reverted to the indirect descendants of the man who had adopted them—male descendants of his brothers to start with and then his cousins and their male descendants (Solon *Laws* F47–57 Leão and Rhodes; C. Patterson 1998: 86–91, 97–101).

These inheritance laws had consequences for the nature of families and their property. Property was split between sons and, in the event of there being no sons and only daughters, passed out of the direct family line to the nearest kin who were obliged to marry the heiress. But the effect of this, when it brought about marriage of cousins, was often at least partially to reunite property that had been divided by partible inheritance in a previous generation. Model life tables suggest that in about one in five cases a man would die with no sons but only one or more daughters, so the potential proportion of cases where property would pass outside the direct family line was significant (Osborne 1988b: 308–9). By the Classical period we find many families with property portfolios spread across many locations, and this is most plausibly a consequence of the working of partible inheritance and the uniting of different family properties through marriage to heiresses (Osborne 1985: 47–63; Cox 1988).

9.3 Education

We can trace back education at Athens to the eighth or early seventh century. From the Sanctuary of Zeus on Mt. Hymettos (map 19) come seven sherds of pottery with parts of abecedaria, and another five such sherds come from the Athenian

---

10. Our evidence comes from fourth-century orators, but they seem to quote the form of the law that went back to Solon—despite fourth-century practice having itself evolved: [Dem.] 43.51; Isae. 3.42, 68; 6.28; 10.13; 11.2, 11–12; Harrison 1968: 122–62.

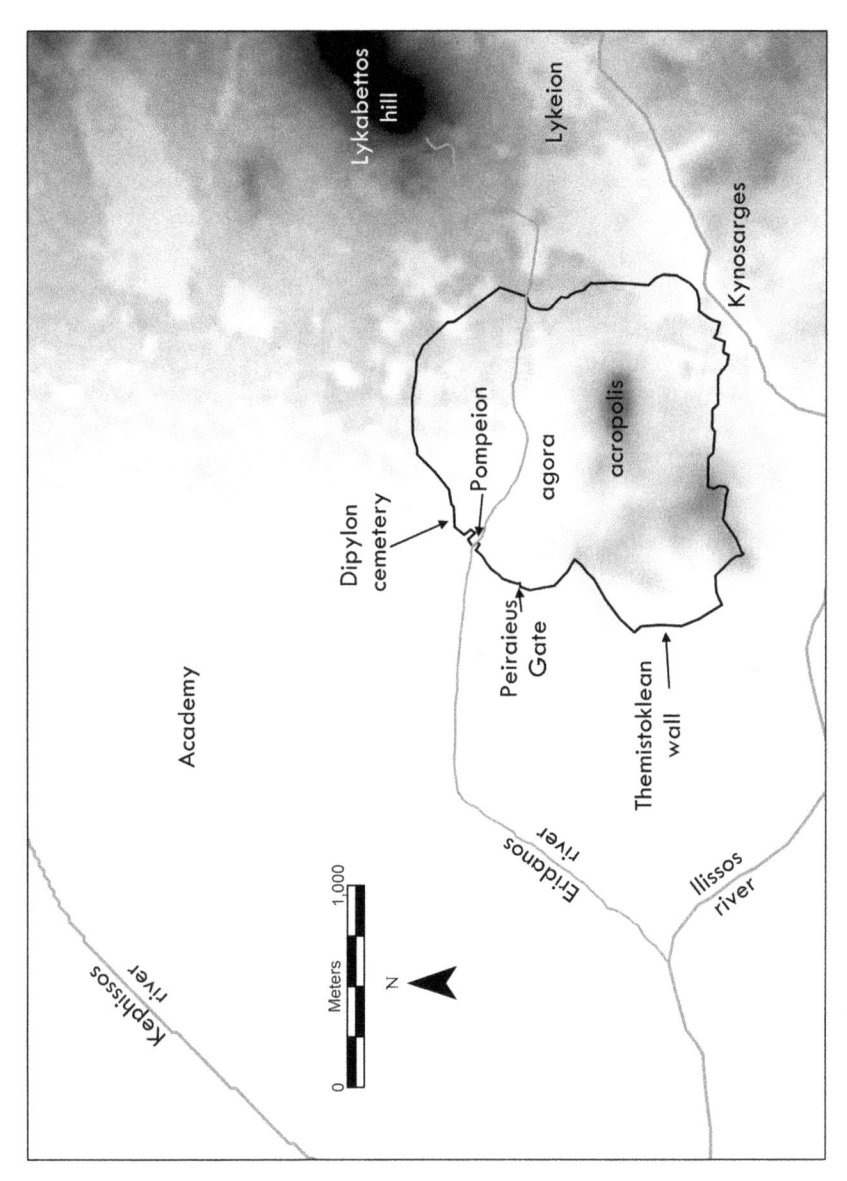

MAP 19 Some key sites in and around Athens mentioned in Sections 9.3 and Section 10. © Paul Christesen 2022.

Agora, dating from c. 700 to the early fifth century. One of these examples has the alphabet written twice, plausibly with the second line copying the first. These inscriptions attest, first, the existence of a set order in which the letters of the alphabet were written, and presumably learned (although one Agora fragment has the final letters of the alphabet (those additional to the Phoenician alphabet) written in a unique order). Second, they show that the alphabet that was learned included letters that were never used to write Attic, because Attic did not have the sounds corresponding to those letters. The prime example is the *digamma*, which the Athenians used when employing letters to designate a sequence (as when marking up building blocks in the fifth-century Hephaisteion), but did not use for writing words (with the exception of one possible name that is probably non-Athenian). Third, they show that the process of writing and learning to write was sufficiently special that the evidence of learning to write made an appropriate dedication in a sanctuary.[11]

We know neither the circumstances in which Athenians learned to write nor the extent of literacy. The casual nature of the earliest graffiti, including that on the jug from the Dipylon cemetery from the third quarter of the eighth century (see further Sections 2.2.1 and 10 in this text), and the use of writing for ownership inscriptions (and not simply for dedications, where the gods could be expected to be literate), suggests that those who wrote them assumed some minimal level of literacy from a significant number of those with whom they mixed (H. R. Immerwahr 1990: 7 #1, 9 #13; cf. also M. K. Langdon 1976: 22 #36; Arrington 2021: 200–5).[12] From the seventh century onward we have evidence for painters of pottery writing on their pots. This writing shows, in some cases, a certain amount of orthographic uncertainty, but in other cases considerable sophistication (cf. Exekias' use of the Sikyonian alphabet in recording a gift from one Epainetos to a Charopos on what appears to be a bespoke dinos; H. R. Immerwahr 1990: 34 #142). There are some cases where pot painters make errors that appear to be consequent on inaccurate copying, and some painters whose grasp of Greek and indeed of what it is they were painting seems at times insecure. The notable examples include signs of copying on the François vase, which is notoriously covered with writing, and errors in Greek and in mythology by Lydos, whose name itself suggests a non-Greek slave origin (H. R. Immerwahr 1990: 171–5) (see Section 4.5.4).

---

11. Hymettos sherds: M. K. Langdon 1976: 11–18, #20–25 (the double alphabet, including *digamma*, is #20). Agora material: Lang 1976. For further discussion, see H. R. Immerwahr 1990: 8, 12, 81, 140.

12. On literacy, see M. K. Langdon 1976: 49; Pébarthe 2006: 54–6; Missiou 2011: 57–8.

Scholars have sometimes suggested that so-called "nonsense inscriptions" (strings of letters or letter-like symbols that fail to spell out words) that appear particularly on Little Master cups and other pots of the middle of the sixth century indicate illiteracy among the pot-painters or an expectation of illiteracy among those buying the pots. Neither seems necessarily the case; strings of letter-like symbols act as cues to articulate what is happening in the scene shown, while at the same time not constraining the interpreter's imagination (Heesen 2016; Yatromanolakis 2016; Chiarini 2018) (see further Section 4.5.4).

It is important that not only did Athenian democracy, from its Kleisthenic inception, choose to advertise some, at least, of its decisions on stone, but from at latest the 480s one major democratic institution, ostracism, relied on the principle that Athenians in general could write (or read) a name of their choice upon a pot sherd, or easily find someone who could write it for them. While this does not indicate universal basic literacy, it implies that expecting people to be able to write a name was not unreasonable. Learning at least that degree of literacy must have been normal. Comments on *ostraka* (Section 7.1.2) suggest that many Athenians had more than just that basic ability.[13]

Attic black-figure pottery takes no interest in "school scenes," but from c. 500 onward we have such scenes on red-figure cups signed by or attributed in particular to Onesimos and Douris (see Figure 35). These show youths playing the lyre along with an older man, singing while older men play the aulos, reading from a text that an older man holds out, or writing on tablets. In a few cases the scroll from which the boy is reading bears legible writing, normally quoting from or alluding to epic poetry (Beazley 1948b; H. R. Immerwahr 1964; H. R. Immerwahr 1990: 99 n.6). From this point on scenes of boys carrying writing tablets or scrolls or reading from scrolls come to be relatively frequently shown. It is not at all clear that we should draw any significant conclusions from the absence of such scenes in black-figure pottery, which may be about general subject preferences, and the technical limitations of what can easily be shown in black-figure, as about any changing historical place for, or changing methods in, education.[14]

Although stories in Herodotos suggest the existence of spaces identified as, if not built to be, schools already in the Archaic period (Hdt. 6.27 with reference to Chios in 494; cf. Pausanias 6.9.6 of Astypalaia in 496), we can identify no such

---

13. The argument for democracy needing literacy is most developed in Missiou 2011; see also Pébarthe 2006: 243–344.

14. Images of education scenes on pottery are collected in F. A. G. Beck 1975. Note that from the second quarter of the fifth century we get images of girls and women reading from scrolls (F. A. G. Beck 1975: 55–6).

FIGURE 35 Athenian red-figure kylix signed by Douris as painter; c. 480; diameter 28.5 cm; from Cerveteri. Berlin Staatliche Museum Antikensammlung F2285. Photo by Johannes Laurentius.

spaces in Attica. We are not in a much better position when it comes to spaces for physical education. The Academy (sanctuary of the hero Hekademos) seems to have been used as a gymnasium already in at least the sixth century, with a boundary stone preserved from the end of the sixth century (*IG* I³.1091) (Kyle 1987: 71–7; Marchiandi 2003; Doronzio 2018: 244). The Lykeion gymnasium also seems to have been in use already by the sixth century, although we know most about its use as a general meeting point for the Athenian people and military muster-point for Athenian troops (Kyle 1987: 77–84; *IG* I³.105.34 [= Osborne and Rhodes 2017: #183B]; *IG* I³.105.137; Jameson 1980; Doronzio 2018: 244). A third gymnasium, at Kynosarges on the south bank of the Ilissos, was also in operation in the late Archaic period, if a story in Plutarch's *Themistokles* 1.3 has any basis. According to this story, Themistokles, because he had a foreign mother, was limited to using the Kynosarges gymnasium, but he attracted well-born Athenians to join him there. However, such discrimination on grounds of having a foreign mother is extremely unlikely before Perikles' citizenship law of 451/0, and the basis on which an association with Kynosarges has been back-projected onto Themistokles is not clear (Humphreys 1974; Doronzio 2018: 240–5).

Wherever they trained, there is no doubt that athletes and athletics were prominent in Archaic Athens, at least among wealthy families. The earliest Athenian victor recorded in the Olympic victor lists is Pantakles, listed as victor in running at the Olympics of 696 and 692. Between then and 480 a further 28 Athenians active in athletics and chariot racing are known, almost all of them associated with wealthy Athenian families (Kyle 1987: 102–13). A law ascribed to Solon, and reprised in the fifth century, assigns monetary rewards to those successful in the Olympic and other major Panhellenic competitions (Solon *Laws* F89 Leão and Rhodes); although the quoted law is anachronistic in some details, the principle of topping up rewards may have been instituted by Solon.[15]

The link between the gymnasium and status is emphasized by Solonian regulations about the behavior of slaves. In a law the Archaic date of which seems guaranteed by its use of a term obsolete in the Classical period, slaves are forbidden to ξηραλοιφεῖν in the *palaistra*, where *xēraloiphein* refers to using oil to clean oneself after exercise (Solon *Laws* F74 Leão and Rhodes). This law is widely referred to later in antiquity, and always in association with a prohibition on a slave becoming the lover of a boy. The law seems concerned that slaves will not merely accompany young men to the *palaistra* and gymnasium but will end up taking part in the activities there and mixing in as equals. That the gymnasium was associated with homoeroticism is confirmed by the story of an altar and statue of Eros being set up at the entrance to the Academy by Charmos who is variously described as having been erotically involved with either Peisistratos or Hippias (Plut. *Sol.* 1.4; Ath. 609d; Paus. 1.30).

Solon's other legislative intervention regarding education was his absolving sons not taught a skill (τέχνη) by their fathers from the obligation to maintain those fathers in their old age (Solon *Laws* F56 Leão and Rhodes). This presumably covered not merely technical "trade" skills, but also any way of earning a living, including farming, and need involve no developed educational structure.

Aeschines ascribes to "the old lawgivers" a set of laws about the education of children that forbid schools and *palaistrai* to open before sunrise or stay open after sunset and prescribe the age of children attending school; who could visit the school (only the schoolmaster's close relatives); and the conduct of festivals involving children, including those in which children engaged in dithyrambic dancing (Aeschin. 1.9–10). What lies behind Aeschines' claims is not clear, particularly since it is extremely unlikely that where children went at what times was regulated by law (and so close control on schooling would be largely in vain). But the implausibility of formal legislation is no argument against the existence

---

15. For the broader context of this law, see Kurke 1993.

of schools, and there is, for instance, no reason to doubt that the use of skilled slaves to oversee a child's education was already a feature of the life of wealthy Athenians in the Archaic period. Our best glimpse of such a man comes with Sikinnos, the non-Greek slave said by Herodotos to have been responsible for the education of Themistokles' children, who was used by Themistokles as a messenger to the Persians, and who later became a citizen of Thespiai when that city was recruiting to make up its losses in the Persian wars (Hdt. 8.75.1).

Social Customs and Institutions

MOST OF THE aspects of Athenian social life in the Archaic period about which we know something are aspects that were institutionally determined. The various sub-groups—*genē*, phratries, tribes (see Section 5.3)—acted as fora for social interaction, and the same is true of religious festivals more generally, as discussed in Section 11. In this section I will therefore primarily discuss what we know of personal interactions occurring either under the umbrella of these institutionalized gatherings or independently.

One Greek social custom has over the past 40 years absorbed far more scholarly energy than any other: the symposion. Subject in antiquity to compendious attention from Athenaeus in his *Deipnosophistai* (*Learned Banqueters* in Olson's translation), the symposion was, for a very long time, taken more or less for granted by ancient historians until attention was drawn back to it primarily by Oswyn Murray.[1] One consequence of this attention has been a tendency to reckon the symposion to have been a uniform practice that followed strict and standardized conventions. The truth is, however, that the evidence that we have from the Archaic period does not justify this assumption of uniformity. Rather than impose an ideal type upon the evidence, it is important to see what that evidence indicates.[2]

Our earliest evidence is provided by the Dipylon jug (see Figure 1), a LG I oinochoe, dated to the third quarter of the eighth century and decorated with a bird and a grazing deer on the neck that was found in a tomb in the Dipylon cemetery (Athens NM 192). What connects this with the drinking party is not simply its function as a wine jug, but also the writing scratched in the black glaze of the shoulder of the jug, which declares this a prize for "whoever of all the dancers

---

[1] Murray's contributions are collected in O. Murray 2018.

[2] What follows stands with Corner 2015 against both Wecowski 2014 and O. Murray 2018.

sports most? friskily" (further letters follow, but there is no scholarly agreement as to their interpretation) (P. A. Hansen 1983–1989: vol. 1: #432).[3] This inscription strongly suggests the existence of a social occasion on which there was both drinking and dancing, and at which the dancing was competitive. This is not simply a party at which existing social relations were reinforced, but one at which there was a possibility of social relations being changed.

One jug inscribed on one occasion by one participant challenging those present to perform in what might be no more than a single dance is fragile evidence on which to build a general social practice. What makes this plausible evidence for more than a one-off occasion, however, is the later evidence for the prominent role played by dancing on occasions of drinking. To cite two examples treated elsewhere in this volume, Athenian potters took up the painting of cups displaying padded dancers in the early sixth century (see Section 4.5.4), and Herodotos' story of the extended courtship of Agariste finds its denouement in a final banquet at which the Athenian Hippokleides dances away his marriage (Hdt. 6.130; Section 13.1). Drinking parties are also repeatedly represented as competitive occasions (consider, for example, scenes of the game *kottabos* being played at drinking parties) (Csapo and Miller 1991).[4] The Dipylon jug at least shows that drinking parties with dancing and a competitive edge were a possible feature of Athenian life already by the third quarter of the eighth century.

A second famous Late Geometric jug may offer some further evidence for the nature of eighth-century drinking parties. Painted a decade or two later than the Dipylon jug, a Late Geometric II oinochoe, with friezes of birds around the body and coursing animals around the shoulder, carries on its neck a scene of shipwreck (see Figure 36). Scholars have long debated whether or not the shipwreck is specifically that of Odysseus—a question that cannot be resolved on the basis of this image alone (for absence of myth from Geometric figure scenes at Athens see Section 4.5.2).[5] But it is worth asking why the artist chose to show an image of a shipwreck on a wine jug. Again, a plausible answer is suggested by later works of art and literature: association between the experience of sailing on a rough sea and the experience of intoxication is widely found in Archaic literature (Slater 1976; M. I. Davies 1978). If this shipwreck is wrought by the effects of alcohol,

---

3. Binek 2017 is the most recent discussion.

4. On sympotic competition in general, see Wecowski 2014: 52–5. On the symposion as an occasion for projecting identities, see Osborne 2007b.

5. See most recently Hurwit 2011.

FIGURE 36 Athenian Late Geometric II oinochoe; c. 730; height: 21.5 cm. Munich, Staatliche Antikensammlungen und Glyptothek 8696.

then the sole figure astride the keel of the upturned boat is best seen as the last man standing at the party.[6]

At least one location for eighth-century drinking parties can be identified archaeologically. This is the so-called "Sacred House" at the site of the Academy (see Section 9.3), just outside the urban core of Athens. Excavation here has yielded a great deal of late-eighth-century evidence, including sacrificial pyres,

6. For this interpretation, see Osborne 1998: 35–7; cf. Osborne 2014. On the competition to stay standing (or awake), see Wecowski 2014: 53.

kraters, and skyphoi and kotylai of various forms, an assemblage that suggests drinking parties, perhaps in association with funerary cult. Other structures with similar assemblages point to possible facilities for such parties elsewhere in Athens and Attica—at Herakleidon Street near Athens' Peiraieus gate, at Eleusis (below Section 11.1), at Thorikos, and perhaps elsewhere (Alexandridou 2015a; Alexandridou 2018; van den Eijnde 2018: 78). At the end of the eighth century all these buildings except that at Eleusis were abandoned. Scholars have talked of the removal of banqueting to sacred precincts with a view limiting the extent to which feasting was a form of power-play, but the belief that feasts in sanctuaries were feasts without patrons seems naïve, not least in the context of the responsibility of *genē* for cult activity (Alexandridou 2018; van den Eijnde 2018: 84).

For more than a century after the Dipylon jug was buried there is little more we can say about drinking parties at Athens. It is, in fact, a striking feature of the changes in ceramics around 700 that the new style of fine pottery, which we call Protoattic (on which see Section 4.5.3), is a style predominantly of closed vessels. We find some Protoattic kraters, but there is no Protoattic cup tradition. It is only with the komast cups of early black-figure that the great series of Athenian cups made for drinking parties, and often referring directly or obliquely to them, begins.[7] Seventh-century drinking parties at Athens must have used cups without figurative decoration and evidently had a somewhat different dynamic.

In the late seventh century a new practice seems to have arrived at the mainland Greek drinking party—reclining to drink. Reclining is not a feature of any social gathering described in the *Iliad* and *Odyssey*. In our texts the first clear reference is in the late-seventh-century poetry of the Spartan poet Alkman (F11 Calame/19 Page *apud* Ath. 110f–111a).[8] The practice of reclining derived from the Phoenician world, where it is found depicted on silver and bronze bowls. Within the Greek world, eighth-century Cretan shield fragments, heavily influenced by Phoenician metalwork, also show scenes of reclined drinking, plausibly introduced by the Phoenicians resident on Crete. It is unsurprising, therefore, that on the Greek mainland it should be found first at Sparta, which enjoyed particularly close relations to Crete. The first appearance of reclined drinking on ceramic vessels used at the drinking parties themselves is on Corinthian kraters painted shortly before and after 600.[9] Like other aspects of Near Eastern culture,

---

7. The imagery associated with drinking parties received its classic exploration in Lissarrague 1987.

8. The word συμπόσιον itself is first found at approximately the same date, in the poetry of Alkaios (F70.3 Page).

9. For the Near Eastern origins, see Fehr 1971; Dentzer 1982; Matthäus 1999; Wecowski 2014: 141–59; O. Murray 2018: 77–88.

we should allow that reclining drinking may not have been adopted by all Greeks on their first acquaintance with it, but that it was adopted at the point that it enabled changes in social relations that were otherwise desired.

More or less contemporaneous with the first Corinthian scenes of reclining drinking parties and with the Attic komast cups is the poetry of Solon. Although there are traditions of Solon performing poetry in the Agora to draw attention to the crisis over Salamis (Plut. *Sol.* 8.1–2; see Section 7.1.1), little credence can be given to these. The predominant, if not the only, context for Solon's poetry (variously written in elegiac meter, trimeters, or tetrameters) must have been the drinking party (E. L. Bowie 1986; E. L. Bowie 1990; Irwin 2005: 32–3).[10] Solon's poems bring the language of politics into poetry, both to point the finger at the problems facing the Athenian community (notably F4 West, perhaps 6, 9–11, 15) and to offer an explanation and defense of what Solon himself has done (F5 West, perhaps 6, 32, 34, 36–7). F4 begins (lines 5–7) with a complaint that "the citizens (*astoi*) themselves want to destroy a great city by mindless acts, persuaded by money, and the mind of the leaders of the people is unjust," treating the drinking party as a place for raising consciousness (a role it is also given in the elegiacs of Theognis of Megara). In F5 it serves as a place for rehearsing what has happened: "I gave the people [*demos*] as much privilege as sufficed, neither taking away from their honor nor adding to it" (F5.1–2 West). Solon's poetry also engages with the nature of the good life in general (F13, 23–4 West [lines also attributed to Theognis]); mortality (F20, 27 West); and the pleasures of the drinking party itself, including food, drink, and sex (F25–6, 38 West; cf. 23), but Solon distances himself from, and criticizes, martial elegy (Irwin 2005: esp. 91–111).

We have already seen that the pleasures of the drinking party were plausibly being themselves celebrated at drinking parties in the eighth century. What is manifest with Solon is the intrusion of politics into the drinking party. While the outsized kraters used to mark male burials in the eighth century frequently carry scenes of heavily armed soldiers or of ships and fighting (Section 4.4.2), the vessels that were plausibly actually used for drinking parties—even if found in graves—seem much more interested, throughout the eighth and seventh centuries, in thinking about what it is to be human than in thinking about how one human group might relate to another (Osborne 2018a). Solon's drinking parties are clearly different. While general thoughts about being human, its pleasures and limitations, are present, so are very particular considerations of contemporary behavior.

---

10. One pair of hexameter lines is attributed to Solon and to a poem in which he versified his laws (Solon F31 West, from Plut. *Sol.* 3.5).

If reclining was indeed a new practice introduced at the end of the seventh century, it is not hard to see why it might have led to new sorts of drinking party becoming possible. Reclining drinking takes a large amount of space and so restricts the size of the party (scholars talk of seven-couch and eleven-couch types of dining rooms, both of which are found in the Archaic period [Bergquist 1990]). It also establishes two different levels of intimacy—sharing a couch or occupying a separate couch. The inscription on Nestor's cup from Pithekoussai (Meiggs and Lewis 1988: #1), with its wish that anyone who drinks from it should experience Aphrodite, shows sexual intimacy to have been on the agenda at drinking parties from the eighth century, but reclining created new opportunities of which representations on Phoenician bowls already take advantage.[11] Sexual allusions are certainly a striking feature of Corinthian representations of so-called "padded dancers" (see Section 4.5.4), from which the imagery on Athenian komast cups takes its inspiration, and "bottom slapping" motifs are prominent on Athenian cups and skyphoi, although never as sexually explicit as those on Corinithian pottery.[12]

Not the least reason for resisting attempts to restrict Athenian drinking parties to any single type is the variety of pottery, both in shape and in imagery, that was made for the symposion by Attic potters in the sixth century. Those organizing drinking parties could offer the participants cups of different sizes and with very different imagery, and jugs and kraters with a similar range of images, some of them alluding to myth and some to the activities of life (see Section 4.5.4). We can rarely be sure in the case of particular cups or kraters that they were either made for or ever used at a symposion, given that large cups, in particular, seem to have been favored as showy dedications, but the general run of cup and krater decoration surely indicates something of the mood and interests of those at drinking parties.[13] We have no Athenian sympotic poets after Solon to offer us particular Athenian selections of sympotic topics, but we hear of famous poets being invited to Athens from abroad, in particular Anacreon, a poet known for the sexual allusiveness of his poetry (Pl. [*Hipparch.*] 228b–c, *Chrm.* 157e).

---

11. Osborne 2009: 108–10. See Wecowski 2014: 127–41 for the so-called cup of Nestor. See Matthäus 1999: 257 for sexual imagery on Phoenician bowls.

12. On the Corinthian material, see Wannagat 2015. On the Athenian material, see Smith 2010: 33–68.

13. On cups as dedications, see Tsingarida 2009. Although many cups and kraters end up being sold abroad, in particular in Etruria, there are reasons for thinking that the choice of subject matter on Athenian pots was determined by Athenian rather than Etruscan taste; see Osborne 2001; Reusser 2002; Osborne 2018c; cf. Section 4.5.5.

Athenian sanctuaries, unlike sanctuaries in other parts of Greece, have yielded no Archaic buildings that are clearly purpose-built for drinking parties.[14] We must wait for the fifth century and the building of the picture-gallery at the Propylaia entrance of the Acropolis, and the Pi Stoa at Brauron (cf. the dining room at the Pompeion). But there is no reason to think that in sanctuaries such provision of permanent facilities was required. Just as the sacrificial feast could be consumed, and normally was consumed, essentially as a picnic, so too drinking parties could take place *al fresco*: our texts suggest that reclining on straw-filled cushions outside was the less sophisticated option, but it remained an option (O. Murray 2018: 130–1).

Similar arrangements may have applied to drinking parties outside domestic contexts. Whereas in Classical houses it has frequently been possible to identify a room that seems to have been specially designed, decorated, and equipped to be used for drinking parties, no such rooms can be identified in Archaic Greek houses. Indeed, there was a radical change in house size across the Greek world at the end of the Archaic period, with the mean number of rooms, which had been between two and three from the ninth century to the sixth century, rising to nine rooms in the fifth and a staggering sixteen rooms in the fourth century, and with mean area, which had been at or below 100 sq m down to c. 500 doubling in the fifth century and then rising by a factor of five to more than 1000 sq m in the fourth. The way in which houses were used must have been very different in 350 from at any period down to 480 (Nevett 2010: 50–7, 61–2). This is yet another reason for being careful not to project back onto the Archaic period the types of drinking party one might expect to find in the *andron* of a private house in the Classical period—that is the type of drinking party described by Plato or Xenophon in their works entitled *Symposion*.

From late Archaic Athens, however, we have, courtesy of the Persian sack, a wonderful glimpse, if not of the surroundings and furniture of a drinking party, then at least of its pottery. A well in a late Archaic house north of the Athenian Agora excavated in 1995 yielded a complete assemblage of household pottery including three or perhaps four sets of drinking cups (Lynch 2011). There seems to be a set of six red-figure cups linked by shape, by the workshops that made them, and by their iconography (with the caveats that one cup is smaller than the rest and that four of those six cups show in their tondos a single male figure, while the other two show in one case an owl and in the other an eight-spoked wheel). Five plain black-glazed cups seem, based on their profiles, to belong to

---

14. For dining rooms as a sixth-century development at Perachora and elsewhere, see Tomlinson 1990.

the same set. In addition to these, there are two coral red cups and five black-figure skyphoi, all work of the Haimon Painter's workshop and perhaps all by the same hand. The skyphoi are decorated in silhouette technique without incision, with scenes, largely typical of the shape, of bovines, reclining figures, Dionysos, and a winged female. The household pottery also included a small black-figure amphora showing Dionysos, a black-figure wine jug showing Herakles, a red-figure pelike showing a bearded man with a stringed musical instrument and a youth being sick as well as amphoras and pelikai in plain black glaze. There was no krater, either because the inhabitants of the house took it with them (perhaps because it was bronze) or because some other vessel was used instead for mixing the wine and water. We simply do not know how typical this household was in its sympotic assemblage, but the scenes on the pots here predominantly encourage reflection upon the sorts of actions in which the drinkers themselves are or will at some point be engaged.

The images on the pots from this late Archaic household are short of representations that encourage discussion of social relations, although one black-figure "Heron Class" skyphos (so large it may have been used for mixing wine rather than to drink from) shows a sympotic scene on both sides (Lynch 2011: 111–18, 97–200). But alongside many further images of solo revelers or individual soldiers, etc., the wider corpus of late Archaic figured pottery produced in Athens includes numerous images that encourage drinkers to think about their relationship to others. One group of these images shows erotic relationships between older and younger men.

Not surprisingly these homoerotic images have attracted much discussion, not least because of the place that Greek homoeroticism has played in the arguments over homosexuality in the modern world (Blanshard 2010: 143–63; Orrells 2015). What, if anything, do these images tell us about sexual relations between older and younger men in Archaic Athens? The images that are of interest here are not so much the small number that show sexual intercourse (heterosexual intercourse received rather more attention), but those that show "courtship." "Courtship" scenes between older and younger men divide into two types. In one type the older man, his age indicated by the presence of a beard, seeks physical intimacy with the younger man, who is beardless and physically smaller, with the older man typically stretching out his hands to feel the chin and genitals of the younger man or positioning his body to make genital contact with the younger man (Osborne 2018b). In the other, which is often combined with the first in the sixth century, older men offer gifts to younger men, or younger men stand with gifts we are to believe they have just received from the older man. The earliest black-figure pots to show such scenes depict fighting cocks and animals captured in the hunt (hares, foxes) as love-gifts, but the equipment of the gymnasium (aryballos, javelins) also appears, along with flowers and wreaths. In what is surely an exaggerated parody of these scenes, the Amasis Painter shows a large feline (panther or cheetah?), a stag, and a waterbird being offered along with hare and hen, and shows naked women being similarly courted (with flowers and wreaths) along with young men (see Figure 25). This parody draws attention to the implicit competition involved in offering any particular love-gift (Dover 1978: 92–3; Lear and Cantarella 2008: 38–52, with catalog of Archaic scenes on 195–220).

But if the giving of large felines is parody, what exactly is the homoerotic practice being parodied? Two issues have figured large in the debate. One concerns the age of the younger men, the other whether we are dealing with a standard ritual of initiation. There are contexts in which early red-figure artists seem to show great interest in depicting a particular stage in the development of facial hair, and this has been used, alongside a particularly rich Greek vocabulary for the onset of the beard, to pinpoint the age of the young men in receipt of the erotic attention of older men. However, it is the absence of interest in picking out age at all precisely that is actually the more notable—youthful figures like Triptolemos or Apollo can be shown bearded, full-grown men like Achilles beardless. Equally there are depictions of courtship where the couples are beardless (see Figure 37). It is hard to think that such "careless" practice is compatible with a society in which there was great sensitivity either to the younger partner being of a certain age or to distinguishing sharply the active and the passive role in the relationship—for all the attempts of some later Classical sources to do so. Whatever the situation may have been in Crete, where Strabo (10.4.21) preserves, from the fourth-century historian Ephoros (*FGrH* 70 F149), an account of "their peculiar custom about love" that involves a highly institutionalized pursuit, nothing in Athenian homoerotic imagery hints in any way at a particular ritual context for courtship at Athens.[15]

What then should we imagine to be the contexts in which Archaic Athenian homoerotic bonds were formed? Archaic Athenian society was markedly gendered, to the extent that we have seen that primary cremation may have been a mode of disposal of the dead reserved for men in the seventh century (Section 4.4.3). All our images suggest that only boys went to school; certainly, only male youths went to the gymnasium; only men served in the army and navy; only men took on political responsibilities, locally or at state level, whether serving in judicial capacity, on the Councils of 400 and 500, or as captain or a naukrary or

---

15. The standard work on ritualized homoeroticism is Bremmer 1980. Davidson 2007: 68–98 is insistent on homoeroticism involving youths of a particular age. The best exposition of the evidence on facial hair is Ferrari 2002: 127–61 and especially pp. 132–8, by whose conclusions, which seem to me to ignore the significance of the inconsistent evidence and of the difference in date between the visual and the textual evidence, I nevertheless remain unpersuaded.

FIGURE 37 Athenian red-figure kylix signed by Peithinos as painter; c. 500; diameter: 34 cm; from Vulci. Berlin Staaliche Museum Antikensammlung 2279. Photo by ArchaiOptix.

archon of the city. The formal and informal contexts in which males, and only males, were intimate were numerous: male homosociality ruled, and only in the context of (some) religious festivals was company mixed in gender (Goldhill 1994; Osborne 2019a). Added to this, there were social expectations, related in part to patterns of inheritance, that men would not marry until they were around 30, and that they would marry women much younger than themselves who would have a long reproductive life. All these circumstances favored strong social bonds of young men, both with older men and with each other. That this social intimacy might also involve sexual intimacy should cause no surprise, any more than the "lewdness" of some Archaic imagery should cause surprise. Nor should the fact that more or less elaborate protocols were developed by which sexual desire might be signaled and then welcomed or rebuffed.[16] The scenes on Archaic Athenian pottery show those protocols in action.

---

16. The term "protocol" was brought into play in this connection by Winkler 1990: 4–5, 39–41, 45–7. It exactly captures the diplomacy and the delicate power relations involved. Note also Winkler 1990: 5 on the non-negotiable androcentrism of ancient Greek society.

The gifts offered in these courtship scenes reveal the importance of one other "institution" in Archaic Athenian social life: the hunt (Schnapp 1989: 71–81; Schnapp 1997: 247–67, Barringer 2001: 70–124 for hunting and courtship). We have effectively no literary evidence for hunting in Attica prior to the Classical period (for the Classical period itself we have a treatise on hunting by Xenophon). The hunt features significantly in a range of Greek myths, however, and there can be no doubt about the importance of the taming of wild nature in Greek ways of thinking about the place of humans in the world. But our best evidence for the day-to-day engagement, in thought if not in practice, of Athenians with the hunt comes from images on pots. Those images show hunters, both bearded and beardless, on foot on horseback, with dogs, using both spears and throwing sticks (*lagōbola*) and nets while hunting hares, foxes, boar, and deer. The hunter with his dog bringing home the animals he has killed is equally popular. One lekythos from c. 550 has three friezes that show from bottom to top a hare being hunted and fighting cocks, young men on horseback, and the bringing of hunted animals as gifts for a young man (who is being courted by a bearded man accompanied by his dog). The hunt clearly figured as prominently as the gymnasium as an arena in which manliness was tested and prowess was displayed; younger men attracted attention by their performance in the hunt and older men proved themselves worthy of younger men's company.

Religious Customs and Institutions

11.1 The Eighth Century

Cult activity can be traced back to the Bronze Age at Eleusis, and although no clear evidence for cult activity during that period survives from the Athenian Acropolis, it must be suspected there, too. At Eleusis the remains that attest to Bronze Age activity, including cult activity, are extensive: a megaron (Megaron B), built on the east side of the hill in LHII A2 (c. 1475), was extended twice (c. 1400, c. 1300). From the tenth and ninth centuries there is evidence for cult activities on Agrieleki above Marathon, at the top of Hymettos and Parnes, and also at the Sanctuary of Artemis Mounychia and perhaps Brauron (map 20).[1]

Finds of pottery and other votive offerings from the eighth century, and occasionally of sacrificial pyres, enable us to add to these sites the Athenian acropolis, the Academy, Acharnai, Eleusis, Kiapha Thiti, Rhamnous, Sounion, Tourkovouni, and further hilltop sites. Again, the most extensive evidence comes from Eleusis. In the middle of the eighth century a polygonal terrace wall was built in the vicinity of Megaron B, which was at that point in time still standing. A long wall, which has been identified by some scholars as a fortification, was situated to the south of the terrace, and a deposit of Late Geometric and early Archaic figurines and a ritual pyre were found near the Megaron. In the late eighth century, the so-called Sacred House was built c. 50 m south of Megaron B; this mud-brick structure measured 13 x 10 m and consisted of four rooms connected by a corridor. The finds from the interior include large vases filled with ashes. A few meters to the southeast of the Sacred House a tomb was excavated, on top of which was found an earth mound with sacrificial pyres from the end of the eighth through the end of the seventh century. The functions of Megaron B

---

1. On Eleusis, see Cosmopoulos 2015. On other sites, see D'Onofrio 1995a; Parker 1996: 18. On hill-top sites see Rönnberg 2021a: 219–25.

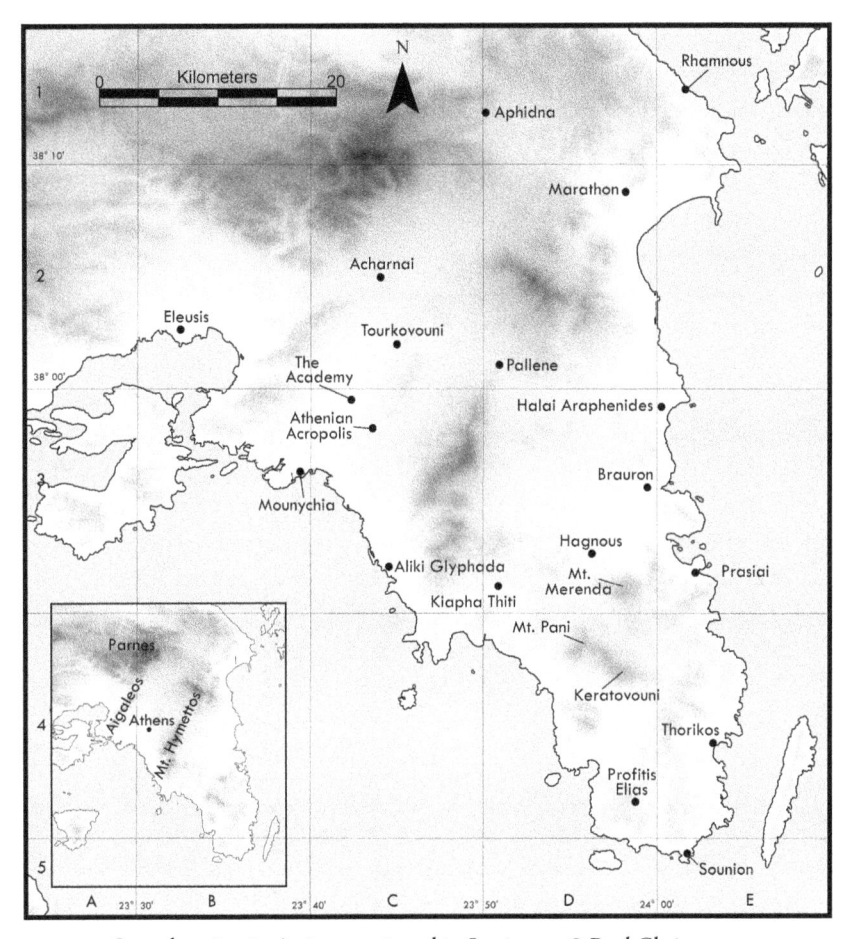

MAP 20 Some key sites in Attica mentioned in Section 11. © Paul Christesen 2022.

and the Sacred House in the eighth century are unclear, and the pyres on top of the tomb and the finds from and around Megaron B and the Sacred House, all of which may relate primarily to rituals concerning the dead rather than concerning the gods, are the only certain signs of religious activity at Eleusis between the end of the Bronze Age and c. 700. Exploration of the surrounding area suggests that several residential clusters and cemeteries were located in the vicinity of Megaron B and the Sacred House, and there was a large apsidal building, under the later temple of Artemis (Mazarakis Ainian 1997: 150–4; Cosmopoulos 2015: 132–9; Alexandridou 2017a).

Although there is significantly more evidence for cult activity in Attica in the seventh century, that increase is primarily in evidence from further hilltop sites (D'Onofrio 1995a; Parker 1996: 18–19; Hurwit 1999: 91–4; Scholl 2006: 49–67,

90–105; Cosmopoulos 2015: 132–9), and through the eighth and seventh centuries two phenomena that stand out are the prominence of these hilltop sites, and the appearance of offerings at old tombs.

The evidence from hilltop sites is generally relatively sparse and not well published, but the cult site of Zeus (named on various inscribed sherds) at the top of Hymettos is well known (M. K. Langdon 1976). We can trace the history of cult on Hymettos in some detail, from a substantial manifestation marked by dedications of wine jugs, kraters, and kantharoi in the Protogeometric period; through a distinct rise in activity at the end of the eighth century, when kraters disappeared but drinking vessels continued to more or less monopolize the assemblage (with one-handled cups the most common offering); to a seventh-century peak, when hundreds of kotylai were dedicated; and then to a distinct sixth-century decline. The pattern of deposition suggests individual worshippers making their own offerings at an altar (and discarding earlier offerings to do so). The offerings seem to have been accompanied by animal sacrifice, although the bone material recovered in the excavations was not kept for analysis (M. K. Langdon 1976: 74–8). The only sherd to give Zeus an epithet calls him Zeus Semios, but Pausanias (1.32.2) makes reference to a cult site of Zeus Ombrios (the "rain bringer") on Hymettos that is likely to be this shrine, and the cult was plausibly concerned with human attempts to influence the gods' determination of the weather rather than with relations between humans or issues of maturation.[2]

A similar pattern of feasting seems to have prevailed at a number of sites. At Parnes, Kiapha Thiti, the Academy, and perhaps Tourkovouni the assemblage is dominated by open Subgeometric cups and household wares, and at other peak sanctuaries such as Keratovouni, Mt. Pani, and perhaps Mt. Merenda the assemblage is dominated by Geometric and Subgeometric cups, although Parnes is marked out by the exceptional presence of more than 3,000 iron daggers. At Hymettos and Parnes there is also evidence for a change from individual drinking to communal drinking practices marked by a single mixing bowl. We move during the ninth and eighth centuries from individual skyphoi, through an intermediate form halfway between krater and skyphos that may mark drinking in small groups, to separate kraters and skyphoi. In the eighth century these sites seem to have been places of gathering, rather than places for making conspicuous dedications to the god (van den Eijnde 2018: 67–75).[3] Indeed one might note that, were it not for their locations and for the presence of later dedications that

---

2. Pausanias also notes the existence of a cult of Zeus Hymettios on Hymettos.

3. On Tourkovouni, see Lauter 1985a; Christiansen 2000: 82–3.

are distinctive, we would not necessarily recognize these as cult sites simply from the pottery.

The deposition of offerings at Bronze Age tombs is a feature found in a number of areas of southern Greece.[4] The earliest examples date to the tenth century, but the peak of activity is in the eighth century, with declining instances in the seventh and sixth centuries. In Attica the earliest examples belong to the eighth century, when offerings began to be made at the tholos tombs at Acharnai (Menidhi; the site is sometimes referred to as Lykotrypa), and perhaps at Thorikos (just one eighth-century sherd). The treatment of earlier tombs both in the Athenian Agora (especially the building of stone platforms that might be associated with ritual meals) and the west cemetery at Eleusis, where an enclosure is built round a group of Middle Helladic tombs, may also imply creation of deliberate links with the past (Antonaccio 1995: 102–26 [who is skeptical about the Eleusis case], Parker 1996: 33–9; Boehringer 2001, 47–131; Deoudi 2005; Papadopoulos, Smithson, and Strack 2017: 233–4; Rönnberg 2021a: 227–30).

At Acharnai and Thorikos the quantity of material deposited increases from the eighth to the seventh and then from the seventh to the sixth centuries, with the sixth century yielding the largest body of material, before activity fades out in the Classical period. In both cases Corinthian as well as Attic ceramics are found—indeed at Thorikos Corinthian material predominates in the seventh and early sixth century. But the characteristic shapes of pot deposited are different in the two cases, with the Acharnai deposit featuring more louteria (large bowls) than anything else, and the Thorikos deposit dominated by small, closed vessels and by miniature forms. The total number of vessels dedicated, and the nature of the worshipping groups, are quite different in the two cases, with the involvement of the whole community possible at Thorikos. The different cults seem to have served cult groups that were drawn from very different social and economic circumstances and that worshipped heroes for rather different purposes (Boehringer 2001: 103–19, 30–1). Groups of different sorts seem to have coalesced around hero cults as ways of establishing and advertising their particular, but different, identities.

Elsewhere in Attica (at Aliki Glyphada and perhaps at Marathon [Antonaccio 1995: 118–9], as well as at Athens and perhaps Eleusis), we have one-off cases of material being deposited in old graves, but we have no persistent cult. What seems to have marked off the Thorikos and Acharnai examples is the monumentality of the tholos tombs, which were a feature of the local landscape that could not be

---

4. On the phenomenon in general, see I. Morris 1988; Antonaccio 1993: 46–70; Whitley 2001: 150–6.

ignored. But in neither case is there any sign that the tholos tomb was associated with a particular named hero.

The relationship between the worship of gods and heroes and the archaeological evidence for that worship present major interpretative challenges. Scholars have been keen to see the great increase in the number of cults at tombs in the eighth century as marking if not the birth then at least the rise of the hero (e.g., Kearns 1989: 136). But the number of places in general from which there is evidence for cultic activity increases markedly in the eighth and seventh centuries, and just as we are confident (from the continuity of divine names from Linear B evidence) that some gods were continuously venerated, even while we have no archaeological evidence for cult (Parker 2017: 1–32), there is no reason to think that recognition of heroes coincided with archaeological evidence for hero cult. Explanations of the increase of archaeologically visible cult at tombs need to focus not on the motivations for engaging with ancestors or heroes, but on the motivations for engaging in those sorts of cult practice.

Our best chance of gaining further insight into eighth-century Athenian engagement with the gods comes from the iconography of Attic pottery. Until recently discussion of the iconography of Athenian Geometric pottery has been largely limited to scenes that more or less certainly have a connection with the funerary context in which most of the pottery is found (see Sections 4.4.2 and 4.5.2). But although monumental vessels were specially made to mark graves, much Geometric pottery in graves is pottery that was originally made for other purposes, and its iconography needs to be understood in contexts of life, rather than death. Two particular motifs are prominent and important: the centaur and male and female dancers (Section 4.5.2).

Centaurs appear in the last quarter of the eighth century on Late Geometric II pottery of various shapes, particularly pottery associated with the workshop of Athens 894, sometimes as isolated figures, sometimes in procession, and sometimes as opposing pairs, carrying branches, and sometimes in the company of men carrying branches. They also appear, accompanying dancers and men, on Attic gold diadems. Susan Langdon has argued that we should see the centaur here as primarily an educator figure, like the centaur Cheiron who appears with Peleus and the infant Achilles on some Protoattic fragments (S. Langdon 2008 95–110).

Female dancers (distinguished either by clothing or by presence of breasts), and mixed groups of male and female dancers, are also prominent in Attic Late Geometric pottery independently of centaurs. The relevant scenes begin in LG Ib and become more prominent in LG II, again with the workshop of Athens 894 taking a lead. The dancers often carry garlands or branches and may be accompanied by a lyre player. Langdon has suggested that the LG II shift to showing women with hair relates to hair as a sexual symbol, as seen both in its prominence in epithets of women in early Greek poetry and in what seems to have been the cultural norm of expecting women to cover their hair. These scenes of dancing are no more snapshots of reality than are the scenes of centaurs, but both draw attention to ways in which the world, and in particular the world of male and female maturation, was conceptualized (S. Langdon 2008: 125–30, 43–56, 66–74).

These pots indicate that collective ritual dances were part of that conceptualization, and that growing up for young girls involved participation in group activity that drew attention to their marriageability. That theme is further explored in the motif of abduction famously shown on a Late Geometric louterion in the British Museum (1899.0219.1), said to be from Thebes but apparently of Attic origin. The louterion depicts, among other things, a woman being led by a man onto an oared ship, and that scene has been linked to a variety of different mythological abductions (e.g., Ariadne, Helen, Medea, Andromache) or interpreted as a reflection of real-life abduction marriages or women bidding seafaring husbands farewell (S. Langdon 2008: 19–32).

The arrival of new iconography on Attic pottery coincides with the arrival of a new type of dedication in Attic sanctuaries. Although, from the late eighth-century onward "raw" dedications, that is the deposit in a sanctuary of items that were used in other aspects of life (cups, tools, arms and armor, etc.), continue to dominate in some assemblages of dedications, they were joined in other sanctuaries by "converted" dedications, that is objects specially made for giving to the gods.[5] Human and animal figurines, votive plaques, and miniature votive shields appear at numerous sites in Attica: on the Athenian acropolis; in a variety of contexts in and around the later Agora; at what will become major cult sites at Brauron, Eleusis, Pallene, and Sounion; at Kiapha Thiti; and at the Acharnai (Menidhi) tholos (Schulze 2004; Doronzio 2018: 206–7). The tripods that are found on the Athenian acropolis (see further below and Section 12.1) should probably be seen in the same category. What these dedications suggest is a newly complex relationship to the gods: no longer is worshipping the gods merely a matter of sharing with them in food and drink and inviting the gods to participate in the equipment deployed in human daily life; it is also a matter of showing the gods that one is thinking about them and about their life and directing the gods' attention to particular aspects of their involvement with the world.

But if the evidence of painted pottery and the changing nature of finds in sanctuaries gives us a good sense of the contexts and ways in which the residents of Attica engaged with gods and heroes in the eighth century, it gives us little

---

5. For the distinction between "raw" and "converted," see Snodgrass 1989–1990. For the appearance of "converted" objects in Attic sanctuaries in the late eighth century, see van den Eijnde 2018: 76–82. For the theological force of the distinction, see Parikh 2020.

evidence for the overall organization of cult. What is more, the exceptional phenomena of hilltop sanctuaries and hero cults can obscure the evidence for cults of major deities attached to significant settlements. Elsewhere in the Greek world, and particularly in the Peloponnese, the late eighth century and the early seventh century saw a great deal of temple building in connection with sanctuaries of major deities (Kotsonas 2017). Attica in general shows little sign of building in sanctuaries, and even on the Acropolis (Section 4.3) actual remains of a temple are almost impossible to identify, although scholars are convinced that by around 700 there was indeed a temple of some sort in the vicinity of the later Erechtheion. Two *poros* limestone column-bases, found embedded in the sixth-century foundations to the south of the Erechtheion, are likely to have been part of a temple building (Nylander 1962). A large circular bronze relief of a Gorgon (Athens NM 13050) may have come from this building, but whether this was indeed the akroterion of a temple is unclear. That there was some form of enclosed space on the Acropolis in the seventh century is implied by two terracotta female statues, one of them more or less life-sized, and by a bronze candelabrum and two large late seventh-century marble lamps (Scholl 2006: 21; Doronzio 2018: 42–9). The existence of a temple of some sort on the Acropolis by c. 700 may be reflected in the reference in the *Odyssey* (7.78–81; cf. *Il.* 2.546–52) to Athena entering the "strong-built house of Erechtheus" in Athens. In their descriptions of the Kylonian coup of 632, Herodotos (5.71) and Thucydides (1.126) refer to a statue of Athena, an altar, and a *hieron* on the Acropolis (Hurwit 1999: 20–1).

It is not architectural features but the exceptional dedications—and most particularly the tripods (see Section 12.1.1)—made there that show that the Acropolis was a major place of cult by 750. The Acropolis is the only site in Attica at which full-sized tripods have been found, suggesting that it was recognized as a singularly important place of cult for the whole region, not merely those who resided in its immediate vicinity. Dedicating such objects implies both the importance of the deity to whom they are dedicated and the prominence of the cult place in terms of others who visited and would see the dedication. Less spectacular, but nevertheless extremely impressive are the pottery fragments surviving from the late eighth-century Acropolis. They include a fragment with part of the earliest dedicatory inscription from the Acropolis, a votive plaque with a female figure, part of a clay box decorated with a row of dancing women, and a number of fragments of pots showing ships. The quality of the decoration on some of these pots, and in particular of some seventh-century fragments, is extremely high. By the end of the seventh century we have our first explicit evidence that the object of cult is Athena, in sherds inscribed as dedicated to the gray-eyed daughter of Zeus (Doronzio 2018: 12–32), and our first clear evidence of cult at the site of the Nike bastion, in the form of female goddess figurines (Schulze 2004; Lempidaki 2013: 372–5; Doronzio 2018: 53–4).

11.2 The Seventh Century

There may have been cult buildings at Eleusis already in the eighth century, but the only certain signs of religious activity at Eleusis before 700 are the pyre and the evidence from the so-called Sacred House, discussed in Section 11.1. During the seventh century, the terrace in the area of Megaron B was expanded, and a rectangular temple (c. 24 x 14 m) to Demeter and Persephone was built on top; this is the only cult building from anywhere in Attica that can be securely dated to the seventh century. The mud-brick temple had a gabled roof and painted terracotta tiles, and the interior probably included an adyton. It likely played a key role in Eleusinian Mysteries and can be plausibly identified as a *telestērion* ("initiation hall"). The importance of the cult at Eleusis in the seventh century is further shown by the composition of the *Homeric Hymn to Demeter*. Although the date of that poem cannot be securely assessed, most recent discussions lean toward the later part of the seventh century. The poem is heavily indebted to Hesiod's *Theogony* and has a close relationship also to the *Homeric Hymn to Aphrodite*. Eleusinian cultic life is particularly closely interwoven into the *Homeric Hymn to Demeter*, and the poem can itself be seen to have a revelatory structure that mirrors the structure of the initiatory cult (Richardson 1974: 5–12; Parker 1991; Foley 1994: 29–30, 169–78; Richardson 2011 49–53). There are, therefore, good reasons for thinking that Eleusis had established itself not simply locally but more widely as *the* center of cult for Demeter.

Votive material of seventh-century date is also known from the Eleusinion in Athens, located east of the Panathenaic Way as the ground begins to rise to the Acropolis. Terracotta horse figurines, plaques, and miniature shields have been found, along with Protoattic and Corinthian pottery (Miles 1998: 16–19; Doronzio 2018: 192–5; see further below). Assuming that we are already dealing with the worship of Demeter and Kore here, the very existence of this sanctuary, and its central position, attests to the status that the cult at Eleusis had achieved.

Outside Athens a number of sanctuaries, in addition to the sanctuaries on Parnes and Hymettos discussed above (Section 11.1), have produced extremely rich votive assemblages (map 21). Some 1,500 sherds of pottery from Mounychia can be attributed to the seventh century, attesting in particular to the dedication of Protoattic pedestaled kraters and Subgeometric krateriskoi, vessels that seem to be for the most part restricted to sanctuaries of Artemis. In addition there are fragments of terracotta figurines and a small number of imported objects, both from elsewhere within the Greek world and from beyond (Palaiokrassa 1989; Palaiokrassa 1991; Palaiokrassa-Kopitsa and Vivliodetis 2015; Palaiokrassa-Kopitsa 2017). The material from Brauron is less well published, but it is clear that large quantities of seventh-century pottery, including Protoattic, and figurines were recovered from several different locations in the sanctuary, with a notable collection of Subgeometric mugs (Ekroth 2003: 103).

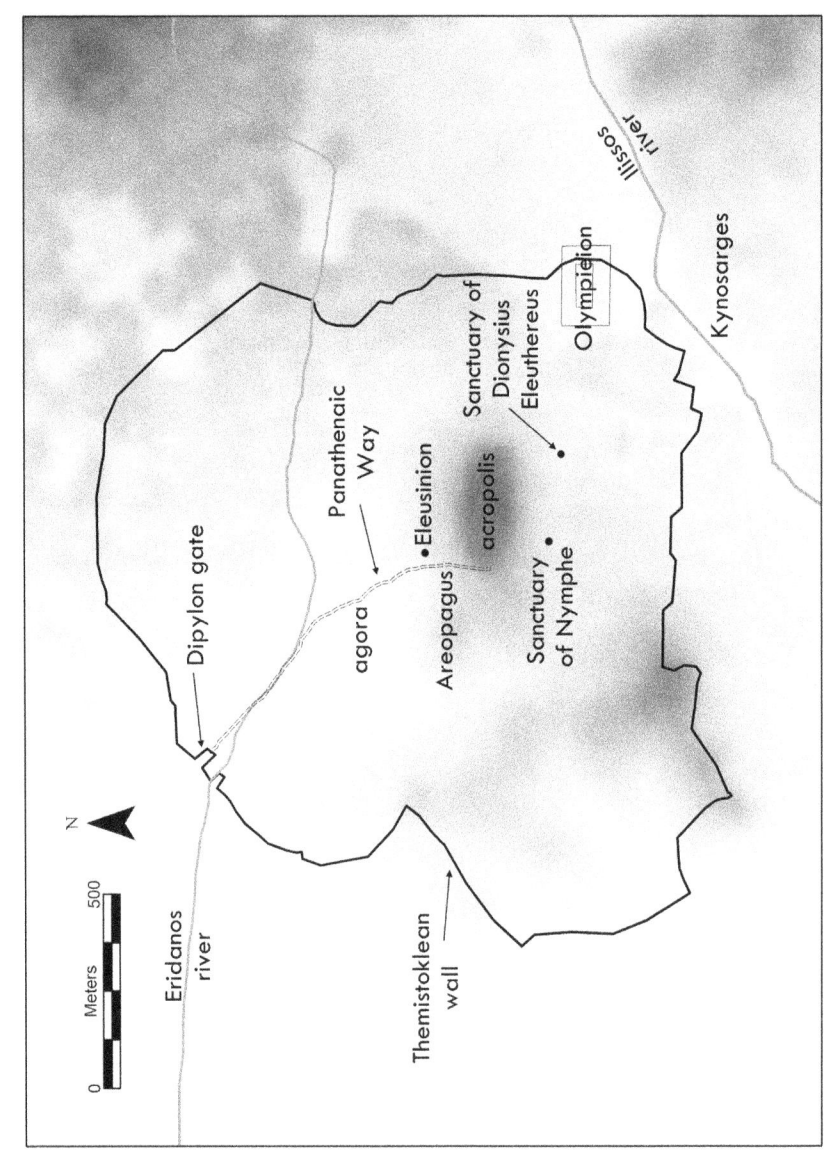

MAP 21 Some key sites in Athens mentioned in Sections 11.2–3. © Paul Christesen 2022.

Abundant pottery was recovered from pits during excavations at Sounion in the early twentieth century, but it is not clear that all the pottery that was excavated has been preserved. What has been preserved is very different from the pottery from Mounychia and Brauron, consisting largely of closed shapes, in particular aryballoi, and of material that is either Corinthian or imitates Corinthian pottery. The earliest pottery is Middle Protocorinthian (c. 690–670), and from Early Corinthian on (620–595) the imagery is dominated by human figures of hoplites and of padded dancers (Theodoropoulou-Polychroniadis 2015: 258–67). Attic work is, however, present in a number of painted plaques, the best preserved of which has been attributed to the Analatos Painter and so to c. 700. The surviving part of the plaque by the Analatos Painter (see Figure 38) shows the rear of a ship, with five rowers and a steersman, with the steersman picked out with a different garment and without the shield and spears that mark the rowers. Because of the prominence of the steersman he has been speculatively identified with the Phrontis whose burial at Sounion is mentioned in *Odyssey* 3.276–85 (Abramson 1979; Theodoropoulou-Polychroniadis 2015: 64–5, 202).

There are also several terracotta relief plaques from the seventh century, in particular showing Herakles and the Nemean lion. The clay appears to be Attic. Large numbers of terracotta female figurines, and some male figurines, have been found, many of them of late seventh- or early sixth-century date. Two miniature bronze shields may be, and four miniature tripods almost certainly are, of seventh-century date (Theodoropoulou-Polychroniadis 2015: 29–45, 58–74, 101–3).

FIGURE 38 Protoattic plaque attributed to the Analatos Painter; first quarter of seventh century: height: 90 cm; from the artificial fill of the Athena sanctuary at Sounion. Athens National Museum 14935.3. Photo by Eleftherios Galanopoulos.

Different again is the votive assemblage from Kiapha Thiti (c. 18 km south-east of Athens, near the modern village of Vourvatsi). That assemblage includes almost 50 terracotta figurines with outstretched arms, which have become known as "Stempelidole." Figurines of that type are found only in the seventh century and only in southern and western Attica—at numerous locations from Eleusis to Sounion down the west coast of Attica, but otherwise only at Brauron and Loutsa (Küpper 1989; Parisi 2014: 28; Rönnberg 2019). There are also a smaller number of female protomes, two miniature clay votive shields, and three objects that might be miniature clay votive *poloi*. Alongside these "converted" dedications from Kiapha Thiti, however, there was also a large quantity of "raw" pottery largely consisting of Subgeometric Attic and Corinthian skyphoi, aryballoi, and kotylai (Christiansen 2000). Given the presence of female figurines, Jette Christiansen has suggested that, despite the similarities with the assemblages at hilltop feasting places like Hymettos, this may have been a sanctuary of the nymphs frequented by women in which the cups were used to pour libations of milk or honey. But this will not account for all the finds (notably the votive shields) and may be too restrictive. Protocorinthian aryballoi and Subgeometric (Phaleron) cups are also a feature of the unexcavated peak sanctuary on Profitis Elias, close to the area of the Laurion mines (Lohmann 1993: 12, 415).

In Athens itself, outside the Acropolis, cult activity is attested by a number of deposits of votive objects. In several cases the deposits have been discovered at some distance from whatever shrine they belonged to. This is true of a deposit found on the north slope of Areopagus close to the "Oval House," but probably originally from the Eleusinion, which contained fragments of miniature tripods of bronze and clay, figurines of horses, late eighth-century and Protoattic pottery dating down to about 630, a terracotta figurine that may be an armed Athena, and a votive plaque with a female figure with upraised arms and flanked by snakes (Burr 1933; D'Onofrio 2001; Doronzio 2018: 176–89; Laughy 2018). It is true also of a deposit of votive material from a pit on the west side of the Panathenaic Way that similarly contained terracotta horse figurines and a votive plaque as well as gold foil and an ivory fibula plate, a protome from a tripod, Protocorinthian and Middle Corinthian pottery, and an Argive bronze shield of early fifth-century date (Doronzio 2018: 189–92). This appears to have been material from a shrine that was destroyed in the Persian sack. In the Agora itself votive material of seventh-century date has been found in a large number of wells (A. Sassù 2014).

On the south side of the Acropolis, the earliest votive material from the Sanctuary of Nymphe (protectress of marriage), along with an altar, dates to the seventh century and is marked particularly by loutrophoroi and figurines, which guarantee that the cult was already focused upon marriage, although whether it served a merely local or also a wider role for Athenians generally it is impossible to tell (Kyrkou 1997; Doronzio 2018: 255–64). Whether the archaeological evidence establishes the presence of cult activity also in the area of the Olympieion and Kynosarges is not clear.[6]

If the seventh-century material record reveals cult activity at a greater number of places and with a greater range of votives, the iconography of seventh-century pottery is far more reticent about cult, but far more explicit about theology. Scenes of dancing and music making, and even the scenes of laying out the corpse for burial, vanish from Attic pottery at the end of Late Geometric. Scenes of procession continue into the seventh century but become detached from burial and gradually turn into processions of animals. With regard to theology, the iconography of Protoattic, which is generally at the very least oblique in its reference to life, makes much more explicit reference to myth (see Section 4.5.3).[7] The world of Protoattic imagery is a world dominated by animals and story, and the story element shows or implies beneficent divine intervention (as in the presence of Athena standing between Perseus and the pursuing Gorgon sisters on the Eleusis amphora, Figure 18). Just as dedicating converted rather than raw objects involved thinking about the world of the gods as not simply an extension of the human world, but a world with its own rules, so Protoattic imagery produces a world of its own. The assemblages at seventh-century cult places, with their broad division between sanctuaries dominated by Subgeometric cups and sanctuaries dominated by Protoattic pottery and converted dedications, suggest a world in which conceptions were changing, but changing in different groups at different rates (D'Onofrio 1995a: 74–6; Palaiokrassa-Kopitsa 2017: 248).[8]

Was the world of Attic sanctuaries in the seventh century part of a single system centered on Athens itself? That the Athenian Acropolis was a cult place like no other in Attica is clear from the finds. But then Athens was quite clearly the largest community in Attica. Equally, the establishment of an Eleusinion in Athens in the wake of the increased fame of the cult of Demeter at Eleusis, the similarity in the votive assemblage between Mounychia and Brauron, and the limited distribution of female figurines of the Stempelidole type, suggest that communication between sites in southern and western Attica was strong (and we simply lack adequate evidence currently for the northeast of Attica). But if these sanctuaries plug in to the same material world and the same ways of thinking,

---

6. For the argument that it might, see Doronzio 2018: 221–2, 40–5.

7. For full discussion, see Rocco 2008: 207–11.

8. While acknowledging the deficiencies in the data I used in Osborne 1989, I continue to insist that to properly understand seventh-century Athenian religion we must take account of the imagery on the pottery (and the textual evidence), alongside the archaeological evidence.

they remain diverse in their particular assemblages, and there is no sense of hier-archy, and only a limited sense of functions being performed in Athens itself that are not performed outside Athens.

11.3 The Sixth Century

The degree to which Athens operated as a single religious unit by 600 is evident from Solon's laws, which make it clear that the Athenians as a whole thought it proper to establish regulations about religious practice (Solon *Laws* F83–6 Leão and Rhodes). Those laws included a religious calendar establishing where, when, to whom, with what victim, and at what expense sacrifices should be made. Fragments of that calendar remain from its late fifth-century re-inscription (Lambert 2002). Reference to the Ionian tribes and *trittyes* (3.33–7 "from the instructions of the Tribe-kings [*phylobasileis*]: for the tribe Geleontes and for the trittys Leukotainioi . . .": see sec. 5.3) guarantees that the version re-inscribed was essentially the version established by Solon, and what survives refers to the festi-vals of the Genesia, Pythais, Plynteria, Synoikia, Eleusinia, Hermaia, Dipolieia, Epidauria, and probably the Panathenaia. It is clear that already in Solon's time Athenians celebrated a large number of festivals and spent significant sums of money on them—so in the case of the Eleusinia we seem to have 16 sheep (in one case, a ram) sacrificed plus a piglet, and in the case of the Epidauria there is an allocation of 300 *drachmai* for expenses.

That this calendar could be re-inscribed in the late fifth century says some-thing about the conservatism of religious practice—and of the freezing effect of putting arrangements into writing. But if the structure of the religious year was already set by 594, the physical setting in which its festivals took place came to be completely transformed. It was transformed not least by the arrival of monumen-tal temple building. By 500 there were significant temple buildings in sanctuaries across Attica, and the Athenian Acropolis featured a dense array of temples. But the monumentalization of the Attic sanctuary began slowly and began not with buildings but with sculpture, and not in Athens but in Attica. The colossal *kouroi* from Sounion, found in a pit just east of the sanctuary of Poseidon and dated close to 600, are by some way the earliest *kouroi* found in an Attic sanctuary.[9]

On the Athenian Acropolis the earliest monumental dedications of stone begin only in the second quarter of the sixth century and include the Moschophoros and the earliest of the great series of *korai* (Acropolis Museum

---

9. For their finding, see Theodoropoulou-Polychroniadis 2015: 23; for the date of the small temple of Athena at Sounion, see Barletta 2015: 72–3.

589, 593, 617, 677). There is also a fine marble perirhantērion, two large votive reliefs, and a marble sphinx. Only in the last third of the century did the quantity of marble dedications on the Acropolis become large.[10]

The history of monumental buildings on the Acropolis remains a fraught subject (see Table 2 for a listing of relevant physical evidence). Some sort of early sixth-century building is attested by surviving terracotta antefixes (N. A. Winter 1993: 213–4). If the context for a surviving frontal four-horse chariot group (Hurwit 1999: 104; Acropolis Museum 575–580) was a pediment or metope, rather than a votive relief, as all the parallels suggest, then there was already a monumental building of some sort in the second quarter of the century. It was at this period that access was facilitated by building a long ramp up the west slope, and an altar and statue of Athena Nike set up on a remodeled bastion from the Mycenaean fortifications. The ramp was probably built to enable building construction, but, once there, it enabled the development of cult activities involving very large numbers of people (Hurwit 1999, 341 n.42). The most spectacular of these was the remodeled Panathenaia.

Late sources variously date a remodeling of the Panathenaia to 566/5, to the archonship of Hippokleides, and to the tyranny of Peisistratos (Arist. F637 Rose [scholiast to Aelius Aristides 1.189]; Jerome/Eusebius 01.53.3 pg. 302b4–5 Helm; Pherekydes *FGrH* 3 F2 [Marcell. *Vita Thucydidis* 3]; Shear 2021: 5–6 n.9). The first and third of these dates are incompatible; Hippokleides' archonship is not otherwise datable. Archaeologists have had no problem dating to the 560s the earliest surviving Panathenaic amphoras (Figure 49), awarded, full of oil, as prizes, and that the Athenians should enhance a pre-existing festival with games at roughly this time is entirely unsurprising, given the founding or re-founding of Panhellenic festivals at Delphi, Corinth, and Nemea (the Pythian, Isthmian, and Nemean games) in the 580s and 570s (Shapiro 1989: 18–47; Parker 1996: 75–6, 89–92).[11] Unlike those games, in which famously the prizes were only symbolic wreaths, the prizes at the Panathenaic festival were of substantial value. Certainly, by the fourth century they included gold crowns, oxen, and cash sums as well as amphoras of oil, and the amphoras of oil were awarded in very large quantities (the fourth-century winner of the two-horse chariot race won 140 amphoras of oil, the second-placed competitor 40 amphoras). The Panathenaic amphoras containing the oil seem, from their distribution across the Greek world, to have become significant trophies, even, perhaps, collectors' pieces, and they served to

---

10. For the monumental dedications on the Acropolis 570–550, see Hurwit 1999: 104. For the late and massive growth of votives, see D'Onofrio 1995b: 185–90.

11. For Panathenaic amphoras, see Bentz 1998 (the earliest amphoras are catalogued on p. 123).

Table 2 Physical Evidence for building on the Archaic Acropolis (after N. A. Winter 1993: 204–32; Hurwit 1999: 104–36; Kissas 2008).

Date	Evidence	Nature of building
c. 700	Two *poros* limestone column bases	temple (?)
c. 700	Bronze disk with Gorgon (acroterion or pedimental decoration?) (NM 13050)	temple (?)
c. 600	Laconian roof of Naxian marble	temple (possibly original roof of "Hekatompedon"/ "H-Architecture" of 570–550 replaced after some problem)
590–580	Terracotta antefix and eaves tile (one fragment inscribed AΘH) (Akr. K120 9582, K121 9659, K241 9667, K246 9668) from Argive system roof	
580–560	Rubble masonry of rebuilding of bastion	South-west bastion supporting altar and statue of Athena Nike
570–560	Antefix and eaves tile (Akr. K247–K275)	Unknown building
570–550	Frontal four-horse chariot group (Akr. 575–580)	Pediment, metope, or votive monument
570–550	Retaining wall of straight, 80 m. long ramp up to west entrance of Acropolis	Entrance ramp
570–550	Limestone column capitals, marble sima fragments, limestone pedimental sculptures, Hymettan marble sculpted metopes, Corinthian roof, akroteria. Undated ("Dörpfeld foundations") may have been first used for this building	Peripteral temple, 6 x 12 or 13 columns, 40 m+ x 20 m. "Hekatompedon"/ "H-architecture"
570–550	Sima, antefix, and eaves tiles (Akr. K11–K13 118).	One or two unknown buildings
560–550	Low relief pedimental sculpture of Herakles and the Lernaian hydra	Temple of unknown location
560–550	Red-painted pedimental group of Herakles and Triton	Temple of unknown location
550	Sima and eaves tiles (Akr. K1–K2 93)	Unknown building
550	Sima and antefix, Central Greek workshop (Akr. K3–10a, K295–K297)	Treasury

Table 2   Continued

Date	Evidence	Nature of building
550–540	Pedimental group showing introduction of Herakles to the gods on Olympus	Unknown temple
550–540	So-called "Olive tree pediment"	Unknown temple
540	Sima and eaves tile (Akr. K15 9468)	Unknown building
540	Antefix (Akr. K127)	Unknown building
540	Karyatid ("Lyons *korē*") Akr. 269	Unknown building
540–530	Antefix and eaves tile (Akr. K276–K282, K128); replaced by simas, antefixes, and eaves tiles (Akr. K16 9461, K17 9462, K283–K293)	Unknown building, reroofed c.510
520	Gorgoneion antefix and eaves tile (Akr. K292–K294, K500–K507, perhaps K122)	Unknown building
500	Sima, ridge tile, antefix, and geison tile (Akr. K18–K23, K152 9577, K301–K380, K437–K446)	Unknown building
500–480	Antefix (Akr. K. 298 9714)	Unknown building
500–480	Corner akroterion antefix (Akr. K299 10093)	Unknown building
510–500	Marble pedimental sculpture, possible marble frieze sculpture, marble sima from temple on (undated) "Dörpfeld foundations"	Peripteral temple of Athena Polias ("*archaios neos*"), 6 x 12 columns, 43.5 x 21.3 m
500	*Poros* blocks from tristyle *in antis* façade and apsidal rear wall, some found in Propylaia foundations.	"Building B" (purpose and location uncertain)
500	*Poros*-limestone steps, marble benches, and re-used metope dado	Forecourt at west entrance
490–480	Cuttings, anta blocks, *poros* ashlar blocks.	Possible Older Propylon 4 columns on each façade, three interior columns flanking passageway, 20 x 16.5 m
490–480	Podium of 8,000 large blocks of Peiraieus limestone; numerous marble superstructure fragments, including column capitals	Older Parthenon, 6 x 16 columns, 26.2 x 69.8 m

spread Athens' renown and advertise the festival as if it was in fact Panhellenic rather than a civic festival (see Section 13.1 for further discussion). The team events, for which the teams were later provided by the Kleisthenic tribes, were probably always restricted to Athenians, but non-Athenian competitors are found in the individual athletic events, and "cultural" competitions, of which the most notable were playing and singing to the lyre, and recitation of the Homeric poems by rhapsodes.[12]

A series of inscribed pillars survives on which the five officials in charge of the Panathenaic festival celebrate their part in enabling the competitions by laying down the running track (τὸν δρόμον) (IG I³ 507–509bis). The best preserved of these explicitly identifies the competition as the first ("who established the contest for the first time for the gray-eyed maiden" [hoὶ τὸν ἀγõ[να θέσ]αν πρõτο[ι] γλ|αυ[ϙ]όπιδι ⋮ ϙόρ[ει]), and the script is entirely compatible with a date in the 560s.[13]

There is little doubt that a large new temple was, or very shortly became, the focus of the re-organized festival, but such is the confusion caused by later building that we cannot in fact certainly place that temple on a particular spot on the Acropolis, though we can be confident of both its existence and its scale (about 40 m x 20 m) from the remains of its marble and limestone architecture and its architectural sculpture, including pedimental groups with lions and the so-called "bluebeard" triple-headed, snake-bodied figure from the pediment's narrow angle (see Figure 42; Plommer 1960; Shapiro 1989: 21–4; Hurwit 1999: 106–11).[14] In addition there are remains of limestone and terracotta architectural elements from a large number of small buildings, all constructed before the Persian wars: Winter's study of the roof tiles revealed one roof dating before 570, six or seven to between 570 and 540, and four additional roofs before 480 (N. A. Winter 1993: 204–32). There are further limestone pedimental sculptures that must belong to these buildings, including one showing the introduction of Herakles to Olympus and another which appears to represent the Acropolis itself, with olive tree, temple building and various figures from Athenian myth depicted (Hurwit 1999: 112–15).

---

12. Our fourth-century data come from IG II².2311. See generally Neils 1992, Shear 2021: 171–211, and on prizes Kyle 1996: 116–23.

13. Jeffery 1990: 72; https://www.atticinscriptions.com/inscription/IGI3/507.

14. Plommer 1960; Shapiro 1989: 21–4; Hurwit 1999: 106–11; Kissas 2008: 39–50, 99–112. The work of Kissas has shown that the main argument against placing this large temple on the site of the later Athena Polias temple is not valid. The arguments in favor of dating the so-called Hekatompedon inscription to the end of the sixth century (Butz 2010) support the view that the Athena Polias temple was the successor to this temple. However, definitive proof that the earlier temple was on the same foundations is still lacking.

Regardless of their precise date, and indeed function, the structures erected on the Acropolis in the second quarter of the sixth century and the rich sequence of votives, with the number of *korai* increasing as the century progresses, show the Acropolis becoming the focus of unprecedented levels of religious activity. From the middle of the century an inscription on a bronze plaque (*IG* I³.510; R. Sassù 2014, 109 and fig. 2) records a dedication by the *tamiai* to mark their having brought together the precious objects (χαλκία).[15] It is unfortunate that the dating of the building activity remains unclear; given the degree of competitive investment and display involved, the question of whether this was or was not at a time when Peisistratos had claimed political control is important for our understanding of Athenian politics, as well as of Athenian religion. Although the interest of Peisistratos' son Hipparchos in the Panathenaia (regulating the performance of the Homeric poems; see, for example, Pl. [*Hipparch.*] 228b) is well attested, the hand of the Peisistratos himself is hard to discern. Competition between members of the Athenian elite is much more patent, above all through the increasing number of surviving dedicatory inscriptions as the century progresses (Raubitschek and Jeffery 1949) (see Section 5.2.3).[16]

Outside the Acropolis, the earliest temple of Zeus Olympios on the Olympieion site seems to date to the first quarter of the sixth century or a little later. At the same period, in the area of the Agora, a fine wall of Acropolis limestone was built around the upper terrace of the Eleusinion, on the north slopes of the Acropolis; subsequently temples of Apollo Patroos (on the west side), and Zeus Agoraios (at the northwest) were constructed in the middle and later part of the century (see Section 4.3).[17] Around 500 there was a major expansion of the Eleusinion onto the middle and lower terraces, and the foundations were laid for an Ionic amphiprostyle tetrastyle temple of Triptolemos, almost certainly in marble and with a fine marble roof, on the middle terrace, although the temple itself was probably constructed only after the Persian Wars (Miles 1998: 33–56). To the south of the Acropolis the earliest temple of Dionysos Eleuthereus seems to date to the second half of the sixth century, and pedimental sculpture from it, showing Dionysos and satyrs, survives (Athens NM 3131). In the Sanctuary of Zeus Olympios building of the colossal temple to replace the first temple, which had been burnt down, seems to have started around 515, though it was never completed (Tölle-Kastenbein 1994b: 168–9).

---

15. As Sassù notes, in Archaic inscriptions χαλκία tends to refer to precious metals or dedications; it was gradually replaced by χρήματα.

16. For the sculpture, see Payne and Young 1936 and Section 12.1.

17. The fullest, if now dated, survey of Athenian building projects is Boersma 1970.

Outside Athens Laconian-style roof tiles and votives attest to cult activity at Rhamnous in the Sanctuary of Nemesis with some sort of building in the early years of the sixth century (Petrakos 1999b: 194–5); on Hymettos, perhaps to Apollo and perhaps in the middle of the century; to Apollo at Cape Zoster around 500; and to Artemis at Brauron around 500. Just north of Brauron, at the site of the Classical temple of Artemis Tauropolos at Halai Araphenides (modern Loutsa), late Archaic pottery may point to an earlier building there (Kalogeropoulos 2013). The existence of a late sixth-century seated cult statue of Dionysos at Ikarion implies the existence there too of a temple (Romano 1982), while at Thorikos the earliest phase of the theater appears to date to the very end of the sixth century or very start of the fifth, and the associated temple may be contemporary (Mussche 1998: 29–32). A temple has also been hypothesized at Prasiai based on textual evidence for cult (Paus. 1.31.2), and of the finding of a head that might come from a cult statue of Apollo.

At Eleusis, the seventh-century *telestērion* was replaced in the second half of the sixth century by a larger (c. 27 x 29 m) structure that remained in use until 480. This was a more elaborate building than its predecessor, with *poros* limestone walls and Parian marble ram heads on the corners of the roof. Twenty-two Ionic columns, supporting the roof, stood in the building's interior, which included a small, separate room in the southwest corner and tiers of nine steps on the north, south, and west walls. At roughly the same time, the sanctuary and parts of the settlement were enclosed by a three-meter thick mud-brick wall with at least seven towers and seven gates.[18] The positioning of the gates in that wall suggests that the main entrance to the site shifted from the south to the north side, which possibly reflects an increasingly close relationship between Eleusis and Athens (Cosmopoulos 2015: 139–42; Paga 2015: 109–12). Scholars have speculated that the procession from Athens to Eleusis as part of the celebration of the Eleusinian Mysteries started in the first half of the sixth century, but there is no secure evidence for this (Rönnberg 2021a: 256).

Scholars have long tried to link cult developments in sixth-century Athens and Attica to Peisistratos, but this has proved frustratingly difficult. Despite literary traditions that mention Peisistratos in relation to the Panathenaia, the reorganization of that festival undoubtedly fell before Peisistratos was tyrant, as did the construction of the Bluebeard temple. Only Photius' *Lexicon* (s.v. Βραυρωνία [β 264]) links Peisistratos with the temple at Brauron, which cannot be dated

---

18. Paga (2015: 109–12) argues that both the temple and the fortification wall were built late in the sixth century and that their traditional association with the Peisistratids should be abandoned; cf. Miles 1998: 27–8.

archaeologically with any precision. A number of lexicons variously record that Peisistratos built a sanctuary or temple to Apollo Pythios (Wilson 2007: 153), but no temple has yet been discovered, and confusion with the activities of his homonymous grandson cannot be ruled out. The building of the great temple of Zeus Olympios was undoubtedly started after Peisistratos's own death.

Although some chronologies would put the inception of dramatic festivals into the last years of Peisistratos, the chronology of early tragedy is fraught.[19] The first temple of Dionysos on the south slope of the Acropolis was built sometime in the second half of the sixth century, but whether dramatic performances initially took place at the site is disputed. A long scholarly tradition puts the earliest performances in the Agora, with temporary wooden seating, an arrangement abandoned only after the seating collapsed, but the basis of this is flimsy, and performances may have been at the later theater site from the start (Pickard-Cambridge 1946: 11–13; Kampourelli 2016: 39–40). The abundant presence of Dionysos in the imagery of Athenian pottery from the very start of the sixth century makes it clear that, although for the Athenians, as for other Greeks, Dionysos was thought of as a god come from elsewhere (enacted by bringing the image of Dionysos from Eleutherai, on the Boiotian border, to Athens [Paus. 1.20.3, 1.38.8]), he was fully at home in Attica well before we can demonstrate his worship either at Ikarion or in Athens itself.

The one religious intervention of Peisistratos that is beyond doubt is that on Delos. Peisistratos' purification of Delos is attested both by Herodotos and Thucydides (Hdt. 1.64.2; Thuc. 3.104). Athens' interest in and religious connections with Delos seem to have started at an earlier date, given the mention of "Deliastai" in Solon's laws (F88 Rhodes and Leāo), but Peisistratos' intervention represented a claim of Athenian responsibility over Delos that must reflect a wider claim to an Ionian heritage, and that is the precursor to Athenian support for the Ionian rebellion as well as for what modern scholars have named the Delian League (Parker 1996: 87–8; Constantakopoulou 2007: 63–6). Two buildings on Delos, the so-called Porinos Naos ("temple made of *poros* stone") and Treasury 5 have been associated with the Athenians, but whether correctly, and whether they date to the time of Peisistratos or of his sons, is unclear (Chankowski 2008: 11).

In Attica it is much easier to see the impact of Peisistratos' sons, and indeed grandson, on Athens' religious life. Not only is Hipparchos associated with regulating Homeric performance at the Panathenaia, but he is credited, most clearly in Plato's *Hipparchos*, with having herms placed half-way between Athens and

---

19. For questioning of the traditional dating, see Connor 1990. Sourvinou-Inwood's defense of the 530s seems to me inconclusive (Sourvinou-Inwood 2003: 103–4).

each of the villages of Attica, recording on one side where one was half-way to (as on the preserved example, I³ 1023 = P. A. Hansen 1983–1989: vol. 1: #304), and on the other giving an improving maxim (e.g. "Pass, thinking just thoughts," Pl. [*Hipparch.*] 229a) (Section 5.2.3). These herms both gave Hermes a special relationship to the Athenian countryside, and gave Athenians a special relationship with herms, a relationship that comes to be reflected in Athenian painted pottery, particularly in the second quarter of the fifth century.[20] The concern for what we might think of as the divine mapping out of Attica is also revealed by the establishment of the Altar of the Twelve Gods on the south side of the Agora (see Section 4.3), which was established by Peisistratos' grandson, also named Peisistratos, who was eponymous archon in 522/1 (Develin 1989: 47). This was the point from which all distances were measured (Hdt. 2.7.1; I³ 1092bis). The younger Peisistratos also dedicated, in the year of his archonship, an altar of Apollo Pythios at the sanctuary to that deity, which was situated at an unknown located just to the south of the other great building project begun in the immediately following years, the never-finished temple of Zeus Olympios, the Olympieion (Parker 1996: 72–3).

11.4 Kleisthenes and After

The years after Kleisthenes certainly saw significant building on the Acropolis. A new and very substantial temple of Athena Polias was probably begun before 500, and in the 480s the all-marble earlier Parthenon, unfinished when sacked by the Persians in 480, was begun (see Figure 39). It was sited immediately south of and parallel to the Athena Polias temple, but it was half as long again. Accompanying this building was a monumental gateway, the older Propylon (Hurwit 1999: 121–35).[21] Outside Athens, finds suggest that a cult of Athena was active at Sounion by the middle of the sixth century, and a small, distyle prostyle temple on the north hill, dedicated to Athena Sounias, seems to date c. 500 (Barletta 2015: 53–84). In the early years of the fifth century, construction was begun on a *poros* limestone temple in the Poseidon sanctuary. That temple, a conventional 6 x 13 Doric structure measuring 13 x 30 m, was unfinished when the Persians destroyed it in 480 (Sinn 1992; Camp II 2001: 305–9; Theodoropoulou-Polychroniadis 2015; Paga and Miles 2016). A distyle *in antis* temple, probably

---

20. For further discussion, see Parker 1996: 80–3; Osborne 2010: 341–67.

21. The existence of the Older Propylon is denied by Eiteljorg (1995), who dates the remodeling of the entrance court to the decade after Marathon, with subsequent repairs consequent on the Persian destruction of 480–79.

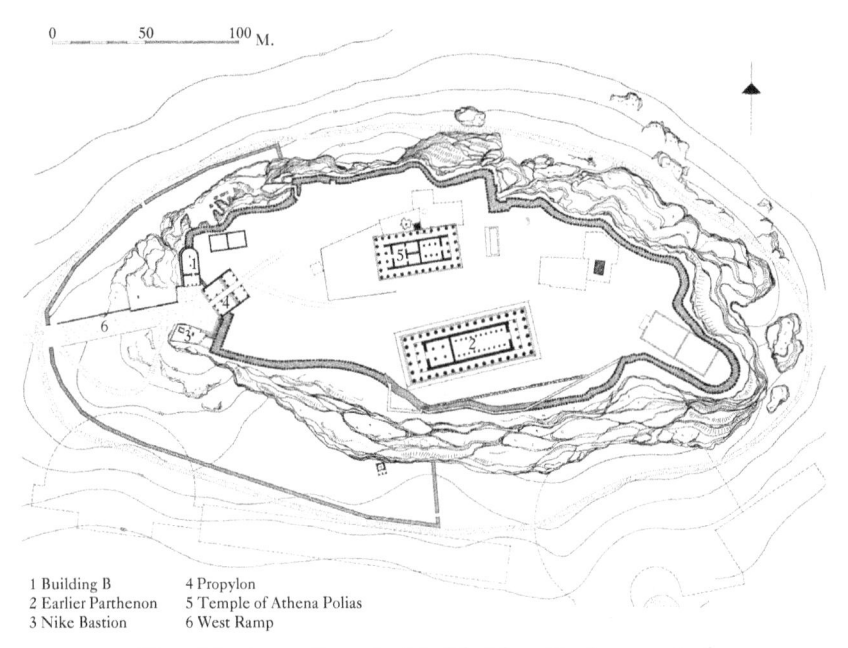

0   50   100 M.

1 Building B	4 Propylon
2 Earlier Parthenon	5 Temple of Athena Polias
3 Nike Bastion	6 West Ramp

FIGURE 39 Plan of the Acropolis c. 489. Modified from Travlos 1971: 61, fig. 71.

dedicated to Nemesis, was built in the sanctuary at Rhamnous from *poros* lime-stone at the end of the sixth century, and it too was subsequently destroyed by the Persians. Shortly after 480, a small (c. 10 x 6 m), non-peripteral temple, possibly dedicated to Themis, was built from local marble in polygonal masonry (Petrakos 1999a: vol. 1: 192–204 and *passim*; Camp II 2001: 301–5; Paga 2015: 112–16).

The Persians saw to it that these monumental temples had but a short life, but for Rhamnous they significantly boosted the cult. Pausanias says of Rhamnous that: "The dwellings of the people are beside the sea, but a little above the sea is a sanctuary of Nemesis, who of all deities is most inexorable toward the proud" (1.33.2; trans. J. G. Frazer), and then goes on to say that when the Persians landed at Marathon in 490 they brought with them a block of Parian marble for a trophy to commemorate the victory they expected to win, and that after the Persians' defeat, Pheidias carved a statue of Nemesis from that very block of marble. However one assesses the truth of that tale (the shattered remains of the statue of Nemesis from the site did indeed all come from a single block of Parian marble but considerably post-date 490; Despinis 1971), it is apparent that the Athenians' victory at nearby Marathon elevated the standing of the cult of Nemesis.

What had a much longer life than the temples begun shortly after 500 was the religious reorganization that went along with Kleisthenes' reforms of civic orga-nization. The four Ionian tribes had undoubtedly had some religious roles—and indeed seem to have retained them, to judge by the fragments of Athens' religious calendar that survive from its late fifth-century re-inscription (Lambert 1993: 251–61; see Sections 5.3 and 11.3). But Kleisthenes' ten new tribes also acquired a distinct role in Athenian religious life, as the basis of competitions at festivals, and not just at existing festivals, such as the Panathenaia, Eleusinia, Thargelia, and City Dionysia, but at a whole range of new festivals—festivals of Prometheus, Hephaistos, and Herakles in the 490s, of Pan in the 480s (Osborne 1993; Fisher 2011).[22] These tribal competitions ensured mass participation in Athenian festival life, and were one of the ways in which festivals came to play a peculiarly large part in Athenian life ([Xen.] *Constitution of the Athenians* 3.2; cf. Thuc. 2.38.1). They also ensured that Athenian life was significantly focused upon the gods and goddesses.

If the Kleisthenic tribes were of crucial importance to the nature of and participation in religious festivals, so too were the Kleisthenic demes to local religious life.[23] Already by 500 the deme of Rhamnous is recording financial transactions on a lead tablet, has officials that it calls *epistatai*, and puts money in the hands of *hieropoioi* (*IG* I³.247bis: 957). This very much looks like deme control of sanctuary finances—something very clear from later fifth-century deme documents (Osborne and Rhodes 2017: #134, 59). The rapidity with which the local community had assumed responsibility for the financial side of the local sanctuary is striking, and testimony to the centrality of religious matters to local life.

The earliest deme decrees that we have concern religious events. Earliest of all is a decree from the urban deme Skambonidai, dated to c. 460 (Osborne and Rhodes 2017: #107). This inscription reveals Skambonidai to have *hieropoioi* who assist the demarch with his religious responsibilities, and lists the sacrifices for which they are responsible, including one to the eponymous hero of their tribe, Leos, and others that are associated, at least in part, with city festivals, including the Panathenaia, Synoikia, and the Dipolieia. Since demes were not themselves new—what Kleisthenes had done was to give newly defined political rights to existing communities—it is plausible that the communities that became demes had some religious identity even before Kleisthenes' reforms, but those communities are unlikely to have had their own formally appointed officials. Distributing responsibilities to the new deme officials—officials who could be held responsible for what went on—seems to have happened quite rapidly after Kleisthenes'

---

22. Fisher (cf. Christesen 2012: 153–63) seems to me to have successfully established mass participation against the variously expressed skepticism of N. F. Jones 1999 and Pritchard 2004.

23. For the religious life of the Classical deme, see Osborne 1985: 178–81; Whitehead 1986: 176–222; Parker 2005: 50–78. For the religious impact of the Kleisthenic deme, see Parker 1996: 102–17.

reforms. Evidence for demes also forming local religious associations with one or more of their neighbors, so as to celebrate various festivals jointly, comes only from the fourth century, but such associations too may have formed much earlier, and in some cases, at least, may go back to pre-deme communities.[24]

What the Kleisthenic reforms did not do, as is emphasized by [Arist.] *Constitution of the Athenians* 21.6, is change where the key responsibilities for performing cult activity lay. Although Aristotle's list of devices employed to facilitate the establishment of democracy in Athens (by Kleisthenes) and in Cyrene include creating more and different tribes and phratries and amalgamating many private cults into a few public ones (*Pol.* 1319b19–27), Kleisthenes in fact left both the phratries and the *genē* untouched, so that the families in charge of cults did not change (Kearns 1985). Although the tribes were new, most, if not all, of the heroes after whom they were named had existing cult, and that cult seems to have been left in the hands of the *genos* already responsible for it. According to the Aristotelian *Constitution of the Athenians* 21.6, the tribal heroes were chosen by Apollo at Delphi by lot from a hundred possible names sent to Delphi by the Athenians, and presumably this hundred deliberately encompassed all major Athenian hero cults. We know of some 130 male heroes who certainly or probably received cult in Attica, and there is no doubt at all that there were many more hero cults than that (every deme calendar discovered adds to the list).[25]

We do not know how extensive intervention in religious practice had been during the sixth century. But with Kleisthenes' reforms the beginning of inscribing public decisions on stone reveals the constant interplay between the political and religious sides of Athenian life. Of the five Athenian public decisions inscribed on stone that are plausibly dated before 480, four concern matters religious: two different episodes of regulation with regard to the Herakleia at Marathon are preserved on two sides of the same stone (*IG* I[3].2–3); a set of regulations about what may or may not be done by whom on the Acropolis and what the penalties are for transgression (*IG* I[3].4); and a set of regulations about what animals are to be sacrificed to whom on the occasion of the Eleusinia (*IG* I[3].5).

Do the new types of evidence, such as public decrees, actually mean that there was an increased engagement with religious cult after the Kleisthenic reforms? A positive answer is suggested by dedicatory activity on the Athenian acropolis. Although the dating of inscriptions and *korai* is at best approximate, the dates that scholars have given both to sculpture and to dedications tells the same basic

---

24. For the Marathonian tetrapolis, see Lambert 2018. Note also Kydantidai and Ionidai celebrating festivals of Herakles together, *SEG* 39.148.

25. I base my count upon information drawn from Kearns 1989 Appendix 1.

story, and that is the story of a massive growth of numbers in the late sixth century, leading to a high point around 500 and with a sudden decline with the Persian invasion of 480.[26] For *korai* the steep rise begins around 520, the peak is reached shortly after 510, and the steep decline begins already around 490. For dedicatory inscriptions, the steep rise begins around 510, the peak is reached only about 490, and the decline is very sudden with the Persian sack. At Eleusis similarly, one *korē* is dedicated in the second quarter of the sixth century, but the other five all date to after 525.[27]

That the peak numbers of dedications of *korai* and of dedicatory inscriptions come after Kleisthenes does not mean that they therefore come as a result of Kleisthenes' reforms, and indeed one striking feature of the distribution is that, were one not to know that there was a major political dislocation in the years 510 to 507, one would not predict it from these results—Kleisthenes comes in the middle of a trend, not at its start.

Although Kleisthenes' reforms cannot underlie the increase in monumental dedicatory activity on the Acropolis, the increase in dedications and the political upheaval in Athens should not be considered as independent phenomena. Peisistratos had taken some care to reduce the level of interaction between town and countryside. His introduction of traveling judges and his own frequent visits to the countryside ([Arist.] *Constitution of the Athenians* 16.5) are said to have been aimed at reducing the need for those in the country to coming into town for judicial or administrative reasons (see Section 6.3), and the anecdote that [Aristotle] tells about Peisistratos exempting a poor farmer from tax similarly points to the desire to prevent rural unrest impinging on urban politics (*Constitution of the Athenians* 16. 6–7).

The story Herodotos (6.103) is about Kimon son of Stesagoras being murdered by the sons of Peisistratos after his third successive Olympic chariot race victory with the same horses, despite the fact that Kimon had the second of the victories announced as a victory of Peisistratos, reveals how sensitive the tyrant family was to others rivaling their prestige. So too the succession of eponymous archons from different major families revealed by a surviving fragment (inscribed c. 425) of the Athenian archon list (Meiggs and Lewis 1988: #6; Develin 1989: 35–48; see also Section 6.3) reveals a delicate balancing act going on, wherein the archonship, the one publicly bestowed honor that could not be abolished if the constitution was to be advertised as still operative, was made to circulate in a way

---

26. See most conveniently Wagner 1997: fig. 91.

27. On the chronological distribution of *korai*, see Karakasi 2003: 115–17.

encouraging potential rivals to focus their rivalry on each other rather than on the Peisistratids.

But the promotion of the town as the cultural center that we see with Hipparchos' Panathenaic reforms, and with the encouragement to think of the Agora as the center around which the world of Attica revolved, inevitably encouraged the elite to display their wealth to the people. The story of Hipparchos' murder being a product of rivalry for the affections of a handsome young of elite male between one of the Peisistratids and a member of an elite family from Aphidna, not from the town itself, is in a sense overdetermined by the situation that Peisistratos' sons had effectively created (Hdt. 5.55–6; Thuc. 6.54–9; Plutarch *Mor.* 628d–e; J. K. Davies 1971: 472–4).[28] It is a further sign of the prominence of rivalry between elite families in these years that the Alkmaionidai wanted to claim particular prominence in bringing about the final removal of Hippias (Hdt. 6.123.2), and that, once Hippias was removed, Athens collapsed into family-led factional strife between Kleisthenes and Isagoras.

The bulge in dedications on the Athenian Acropolis between 520 and 480 is a monumental reflection of a world in which elite families were seeking every opportunity to display their wealth and cultural prestige. Such elite family competition was not ended by Kleisthenes' democratic reforms—indeed, rather to the contrary, what those reforms did was to open up opportunities for participation, and thereby for competition, to a much wider range of individuals.

But if the increased pace of dedicatory activity on the Acropolis was in part political, it was not the less a religious phenomenon. The choice to make one's mark in a sanctuary may have been determined in part by the absence of other options—cemeteries were the only other spaces available, and although they were indeed used, not least in this period, family deaths were not always timed for optimal political effect. But the decision of the wealthy to show off in a sanctuary undoubtedly drew attention to the gods. It is worth noting, in this context, the high quality of the pottery dedications found on the Athenian Acropolis (see Section 4.5.4). Repeatedly the finest of the pots known from a painter's hand are the pots excavated from the Acropolis (Wagner 1997: 85–6). As we have seen, some of these dedications are explicitly made by the potter or painter himself (most explicitly Athens NM 2134, a kantharos by Nearchos), and many more may also be. However wealthy potters could become, and Nearchos seems to have been wealthy enough to dedicate a particularly large (2 m tall) and fine *korē* by the

---

28. The puzzlement scholars (see, for example, Gray 2007) have felt at the space Herodotos devotes to the origins of the family, the Gephyraioi, to which Harmodios and Aristogeiton belonged, is, in my view, to be explained by the importance of elite politics and of the balance of Athenian politics being changed by the greater involvement of families from Attica.

sculptor Antenor (Athens Acropolis Museum 681 with *IG* I³.628),[29] they were not members of the elite; just as the Pioneers of red-figure pottery like to picture themselves at the symposion, so by their dedications they and other potters inserted themselves into, and thereby reinforced, the competitive practices of the elite. Kleisthenes' reforms, on this reckoning, only further encouraged competitive display across Athenian society and, with it, competition to give pleasure to Athena.

11.5 Gods, Heroes, and Festivals

What by the end of the Archaic period was religious life like for Athenians? What sorts of religious acts did Athenians perform? Whom did they perform them with? How often did they perform them? Whom did they perform them for?

Scholars have regularly treated the central religious action as animal blood-sacrifice, largely because animal sacrifice was the action that ancient writers themselves thought most in need of theological explanation. Hesiod's explanation, in terms of the actions of Prometheus (*Op.* 47–59, *Theog.* 535–70), has drawn most scholarly attention, but the Athenians seem to have had their own account. Although this account, concerned to explain the particular actions performed at the festival of the Dipolieia and the sacrifice known as the Bouphonia ("Cow-slaying") is primarily preserved for us in Porphyry's late antique treatise on veg-etarianism, *De Abstinentia* (2.29–30), Porphyry quotes Theophrastus, and we know the festival also to have been discussed by the Atthidographer Androtion (*FGrH* 324 F16). The story told concerns an ox killed with an axe for eating cakes intended for the gods, a subsequent drought, and the ending of that drought through punishing the axe and through ritualizing the killing. It differs from the Hesiodic story in its focus, interested not in the unequal division of the sacrificed animal but in why one might kill a useful animal in the first place, and it differs also in making the issue not one that arose back in mythical times, but one that takes place in contemporary circumstances and is settled by contemporary means—both the trial and the ritualized play-acting imitation of the act of killing the ox. Indeed, the explanation is as much a justification for and authorization of civic activities as it is an explanation of sacrifice itself.

Animal sacrifice did not occur only at festivals of the whole city, but it did demand the presence of a group that would then consume the meat (barring occasions such as the holocaust sacrifice of a piglet, attested in the fifth-century Thorikos calendar [Osborne and Rhodes 2017: #146]). That group might be local

---

29. On the *korai* from the Acropolis, see Section 12.1.2.

(as institutionalized in deme calendars) or familial, either centered on the more or less extended family group or involving the whole of a descent group (as in the *genos* or the phratry). Such a group was needed, too, for various acts that celebrated the gods, in particular dancing and drama: one cannot have much of a festival without a crowd. But other religious activities could be performed by individuals or groups too small to support sacrifice. These included prayer, which could be performed by anyone anywhere and did not require utterance aloud; libation, the pouring of a liquid offering of wine or milk and honey; and dedication of an object, often in conjunction with prayer (either giving a gift in hope of a reciprocal reward or to recognize good things already granted, or both).

Sacrificial activity is archaeologically visible, requiring an altar and producing long-lasting remains (in the form of bones). Bones offer a history of changing sacrificial practices over time in terms of preferred victims, but no Archaic Attic sanctuary has produced a rich animal bone sequence.[30] Dedications are one of our prime sources of evidence, not simply of cult behavior, but also of what was available to Athenians when and in what quantities, and dedications have been deployed repeatedly throughout this account. We should, however, be aware that many items that were dedicated were perishable and that the archaeological picture is far from complete. Libations leave no lasting trace, unless through the dedication of the libation vessel, which seems to have been a localized practice (cf. Tomlinson 1990: 99–100 on Perachora). Similarly, only associated dedications give evidence for prayer.

Differential archaeological visibility is reinforced by the fact that the religious activities of larger groups are much better attested in texts than are the religious activities of smaller groups and individuals. Larger groups need to communicate to co-ordinate their actions, and this encourages writing down what is to happen and making that writing available to those who need to know—and hence potentially to us. Individuals, families, and small groups have no such need. So, too, things that need to happen regularly have much more chance of being recorded than one-off acts—except in as far as idiosyncratic one-off acts may be recorded for the purpose of mocking them (as with Theophrastus' sketch of the Superstitious Man [*Char.* 16]). In all these ways, our picture of religious life is heavily weighted toward the institutionalized religious acts.[31] It is important

---

30. But see Reese 1989 for the predominantly sheep and goat bones from an altar of Aphrodite Ourania in the Athenian Agora, which began to be used c. 500.

31. This has been both responsible for and exacerbated by the focus for the last generation on "*polis* religion," a focus that is particularly evident in Parker 1996; Parker 2005. For critique, see Kindt 2012.

both to acknowledge this bias, and at the same time to give due weight to this evidence.

What the archaeological and textual evidence does is to show how much time and energy (and expense) Athenians devoted to their gods. Although introducing new gods (and with them new festivals) never ceased in Athens (Garland 1991; Parker 1996: 152–87), by the end of the Archaic period the great majority of Athens' Classical festival calendar was in place. There were festival days for various gods at the beginning of every month, so that the first to fourth and sixth to eighth of every month were festival days—important enough for the Athenian Assembly and law courts never to meet on those days. In addition, we know of some 37 days devoted to festivals that occurred just once a year; those festivals lasted between one and seven (the Eleusinian Mysteries) days (Mikalson 1975: 186–8). These were just the city festivals; there was also the phratry festival of the Apatouria, and individual *genē* and demes had their own calendars of festivals, some of which mirrored the festivals of the city, but most of which were additional. The Athenians were conscious that they celebrated more festivals than other Greek cities ([Xen.] *Constitution of the Athenians* 3.2, 3.8, cf. 2.9; Thuc. 2.38.1). Of course, nothing like the entire populace of Attica attended any particular city festival, and within the demes too there were no doubt moments in the year when most of the community came together and moments when individual demesmen were content to let others celebrate. But for everyone, as the timing of Assembly meetings shows, these festivals structured the year.

Most of the Olympian gods were celebrated monthly—Athena, Hermes, Aphrodite, Artemis, Apollo, Poseidon—as was Herakles, with Apollo, Artemis, and Athena also being celebrated at various annual festivals. Of the others, Demeter was celebrated at the Thesmophoria, Skira, and Haloa as well as the Eleusinian Mysteries, Dionysos was celebrated at the Oschophoria and Lenaia as well as the City and Rural Dionysia, Zeus was celebrated in the Dipolieia and Diasia. Even Hera, who shows up very little in Athens, was celebrated with Zeus in the Theogamia.

But just as cultic activity was not limited to festivals, so it was not limited to the Olympian gods. From the Classical period and later there is a great deal of textual and archaeological evidence for the worship of named heroes in Classical Attica (Section 11.4). Such textual evidence is largely lacking for earlier periods, and the relevant archaeological evidence is also relatively scanty.[32] Although attempts have been made to identify at Sounion a cult of Phrontis, the steersman of Menelaos buried at Sounion (*Od.* 3.278–85), the evidence (Section 11.2)

---

32. The textual evidence is collected in Kearns 1989.

is inconclusive (Abramson 1979; Parker 1996: 35; Barletta 2015: 81–2). In Athens the locations of the cult of Aglauros and of the cult of Amynos are known, but in neither case can we trace this confidently back into the Archaic period.[33] Since we also lack local sacrificial calendars from demes or other cult organizations from the Archaic period, of the sort that tells us so much of local hero cult in the Classical period, it is extremely hard to know how important a place hero cult had for Athenians in the Archaic period. The extant fragments of Solon's calendar (Section 11.3) include a sacrifice to the hero Leos at Hagnous (Solon *Laws* F83 Leão and Rhodes; Parker 1996: 52–3). Had the entire calendar been preserved, we would have a much richer picture of hero cults in Archaic Athens.

The absence of specific Archaic evidence for the great majority of heroes should not lead to our under-estimating the place they had in life in Archaic Athens. The fact that Kleisthenes could be held by the *Constitution of the Athenians* (21.6) to have given Delphi a list of 100 possible heroes from which to choose the ten tribal eponyms is a sign of the rich supply of heroes available. For although we do not know whether each of the heroes chosen as tribal eponyms had a pre-existing cult, it is certain that there was pre-existing cult in some cases and likely that there was some cultic presence in all cases, and all of the eponymous tribal heroes certainly had a cult after the creation of the tribes (Kearns 1985: 192–8; cf. Kron 1976; Section 11.4).

Some hero cult seems to have been associated with "civic" issues, their stories good to think within the context of how individuals' interests and those of the city aligned and providing models of putting the city before individual interests. Heroes also offered an explanation and an identity for groups of various kinds— at one level simply an excuse for commensality. But many hero cults seem to have been more closely tied with the life of an individual, whether associated with life crises (coming of age, in particular) or with health, or with the undertaking of dangerous tasks (going to sea). Heroes—male and female—offered power-ful models whom communities and individuals could, by their cult activity, link themselves to and enlist in their own support (Kearns 1989; Kearns 1990).

But if by the end of the Archaic period Athenian religious life already looked very much like the religious life of the Classical period, how long had that been the case? We have seen (Section 11.3) that much of the structure of the city's fes-tival year can be traced back to Solon, but we have also seen that at that date in Attica temple buildings were few, monumental stone dedications only beginning to appear, and the competitive program of the Panathenaia lay in the future. By

---

33. Aglauros was worshipped in a cave located on the eastern side of the Acropolis (Hdt. 8.53; Kearns 1989: 139). Amynos was worshipped on the south slopes of the Areopagus (Kearns 1989: 146–7).

Solon's time cult activity was widespread across Attica, and had been for more than a century, but, compared with later periods, the physical context of that activity was quite different, and the range of ways of worshipping the gods more restricted. The changing iconography of Athenian pottery found in cult contexts, or otherwise associated with the gods and their worship, suggests changing emphasis within worship from the celebrating with the gods in the eighth century, marked by dancing and giving the gods the objects one used oneself, through the acknowledgement of the otherness of the divine world, in the encounters with the monstrous that figure large in the seventh, to the exploration in the sixth of divine power, through developed mythology. Within a structure that changed slowly, the Athenian experience of the gods varied markedly over time.

12

Cultural History

DO ATHENS AND Attica have a distinct cultural history during the Archaic period? The clearest case for Athens standing apart in cultural terms is to be found in the Attic alphabet. The Attic alphabet is very close to the alphabet of Aegina, but it differs in adopting a form of *lambda* and *digamma* found not in Aeginetan writing but at Eretria, and a form of *gamma* that is found at neither Aegina nor Eretria (Jeffery 1990: 66–7, 79–81, 110). The earliest Attic inscription of any length, that on the Dipylon oinochoe, is anomalous in some of its letter forms (including *alpha*, *iota*, and *lambda*).[1] Like other Greek communities, eighth-century Athens seems from the beginning to have used the letter forms it adopted as a way to mark itself out as distinctive.[2]

Conscious adoption of a distinctive visual style is also apparent in painted pottery, and again already from as early as we have Iron Age evidence.[3] That distinctive style was a matter of potting as well as of painting. That is, Athens maintained a distinct repertoire of pot shapes as well as a distinct set of decorative choices. This is quickly revealed by comparisons with her neighbors. For all the evident commercial success of Euboian pendant semicircle skyphoi in the eighth century, or of Corinthian aryballoi in the seventh, Athens emulates neither shape, nor does she offer anything comparable to the decorative modes employed in either case. So, too, the Athenian repertoire of funerary imagery and ship imagery on Late Geometric pottery is not found in the pottery of her neighbors; and although broadly geometric decorative and figure styles

---

1. On the Dipylon oinochoe, see Binek 2017. For discussion of that inscription in the context of the symposion, see Section 10. For the earliest inscriptions from Attica, see Section 2.2.1.

2. On this deliberate cultural self-differentiation, see Osborne 2019b.

3. For an outline history of Athenian pottery, see Section 4.5.

The Oxford History of the Archaic Greek World. Robin Osborne, Oxford University Press. © Oxford University Press 2023.
DOI: 10.1093/oso/9780197644423.003.0012

are produced in many eighth-century Greek communities, and there is some overlap in scenes related to ritual, the overall organization of decoration makes Athenian products distinctive.[4] Athens' seventh-century Protoattic figure style is quite different from figure styles used elsewhere, as is also, beyond a common interest in the scene of the blinding of Polyphemos, the mythological subject matter shown.

Although the techniques of Athenian black-figure and, later, red-figure pottery were widely imitated, the repertoire of shapes and images of Athenian pottery remained distinct until at least well into the fifth century, when some South Italian pottery closely follows Athenian choices. For all that Athens' development of black-figure pottery owed a great deal to Corinth, the Athenian products remain clearly distinct, even when that debt was closest, as in the komast cups. Similarly, even those potters who deliberately imitated aspects of pottery outside Athens to make their pottery more attractive to non-Athenian customers—and the Nikosthenes workshop (see Section 4.5.4) is outstanding here—produced pots that were anything but reproductions of the material that they emulated. Nikosthenes takes over shapes from Etruscan bucchero, but continues to decorate those shapes in a distinctively Athenian manner (Tosto 1999).

But did the Athenians' distinctive pottery reflect purely Athenian cultural history, or was it a product, at least in part, of the cultural history of those who purchased it? That Athenian potters and painters had an eye to the market is clear, not simply from what potters such as Nikosthenes did, but also from the distribution of Athenian pottery around the Mediterranean, which suggests the targeting of particular demand (see Section 8.3). We might wonder, indeed, whether the rapid sequence of different shapes for drinking cups during the sixth century (Section 4.5.4) did not stem, at least in part, from Athenian potters wishing to create new fashions that would lead to purchasers discarding perfectly good pots that were out of fashion to be seen to be up with the latest trends. But the initiative for all these changes was Athenian, and it is properly a part of Athenian cultural history.

The question is whether there were any aspects of Athenian pottery production that were determined from outside. That particular pots might be commissioned is clear, but how extensive was such commissioning? Scholars have suggested that not simply some individual scenes (of athletes and symposiasts in loincloths and of particular myths) but some whole categories of scenes (notably

---

4. For Geometric, the organization of Coldstream 2008 enables the differences from other regional styles to be easily seen. For common interest in certain scenes with a relation to ritual, see S. Langdon 2008.

scenes of explicit sexual intercourse) were part of the Athenian repertory significantly because they were in demand by the Etruscans (Shapiro 2000; de la Genière 2006; de la Genière 2009; Lynch 2009). While the case for particular painters cultivating scenes that they know attracted Etruscan purchasers is strong, the case for more general influence is weak. The changes that occur in the types of image being painted on Athenian pottery are so coordinated across all types of scene that there can be no doubt that they reflect, not responses to demand from outside Athens, but changing interests and values among those resident at Athens.[5]

12.1 Sculpture

A distinctively Athenian history of sculpture is much harder to discern than a distinctively Athenian alphabet or a distinctively Athenian production of pottery. This is in part because of the very much smaller number of statues that survive by comparison with either pots or painted, scratched, or inscribed letters. But it is arguably also because, whereas pots were created from local resources, and writing appears on materials that were to hand in Attica, sculpture regularly demanded either technologies developed outside Attica or materials acquired from beyond Attica (whether that be fine marble, or the ingredients needed to create bronze). Sculptors were therefore part of a world that transcended the boundaries of Athens and Attica.[6] This becomes clear once sculptors begin to sign their work: whereas the names of painters of pottery and of the potters suggest Athenians or non-Greeks who had presumably come to Athens as slaves, sculptors proudly identify themselves as from other Greek cities.

12.1.1 The Beginnings of Sculpture in Attica

In Athens, as in other Greek cities, sculpture appears in two main locations: cemeteries and sanctuaries. There were plentiful Greek traditions of images of the gods existing in mythological time. For Athens, Pausanias records traditions that the mythical king Kekrops had dedicated a wooden statue of Hermes that was to be found in his own day (later second century CE) in the temple of Athena Polias (Paus. 1.27.1). That temple was also reckoned to house a statue of Athena that had fallen from heaven some time before the synoecism of Attica (1.26.6; cf. reference

---

5. For coordinated changes, Osborne 2018c; for the implications of this for relations with the Etruscan market, Osborne 2018c: 46–8.

6. For general histories of Archaic Greek sculpture, see Boardman 1978; Stewart 1990; Ridgway 1993; Rolley 1994; Fullerton 2016.

to the wooden statue of Athena Polias set up "by the *autochthones*" in Plut. *apud* Euseb. *Praep. evang.* 3.8). Pausanias also records an aniconic *xoanon* of wingless Victory (5.26.6), a *xoanon* of Artemis at Brauron (1.23.7, 1.33.1), and a *xoanon* of Dionysos brought from Eleutherai (1.38.8).[7]

From the eighth century, four small ivory statues (the largest 24 cm in height) of a naked woman wearing a *polos* hat were recovered from grave 13 of the Dipylon cemetery, a small terracotta statue (13 cm high) of a naked woman from a child's grave at Merenda, and a bronze statuette of a naked woman (16 cm high) from the Athenian Acropolis (Carter 1985: 1–7; Böhm 1990: 149, 51, 56–7; Rolley 1994: 96; Zosi 2012: 146–52; Doronzio 2018: 24–5). The ivory statues have attracted much attention since, although recognizably derived from a Syrian tradition via the southeast Aegean, they are local products (albeit in exotic material). The Acropolis statue seems to belong to the same tradition—although given the absence of predecessors or successors, the sense of "tradition" is rather weak.

The other human figures in bronze recovered from the Acropolis seem to have belonged to bronze tripods that were dedicated there in some numbers (fragments of some 70 tripods have been identified, Holtzmann 2003: 38–40) during the later eighth century and into the seventh (Section 11.1). These figures include both helmeted and bare-headed figures: for example, a figure that once wielded a spear, and a bull-headed figure (both from the eighth century), and a second spear thrower (from the early seventh). From the early seventh various orientalizing attachments (griffin heads, sirens) are also found (Weber 1974; Hurwit 1999: 91–4; Scholl 2006: 49–67, 90–105).

The tripods are good evidence for the importance, indeed arguably centrality, of the Acropolis to Athenian cult by the late eighth century, but it is not clear that independent sculpture played any significant part in the material dedicated on the Acropolis during that time period. In addition to the aforementioned naked bronze woman, a bronze charioteer (11.1 cm high) from the early seventh century survives from a chariot group that may have adorned a tripod, along with a bronze winged goddess (9.2 cm high), and—a rare import—a Cretan bronze figure of a man bringing some form of offering (17.2 cm high) (Hurwit 1999: 94–8; Scholl 2006: 66–7, 106–10; Doronzio 2018: 35–41, 50–1; for dedications on the Athenian acropolis, see further Section 11.1). During the seventh century the dedication of two female terracotta statues points toward the increasing importance of sculpture (Section 11.1).

---

7. This evidence for *xoana* is collected in Papadopoulos 1980: 27–30; see also Donohue 1988.

12.1.2 *Kouroi* and *Korai*

At the end of the seventh century the situation changes dramatically with the appearance in Attica of monumental stone sculpture, first in the form of *kouroi*, then of *korai* and grave *stēlai* (see Section 4.4.4). Elsewhere in the Greek world *korai*, life-sized and under life-sized stone figures of standing women, first appeared on Delos, on Thera, and on Crete in the middle of the seventh century (Karakasi 2003: 67–8). *Kouroi*, statues of naked males, standing with their arms by their sides and one foot slightly advanced, looking straight ahead, followed before the end of the century. Early examples of *kouroi* and some at least of the earliest *korai* are made of Naxian marble, even if found on Thera and Delos. *The kouroi differ from the korai in being, in many instances, colossal.*

The Attic *kouroi* from the end of the seventh century belong to the same colossal tradition, and seem, from the examples found in and around the Kerameikos, immediately to have been used as grave markers (as they probably were on Thera), as well as for dedications (as they were on Delos), as in the series of four *kouroi* (see Figure 40) in the Sanctuary of Poseidon at Sounion (see Section 11.1) (Theodoropoulou-Polychroniadis 2015: 114–15, 18–19).[8] Unlike the earliest *korai*—Nikandre, from Delos, and the Auxerre Goddess, perhaps originally from Crete—the early Athenian *kouroi* are not strongly indebted to the Daedalic tradition: their faces are not triangular, and the hair, although highly formalized, does not have the same wig-like appearance. Scholars have debated whether there was a single workshop responsible for all the over-life-sized early Attic *kouroi* or whether one should separate the Sounion *kouroi* from those of similar date found in Athens (Section 4.4.4); but, despite differences in detail, especially in the shape of the face, the overall conception of the body in space is shared and distinctive. Parallels with Athenian late Protoattic and early black-figure pottery, particularly work ascribed to the Nessos Painter, show how firmly rooted these *kouroi* are in local traditions of representation. But the idea of monumental marble sculpture, the idea of using it for dedications in a sanctuary, and such practices as inscription upon the limbs of the statue came from elsewhere in the Aegean, as did the marble, which is Naxian (Richter 1970: 30–58; Pedley 1978; Karakatsanis 1986; Rolley 1994: 165–7; Sturgeon 2006; D'Onofrio 2008; Hochscheid 2015: 93–156; Palagia and Maniatis 2015). Recent work has concluded that, despite an ancient tradition that Greek sculpture borrowed their canon of proportions from Egypt, not a single *kouros* can be found that fits the Egyptian canon (Carter and Steinberg 2010).

---

8. On the late seventh- rather than early sixth-century date of the colossal *kouroi* dedicated to Poseidon, see D'Onofrio 2008: 207, 11.

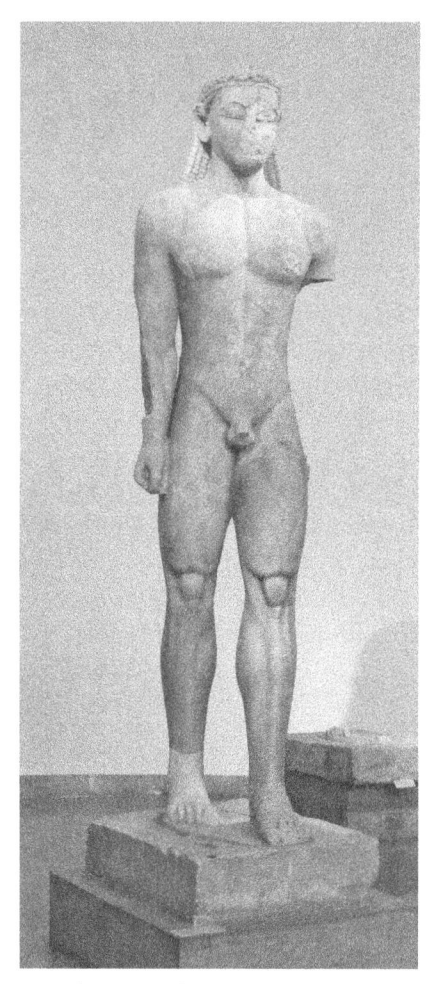

FIGURE 40 Naxian marble *kouros* from the Sanctuary of Poseidon at Sounion; c. 600: height: 3.05 m. Athens National Archaeological Museum 2720. Photo by Sharon Mollerus.

A number of *kouroi* and bases for *kouroi* used as grave markers survive from both Athens and Attica. Notable among the more than 25 examples known are: (1) very similar *kouroi* from c. 560 found at Kalyvia Kouvara ("Volomandra") (Athens NM 1906) and at an unknown location (Florence Museo Archeologico); (2) a *kouros* of mid-century date found in a cemetery at Merenda (Athens NM 4890) together with the Phrasikleia *korē* (see below); (3) a *kouros* from Anavyssos, dated to around 530, that has traditionally, but probably wrongly, been associated with a base (found in the same grave plot) commemorating one Kroisos (Athens NM 3851); and (4) a *kouros* dating to the end of the century from the Olymbos area north of Anavyssos, the base of which reads "Of Aristodikos" (Athens NM 3938, Karusos 1961).[9]

Despite the strength of the early *kouros* production in Attica, *kouroi* play a relatively small role in Athenian sculpture after c. 550, although they continue to be used occasionally in sanctuaries as well as on graves. As elsewhere, after the first third of the sixth century production of colossal *kouroi* ceased in Attica; later examples were never more than slightly larger than life-sized. Small fragments indicate that there were nine *kouroi* put up in the Sanctuary of Athena at Sounion ranging in date from around 575 to 490, and all of them were under-life-sized. On the Athenian Acropolis a small number of *kouroi* were dedicated in the second half of the sixth century and at the start of the fifth, along with a curious draped male statue in the pose of a *korē* (Acropolis Museum 633; Barletta 1987: 246 #34).

The *korai* found in Attica (including Athens) greatly outnumber *kouroi* thanks to an extraordinary sequence of more than 120 examples (although many are preserved only in small fragments) from the Acropolis, starting around 560 and continuing right down to 480. These are as remarkable for their variety as for their number. They vary in size from well under-life-size (the smallest is 40 cm high) to considerably over life-size (the largest example being the 2-meter-tall statue known as Antenor's *korē*; Acropolis Museum 681 with *IG* I³.628), but they vary too in their dress. Not only is there the one famous example dressed in a peplos rather than the usual chiton and himation (Acropolis Museum 679), but even those that are similarly attired render the garments involved in quite different ways. Together they must have put on a fashion display that was continuously renewed.[10]

Two early Acropolis *korai* are of Naxian marble, but the vast majority are of Parian marble. Pentelic marble is used occasionally from the beginning, but it becomes more common in the last quarter of the sixth century; nevertheless, island marble continues to dominate. In terms of function, these *korai* both recognize the maiden to whom they are dedicated (in this case Athena) and offer her that most essential exchange gift, the marriageable maiden, without whom society would cease to exist. In doing so they acknowledge both the similarity of goddess and human maidens and the fundamental difference between ephemeral human maidenhood and Athena's undying maidenhood (Osborne 1994b;

---

9. *Kouroi* are usefully cataloged in Meyer and Brüggemann 2007: 133–5, 66–72, 99–208, 15–7. Karusos 1961: 59–66 catalogs those *kouroi* certainly or probably from graves, including those known only from surviving bases.

10. On Attic *korai*, see Payne and Young 1936; Rolley 1994: 181–7; Karakasi 2003: 115–41; Keesling 2003; Stieber 2004; Meyer and Brüggemann 2007: 15–50; Franssen 2011: 140 (for the number of korai), 50–4 (for size and variety).

Meyer and Brüggemann 2007). In terms of sculptural history, these *korai* show Athenian sculptors both aware of and learning from sculptors working elsewhere, and then manifesting their own distinct idiom.

The same story can be read from *korai* found elsewhere in Attica, where eight are known to have been dedicated in the Sanctuary of Demeter at Eleusis, and five from across Attica. The latter five seem to have been used as grave markers, a use to which *korai* seem not to have been put in Athens itself and rarely in other parts of Greece, and all of them belong to the period 580–540, including what may be the earliest of all Attic *korai*, which was found at Agios Ioannis Rentis near the Peiraieus (Peiraieus Museum 2530, Karakasi 2003: 116). Two of the five *korai* used as grave markers are particularly notable. These were found, not many miles apart from each other, in cemeteries at Keratea and at Merenda. The over-life-sized Keratea statue, now in Berlin and often known as the Berlin Standing Goddess (Antikenmuseen 1800), wears a *polos* hat with incised and painted mae-ander and lotos decoration, a heavy chiton (once brightly colored) with a scarf over it, and sandals with their relief straps (once painted). Her bulging eyes and cheeks give her a particularly individual expression. She has a band round the back of her hair, bud-shaped earrings, a necklace of buds and a bracelet, and car-ries a pomegranate in her right hand. She probably dates to around 570, one or two decades earlier than the statue from Merenda, known from her surviving base as Phrasikleia (see Figure 41).

Phrasikleia belongs to the same sculptural tradition as the Berlin Standing Goddess and has many similarities—her *polos* hat with lotos blossoms and buds, a band round the back of her hair, earrings, necklace, bracelet, sandals, and the fact that she carries a natural symbol, here a bud, in her hand. Her chiton bears abundant signs of having been brightly colored and elaborately decorated. She has slightly different proportions (longer legs), greater hints of a body beneath the clothing, and a less individual face (Karakasi 2003: 117–29).[11]

Phrasikleia's surviving base gives important information. Not only does it have an epigram, in which Phrasikleia declares that she will always be called *korē* (maiden, but also the name of Demeter's daughter, snatched away by Hades), since she obtained that name from the gods instead of marriage, but it also has a sculptor's signature: "Aristion of Paros made me." This is the only case of a sig-nature from Archaic Athens in which the sculptor declares himself Parian, and it is noteworthy that the sculpture itself was carved from Parian marble. While Phrasikleia has distinct similarities to the Berlin Standing Goddess, the details of

---

11. On *korai* as grave markers, see Sourvinou-Inwood 1995: 147–79, 217–77; Meyer and Brüggemann 2007: 47.

FIGURE 41 Parian marble *korē* from the cemetery at Merenda; c. 550–540; height: 2.11 m. Inscriptions on the statue identify it as a marker on the tomb of Phrasikleia and as the work of the sculptor Ariston. Athens National Archaeological Museum 4889. Photo by Zde.

the drapery, and the way in which it relates to the body, find parallels instead in *korai* from Paros (Karakasi 2003: 126).

Phrasikleia is distinctly similar in some respects to a *korē*, carved in Pentelic marble, that originally stood on the Acropolis but is now in Lyon.[12] This is the earliest Athenian *korē* in Ionic dress (marked by a linen rather than woolen chiton), and there is certainly influence from Ionia, but the closest parallels with respect to the relationship of drapery to body are with Phrasikleia and *korai* from Paros. The face of the Lyon *korē* has similarities with the *kouros* found at Merenda along with Phrasikleia, and Katerina Karakasi has suggested that we should think of Phrasikleia, the Merenda *kouros*, and the Lyon *korē* all as products of Parian sculptors, with a Parian sculptor taking on a commission for a *korē* in local marble once the *kouros* (carved in Parian marble) was complete (Karakasi 2003: 127–9).

Another large *korē* from Attica, of which, unfortunately, only the feet remain, was put up in a cemetery at Vourva in the northeastern part of the Mesogeia. An inscription on its base declared not only that the deceased was named Phile, but also that the sculptor was one Phaidimos (Athens NM 81; Jeffery 1962: #44; Kissas 2000: A13). Phaidimos' signature survives on two further funerary monuments, a statue base probably from the Kerameikos (Jeffery 1962: #2; Kissas 2000, A9) and a fragment of a *stēlē* from Kalyvia Kouvara (Jeffery 1962: #48). The skilled hand of the mason who carved the Kerameikos and Vourva inscriptions has been identified as also responsible for the inscription on the dedication of the Moschophoros (the statue from c. 560, found on the Athenian Acropolis, of a man carrying a calf on his shoulders; Acropolis Museum 624) and for the inscription on Phrasikleia's base; but attempts to identify preserved work from the hand of Phaidimos on the basis of Phile's feet and the lower part of a *stēlē* said to have been found with the Kerameikos base have not commanded general assent.[13]

Sculptors' signatures survive in quantity from bases that cannot be associated with individual sculptures, and, coupled with later literary traditions about those responsible for Archaic sculptures on the Athenian Acropolis, they reveal the size of the sculpture industry. From the Acropolis alone the names of 16 different sculptors survive, four of them on more than one inscription. Some of these names are known also from ancient literature—Antenor, son of Eumares (and perhaps also Eumares himself); Endoios; Euthykles; Hegias; Polli(a)s, father of Euythmides;

---

12. More precisely, the upper part is in the Musée des Beaux Art in Lyon, while the lower part is in the Acropolis Museum in Athens (inv. # 269).

13. See Jeffery 1962: 118 for "Mason A." See Dörig 1967 and Deyhle 1969: 46–56 for disputed attributions to Phaidimos.

Archermos of Chios; Bion, son of Diodoros of Miletos; Euenor, father of Parrhasios of Ephesos (perhaps); Gorgias of Sparta; Kalon of Aegina; and Onatas son of Mikon of Aegina. Others, like Hermippos, Leobios, or Pythis (who seems to have been Ionian), are known only from epigraphy, although sometimes, as in the case of Diopeithes of Athens, from outside Athens as well as at Athens itself. Both the high proportion of names that appear in later literature and the high proportion of non-Athenians are testimony to the degree to which sculpture was a specialist craft, and those famed for it in wide demand (Raubitschek and Jeffery 1949: 479–524; Viviers 1992; Hochscheid 2015: 157–236).

12.1.3 Other Stone Sculpture

Although *korai* and *kouroi* have dominated accounts of Athenian sculpture, from the beginning stone sculpture took a wide variety of forms. On the Athenian Acropolis from the middle of the sixth century onward we find among free-standing sculpture, in addition to *korai* and *kouroi* and to such figures as the Moschophoros, riders (most famously the Rampin horseman),[14] figures of Victory, statues of Athena, seated figures, sphinxes, and free-standing groups likely to have represented some mythical encounter (although identification of specific figures is mostly uncertain) (Franssen 2011: 139–40, 60–201 [194, 96–8 on Theseus]); Eaverly 1995 on equestrian statues). All the forms taken by Athenian stone sculpture can be paralleled, more or less, elsewhere—that is, we have seated figures elsewhere, figures carrying animals across their shoulders, figures of Victory, sphinxes, and so on. Where there is distinction, it is in the style. In what remains an unsurpassed description of the marble sculpture of the Acropolis, Humfrey Payne set out the features that set the core body of material from the Acropolis apart as Attic (while recognizing that there were also pieces that belonged to other sculptural traditions), both in terms of how bodies and drapery are conceived and in terms of the whole approach to the figure (Payne and Young 1936: 3–6, 12–13, 26–7, 46–7, 55–63).

Architectural sculpture, some in marble and some in limestone, seems to have been important from the beginning of at least the second quarter of the sixth century, from which we have both a Gorgon head and a relief lion, apparently from a frieze as well as a lion attacking a bull from a pediment (Section 11.3). We also have pediments showing Herakles attacking the Hydra and Triton, and the three-headed snake-bodied monster, who has become known as Bluebeard (see

---

14. The head of the Rampin rider is Louvre #3104; the body of the rider and horse Acropolis Museum 590.

FIGURE 42 Limestone pedimental group of a three-bodied monster with snaky tail ("Bluebeard") from Athenian Acropolis; second quarter of sixth century; height: 80 cm. Athens, Acropolis Museum 35. Photo by Yiannis Koulelis. Acr. 3.

Figure 42). Both are designed to fill the corner of a pediment of quite a large building and may have come from the same building, perhaps flanking lions attacking a bull. A further group of Herakles being introduced to the gods on Olympus might have come from the other end of the same building. In addition, at the same date, we have complete pedimental groups showing Herakles battling with the Hydra, and then a little later what is known as the "Olive Tree" pediment (Stewart 1990: vol. 1: 114–15, Hurwit 1999: 107–13).

In the last quarter of the century, in a decisive advance, technically and stylistically, Athena was presented as the central figure in a pedimental representation in marble of a gigantomachy (see Figure 43); this group, carved completely in the round, was from a substantial building—almost certainly the new temple of Athena Polias the foundations of which remain visible between the Erechtheion and Parthenon (Section 11.4). We also have fragments of a marble frieze of uncertain subject matter, showing a keenly driven chariot, but whether it is from that temple or from an altar we do not know (Hurwit 1999: 121–4). The puzzle of fitting all the surviving sculpture to the buildings for which there is archaeological evidence remains to be satisfactorily solved.

Once again, most of the subject matter of Athenian architectural sculpture can be paralleled elsewhere, but some distinctiveness can be seen in the style of the Acropolis sculpture. These architectural sculptures not only display vibrant use of polychromy, but also an increasing sense of how to make the peculiar shape of the pediment work to give hierarchy and climax to a scene.

Vibrant polychromy seems also to have been a feature of the *stēlē* tradition of funerary monuments that existed side by side with free standing sculptural tomb markers (*kouroi*, *korai*, and equestrian figures [Eaverly 1995: 53–4]) as an alternative way of engaging cemetery visitors—or simply those passing roadside cemeteries—with the dead (see Section 4.4.4). Along with the use as grave

FIGURE 43 Marble figure of Athena fighting the giants from a pedimental group; c. 510–500; height: 2.00 m; found on the Acropolis. Athens, Acropolis Museum 631A. Photo by Fcgsccac.

markers of *kouroi* and, to a limited extent, of *korai*, tall narrow *stēlai* featuring a man shown in profile seem to have been a distinctly Athenian form of funerary monument, although a limited number of funerary *kouroi* are found elsewhere and Boiotian *stēlai* bear some relation to Attic (Richter 1961; D'Onofrio 1988: 86–7; Viviers 1992: 115–47; Brinkmann and Wünsche 2003: 60–4). Painting was one way that these Attic funerary *stēlai* had of attracting attention, just as the bright colors of Phrasikleia's *korē* attracted attention. Some figures on *stēlai* seem simply to have been incised, leaving painting to carry more or less the whole burden of display. On other occasions the relief itself was highly colored. A second method deployed on the *stēlai* was vivid characterization of the deceased, whether this was a young habitué of the gymnasium, characterized by the aryballos suspended from his wrist, a discus-thrower, holding the discus behind his head, a boxer with cauliflower ear, or a warrior.

Two examples that once stood close to each other in the same cemetery at Velanideza in the Mesogeia (and that may have commemorated two men who had made a dedication together on the Athenian Acropolis) show off these two different ways of attracting attention. The decoration on the *stēlē* of Lyseas (see Figure 44) is executed solely with paint, and shows the deceased bearded, clad in chiton and himation and carrying a kantharos and a branch; below him is a scene of a small figure on a galloping horse. The *stēlē* of Aristion (see Figure 45) shows him in armor but without his helmet, simply with the cap that goes under a helmet. This too seems to have been brightly painted, and, unlike the *stēlē* of Lyseas, it is signed by its sculptor, Aristokles, whose name is found on three other funerary bases from the Kerameikos and elsewhere in Athens, as well as on a dedication in Attica. The very stillness of these figures lends them pathos, and the careful details with which Aristion is portrayed further emphasizes this; now dead, this man, the details seem to suggest, was once immaculately turned out, even when he went to war.

The tall narrow *stēlai* seem to have been complemented by wider *stēlai*. That wider *stēlai* were not uncommon is indicated by surviving bases, although not one wider *stēlē* survives complete, and we are therefore unable to assess the iconographic range. One fragment from Anavyssos seems to have shown a mother cradling a child; another fragment, from an unknown location in Attica shows two women, one seated and the other standing in front of her and pulling at her own skirt, their arms suggesting lively exchange. A further fragment, with two soldiers apparently setting an ambush, also seems to come from a wider *stēlē* (Jeffery 1962: 149–50; D'Onofrio 1988: 90).

Wider *stēlai* were not used only for some grave monuments, but also for dedications. Only one votive relief survives complete from the Acropolis; it shows a young male aulos player leading three young women dancing hand in hand and pulling along a small boy after them (Acropolis Museum 702). Fragments of other reliefs show an armed Athena, a family bringing a pig to Athena (apparently by the same hand as the relief of two women from Attica), and a seated, bearded man with a kylix dangling from a finger—presumably he was a potter and is giving thanks for, and advertising, his craft. From the Athenian Agora we have a relief of Herakles carrying off the Erymanthian boar (Athens NM 43) (Payne and Young 1936: 47–50; Boardman 1978: 166, figs 258–61).

Statue bases, too, might be carved in relief, both in sanctuary and in cemetery contexts. Herakles appears on all three carved sides of a statue base from

FIGURE 44 Drawing of marble *stēlē* of Lyseas, from Velanideza in Attica; c. 500; height: 1.96 m. Shaft is Hymettian marble, base is Pentelic marble. Athens, National Archaeological Museum 30. Fom K. Müller 1922: Beilage 1.

FIGURE 45 Pentelic marble *stēlē* of Aristion, from Velanideza in Attica; c. 510; height: 2.02 m.

Athens National Archaeological Museum 29. Photo by Jebulon.

FIGURE 46 Pentelic marble *kouros* base recovered from the Themistoklean wall; c. 510; height: 30 cm. Athens National Archaeological Museum 3476. Photo by Zde.

Lamptrai (Athens NM 42 and 3579). From the Kerameikos (found either there or built into the Themistoklean wall) we find reliefs on bases for *kouroi*, a seated figure, and a *stēlai*. Friezes showing horsemen, soldiers, young men engaged in various athletic activities (see Figure 46), or animals confronting each other are favored for the long oblong shape that these bases offered. The scenes of games and athletics, in particular, have much in common with the scenes on contemporary painted pottery, not just in their subject matter, but also in the ways in which they handle the human body. The emphasis here is very much on the action and on making the action clear and comprehensible (Boardman 1978: 164, figs. 240–3; Kosmopoulou 2002: 162–3 and *passim*).

12.1.4 Bronze Sculpture

As we have seen in Section 11.1, bronze had been used for small statues as early as the eighth century, but it was only in the later sixth century that large-scale sculptures in bronze appear. Until then, statuettes of up to about half a meter in height were fashioned from solid bronze, but the only way to make a larger statue was to beat bronze sheet to shape and then fix the sheets together, a method known as *sphyrelaton* and visible in a seventh-century figurine of Artemis from Brauron (Brauron Museum BE 119). Some dozen Archaic bronze statuettes, primarily of Athena and of *kouroi*, survive from the Athenian Acropolis (Niemeyer 1964).

Experiments with hollow casting seem to have been carried out as early as the eighth century, but hollow-cast statues of any size are found only from the sixth century. From the middle of the sixth century we have fragments of a mold for a *kouros* of about half life-size from the Athenian Agora, along with fragments of two molds for heads and evidence of the casting pit (Mattusch 1988: 54–60).

Then, from the last decade of the sixth century, we have good literary evidence for a bronze four-horse chariot erected just inside the entrance to the Acropolis to commemorate Athenian victory over the Boiotians and Chalkidians (see Section 7.1.2).

Archaeologically, the main evidence for larger bronzes is their bases; some 40 low bases dating before 480 that once carried bronze statues were identified by Raubitschek, along with four further pillar bases (Raubitschek and Jeffery 1949: 87–120, 267–72). A life-sized, bearded, bronze head of early fifth-century date survives from the Acropolis (NM 6446), and in 1959 a bronze Apollo was excavated from the harbor of the Peiraieus (see Figure 47). The

FIGURE 47 Bronze statue of Apollo; height 1.92 m; found in the Peiraieus. Peiraieus Museum 4645. Photo by George E. Koronaios.

precise date of the latter statue is disputed, but there are technical as well as stylistic reasons to consider it Archaic, rather than archaistic. Anatomically this statue belongs with late Archaic *kouroi*, but both the marked inclination of the head and the hands extended, one originally to hold a bow and one an offering bowl, distinguish this figure and bring about a quite different relationship between statue and viewer, one that does not involve eye-contact. Technically, the body and legs of this statue were cast together, the arms and head separately and then joined. It is likely that, just as this Apollo largely follows the precedents of stone sculpture, so too most of the bronze sculpture from the late Archaic Acropolis resembled what we know from stone sculpture rather than, yet, taking advantage of the rather different properties and possibilities of bronze (Mattusch 1988: 74–9; Dafas 2019: 96–115; for a contrary view on date see Palagia 2016).

12.2 Minor Arts

The survival of jewelry from the Greek world is closely dependent on the nature of burial practices. In the case of Athens, the burial practices of the eighth century, like those in the Early Iron Age, preserved some jewelry, giving us an impression of what was present, even if no way to judge in what quantities it was present. After 700, however, the evidence we have is at best indirect.

The most striking gold jewelry of the eighth century comes from a grave in the south cemetery at Eleusis, which has become known as the "Isis tomb." Dating to the first half of the eighth century, this grave produced Middle Geometric II pottery of unusual shapes (miniature belly amphoras 14 cm or less tall, miniature tripod cauldrons no more than 6 cm high, a small kalathos, and a small krater). But it also produced a small faience figure of the Egyptian goddess Isis, two bronze armlets, nine finger rings (two of silver, three of iron, four of bronze), an ivory pin, a bronze fibula, two necklaces with faience and amber beads, and a set of earrings (see Figure 48). The earrings consist of a crescent-shaped plaque delicately decorated with granulation and filigree, from which hang gold chains on the end of which are tubes with crinkled ends, once covered with glass or amber to turn them into tiny pomegranates.

Other eighth-century tombs from Attica have yielded a series of gold bands— thin strips of gold with impressed decoration made to be placed around the brow. Fragments of a mold for such a band have been found at Eleusis. The embossed decoration variously shows geometric or curvilinear decoration, friezes of animals grazing, or hostile encounters of men and animals or horsemen and centaurs. The style of the figurative decoration varies a great deal, from quite rigidly geometric to heavily Orientalizing. Not the least interesting aspect of this is that

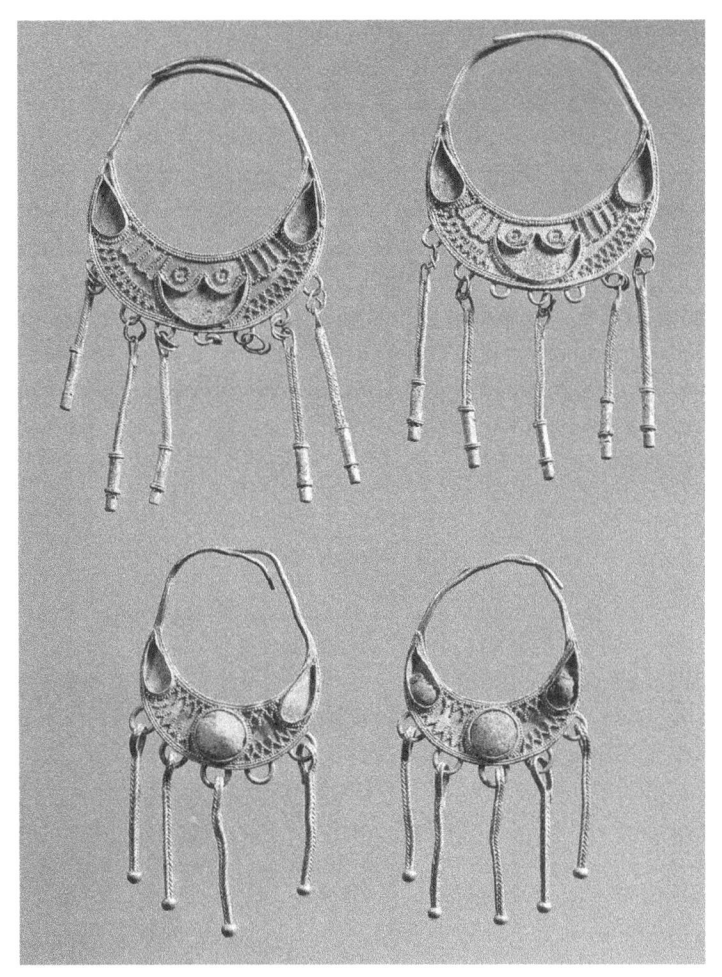

FIGURE 48 Gold earrings from the so-called Isis Tomb in the South cemetery at Eleusis; c. 800; width: 3 cm. Athens National Archaeological Museum. Photo by Gianni Dagli Orti.

the Orientalizing bands seem earlier than the more rigidly geometric bands, and the "Orientalizing" bands were found in graves with Geometric pottery (Ohly 1953; Osborne 2019b).

Much of our knowledge of Athenian jewelry in the two centuries after 700 is indirect, derived from the jewelry displayed on *korai* and other sculpture or on painted pottery. Some jewelry survives from the sanctuaries of Artemis at Brauron and at Halai Araphenides (modern Loutsa). But it is hard to gain much impression of the range or the quantity of jewelry deployed in real life, and we have little sense of the scale of jewelry production.

Although graves before 700 also produce some terracottas, including some elaborate enthroned figures and a mule cart carrying amphoras (R. A. Higgins 1967: plates 7F–G, 8A–B), in Attica as in other parts of the Greek world we largely owe our knowledge of the production of statuettes in terracotta, other than occasional terracotta models, to sanctuaries rather than to graves. The richest and best published collection of Archaic terracotta figurines comes from the Athenian Acropolis, but figurines are regular finds at Attic sanctuaries (at Mounychia, Brauron, Eleusis, Kiapha Thiti, etc.; see Section 11.2).[15]

The earliest terracotta figurines from the Acropolis (including the north slope) are the hand-made standing "Stempelidole" figurines with stump-like arms from the early seventh century (Section 11.2). Figurines of the same type of were found in a foundation deposit uncovered in the area of the Nike bastion (Mark 1993: 22 and fig. 2b). In the late seventh century more carefully made "daedalic" figurines began to be produced, and sixth-century standing figures come to take the form of miniature *korai*. Repeated copies of figurines taken from the same mold are found. Some of the figurines are turned into Athenas by the addition of a helmet or a raised arm with a spear. In terracotta, as not in bronze, seated figures appear occasionally in the seventh century and become common in the sixth, dressed in a chiton and wearing a crown—and sometimes turned into a warlike Athena by the addition of helmet and *gorgoneion*. A small number of figurines from the Acropolis represent other gods and goddesses—seated and standing female figures with kid and fawn seem likely to be Artemis, winged female figures perhaps Nike or Iris, and a figure with a lion-skin Herakles. Terracotta is also used for head protomes, up to about one-third life-size, of uncertain use, some of which are very fine. Apart from the purely local "Stempelidole," it is the particular mix of the terracottas, rather than any individual type, that is distinctly Athenian.

12.3 Athenian Literature

Outside the inscriptional record, no Athenian prose survives from the Archaic period. Nor are we significantly better off regarding poetry. The *Homeric Hymn to Demeter* (see Section 11.2) certainly concerns itself centrally with Attica— primarily with the site of Eleusis but also including Demeter's story of how pirates brought her from Crete to Thorikos[16]—and scholars have thought that

---

15. For terracottas, see F. Winter 1893; Brooke 1921; C. H. Morgan 1935; Alroth 1989: 52–4, 88–90; Hurwit 1999: 91–4; Scholl 2006: 49–67, 90–105; Moustaka 2009; Parisi 2014.

16. Bizarrely both modern commentators (Richardson 1974: 188; Foley 1994, 43) state that Thorikos is on the northeast, rather than southeast, coast of Attica.

its closeness to Hesiod's *Theogony* and the Atticisms detected in its language may point to an Attic poet (Richardson 1974: 5–6, 12, 52–6; Richardson 2011: 49). Otherwise, the only lengthy remains that we have of Athenian poetry are fragments of the poetry of Solon.

Solon's poetry survives only as quoted by later writers. Some 46 fragments have come down to us attributed to Solon, ranging from a single word (F41 West) to a complete elegy of 76 lines quoted by Stobaeus (F13 West). It is likely that not all the attributions to Solon are correct (although some of those who have doubted attributions have done so on the basis of greater confidence about the narrative of Athenian history than it is reasonable to assume).

Some of the material is very specifically Athenian, and some directly addresses Solon's own political actions, explaining and defending what he did (Sections 5.2.2 and 10). The poems talk about the particular situation in Athens, both its situation with regard to its neighbors (as in the fragments concerned with Athenian recovery of Salamis, although some have thought these not genuine) and the social and economic issues that had forced many Athenians to leave Attica. It is not uncommon for Archaic poets to refer explicitly to current politics, but Solon's poetry is different in that it does not target individuals, in the way that Alkaios targets Pittakos, but addresses itself to broader problems of land distribution and inequality.

Other material in Solon's poetry is generalized, and there is a significant overlap between lines attributed to Solon and lines attributed to the Megarian poet Theognis. Rather than treating this as a problem about "false" attribution, we should probably take this to be indicative of the way in which Archaic elegy was composed. That is, it may well have been common for a poet to incorporate well-known lines into a new elegy of his own, enriching his poetry by simultaneously evoking the contexts in which the lines had first become familiar to his audience. Solon certainly makes abundant allusion to the Homeric poems, and in doing so he gives a particular thrust to his own claims.[17]

But if the sharing of lines is a product of the way elegy was composed, it is also indicative of the society that consumed elegy; that is, the sharing of lines is an indication of the degree to which the world explored by elegy, its concerns, and its values were a universe shared across political and regional boundaries. Common themes include the dangers to community life posed by greed and misbehavior on the part of the powerful; the advantages of moderation; the importance of justice; the independence of moral worth from worldly success; the inevitability and unpleasantness of death; and the delights of possessions, horses, and boys.

---

17. See the essays by Lardinois, Irwin, Stehle, Blaise, Noussia, and Martin, in Blok and Lardinois 2006, along with Irwin 2005.

Arguably the importance of Solon's poetry lies not least in its legacy. Just as the concerns of Tyrtaios and Alkman seem to have played a significant part in defining what it was to be Spartan, through their on-going reperformance, so the survival of Solon's poems handed down for the Athenians a political agenda that had at its center the question of what should and what should not be equally shared.

Although some verses that appear in dedications and epitaphs may have been repeated from use elsewhere in the Greek world, the not insubstantial body of Greek verse inscriptions surviving epigraphically from Archaic Athens and Attica gives us further access to the poetic world of Athens. Some 80 verse epitaphs and some 100 dedicatory inscriptions from the Archaic period survive from Athens and Attica (P. A. Hansen 1983–1989: vol. 1: #1–78, 179–265, 81–6, 99–311). Many are fragmentary, but they attest to the widespread desire to express something more about the dead than simply that they had lived, and to say something more to the gods with a dedication than a simple thank you.[18]

---

18. For the inseparability of displays of piety and self-glorification in Archaic dedicatory epigrams, see Day 2010: 185.

Conclusion

THE HISTORY OF ARCHAIC ATHENS, UNIFORMITY, AND DIVERSITY

TWO QUESTIONS STAND out at the conclusion of this study. First, how do these different aspects of the archaeology and history of Archaic Attica hang together? What story should we be telling? Second, how does the history of Archaic Athens sit against the history of other Greek cities in this period?

13.1 The Story of Archaic Athens

Throughout the tenth and ninth centuries Athens never lost touch with a wider world, exporting its pottery to Crete, Euboia, and elsewhere (S. C. Murray 2017: 201–4). But the archaeology of Attica never looks like the archaeology of Lefkandi or Knossos in this period, and, whatever their political relations, those living in Attica already shared a cultural style. Indeed, the apparently coordinated adoption across Attica of what we call the Early Geometric style of pottery to replace Protogeometric around 900 is a clear sign of this cultural unity (Coldstream 2003: 26–35, 376).

Around 800, the date at which, arbitrarily, I began my discussion of "Archaic Athens," social relations in Athens, and indeed across much of Greece, changed significantly. The inhabitants of the eighth-century world sought to communicate at a distance, first through pictures and then shortly afterward through writing, in a way they had not done before, and they used pictures and writing to suggest the world that might be conjured up in oral discourse. For the first time in Iron Age Greece, we can be confident that we have some sense not just of what groups of Athenians did, but also of what they wanted to talk about. And what they wanted to talk about were the formal and informal rituals that they took

The Oxford History of the Archaic Greek World. Robin Osborne, Oxford University Press. © Oxford University Press 2023.
DOI: 10.1093/oso/9780197644423.003.0013

part in (notably dancing, on the one hand, and burial on the other), issues to do with courtship and marriage, humans' relations with the wild and the monstrous, and, at least locally, fighting in ships and individuals' contributions to collective activity. Individual and community is clearly a major theme here, and the ship battles point to imagining, at least, a sizeable community that can manage to organize activities demanding investment and significant coordination (Osborne 2021b: 79–82).

It is against the background of such discursive engagement that we must understand the proliferation of settlement and of funerary practices as the eighth century proceeds. On the one hand, the very considerable local diversity to be observed across Attica by the end of the eighth century shows local desire to be, and be recognized as, distinct. On the other hand, the clustering of settlement around Athens itself, the development of the Athenian Acropolis as a cult center like no other in Attica, and the way in which local variations often seem to be engaging with what is happening in the town of Athens, these, taken together, point to a clear sense of all residents of Attica belonging together and all relating to the major center of Athens itself. And for all the detailed variation that comes to prevail in burial practices, the very marked change in who gets buried over the course of the eighth century, with a steep rise and then an equally steep fall in numbers of archaeologically visible burials, is common to almost all cemeteries across Athens and Attica.

Around 700, further radical changes in material culture become visible. Once more, these are most apparent in the way pottery is painted and the way the dead are buried. The cemetery ritual changes from inhumation to primary cremation, and myths involving figures who feature across the Greek world (and beyond—Odysseus, Herakles, Perseus) burst onto Athenian pottery in a figure style designed to make their identity obvious and unquestionable. For the first time we find outside Athens (at Phaleron) a vast cemetery in which most of those buried receive few grave goods. In the town of Athens, there is a radical reorganization of space that clears burials not only from the Acropolis, but also from a broad area of 200 ha nearby. Town residents continued to cluster at different points around the Acropolis, yet there was now a strong sense that they all (also) belonged to a single large community. However skeptical we may be of the precise date later Athenian writers offered for the earliest archons, the case for a formally organized community—a community capable of carrying out mass executions (Sections 4.4.3 and 5.2.1)—in seventh-century Athens is archaeologically clear.

Whether and in what ways that formal organization encompassed the rest of Attica is less obvious. A florescence of local cult activity, notably at hilltop cult sites, in the later eighth and the seventh centuries might indicate either deepening localism or pan-Attic cult coordination. Certainly, local cult development was not in any way impeded by what was going on in Athens itself, as the *Homeric Hymn to Demeter* and building at Eleusis, on the one hand, and cult investment at Sounion (marked above all by the colossal Sounion *kouroi* from the very end of the seventh century), on the other, make clear.

The judicial infrastructure revealed in Drako's homicide law from the 620s confirms that by then Athens was expecting to deal with dispute settlement across the whole of Attica, just as the sacred calendar embedded in Solon's laws explicitly covered activities across Attica, not simply in Athens itself. Solon's laws indicate a world heavily invested in property ownership and material display, and his poetry indicates that this world was bitterly divided, at least in part, over questions of land and labor. Whatever legal remedies Solon instituted, they were only part of what looks to be a much larger package that also involved opening up opportunities outside Attica, both through the acquisition of Salamis and through settlement abroad, first at Sigeion and later in the Thracian Chersonese. But if such foreign activities were intended as a safety valve, they seem to have been unsuccessful: the competition among the Athenian elite that has long been visible in the archaeological record, and which is strongly hinted at in Drako's surviving law, continued to dominate sixth-century Athenian politics.

Foreign interventions led by the elite, and elite political clashes, came to dominate such narrative history as historians of the Classical period could recover or surmise from the scraps of memory and tradition handed down to them. But the archaeological record reveals other sides of Athens, too. Alongside the elite funerary monuments parading prowess in war and athletics that could be cashed in internationally, and the competitive displays of conspicuous piety that came to dominate the Acropolis, there is another Athenian world in which the petty pot production of the Kerameikos is shipped in large quantities not just around the central Mediterranean but also to its eastern and western reaches, and where demand for Athenian pottery, built perhaps on earlier demand for Athenian oil distributed in SOS amphoras, ensured that Athens was exceptionally well connected across more or less the whole Mediterranean. However trivial the value of individual pots, and whoever manned the ships in which they were transported, their distribution marks the reach and reveals the entanglement of the Athenian economy. But their distribution also meant that the Athenian version of what mattered in the world, explored through changing selections of mythological scenes, was a version with which the whole not only of the Greek but of the Mediterranean world was made familiar, and by which the vision of that wider world was shaped.

One pot shape that came to be widely distributed deserves special attention: the Panathenaic amphora (see Figure 49) (Sections 4.5.4 and 11.3). Given as prizes in what was essentially an Athenian civic festival that brought the Athenians

FIGURE 49 Panathenaic amphora found in Athens in 1813 ("the Burgon Amphora"); c. 560; height: 61.20 cm. Inscribed τōν Ἀθηνήθ<ε>ν ἄθλον ἐμί. British Museum 1842,0728.834.

together to celebrate their patron goddess, we might have expected Panathenaics rarely to have been spread outside Attica. In fact, however, by the end of the sixth century we have 28 examples from Etruria, 10 from south Italy, three from the Black Sea, five from Cyrenaica, and 10 from the Peloponnese (Bentz 1998: 117). Athens had managed to make itself the one city—as opposed to the Panhellenic festival centers—whose civic festival mattered well outside the boundaries of the sponsoring community, and where the local token of success was a desirably exportable item. That goes together with the Herodotean story (6.126–30) that, when in c. 575 Kleisthenes the tyrant of Sikyon held a competition for the hand of his daughter Agariste, both the eventual winner and the front-runner who disgraced himself in the final round by his dirty dancing were Athenians. Sixth-century Athens had made itself distinctive within the Greek world, and indeed beyond.

Only if we give Athenian pottery production a serious place in our understanding of Athenian society in the sixth century can we understand Athenian political history. Despite scholarly resistance, the dedications on the Athenian Acropolis reveal that Athenian craftsmen, and in particular Athenian potters, became significant and wealthy members of Athenian society. Solon had so arranged Athenian public responsibilities that increased wealth gave access to increased power. Whether or not Aristotle's pupil correctly interpreted the dedication by Anthemion ([Arist.] *Constitution of the Athenians* 7.4; Keesling 2015) to mark his rise from thete to *hippeus*, Solon had provided a scale according to which social mobility could be measured and celebrated. The practice of the so-called "Pioneers" of Athenian red-figure pot-painting of showing themselves at sophisticated symposia suggests that there were also informal ways in which one could display that one was enjoying the life of the wealthy (Neer 2002: 83–134). But the important point is that by the end of the sixth century Athenian society was sufficiently complex and intertwined for a reform that promised an opening up of opportunities for political involvement to be irresistible. The powerless realized their power in this earliest of velvet revolutions (cf. Havel 1985).

13.2 *Typical or Extraordinary, Athens in the World of the Archaic Greek City*

By the first decades of the fifth century Athens was not like anywhere else in the Archaic Greek world. The differences are easily enumerated—the democratic governmental structure empowering not only those outside the elite, but also those residing outside the center; the extraordinarily inventive and, in comparative terms, large pottery industry; the massive silver production; the burgeoning navy. Behind these differences lie Athens' size and pattern of settlement. Athens' size had few rivals, but there were city-states with larger territories: Sparta and Syracuse left Athens standing, as far as the extent of their territories was concerned. But Athens' pattern of settlement was unique. What was special about Athens was the continued separate existence of large numbers of villages across Attica, with distinct patterns of local life, manifested above all in cult activity, which were nevertheless tied in to the life of the city as a whole, and not merely by wealthy local families (Osborne 1985 [cf. the use of "discovery" in that title]; Whitehead 1986; N. F. Jones 1999).

How had this settlement pattern come about? Two aspects are particularly notable. One is that although the settlement pattern remained nucleated, not dispersed, it is marked by the proliferation of really rather small communities; in terms of the exploitation of the territory, a pattern of rather fewer, larger settlements would have been possible. The other is the absence of subordination to Athens. Economics seems crucial here. Exploitation of Attica's mosaic of resources—from the forests of Parnes exploited by Acharnian charcoal-burners, through the marble resources of Pendele and Hymettos, the clay beds of Athmonon, and the access to sea from numerous locations along the exceptionally long coastline, to the silver mines of Laurion—required not just being able to supply labor to every part of Attica, but also, in many cases, significant investment on the spot. The exploitation of these resources also offered opportunities for people of all sorts of economic backgrounds. Not just wealthy landed families but a wide range of Athenians were attracted into competitive relationships. There was a lot of luck involved in exploiting the dispersed resources of Laurion; turning fine clay into fine pottery demanded skills that did not depend on family wealth; making the most of the communications opened up by easy access to the sea required picking up and exploiting scraps of information. The easy monopoly on wealth that is found when the only significant economic resource is the land seems to have been in some way stymied by Solonian reform but, in any case, this became less and less relevant as Athenians came more and more to exploit the full variety of their resources. And Athens had to work for its position at the center of the web, providing the infrastructure—of roads, of services, and quite simply of demand—that facilitated continued life in the demes.

Geography and history conspired together to create the unique phenomenon that Athens had become by 480. Thucydides (1.2.5) was right that Attica was shaped in part by not being invaded and was shaped by being marginal for arable agriculture and so compelled to diversity. It was shaped, too, by its place in the Greek peninsula that made it central, able to compete with other potential central places (Aegina, Delos) to provide more, better, or cheaper services. But it was not geography that produced Solon, and only indirectly was it geography that ensured that the coincident threats from Aegina and Persia persuaded the Athenians to build an outsize fleet.

We cannot hope to understand the political history of Athens without understanding her peculiar resource base and what the Athenians made of those resources. It is this that justifies and requires the attempt to put together the history and the archaeology in the way in which this discussion has attempted to do. But the material culture was never produced in a vacuum, and the decisions made by craftsmen must be put back into the wider historical context if they are themselves to be understood. There is a great deal which we do not understand of what went on in Athens between 800 and 480, but, if we are to have a chance of answering the outstanding questions, we need both to look more closely at each particular element, and to keep in mind the place of each element in the whole. This book has attempted to make a start on that task.

Guide to Further Reading

No other volume covers the ground of this book. Inevitably, general treatments of archaic Greek history and archaeology spend significant amounts of time on Athens, and for the broader context Hurwit 1985b, Whitley 2001, and my own Osborne 2009 are all valuable.

For an introduction to Athenian archaeology in the sense of monuments see Camp 2001, and Travlos 1971, 1988). For comprehensive collections of the archaeological evidence for Athens and/or Attica for the eighth and seventh centuries see now Dimitriadou 2019, Doronzio 2018, and Rönnberg 2021a. Of older discussions the most important is Morris 1987.

There is no treatment of Athenian art and sculpture separate from the art and sculpture of Greece more generally, but Athenian ceramics and sculpture play a large part in general histories of archaic Greek art, including Osborne 1998. Particularly valuable for their judicious choice of visual evidence are the "handbooks" by John Boardman: Boardman 1974, 1975, 1978, 1998a. Still worth consulting is Beazley 1986 (original edition 1951).

The story of Athenian political history in the archaic period has frequently been told, almost always as a story that leads to Athenian democracy, but there is no single "classic" account. For an interesting recent account which ties together political and economic history, see van Wees 2013. The history of Athenian religion in this period has been told just once, in Parker 1996.

Contributor Biography

Robin Osborne is Professor of Ancient History at the University of Cambridge and a Fellow of King's College and of the British Academy. His work ranges across the archaeology and history of the archaic and classical Greek world. His first book was *Demos: The Discovery of Classical Attika* (1985), and this has been followed by *Classical Landscape with Figures: The Ancient Greek City and its Countryside* (1987), *Greece in the Making, 1200–479 B.C.* (1996; 2nd ed. 2009), *Archaic and Classical Greek Art* (1998), *Greek History* (2004) (2nd ed. *Greek History: The Basics* 2014); *Athens and Athenian Democracy* (2010); *The History Written on the Classical Greek Body* (2011); *The Transformation of Athens: Painted Pottery and the Creation of Classical Greece* (2018), two volumes of *Greek Historical Inscriptions* (with P. J. Rhodes), *404–323 B.C.* (2003), *478–404 B.C.* (2017), and many articles in journals and edited collections. He is a past President of the Society for the Promotion of Hellenic Studies, and of the Classical Association, and a past Chairman of the Council of University Classical Departments.

Gazetteer

Location	Map	Grid Number
23–5 Lekka Street, Athens	16	—
8th–7th Century Burials, Agora, Athens	Figure 2	
Academy (gymnasium)	11	C3
—	19	—
Acharnai	9	C2
—	10	C2
—	11	C2
—	12	C2
—	17	C2
—	20	C2
Acharnai Gate, Athens	1	—
	15	—
Acropolis, Athens	13	—
—	14	—
—	16	—
—	19	—
—	20	C3
—	21	—
Aegina	2	E3
Agia Paraskevi	11	C2
Agios Ioannis Rentis	17	C3
Agora (Village)	4	E1
Agrieliki	10	D2

Location	Map	Grid Number
Athens	2	E3, inset
—	4	C3/4
—	5	A3
—	6	F3
—	7	C3, inset
—	8	C3, inset
—	9	C3
—	10	C3, inset
—	11	C3, inset
—	12	C3, inset
—	17	C3, inset
—	20	inset
—	Figure 34	bottom
Athmonon	12	C2
Aixone	12	C3
Beirut	5	D4
Berezan	5	C1
Besa	12	E4
Boiotia	3	C3
Brauron	9	D3
—	10	D3
—	12	D3
—	20	D3
Building B, Acropolis, Athens	Figure 39	—
Building C, Agora, Athens	Figure 2	—
Building D, Agora, Athens	Figure 2	—
Building F, Agora, Athens	Figure 2	—
—	Figure 3	—
Burials at juncture of Dimitrakopoulou and Meïntani Streets, Athens	13	—
Burials at Nileos Street, Athens	14	—
Camirus	3	G5
Cape Kolias	8	inset
Cape Zoster	8	C4

Location	Map	Grid Number
Cemetery at Juncture of Erysichthonos and Nileos Streets, Athens	18	—
Cerveteri	6	C2
Chalandri	17	C2
Chalkis	2	inset
Charvati	17	D2/3
Chios	3	E/F3
Classical Agora, Athens	1	—
—	13	—
—	14	—
—	16	—
—	19	—
—	21	—
Corfu	2	A1
—	6	E2
Corinth	2	D3, inset
—	3	B4
Cyprus	5	C3/4
Cyrenaica	5	A4
Cyrene	5	A4
Deiradiotai	12	E4
Dekeleia	9	C2
Delos	3	E4
Delphi	2	D2
Dipylon Cemetery, Athens	1	—
—	13	—
—	14	—
—	15	—
—	18	inset
—	19	—
Dipylon Gate, Athens	1	—
—	18	inset
—	21	—
Drain, Agora, Athens	Figure 3	—
Draphi	11	D2

Location	Map	Grid Number
Drosia	11	D2
Earlier Parthenon, Acropolis, Athens	Figure 39	—
Eetioneia, Peiraieus	Figure 34	top
Elaious	12	B2
Eleusinion, Athens	16	—
—	21	—
Eleusis	7	B2
—	8	B2
—	9	B2
—	10	B2
—	11	B2
—	12	B2
—	17	B2
—	20	B2
Eleutherai	9	A1
Elleniko	11	C3
Ephesos	3	G4
Epidaurus	2	E3
Erchia	12	D3
Erechtheiou Street Burials, Athens	13	—
Eretria	2	inset
Eriai Gate, Athens	1	—
—	15	—
—	18	inset
Eridanos river	1	—
—	8	inset
—	13	—
—	14	—
—	18	inset
—	19	—
—	21	—
—	Figure 2	—
Essaouira	6	inset
Etruria	6	B1/C1/C2
Euboia	3	C/D3

Location	Map	Grid Number
Iolkos	3	B2
Ionidai	12	D2
Kallithea	11	C3
Kalyvia Kouvara	11	D3
—	17	D3
Kantharos	See Great Harbor, Peiraieus	
Karystos	2	F2
—	3	D3
Kato Souli	11	E1
Keos	2	F3
—	3	D4
Kephale	12	D4
Kephisia	9	C2
—	12	C2
Kephissos river	8	inset
—	19	—
Kerameikos Cemetery, Athens	1	—
—	13	—
—	14	—
—	15	—
—	16	—
—	18	inset
Keratea	11	D4
—	17	D4
Keratovouni	8	D4
—	20	D4
Kiapha Thiti	11	D3
—	20	D3
Klazomenai	3	F3
Knossos	5	B3
Kokkinos Mylos	11	C2
Kolonai	12	D1
Kolonos Agoraios, Athens	Figure 3	—
Konthyle	12	D3

Location	Map	Grid Number
Kopros	12	B2
Koropi	11	D3
—	17	D3
Kothokidai	12	B2
Kotzias Square, Athens	14	—
Koukaki, Athens	14	—
Koukouvaones	11	C2
Kriezi Street, Athens	18	inset
Kropidai	12	C2
Kynos	2	E2
Kynosarges, Athens	14	—
—	15	—
—	16	—
—	18	—
—	19	—
—	21	—
Kynthos	3	D4
Kytheros	9	D3
Kyzikos	4	F1
Lambrika	11	D3
Lampsakos	4	E1
Lathouresa	11	C4
—	17	C4
Laurion	7	E4
—	8	E4
—	9	E4
—	11	E4
Lefkandi	2	inset
Leipsydrion	9	C2
Lemnos	3	E2
—	4	D2
Lesbos	3	E/F2
—	4	D/E2
Leukas	2	B2

Location	Map	Grid Number
Ligori	9	D3
Lindos	3	H5
Liossia	11	C2
Lokris	3	C3
Long Walls	Figure 34	bottom
Lower Lamptrai	12	D3
Lower Paiania	12	D3
Lykabettos Hill	1	—
—	8	inset
—	19	—
Lykeion	19	—
Lykotrypa	11	C2
Makrygianni district, Athens	14	—
Makrygianni Street burials, Athens	13	—
Marathon	7	D2
—	8	D2
—	9	D2
—	10	D2
—	11	D2
—	12	D2
—	17	D2
—	20	D2
Markopoulo	10	D3
—	11	D3
Marousi	8	C2
Megara	2	inset
Megara Hyblaia	6	D3
Melos	2	F4
—	3	D5
Merenda	9	D3
—	10	D3
—	11	D3
—	17	D3
Mesogeia	8	D3
Messina	6	D3

Location	Map	Grid Number
Miletos	3	G4
Moschato	11	C3
—	17	C3
Motya	6	C3
Mounychia	9	B3
—	10	B3
—	20	B3
Mounychia harbor, Peiraieus	Figure 34	top
Mt. Merenda	8	D3
—	20	D3
Mt. Pangaion	4	C1
Mt. Pani	8	D4
—	20	D4
Mt. Trikeraton	8	A2
Mycale	3	G4
Mycenae	2	D3
Myrrhinous	12	D3
Myrrhinoutta	12	D2
Mytilene	3	F2
—	4	E2
National Garden, Athens	13	—
—	14	—
Naukratis	5	C4
Naxos	3	E4
Nemea	2	D3
Nikaia	11	B3
Nike Bastion, Acropolis, Athens	Figure 39	—
Nisaia	2	inset
Oa	12	D3
Oe	12	B2
Oinoe	7	A1/2
—	10	D2
—	12	D2
Oion Dekeleikon	12	D2

Location	Map	Grid Number
Old Bouleuterion, Agora, Athens	Figure 2	—
—	Figure 3	—
Olymbos	17	D4
Olympieion, Athens	1	—
—	13	—
—	14	—
—	16	—
—	21	—
Oropos	8	C1
Orphryneion	4	E1
Paiania	11	D3
Palaia Kokkinia	10	B3
Pallene	9	D2
—	11	D2
—	12	D2
—	20	D2
Panathenaic Way, Athens	21	—
—	Figure 3	—
Parnes	7	inset
—	8	C1/2
—	9	C1
—	10	inset
—	11	inset
—	12	inset
—	17	inset
—	20	inset
Paros	3	E4
Patissia	10	C2
Peiraieus	7	B3
—	8	inset
—	9	B3
—	12	B3
—	Figure 34	bottom
Peiraieus Gate, Athens	1	—
—	15	—
—	19	—

Location	Map	Grid Number
Pendele	8	D2
Perati	7	E3
—	17	E3
Phaleron	7	C3
—	8	inset
—	9	C3
—	10	C3
—	12	C3
—	17	C3
Pharsalos	3	B2
Phegaia	12	D2
Philaidai	12	D3
Philopappos hill, Athens	1	—
Phoinikia	11	D4
Phokaia	3	F3
—	4	E3
Phrearrhioi	12	D4
Phyla	12	C2
Pithekoussai	6	C2
Plaka, Athens	14	—
Plataia	2	inset
Plotheia	12	D2
Pnyx, Athens	1	—
Pompeion, Athens	18	inset
—	19	—
Poros	12	D4
Porto Raphti	9	E3
Potamos Deiradiotes	12	E4
Poteidaia	4	B1
Pousi Kalogerou	11	E3
Prasiai	20	E3
Probalinthos	12	D2
Profitis Elias, near Laurion	20	D4

Location	Map	Grid Number
Prokonessos	4	F1
Propylon, Acropolis, Athens	Figure 39	—
Pylos	2	C4
Ragusa	6	C3
Raikelos	3	B1
—	4	A1
Raphina	9	E2
Rhamnous	7	E1
—	8	E1
—	9	E1
—	12	E1
—	20	E1
Rheneia	3	E4
Rhodes	3	G5/H5
Sacred Gate, Athens	18	inset
Sacred Road	7	B2/C3
Salamis	7	A/B3
—	8	A/B3
—	9	A/B3
—	11	A/B3
—	12	A/B3
—	17	A/B3
Samos	3	F4
Sanctuary of Artemis Mounychia, Peiraieus	Figure 34	top
Sanctuary of Dionysos Eleuthereus, Athens	16	—
—	21	—
Sanctuary of Nymphe, Athens	21	—
Sardis	3	H3
—	5	B3
Sigeion	4	E2
Sikyon	2	D3
Siphnos	3	D5
Skaleza	11	D1/2
Skourta	7	B1

Location	Map	Grid Number
Skourta plain	8	B1
Sounion	7	E5
—	8	E5
—	9	E5
—	11	E5
—	12	E5
—	20	E5
Sparta	2	D3
—	3	B4
Spata	11	D3
—	17	D3
Sphettos	9	D3
Stoa Basileos, Agora, Athens	Figure 3	
Susa	5	F4
Syndagma Square, Athens	13	—
—	14	—
Syracuse	6	D3
Taganrog	5	D1
Taranto	6	D2
Tavros	11	C3
Tegea	2	D3
Tell Defenneh	5	C4
Tempe	3	B2
Temple of Apollo Patroos, Agora, Athens	Figure 3	
Temple of Athena Polias, Acropolis, Athens	Figure 39	
Temple of Zeus Agoraios, Agora, Athens	Figure 3	
Tenos	3	E4
Tharros	6	A2
Thasos	4	C1
The Academy (gymnasium)	11	C3
—	19	—
Thebes	2	inset

Location	Map	Grid Number
Themistoklean Wall, Athens	1	—
—	15	—
—	16	—
—	18	inset
—	19	—
—	21	—
Thera	3	E5
Thermopylai	3	B3
Thespiai	2	inset
Tholos, Agora, Athens	16	—
Tholos Cemetery, Athens	18	—
Thorikos	7	E4
—	8	E4
—	9	E4
—	10	E4
—	11	E4
—	12	E4
—	17	E4
—	20	E4
Thracian Chersonese	4	E1
Thria	12	B2
Thriasian Plain	8	B2
Tourkovouni	20	C2
Trachones	11	C3
—	17	C3
Trikorynthos	12	D2
Trinemeia	12	D2
Troizen	2	E3
Upper and Lower Pergase	12	C2
Upper Lamptrai	12	C3
Upper Paiania	12	D3
Vari	9	C4
—	11	C4
—	17	C4

Location	Map	Grid Number
Velanideza	7	E3
Votanikos	11	C3
Voula	11	C3
Vouliagmeni	9	C4
—	11	C4
Vourva	7	D3
—	17	D3
Vulci	6	B1
West Ramp, Acropolis, Athens	Figure 39	—
Xypete	12	C3
Zea harbor, Peiraieus	Figure 34	Top

Bibliography

Abramson, H. 1979. "A Hero Shrine for Phrontis at Sounion?" *California Studies in Classical Antiquity* 12: 1–19.

Ahlberg-Cornell, G. 1992. *Myth and Epos in Early Greek Art: Representation and Interpretation*. Studies in Mediterranean Archaeology 100. Jonsered: Paul Åströms Förlag.

Ahlberg, G. 1971a. *Fighting on Land and Sea in Greek Geometric Art*. Skrifter utgivna av Svenska institutet i Athen 4° 16. Stockholm: Swedish Institute at Athens.

Ahlberg, G. 1971b. *Prothesis and Ekphora in Greek Geometric Art*. Studies in Mediterranean Archaeology 32. Göteborg: Paul Åströms Förlag.

Alexandridou, A. 2008. "Athens versus Attika: Local Variations in Funerary Practices during the Late Seventh and Early Sixth Centuries BC." In *Essays in Classical Archaeology for Eleni Hatzivassiliou 1977–2007*, edited by D. Kurtz, 65–72. BAR International Series 1796. Oxford: Archaeopress.

Alexandridou, A. 2009. "Offering Trenches and Funerary Ceremonies in the Attic Countryside: The Evidence from the North Necropolis of Vari." In *From Artemis to Diana: The Goddess of Man and Beast*, edited by T. Fischer-Hansen and B. Poulsen, 497–522. *Acta Hyperborea* 12. Copenhagen: Museum Tusculanum Press.

Alexandridou, A. 2011. *The Early Black-Figured Pottery of Attika in Context (c. 630– 570)*. Monumenta Graeca et Romana 17. Leiden: Brill.

Alexandridou, A. 2012a. "Early Sixth-Century Directional Trade: The Evidence of Attic Black-Figured Pottery." In *The Contexts of Painted Pottery in the Ancient Mediterranean World (Seventh–Fourth Centuries BCE)*, edited by D. Paleothodoros, 5–20. BAR International Series 2364. Oxford: Archaeopress.

Alexandridou, A. 2012b. "The North Necropolis of Vari Revisited." Αρχαιολογική εφημερίς: 1–90.

Alexandridou, A. 2015a. "Ritual Utensils or Funerary Vases? Functions of the Late Geometric Pottery from the 'Sacred House' of the Academy in Athens." In *Pots, Workshops and Early Iron Age Society: Function and Role of Ceramics in Early Greece, Proceedings of the International Symposium (Université Libre de Bruxelles, 14–16 November 2013)*, edited by V. Vlachou, 141–54. Études d'archéologie 8. Brussels: CReA-Patrimoine.

Alexandridou, A. 2015b. "Shedding Light on Mortuary Practices in Early Archaic Attica: The Case of the Offering Trenches." In *Classical Archaeology in Context: Theory and Practice in Excavation in the Greek World*, edited by D. Haggis and C. M. Antonaccio, 121–47. Berlin: Walter de Gruyter.

Alexandridou, A. 2016. "Funerary Variability in Late Eighth-Century B.C.E. Attica." *American Journal of Archaeology* 120: 333–60.

Alexandridou, A. 2017a. "Some Insights into the Early Attic Society (10th–7th Centuries BC)." In *Regional Stories: Towards a New Perception of the Early Greek World. Acts of an International Symposium in Honour of Professor Jan Bouzek, Volos 18–21 June 2015*, edited by A. Mazarakis Ainian, A. Alexandridou, and X. Charalambidou, 155–76. Volos: University of Thessaly Press.

Alexandridou, A. 2017b. "Special Burial Treatment for the 'Heroized' Dead in the Attic Countryside: The Case of the Elite Cemetery of Vari." In *Interpreting the Seventh Century BC: Tradition and Innovation. Proceedings of the International Colloquium Conference Held at the British School at Athens, 9th–11th December 2011*, edited by X. Charalambidou and C. A. Morgan, 281–92. Oxford: Archaeopress.

Alexandridou, A. 2018. "Feasting in Early Iron Age Attika: The Evidence from the Site of the Academy." In *Feasting and Polis Institutions*, edited by F. van den Eijnde, J. Blok, and R. Strootman, 28–59. *Mnemosyne* Supplementum 414. Leiden: Brill.

Alroth, B. 1989. *Greek Gods and Figurines: Aspects of the Anthropomorphic Dedications*. Uppsala Studies in Ancient Mediterranean and Near Eastern Civilizations 18. Uppsala: Almqvist & Wiksell.

Ammerman, A. J. 1996. "The Eridanos Valley and the Athenian Agora." *American Journal of Archaeology* 100: 699–715.

Anderson, G. 2003. *The Athenian Experiment: Building an Imagined Political Community in Ancient Attica, 508–490 B.C.* Ann Arbor: University of Michigan Press.

Anderson, J. K. 1995. "The Geometric Catalogue of Ships." In *The Ages of Homer: A Tribute to Emily Townsend Vermeule*, edited by J. P. Carter and S. P. Morris, 181–91. Austin: University of Texas Press.

Andrewes, A. 1961. "Philochoros on Phratries." *Journal of Hellenic Studies* 81: 1–15.

Andrewes, A. 1977. "Kleisthenes' Reform Bill." *Classical Quarterly* 27: 241–48.

Andrewes, A. 1982. "The Growth of the Athenian State." In *The Cambridge Ancient History. Volume III, Part 3. The Expansion of the Greek World, Eighth to Sixth Centuries B.C.*, edited by J. Boardman and N. G. L. Hammond, 360–91. 2nd ed. Cambridge: Cambridge University Press.

Antonaccio, C. M. 1993. "The Archaeology of Ancestors." In *Cultural Poetics in Archaic Greece: Cult, Performance, Politics*, edited by C. Dougherty and L. Kurke, 46–70. Cambridge: Cambridge University Press.

Antonaccio, C. M. 1995. *An Archaeology of Ancestors. Tomb Cult and Hero Cult in Early Iron Age Greece*. Lanham, MD: Rowman and Littlefield.

Arrington, N. T. 2021. *Athens at the Margin: Pottery and People in the Early Mediterranean*. Princeton: Princeton University Press.

Arrington, N. T., G. Spyropoulos, and D. J. Brellas. 2021. "Glimpses of the Invisible Dead: A 7th-century B.C. Burial Plot in Northern Piraeus." *Hesperia* 90: 223–79.

Azoulay, V. 2017. *The Tyrant-Slayers of Ancient Athens: a Tale of Two Statues*. New York: Oxford University Press.

Badian, E. 1971. "Archons and Strategoi." *Antichthon* 5: 1–31.

Badian, E. 1994. "Herodotus on Alexander I of Macedon: A Study in Some Subtle Silences." In *Greek Historiography*, edited by S. Hornblower, 107–30. Oxford: Clarendon Press.

Badian, E. 2000. "Back to Kleisthenic Chronology." In *Polis and Politics: Studies in Ancient Greek History Presented to Mogens Herman Hansen on His Sixtieth Birthday, August 20, 2000*, edited by P. Flensted-Jensen, T. H. Nielsen, and L. Rubinstein, 447–64. Copenhagen: Museum Tusculanum Press.

Bakir, G. 1981. *Sophilos: ein Beitrag zu Seinem Stil*. Keramikforschungen 4. Mainz: Philipp von Zabern.

Banou, E. S., and L. K. Bournias. 2014. *Kerameikos*. Athens: John S. Latsis Public Benefit Foundation.

Barletta, B. A. 1987. "The Draped Kouros Type and the Workshop of the Syracuse Youth." *American Journal of Archaeology* 91: 233–46.

Barletta, B. A. 2015. *The Sanctuary of Athena at Sounion*. Princeton: American School of Classical Studies at Athens.

Barringer, J. M. 2001. *The Hunt in Ancient Greece*. Baltimore: Johns Hopkins University Press.

Baurain-Rebillard, L. 1998. "Les vases 'communicants' à Athènes, des offrandes sur l'Acropole aux premiers banquets sur l'Agora." *Ktèma* 23: 125–36.

Baziotopoulou-Valavani, E. 1994. "Ανασκαφές σε αθηναϊκά κεραμικά εργαστήρια αρχαϊκών και κλασικών χρόνων." In *The Archaeology of Athens and Attica under the Democracy*, edited by W. D. E. Coulson, O. Palagia, T. L. Shear Jr., et al., 45–54. Oxford: Oxbow Books.

Beazley, J. D. 1910. "Kleophrades." *Journal of Hellenic Studies* 30: 38–68.

Beazley, J. D. 1911. "The Master of the Berlin Amphora." *Journal of Hellenic Studies* 31: 276–95.

Beazley, J. D. 1930. *Der Berliner Maler*. Bilder griechischen Vasen 2. Berlin: H. Keller.

Beazley, J. D. 1932. "Little-Master Cups." *Journal of Hellenic Studies* 52: 167–204.

Beazley, J. D. 1933. *Der Kleophrades-Maler*. Bilder griechischen Vasen 6. Berlin: H. Keller.

Beazley, J. D. 1948a. "Hymn to Hermes." *American Journal of Archaeology* 52: 336–40.

Beazley, J. D. 1948b. "Some Attic Vases in the Cyprus Museum." *Proceedings of the British Academy* 33: 195–247.

Beazley, J. D. 1956. *Attic Black-Figure Vase Painters*. Oxford: Clarendon Press.

Beazley, J. D. 1971. *Paralipomena: Additions to Attic Black-Figure Vase-Painters and to Attic Red-Figure Vase-Painters*. 2nd ed. Oxford: Clarendon Press.

Beazley, J. D. 1986. *The Development of Attic Black-Figure Vase Painting*. Rev. ed. Sather Classical Lectures 24. Berkeley: University of California Press.

Beck, F. A. G. 1975. *Album of Greek Education: The Greeks at School and at Play*. Sydney: Cheiron Press.

Beck, H. 2023. "Thebes." In *The Oxford History of the Archaic Greek World*, edited by P. Cartledge and P. Christesen. New York: Oxford University Press.

Bellen, H., H. Heinen, D. Schäfer, et al. 2003. *Bibliographie zur antiken Sklaverei im Auftrag der Kommission für Geschichte des Altertums der Akademie der Wissenschaften und der Literatur*. 2 vols. Forschungen zur antiken Sklaverei 4. Stuttgart: Franz Steiner Verlag.

Belletier, M. -P. 2003. "La 'politique de la mort': observation sur les tombes attiques aux époques géométrique et archaïque." *Pallas* 61: 71–82.

Benson, J. L. 1970. *Horse, Bird and Man: The Origins of Greek Painting*. Amherst: University of Massachusetts Press.

Bentz, M. 1998. *Panathenäische Preisamphoren: eine athenische Vasengattung und ihre Funktion vom 6.–4. Jahrhundert v. Chr.* Beiheft zur Halbjahresschrift *Antike Kunst* 18. Basel: Vereinigung der Freunde antiker Kunst.

Bergquist, B. 1990. "Sympotic Space: A Functional Aspect of Greek Dining Rooms." In *Sympotica: A Symposium on the Symposion*, edited by O. Murray, 37–65. Oxford: Clarendon Press.

Binek, N. M. 2017. "The Dipylon Oinochoe Graffito: Text or Decoration?" *Hesperia* 86: 423–42.

Blanshard, A. J. L. 2010. *Sex: Vice and Love from Antiquity to Modernity*. Chichester: John Wiley and Sons.

Blok, J. 2006. "Solon's Funerary Laws: Questions of Authenticity and Function." In *Solon of Athens: New Historical and Philological Approaches*, edited by J. Blok and A. P. M. H. Lardinois, 197–247. *Mnemosyne* Supplementum 272. Leiden: Brill.

Blok, J. and A. P. M. H. Lardinois, eds. 2006. *Solon of Athens: New Historical and Philological Approaches*. *Mnemosyne* Supplementum 272. Leiden: Brill.

Boardman, J. 1955. "Painted Funerary Plaques and Some Remarks on Prothesis." *Annual of the British School at Athens* 50: 51–66.

Boardman, J. 1974. *Athenian Black Figure Vases*. London: Thames & Hudson.

Boardman, J. 1975. *Athenian Red Figure Vases: The Archaic Period: A Handbook*. London: Thames & Hudson.

Boardman, J. 1978. *Greek Sculpture: The Archaic Period*. London: Thames & Hudson.

Boardman, J. 1983. "Symbol and Story in Geometric Art." In *Ancient Greek Art and Iconography*, edited by W. Moon, 15–36. Madison: University of Wisconsin Press.

Boardman, J. 1998a. *Early Greek Vase Painting: 11th–6th Centuries BC*. London: Thames & Hudson.

Boardman, J. 1998b. "The Ragusa Group." In *In Memoria di Enrico Paribeni*, edited by G. Capecchi, E. Paribeni, and O. Paoletti, 59–65. Archaeologica 125. Rome: Bretschneider.

Boardman, J., ed. 1981–1999. *Lexicon Iconographicum Mythologiae Classicae*. 9 vols. Zurich: Artemis Verlag.

Bodnar, E. W., ed. 2003. *Cyriac of Ancona: Later Travels*. I Tatti Renaissance Library 10. Cambridge, MA: Harvard University Press.

Bodnar, E. W., ed. 2015. *Cyriac of Ancona: Life and Early Travels*. I Tatti Renaissance Library 65. Cambridge, MA: Harvard University Press.

Boehringer, D. 2001. *Heroenkulte in Griechenland von der geometrischen bis zur klassischen Zeit: Attika, Argolis, Messenien. Klio* Beihefte Neue Folge 3. Berlin: Akademie Verlag.

Boersma, J.S. 1970. *Athenian Building Policy from 561–560 to 404–403 B.C.* Scripta Archaeologica Groningana 4. Groningen: Wolters-Noordhoff.

Bohen, B. 2017. *Kratos and Krater: Reconstructing an Athenian Protohistory*. Oxford: Archaeopress.

Böhm, S. 1990. *Die "Nackte Göttin"*. Mainz: Philipp von Zabern.

Borell, B. 1978. *Attisch Geometrische Schalen. Eine spätgeometrische Keramikgattung und ihre Beziehungen zum Orient*. Keramikforschungen 2. Mainz: Philipp von Zabern.

Bournias, L. K. 2017. "A Newly Discovered Funerary Pinax from the Athenian Kerameikos." In *Τέρψις: Studies in Mediterranean Archaeology in Honour of Nota Kourou*, edited by V. Vlachou and A. Gadolou, 247–60. Études d'archéologie 10. Brussels: CReA-Patrimoine.

Bourriot, F. 1976. *Recherches sur la nature du génos: étude d'histoire sociale athénienne: périodes archaïque et classique*. 2 vols. Paris: H. Champion.

Bowie, E. L. 1986. "Early Greek Elegy, Symposium and Public Festival." *Journal of Hellenic Studies* 106: 13–35.

Bowie, E. L. 1990. "Miles Ludens? The Problem of Martial Exhortation in Early Greek Elegy." In *Sympotica: A Symposium on the Symposion*, edited by O. Murray, 221–29. Oxford: Clarendon Press.

Bowie, T., and D. Thimme, eds. 1971. *The Carrey Drawings of the Parthenon*. Bloomington: Indiana University Press.

Bradford, J. 1956. "Fieldwork on Aerial Discoveries in Attica and Rhodes. Part I. The Town Plan of Classical Rhodes." *Antiquaries Journal* 36: 57–69.

Bradford, J. 1957. *Ancient Landscapes*. London: G. Bell and Sons.

Brann, E. T. H. 1962. *Late Geometric and Protoattic Pottery*. Athenian Agora 8. Princeton: American School of Classical Studies at Athens.

Bremmer, J. 1980. "An Enigmatic Indo-European Rite: Paederasty." *Arethusa* 13: 279–98.

Brenne, S. 1992. "'Porträts' auf ostraka." *Mitteilungen des Deutschen Archäologischen Instituts, Athenische Abteilung* 107: 161–75.

Brenne, S. 1994. "Ostraka and the Process of Ostrakophoria." In *The Archaeology of Athens and Attica under the Democracy*, edited by W. D. E. Coulson, O. Palagia, T. L. Shear Jr., et al., 13–24. Oxford: Oxbow Books.

Brenne, S. 2001. *Ostrakismos und Prominenz in Athen: Attische Bürger des 5. Jhs. v. Chr. auf den Ostraka*. Vienna: Holzhausens.

Brenne, S. 2002. "Die Ostraka (487 ca. 416 v. Chr.) als Testimonien." In *Ostrakismos– Testimonien I: Die Zeugnisse antiker Autoren, der Inschriften und Ostraka über das Athenische Scherbengericht aus vorhellenistischer Zeit (487–322 v. Chr.)*, edited by P. Siewert, 36–166. Stuttgart: Franz Steiner Verlag.

Brenne, S. 2019. *Die Ostraka von Kerameikos*. 2 vols. Kerameikos Ergebnisse der Ausgrabungen 20. Wiesbaden: Reichert Verlag.

Bresson, A. 2016. "Aristotle and Foreign Trade." In *The Ancient Economy: Markets, Households, and City-States*, edited by E. M. Harris, D. M. Lewis, and M. Woolmer, 41–65. Cambridge: Cambridge University Press.

Brijder, H. A. G. 1983. *Siana Cups I and Komast Cups*. Allard Pierson Series 4. Amsterdam: Allard Pierson Museum.

Brijder, H. A. G. 1991. *Siana Cups II: The Heidelberg Painter*. Allard Pierson Series 8. Amsterdam: Allard Pierson Museum.

Brijder, H. A. G. 1997. "New Light on the Earliest Attic Black-Figure Drinking-Cups." In *Athenian Potters and Painters: The Conference Proceedings*, edited by J. H. Oakley, W. D. E. Coulson, and O. Palagia, 1–16. Oxbow Monograph 67. Oxford: Oxbow Books.

Brijder, H. A. G. 2000. *Siana Cups III: The Red-Black Painter, Griffin-Bird Painter and Siana Cups Resembling Lip-Cups*. Allard Pierson Series 13. Amsterdam: Allard Pierson Museum.

Brijder, H. A. G. 2008. "Six's Technique and Etruscan Bucchero." In *Papers on Special Techniques in Athenian Vases: Proceedings of a Symposium Held in Connection with the Exhibition "The Colors of Clay: Special Techniques in Athenian Vases," at the Getty Villa, June 15–17, 2006*, edited by K. Lapatin, 35–46. Los Angeles: J. Paul Getty Museum.

Brinkmann, V., and R. Wünsche. 2003. *Bunte Götter: die Farbigkeit antiker Skulptur. Eine Ausstellung der Staatlichen Antikensammlungen und Glyptothek München in Zusammenarbeit mit der Ny Carlsberg Glyptotek Kopenhagen und den Vatikanischen Museen, Rom*. Munich: Staatliche Antikensammlungen und Glypothek.

Brokaw, C. 1963. "Concurrent Styles in Late Geometric and Early Protoattic Vase Painting." *Mitteilungen des Deutschen Archäologischen Instituts, Athenische Abteilung* 78: 63–73.

Brooke, D. 1921. "Catalogue of Terracottas." In *Catalogue of the Acropolis Museum. Volume II: Sculpture and Architectural Fragments*, edited by S. Casson, 315–433. Cambridge: Cambridge University Press.

Brunt, P. A. 1953. "The Hellenic League Against Persia." *Historia* 2: 135–63. Reprinted with addenda in P. A. Brunt, *Studies in Greek History and Thought*, Oxford: Clarendon Press (1993), pp. 47–83.

Brunt, P. A. 1993. *Studies in Greek History and Thought*. Oxford: Clarendon Press.

Buitron-Oliver, D. 1995. *Douris: A Master-Painter of Athenian Red-Figure Vases*. Forschungen zur antiken Keramik Reihe 2, Kerameus 9. Mainz: Philipp von Zabern.

Burford, A. 1993. *Land and Labor in the Greek World*. Baltimore: Johns Hopkins University Press.

Burr, D. 1933. "A Geometric House and a Proto-Attic Votive Deposit." *Hesperia* 2: 542–640.

Butz, P. A. 2010. *The Art of Hekatompedon and the Birth of the Stoikhedon Style*. Monumenta Graeca et Romana 16. Leiden: Brill.

Camp II, J. M. 1986. *The Athenian Agora: Excavations at the Heart of Classical Athens*. London: Thames & Hudson.

Camp II, J. M. 2001. *The Archaeology of Athens*. New Haven: Yale University Press.

Camp II, J. M. 2022. "The Persian Destruction of Athens: Sources and Archaeology." In *Destruction, Survival and Recovery in the Ancient Greek World*, edited by S. Fachard and E. Harris, 70–84. Cambridge: Cambridge University Press.

Carawan, E. M. 1998. *Rhetoric and the Law of Draco*. Oxford: Clarendon Press.

Carpenter, T. H. 1984. "The Tyrrhenian Group: Problems of Provenance." *Oxford Journal of Archaeology* 3: 45–56.

Carpenter, T. H. 1986. *Dionysian Imagery in Archaic Greek Art*. Oxford: Clarendon Press.

Carter, J. B. 1985. *Greek Ivory-Carving in the Orientalizing and Archaic Periods*. New York: Garland.

Carter, J. B., and L. J. Steinberg. 2010. "Kouroi and Statistics." *American Journal of Archaeology* 114: 103–28.

Cartledge, P. 2002. "The Political Economy of Greek Slavery." In *Money, Labour and Land: Approaches to the Economies of Ancient Greece*, edited by P. Cartledge, E. E. Cohen, and L. Foxhall, 156–66. London: Routledge.

Cavanagh, W. G., and C. B. Mee. 1995. "Mourning Before and After the Dark Age." In *Klados: Essays in Honour of J.N. Coldstream*, edited by C. Morris, 45–61. London: Institute of Classical Studies.

Chankowski, V. 2008. *Athènes et Délos à l'époque classique: recherches sur l'administration du sanctuaire d'Apollon délien*. Bibliothèque des Écoles françaises d'Athènes et de Rome 331. Athens: École française d'Athènes.

Chaviara, A. 2019. "A Technical Approach to Pottery Production in Attica During the Historic Period: Use of Raw Materials and Processing Techniques Over Time." PhD diss., University of Cyprus.

Chiarini, S. 2018. *The So-Called Nonsense Inscriptions on Ancient Greek Vases: Between Paideia and Paidiá*. Brill Studies in Greek and Roman Epigraphy 10. Leiden: Brill.

Christesen, P. 2007. *Olympic Victor Lists and Ancient Greek History*. Cambridge: Cambridge University Press.

Christesen, P. 2012. *Sport and Democracy in the Ancient and Modern Worlds*. Cambridge: Cambridge University Press.

Christiansen, J. 2000. *Kiapha Thiti, Ergebnisse der Ausgrabungen III.1 (The Iron-Age Peak Sanctuary)*. Marburg: Selbstverlag der Philipps-Universität.

Cirio, A. M. 1980. "Due iscrizioni del Sigeo e la cronologia dei poeti eolici." *Bollettino dei classici* 3: 108–12.

Clarke, K. 2008. *Making Time for the Past: Local History and the Polis*. Oxford: Oxford University Press.

Cohen, B. 1978. *Attic Bilingual Vases and their Painters*. New York: Garland.

Cohen, B. 2006. *The Colors of Clay: Special Techniques in Athenian Vases*. Los Angeles: J. Paul Getty Museum.

Coldstream, J. N. 2003. *Geometric Greece: 900–700 BC*. 2nd ed. University Paperbacks 680. London: Routledge.

Coldstream, J. N. 2006. "'The Long, Pictureless Hiatus.' Some Thoughts on Greek Figured Art Between Mycenaean Pictorial and Attic Geometric." In *Pictorial Pursuits: Figurative Painting in Mycenaean and Geometric Pottery: Papers from Two Seminars at the Swedish Institute at Athens in 1999 and 2001*, edited by E. Rystedt and B. Wells, 159–63. Skrifter utgivna av Svenska institutet i Athen 4° 53. Stockholm: Swedish Institute at Athens.

Coldstream, J. N. 2008. *Greek Geometric Pottery: A Survey of Ten Local Styles and Their Chronology*. Updated 2nd ed. Exeter: Bristol Phoenix Press.

Connor, W. R. 1990. "City Dionysia and Athenian Democracy." In *Aspects of Athenian Democracy*, edited by J. R. Fears, 7–32. Classica et Mediaevalia Dissertationes 11. Copenhagen: Museum Tusculanum Press.

Conophagos, C. E. 1980. *Le Laurium antique: et la technique de la production de l'argent*. Athens: Εκδοτική Ελλάδος.

Constantakopoulou, C. 2007. *The Dance of the Islands: Insularity, Networks, the Athenian Empire, and the Aegean World*. Oxford: Oxford University Press.

Cook, J. M. 1934–1935. "Protoattic Pottery." *Annual of the British School at Athens* 35: 165–211.

Cook, R. M. 1997. *Greek Painted Pottery*. 3rd ed. London: Routledge.

Corner, S. 2015. "Symposium." In *A Companion to Food in the Ancient World*, edited by J. Wilkins and R. Nadeau, 234–42. Chichester: Wiley-Blackwell.

Cosmopoulos, M. B. 2015. *Bronze Age Eleusis and the Origins of the Eleusinian Mysteries*. New York: Cambridge University Press.

Coulié, A. 2013. *La céramique grecque aux époques géométrique et orientalisante (XIe– Vie siècle av. J. -C)*. Paris: Picard.

Coulié, A. 2015. "L'atelier du Dipylon: style, typologie et chronologie relative." In *Pots, Workshops and Early Iron Age Society: Function and Role of Ceramics in Early*

Greece, Proceedings of the International Symposium (Université Libre de Bruxelles, 14–16 November 2013), edited by V. Vlachou, 37–47. Études d'archéologie 8. Brussels: CReA-Patrimoine.

Cox, C. A. 1988. "Sisters, Daughter and the Deme of Marriage: A Note." *Journal of Hellenic Studies* 108: 185–8.

Crane, E., and A. J. Graham. 1985. *Bee Hives of the Ancient World*. Bee World 66. Gerrards Cross: International Bee Research Association.

Crowley, J. 2012. *The Psychology of the Athenian Hoplite: The Culture of Combat in Classical Athens*. Cambridge: Cambridge University Press.

Csapo, E. 2003. "The Dolphins of Dionysus." In *Poetry, Theory, Praxis: The Social Life of Myth, Word and Image in Ancient Greece. Essays in Honour of William J. Slater*, edited by E. Csapo and M.C. Miller, 69–98. Oxford: Oxbow Books.

Csapo, E., and M. C. Miller. 1991. "The 'Kottabos-Toast' and an Inscribed Red-Figured Cup." *Hesperia* 60: 367–82.

Curtius, E., J. A. Kaupert, and A. Milchhoeffer. 1881–1900. *Karten von Attika: auf Veranlassung des Kaiserlich Deutschen Archäologischen Instituts und mit Unterstützung des K. Preussischen Ministeriums der Geistlichen, Unterrichts- und Medicinal-angelegenheiten aufgenommen durch Offiziere und Beamte des K. Preussischen Grossen Generalstabes, mit erläuterndem*. 10 vols. Berlin: G. Reimer.

D'Onofrio, A. M. 1984. "Korai e kouroi funerari Attici." *AION Annali di Archeologia e Storia Antica* 4: 135–70.

D'Onofrio, A. M. 1984. 1988. "Aspetti e problemi del monumento funerario Attico arcaico." *AION Annali di archeologia e storia antica* 10: 83–96.

D'Onofrio, A. M. 1984. 1993. "Le trasformazioni del costume funerario ateniese nella necropoli pre-soloniana del Kerameikos." *AION Annali di archeologia e storia antica* 15: 143–71.

D'Onofrio, A. M. 1984. 1995a. "Santuari 'rurali' e dinamiche insediative in Attica tra il Protogeometrico e l'Orientalizzante." *AION Annali di Archeologia e Storia Antica* 2: 57–88.

D'Onofrio, A. M. 1984. 1995b. "Soggetti sociali e tipi iconografici nella scultura attica arcaica." In *Culture et cité: l'avènement d'Athènes à l'époque archaïque. Actes du colloque international, organisé à l'Université libre de Bruxelles, du 25 au 27 avril 1991*, edited by A. Verbanck-Piérard and D. Viviers, 185–209. Brussels: de Boccard.

D'Onofrio, A. M. 1984. 1997. "The 7th Century BC in Attica: The Basis of Political Organization." In *Urbanization in the Mediterranean in the 9th to the 6th Centuries B.C.*, edited by H. Damgard Andersen, H. Horsnaes, S. Houby-Nielsen, et al., 63–88. *Acta Hyperborea* 7. Copenhagen: Museum Tusculanum Press.

D'Onofrio, A. M. 1984. 2001. "Immagini di divinità nel materiale votivo dell'edificio ovale geometrico ateniese e indagine sull'area sacra alle pendici settentrionali dell'Areopago." *Mélanges de l'École française de Rome, Antiquité* 113: 257–320.

D'Onofrio, A. M. 1984. 2008. "L'apporto cicladico nella più antica plastica monumentale in Attica." In *La sculpture des Cyclades à l'époque archaïque histoire des ateliers, rayonnement des styles. Actes du colloque international organisé par l'Ephorie des Antiquités Préhistoriques et Classiques des Cyclades et l'Ecole Française d'Athènes (7–9 septembre 1998)*, edited by Y. Kourayos and F. Prost, 201–62. *Bulletin de correspondance hellénique* Supplément 48. Paris: de Boccard.

D'Onofrio, A. M. 1984. 2011. "Athenian Burials with Weapons: The Athenian Warrior Graves Revisited." In *The "Dark Ages" Revisited: Acts of an International Symposium in Memory of William D.E. Coulson, University of Thessaly, Volos, 14–17 June 2007*, edited by A. Mazarakis Ainian, 2: 645–73. 2 vols. Volos: University of Thessaly Press.

D'Onofrio, A. M. 1984. 2017. "Athenian Burial Practices and Cultural Change: The Rundbau Early Plot in the Kerameikos Cemetery Revisited." In *Interpreting the Seventh Century BC: Tradition and Innovation. Proceedings of the International Colloquium Conference Held at the British School at Athens, 9th–11th December 2011*, edited by X. Charalambidou and C.A. Morgan, 260–80. Oxford: Archaeopress.

Dafas, K. A. 2019. *Greek Large-Scale Bronze Statuary of the Late Archaic and Classical Periods. Bulletin of the Institute of Classical Studies* Supplement 138. London: Institute of Classical Studies.

Dahm, M. K. 2007. "Not Twins at All: The Agora Oinochoe Reinterpreted." *Hesperia* 76: 717–30.

Dakoronia, P. 2006. "Mycenaean Pictorial Style at Kynos, East Lokris." In *Pictorial Pursuits: Figurative Painting in Mycenaean and Geometric Pottery: Papers from Two Seminars at the Swedish Institute at Athens in 1999 and 2001*, edited by E. Rystedt and B. Wells, 23–9. Skrifter utgivna av Svenska institutet i Athen 4° 53. Stockholm: Swedish Institute at Athens.

Davidson, J. 2007. *The Greeks and Greek Love: A Radical Reappraisal of Homosexuality in Ancient Greece*. London: Weidenfeld & Nicolson.

Davies, J. K. 1971. *Athenian Propertied Families, 600–300 B.C.* Oxford: Clarendon Press.

Davies, J. K. 1981. *Wealth and the Power of Wealth in Classical Athens*. Reprint ed. New York: Arno Press.

Davies, J. K. 2013. "Corridors, Cleruchies, Commodities, and Coins: The Pre-History of the Athenian Empire." In *Handels- und Finanzgebaren in der Ägäis im 5. Jh. v. Chr.*, edited by A. Slawisch, 43–66. Byzas 18. Istanbul: Zero.

Davies, M. I. 1978. "Sailing, Rowing, and Sporting in One's Cups on the Wine-Dark Sea." In *Athens Comes of Age, from Solon to Salamis*, edited by W. A. P. Childs, 72–95. Princeton: Archaeological Institute of America.

Davis, G., D. B. Gore, K. A. Sheedy, et al. 2020. "Separating Silver Sources of Archaic Athenian Coinage by Comprehensive Compositional Analyses." *Journal of Archaeological Science* 114: 105068.

Dawson, S. E. 1999. "The Athenian Wappenmünzen." *Scholia: Natal Studies in Classical Antiquity* 8: 71–8.

Day, J. 2010. *Archaic Greek Epigram and Dedication: Representation and Performance.* Cambridge: Cambridge University Press.

de Bakker, M. 2019. "A Narratological Comparison of Herodotus and Diodorus on Thermopylae." In *Textual Strategies in Ancient War Narrative: Thermopylae, Cannae and Beyond*, edited by L. W. van Gils, I. J. F. de Jong, and C. H. M. Kroon, 54–90. Amsterdam Studies in Classical Philology 29. Leiden: Brill.

de la Genière, J. 2006. "Clients, potiers et peintres." In *Les clients de la céramique grecque: actes du colloque de l'Académie des inscriptions et belles-lettres, Paris, 30–31 janvier 2004*, edited by J. de la Genière and J. Leclant, 9–15. Cahiers du Corpus vasorum antiquorum. France, 1. Paris: de Boccard.

de la Genière, J. 2009. "Les amateurs des scènes érotiques de l'archaïsme récent." In *Shapes and Uses of Greek Vases (7th–4th centuries B.C.). Proceedings of the Symposium held at the Université de Bruxelles, 27–29 April 2006*, edited by A. Tsingarida, 337–46. Études d'Archéologie 3. Brussels: CReA-Patrimoine.

de Ste. Croix, G. E. M. 2004. *Athenian Democratic Origins and Other Essays.* Edited by David Harvey and Robert Parker. Oxford: Oxford University Press.

Denoyelle, M. 1996. "Le peintre d'Analatos: essai de synthèse et perspectives nouvelles." *Antike Kunst* 39: 71–87.

Dentzer, J. -M. 1982. *Le motif du banquet couché dans le Proche-Orient et le monde grec du VIIe au IVe siècle avant J. -C.* Bibliothéque des Écoles Françaises d'Athènes et de Rome 246. Rome: École française de Rome.

Deoudi, M. 2005. "Keramik und Kult im Dromos der Tholos bei Menidi." *Thetis: Mannheimer Beiträge zur Klassischen Archäologie und Geschichte Griechenlands und Zyperns* 11–12: 33–44.

Desborough, V. R. D. A. 1952. *Protogeometric Pottery.* Oxford: Clarendon Press.

Desborough, V. R. D. A. 1972. *The Greek Dark Ages.* London: Ernest Benn.

Despinis, G. 1971. *Συμβολὴ στὴ μελέτη ἔργου τοῦ Ἀγορακρίτου.* Athens: Hermes.

Develin, R. 1989. *Athenian Officials, 684–321 BC.* Cambridge: Cambridge University Press.

Dewald, C. 2003. "Form and Content: The Question of Tyranny in Herodotus." In *Popular Tyranny: Sovereignty and its Discontents in Ancient Greece*, edited by K. A. Morgan, 25–58. Austin: University of Texas Press.

Deyhle, W. 1969. "Meisterfragen des archaischen Plastik Attikas." *Mitteilungen des Deutschen Archäologischen Instituts, Athenische Abteilung* 84: 1–64.

Dickinson, O. T. P. K. 2006. *The Aegean from Bronze Age to Iron Age: Continuity and Change between the Twelfth and Eighth Centuries B.C.* London: Routledge.

Dimitriadou, E. 2017. "Appendix: The Development of Early Athens from ca. 1125 B.C. to the End of the 8th Century B.C." In *The Early Iron Age: The Cemeteries*, edited by J. K. Papadopoulos and E. L. Smithson, 985–90. Athenian Agora 36. Princeton: American School of Classical Studies at Athens.

Dimitriadou, E. 2019. *Early Athens: Settlements and Cemeteries in the Submycenaean, Geometric and Archaic Periods*. Monumenta archaeologica 42. Los Angeles: Cotsen Institute of Archaeology.

Dimitriadou, E. 2020. "Ὑπομυκηναϊκή Ἀθήνα (1075/1050–1000 π.Χ.): ἀπὸ τὴν προϊστορία στὴν ἱστορία." In *Athens and Attica in Prehistory: Proceedings of the International Conference, Athens, 27–31 May 2015*, edited by N. Papadimitriou, J. C. Wright, S. Fachard, et al., 559–68. Oxford: Archaeopress.

Dittenberger, W. 1917–1920. *Sylloge inscriptionum graecarum*. 3 vols. Leipzig: S. Hirzel.

Domingo Gygax, M. 2016. *Benefactors and Rewards in the Ancient Greek City: The Origins of Euergetism*. Cambridge: Cambridge University Press.

Donohue, A. A. 1988. *Xoana and the Origins of Greek Sculpture*. Athens: Scholars Press.

Dörig, J. 1967. "Phaidimos." *Archäologischer Anzeiger* 1967: 15–28.

Doronzio, A. 2018. *Athen im 7. Jahrhundert v. Chr.: Räume und Funde der frühen Polis*. Urban Spaces 6. Berlin: Walter de Gruyter.

Dover, K. J. 1978. *Greek Homosexuality*. London: Duckworth.

Duplouy, A. 2006. *Le prestige des élites: recherches sur les modes de reconnaissance sociale en Grèce entre les Xe et Ve siècles avant J. -C.* Histoire (Les Belles Lettres, Paris) 77. Paris: Les Belles Lettres.

Duplouy, A. 2014. "The So-Called Solonian Property Classes: Citizenship in Archaic Athens." *Annales: histoire, sciences sociales* 69: 411–39.

Duplouy, A. 2019. *Construire la cité: essai de sociologie historique sur les communautés de l'archaïsme grec*. Mondes anciens 8. Paris: Les Belles Lettres.

Duplouy, A., and R. Brock, eds. 2018. *Defining Citizenship in Archaic Greece*. Oxford: Oxford University Press.

Eaverly, M. A. 1995. *Archaic Greek Equestrian Sculpture*. Ann Arbor: University of Michigan Press.

Eilmann, R., and K. Gebauer. 1938. *Corpus Vasorum Antiquorum, Deutschland: Berlin, Antiquarium, Band 1*. Munich: C. H. Beck.

Eisner, R. 1991. *Travelers to an Antique Land: The History and Literature of Travel to Greece*. Ann Arbor: University of Michigan Press.

Eiteljorg, H. 1995. *The Entrance to the Athenian Acropolis before Mnesicles*. Dubuque, IA: Kendall Hunt Publishing.

Ekroth, G. 2003. "Inventing Iphigeneia? On Euripides and Cultic Construction at Brauron." *Kernos* 16: 59–118.

Eliot, C. W. J. 1962. *The Coastal Demes of Attika: A Study of the Policy of Kleisthenes*. *Phoenix* Supplement 5. Toronto: University of Toronto Press.

Fachard, S. 2016. "Modelling the Territories of Attic Demes: A Computational Approach." In *The Archaeology of Greece and Rome: Studies in Honour of Anthony Snodgrass*, edited by J. L. Bintliff and N. K. Rutter, 192–222. Edinburgh: Edinburgh University Press.

Fachard, S., and A. R. Knodell. 2020. "Out of Attica: Modeling Mobility in the Mycenaean Period." In *Athens and Attica in Prehistory: Proceedings of the International Conference, Athens, 27–31 May 2015*, edited by N. Papadimitriou, J. C. Wright, S. Fachard, et al., 407–16. Oxford: Archaeopress.

Fachard, S., and S. Verdan. 2023. "Chalcis and Eretria." In *The Oxford History of the Archaic Greek World*, edited by P. Cartledge and P. Christesen. New York: Oxford University Press.

Faraguna, M. 2012. "*Hektemoroi, isomoiria, seisachtheia*: ricerche recenti sulle riforme economiche di Solone." *Dike. Rivista di storia del diritto greco ed ellenistico* 15: 171–93.

Fehr, B. 1971. *Orientalische und griechische Gelage*. Abhandlungen zur Kunst–, Musik– und Literaturwissenschaft 94. Bonn: Bouvier Verlag H. Grundmann.

Ferguson, W. S. 1938. "The Salaminioi of Heptaphylai and Sounion." *Hesperia* 7: 1–74.

Ferrari, G. 2002. *Figures of Speech: Men and Maidens in Ancient Greece*. Chicago: University of Chicago Press.

Figueira, T. J. 1984. "The Ten Archontes of 579/8 at Athens." *Hesperia* 53: 447–73.

Figueira, T. J. 1991. *Athens and Aigina in the Age of Imperial Colonization*. Baltimore: Johns Hopkins University Press.

Figueira, T. J. 1993. *Excursions in Epichoric History: Aiginetan Essays*. Lanham, MD: Rowman and Littlefield.

Figueira, T. J. 2015a. "Archaic Naval Warfare." *Historiká: studi di storia greca e romana* 5: 499–514.

Figueira, T. J. 2015b. "Modes of Colonization and Elite Integration in Archaic Greece." In *'Aristocracy' in Antiquity: Redefining Greek and Roman Elites*, edited by N. Fisher and H. van Wees, 313–47. Swansea: Classical Press of Wales.

Fink, D. 2014. *The Battle of Marathon in Scholarship: Research, Theories and Controversies Since 1850*. Jefferson, NC: McFarland.

Finley, M. I. 1951. *Studies in Land and Credit in Ancient Athens, 500–200 B.C.* New Brunswick, NJ: Rutgers University Press.

Finley, M. I. 1973. *The Ancient Economy*. Sather Classical Lectures 43. Berkeley: University of California Press.

Finley, M. I. 1981. "Land, Debt and the Man of Property in Classical Athens." In *Economy and Society in Ancient Greece*, edited by B. Shaw and R. Saller, 62–76. London: Chatto and Windus. Originally published in *Political Science Quarterly* 68 (1953): 249–68.

Finné, M., K. Holmgren, H. S. Sundqvist, et al. 2011. "Climate in the Eastern Mediterranean, and Adjacent Regions, During the Past 6000 Years—A Review." *Journal of Archaeological Science* 38: 3153–73.

Fisher, N. 2001. *Slavery in Classical Greece*. 2nd ed. Bristol: Bristol Classical Press.

Fisher, N. 2011. "Competitive Delights: The Social Effects of the Expanded Programme of Contests in Post-Kleisthenic Athens." In *Competition in the Ancient World*, edited by N. Fisher and H. van Wees, 175–219. Swansea: Classical Press of Wales.

Fisher, N., and H. van Wees, eds. 2015. *'Aristocracy' in Antiquity: Redefining Greek and Roman Elites*. Swansea: Classical Press of Wales.

Flament, C. 2007. *Le monnayage en argent d'Athènes de l'époque archaïque à l'époque hellénistique (c.550–c.40 av. J. -C.)*. Études numismatiques 1. Louvain: Association de numismatique professeur Marcel Hoc.

Flament, C. 2011. "Le Laurion et la cité d'Athènes à la fin de l'époque archaïque." *L'Antiquité classique* 80: 73–94.

Fletcher, R. N. 2008. "A Cypro-Phoenician Oinochoe in Attic Black-Figure." *Ancient West and East* 7: 219–35.

Fletcher, R. N. 2011. "Greek-Levantine Cultural Exchange in Orientalising and Archaic Pottery Shapes." *Ancient West and East* 10: 11–42.

Foley, H. 1994. *The Homeric Hymn to Demeter: Translation, Commentary, and Interpretative Essays*. Princeton: Princeton University Press.

Forsdyke, S. 2005. *Exile, Ostracism, and Democracy: The Politics of Expulsion in Ancient Greece*. Princeton: Princeton University Press.

Forsdyke, S. 2006. "Land, Labor and Economy in Solonian Athens: Breaking the Impasse Between Archaeology and History." In *Solon of Athens: New Historical and Philological Approaches*, edited by J. Blok and A. P. M. H. Lardinois, 334–50. *Mnemosyne* Supplementum 272. Leiden: Brill.

Fowler, R. L. 2000. *Early Greek Mythography, I. Text and Introduction*. Oxford: Oxford University Press.

Fowler, R. L. 2003. "Herodotus and Athens." In *Herodotus and His World: Essays from a Conference in Memory of George Forrest*, edited by P. Derow and R. Parker, 305–18. Oxford: Oxford University Press.

Fowler, R. L. 2013. *Early Greek Mythography, II. Commentary*. Oxford: Oxford University Press.

Foxhall, L. 1997. "A View from the Top: Evaluating the Solonian Property Classes." In *The Development of the Polis in Archaic Greece*, edited by L. G. Mitchell and P. J. Rhodes, 113–36. London: Routledge.

Foxhall, L. 2007. *Olive Cultivation in Ancient Greece: Seeking the Ancient Economy*. Oxford: Oxford University Press.

Franssen, J. 2011. *Votiv und Repräsentation: statuarische Weihungen archaischer Zeit aus Samos und Attika*. Archäologie und Geschichte 13. Heidelberg: Verlag Archäologie und Geschichte.

Frederiksen, R. 2011. *Greek City Walls of the Archaic Period, 900–480 BC*. Oxford: Oxford University Press.

French, A. 1956. "The Economic Background to Solon's Economic Reforms." *Classical Quarterly* 50: 11–25.

Frost, F. 1984. "The Athenian Military Before Cleisthenes." *Historia* 33: 283–94.

Fullerton, M. D. 2016. *Greek Sculpture*. Malden, MA: Wiley-Blackwell.

Gabrielsen, V. 1985. "The Naukrariai and the Athenian Navy." *Classica et mediaevalia* 36: 21–51.

Gabrielsen, V. 1994. *Financing the Athenian Fleet*. Baltimore: Johns Hopkins University Press.

Gagarin, M. 1981. *Drakon and Early Athenian Homicide Law*. Yale Classical Monographs 3. New Haven: Yale University Press.

Gagarin, M. 2006. "Legal Procedure in Solon's Laws." In *Solon of Athens: New Historical and Philological Approaches*, edited by J. Blok and A. P. M. H. Lardinois, 261–75. *Mnemosyne* Supplementum 272. Leiden: Brill.

Gagarin, M. 2008. *Writing Greek Law*. Cambridge: Cambridge University Press.

Gallant, T. W. 1982. "Agricultural Systems, Land Tenure, and the Reforms of Solon." *Annual of the British School at Athens* 77: 111–24.

Gallant, T. W. 1991. *Risk and Survival in Ancient Greece: Reconstructing the Rural Domestic Economy*. Stanford: Stanford University Press.

Garland, R. 1991. *Introducing New Gods: The Politics of Athenian Religion*. London: Duckworth.

Garland, R. 2001. *The Piraeus from the Fifth to the First Century B.C.* 2nd ed. Bristol: Bristol Classical Press.

Garnsey, P. 1985. "Grain for Athens." In *CRUX: Essays in Greek History Presented to G. E. M. de Ste Croix on His 75th Birthday*, edited by P. Cartledge and D. Harvey, 62–75. London: Duckworth. Reprinted with addendum by W. Scheidel in P. Garnsey, *Famine and Food Supply in the Graeco–Roman World: Responses to Risk and Crisis*, Cambridge: Cambridge University Press (1988), pp. 183–200.

Garnsey, P. 1988. *Famine and Food Supply in the Graeco-Roman World: Responses to Risk and Crisis*. Cambridge: Cambridge University Press.

Garnsey, P. 1992. "The Yield of the Land in Ancient Greece." In *Agriculture in Ancient Greece*, edited by B. Wells, 147–53. Göteborg: Paul Åströms Förlag. Reprinted in P. Garnsey, *Cities, Peasants and Food in Classical Antiquity: Essays in Social and Economic History*, Cambridge: Cambridge University Press (1998), pp. 201–13.

Gaspari, N. 2007–2008. "Un monumento funerario attico di età Arcaica: le 'built tombs'." *Agoge* 4–5: 95–118.

Gauss, W., and F. Ruppenstein. 1998. "Die Athener Akropolis in der frühen Eisenzeit." *Mitteilungen des Deutschen Archäologischen Instituts, Athenische Abteilung* 113: 1–60.

Gehrke, H. -J., and P. Sapirstein. 2023. "Corcyra." In *The Oxford History of the Archaic Greek World*, edited by P. Cartledge and P. Christesen. New York: Oxford University Press.

Giuliani, L. 2013. *Image and Myth: A History of Pictorial Narration in Greek Art*. Originally published as *Bild und Mythos: Geschichte der Bilderzählung in der griechischen Kunst* (2003). Translated by J. O'Donnell. Chicago: Chicago University Press.

Goemann, E., L. Giuliani, and W. -D. Heilmeyer. 1991. *Euphronios der Maler: eine Ausstellung in der Sonderausstellungshalle der Staatlichen Museen Preussischer Kulturbesitz: Berlin 20.3–26.5.1991.* Mailand: Fabbri.

Goette, H. R. 2000. *Ο ἀξιόλογος δῆμος Σούνιον: Landeskundliche Studien in Südost–Attika.* Rahden: Verlag Marie Leidorf.

Goiran, J. -P., K. P. Pavlopoulos, E. Fouache, et al. 2011. "Piraeus, the Ancient Island of Athens: Evidence from Holocene Sediments and Historical Archives." *Geology* 39: 531–4.

Goldhill, S. D. 1994. "Representing Democracy: Women at the Great Dionysia." In *Ritual, Finance, Politics: Athenian Democratic Accounts Presented to David Lewis*, edited by R. Osborne and S. Hornblower, 347–69. Oxford: Oxford University Press.

Gomme, A. W. 1933. *The Population of Athens in the Fifth and Fourth centuries B.C.* Oxford: Basil Blackwell.

Gomme, A. W., A. Andrewes, and K. J. Dover. 1945–1981. *A Historical Commentary on Thucydides.* 5 vols. Oxford: Clarendon Press.

Gottesman, A. 2010. "The Beggar and the Clod: The Mythic Notion of Property in Ancient Greece." *Transactions of the American Philological Association* 140: 287–322.

Gray, V. 2007. "Structure and Significance (5.55–69)." In *Reading Herodotus: A Study of the Logoi in Book 5 of Herodotus' Histories*, edited by E. K. Irwin and E. Greenwood, 202–21. Cambridge: Cambridge University Press.

Greco, E. 2014. "L'asty. Per una storia urbanistica di Atene." In *Topografia di Atene: Sviluppo urbano e monumenti dalle origini al III secolo d.C.*, edited by E. Greco, 4: 1521–48. 4 vols. Studi di Archeologia e Topografia di Atene e dell'Attica (SATAA) 1–1.4. Athens: Pandemos.

Green, J. R. 1991. "On Seeing and Depicting the Theatre in Classical Athens." *Greek, Roman, and Byzantine Studies* 32: 15–50.

Green, J. R. 2007. "Let's Hear it for the Fat Man: Padded Dancers and the Prehistory of Drama." In *The Origins of Theater in Ancient Greece and Beyond: From Ritual to Drama*, edited by E. Csapo and M. C. Miller, 96–107. Cambridge: Cambridge University Press.

Grote, O. 2016. *Die griechischen Phylen: Funktion—Entstehung—Leistungen.* Stuttgart: Franz Steiner Verlag.

Grove, A. T., and O. Rackham. 2001. *The Nature of Mediterranean Europe: An Ecological History.* New Haven: Yale University Press.

Haas, C. J. 1985. "Athenian Naval Power Before Themistocles." *Historia* 34: 29–46.

Habicht, C. 1985. *Pausanias' Guide to Ancient Greece.* Berkeley: University of California Press.

Haentjens, A. M. E. 1999. "Attic Geometric Childgraves: More Than Bones in Pots." In *Proceedings of the XVth International Congress of Classical Archaeology, Amsterdam, July 12–17, 1998: Classical Archaeology Towards the Third Millennium: Reflections and Perspectives*, edited by R. F. Docter and E. M. Moormann, 1: 182–3. 2 vols. Allard Pierson Series 12. Amsterdam: Allard Pierson Museum.

Hansen, M. H. 1988. *Three Studies in Athenian Demography*. Copenhagen: Kongelige Danske Videnskabernes Selskab.

Hansen, P. A. 1983–1989. *Carmina Epigraphica Graeca, I–II*. Texte und Kommentare vols. 12, 15. Berlin: Walter de Gruyter.

Harding, P. 2008. *The Story of Athens: The Fragments of the Local Chronicles of Attika*. London: Routledge.

Harding, P., ed. 1994. *Androtion and the Atthis: The Fragments Translated with Introduction and Commentary*. Oxford: Oxford University Press.

Harris, E. M. 2002. "Did Solon Abolish Debt-Bondage?" *Classical Quarterly* 52: 415–30.

Harrison, A. R. W. 1968. *The Law of Athens. [1]. The Family and Property*. Oxford: Clarendon Press.

Hasebroek, J. 1933. *Trade and Politics in Ancient Greece*. Translated by L. M. Fraser and D. C. Macgregor. London: G. Bell and Sons.

Hatzivassiliou, E. 2010. *Athenian Black-Figure Iconography Between 510 and 475 B.C.* Tübinger Archäologische Forschungen 6. Rahden: Verlag Marie Leidorf.

Havel, V. 1985. "The Power of the Powerless." In *The Power of the Powerless: Citizens against the State in Eastern Europe*, edited by J. Keane, 23–96. Contemporary Politics 4. London: Hutchinson.

Hedreen, G. M. 1992. *Silens in Attic Black-Figure Vase-Painting*. Ann Arbor: University of Michigan Press.

Hedreen, G. M. 2013. "The Semantics of Processional Dithyramb: Pindar's Second Dithyramb and Archaic Athenian Vase-Painting." In *Dithyramb in Context*, edited by B. Kowalzig and P. Wilson, 171–97. Oxford: Oxford University Press.

Hedreen, G. M. 2014. "Smikros and Epilykos: Two Comic Inventions in Athenian Vase-Painting." In *Athenian Potters and Painters Volume III*, edited by J. H. Oakley, 49–62. Oxford: Oxbow Books.

Hedreen, G. M. 2016. *The Image of the Artist in Archaic and Classical Greece: Art, Poetry and Subjectivity*. Cambridge: Cambridge University Press.

Heesen, P. 2011. *Athenian Little-Master Cups*. 2 vols. Amsterdam: Pieter Heesen.

Heesen, P. 2016. "Meaningless, But Not Useless! Nonsense Inscriptions on Athenian Little-Master Cups." In *Epigraphy of Art: Ancient Greek Vase-Inscriptions and Vase-Paintings*, edited by D. Yatromanolakis, 91–120. Oxford: Archaeopress.

Henderson, J. 1994. "Timeo Danaos: Amazons in Early Greek Art and Pottery." In *Art and Text in Ancient Greek Culture*, edited by S. D. Goldhill and R. Osborne, 85–137. Cambridge: Cambridge University Press.

Higgins, M. D., and R. A. Higgins. 1996. *A Geological Companion to Greece and the Aegean*. London: Duckworth.

Higgins, R. A. 1967. *Greek Terracottas*. London: Methuen and Co.

Hignett, C. 1952. *A History of the Athenian Constitution to the End of the Fifth Century B.C.* Oxford: Clarendon Press.

Hiller, S. 2006. "The Prothesis Scene: Bronze Age—Dark Age Relations." In *Pictorial Pursuits: Figurative Painting in Mycenaean and Geometric Pottery: Papers from Two Seminars at the Swedish Institute at Athens in 1999 and 2001*, edited by E. Rystedt and B. Wells, 183–190. Skrifter utgivna av Svenska institutet i Athen 4° 53. Stockholm: Swedish Institute at Athens.

Hirayama, T. 2010. *Kleitias and Attic Black-Figure Vases in the Sixth-Century B.C.* Tokyo: Chuokoron Bijutsu Shuppan.

Hochscheid, H. 2015. *Networks of Stone: Sculpture and Society in Archaic and Classical Athens*. Cultural Interactions 35. Bern: Peter Lang.

Hoepfner, W. and E. -L. Schwandner. 1986. *Haus und Stadt im klassischen Griechenland*. Wohnen in der klassischen Polis 1. Munich: Deutscher Kunstverlag.

Hölkeskamp, K. -J. 1992a. "Arbitrators, Lawgivers and the 'Codification of Law' in Archaic Greece: Problems and Perspectives." *Mètis* 7: 49–81.

Hölkeskamp, K. -J. 1992b. "Written Law in Archaic Greece." *Proceedings of the Cambridge Philological Society* 38: 87–117.

Hölkeskamp, K. -J. 1999. *Schiedsrichter, Gesetzgeber und Gesetzgebung im archaischen Griechenland. Historia* Einzelschriften 131. Stuttgart: Franz Steiner Verlag.

Hölkeskamp, K. -J. 2005. "What's in a Code? Solon's Laws Between Complexity, Compilation and Contingency." *Hermes* 133: 280–93.

Holladay, A. J. 1977. "The Followers of Peisistratus." *Greece and Rome* 24: 40–56.

Hölscher, T. 1991. "The City of Athens: Space, Symbol, Structure." In *City-States in Classical Antiquity and Medieval Italy*, edited by A. Molho, K. Raaflaub, J. Emlen, et al., 355–80. Stuttgart: Franz Steiner Verlag.

Holtzmann, B. 2003. *L'Acropole d'Athènes: monuments, cultes et histoire du sanctuaire d'Athèna Polias*. Antiqua 7. Paris: Picard.

Hopper, R. J. 1961. "'Plain,' 'Shore' and 'Hill' in Early Athens." *Annual of the British School at Athens* 56: 189–219.

Hornblower, S. 1991–2008. *A Commentary on Thucydides*. 3 vols. Oxford: Clarendon Press.

Hornblower, S. 2013. *Herodotus Histories Book V*. Cambridge: Cambridge University Press.

Hornblower, S., and C. B. R. Pelling. 2017. *Herodotus Histories Book VI*. Cambridge: Cambridge University Press.

Houby-Nielsen, S. 1992. "Interaction between Chieftains and Citizens? 7th Cent. B.C. Burial Customs in Athens." *Acta Hyperborea* 4: 343–74.

Houby-Nielsen, S. 1996. "The Archaeology of Ideology in the Kerameikos: New Interpretations of the Opferrinnen." In *The Role of Religion in the Early Greek Polis. Proceedings of the Third International Seminar on Ancient Greek Cult, Organized by the Swedish Institute at Athens, 16–18 October 1992*, edited by R. Hägg, 41–54.

Skrifter utgivna av Svenska institutet i Athen 8° 14. Stockholm: Swedish Institute at Athens.

Humphreys, S. C. 1974. "The Nothoi of Kynosarges." *Journal of Hellenic Studies* 94: 88–95.

Humphreys, S. C. 2018. *Kinship in Ancient Athens: An Anthropological Analysis*. 2 vols. Oxford: Oxford University Press.

Hurwit, J. M. 1985a. *The Art and Culture of Early Greece, 1100–480 B.C.* Ithaca: Cornell University Press.

Hurwit, J. M. 1985b. "The Dipylon Shield Once More." *Classical Antiquity* 4: 121–6.

Hurwit, J. M. 1999. *The Athenian Acropolis: History, Mythology, and Archaeology from the Neolithic Era to the Present*. Cambridge: Cambridge University Press.

Hurwit, J. M. 2011. "The Shipwreck of Odysseus: Strong and Weak Imagery in Late Geometric Art." *American Journal of Archaeology* 115: 1–18.

Iakovidis, S. 1969. Περατή. Τὸ Νεκροταφεῖον. 3 vols. Athens: Η εν Αθήναις Αρχαιολογική Εταιρεία.

Igelbrink, C. 2015. *Die Kleruchien und Apoikien Athens im 6. und 5. Jahrhundert v. Chr.: Rechtsformen und politische Funktionen der athenischen Gründungen. Klio* Beihefte Neue Folge 25. Berlin: Walter de Gruyter.

Immerwahr, H. R. 1964. "Book Rolls on Attic Vases." In *Classical, Medieval, and Renaissance Studies in Honor of Berthold Louis Ullman*, edited by B. L. Ullman and C. Henderson Jr., 1: 17–48. 2 vols. Rome: Edizioni di storia e letteratura.

Immerwahr, H. R. 1990. *Attic Script: A Survey*. Oxford: Clarendon Press.

Immerwahr, S. A. 1971. *The Neolithic and Bronze Ages*. Athenian Agora 13. Princeton: American School of Classical Studies at Athens.

Ingvarsson, A., Y. Bäckstrom, S. Chryssoulaki, et al. 2019. "Bioarchaeological Field Analysis of Human Remains from the Mass Graves at Phaleron, Greece." *Opuscula. Annual of the Swedish Institutes at Athens and Rome* 12: 7–158.

Iozzo, M. 2013. "The François Vase: Notes on Technical Aspects and Function." In *The François Vase: New Perspectives. Papers of the International Symposium Villa Spelman, Florence 23–24 May 2003*, edited by H. A. Shapiro and A. Lezzi-Hafter, 1: 53–65. 2 vols. Akanthus Proceedings 3. Kilchberg: Akanthus.

Irwin, E. K. 2005. *Solon and Early Greek Poetry: The Politics of Exhortation*. Cambridge: Cambridge University Press.

Isler-Kerényi, C. 2007. "Komasts, Mythic Imaginary, and Ritual." In *The Origins of Theater in Ancient Greece and Beyond: From Ritual to Drama*, edited by E. Csapo and M. C. Miller, 77–95. Cambridge: Cambridge University Press.

Ismard, P. 2010. *La cité des réseaux: Athènes et ses associations VIe–Ie siècle av. J. -C. Paris*. Histoire ancienne et médievale 105. Paris: Publications de la Sorbonne.

Ismard, P. 2018. "Associations and Citizenship in Attica from Solon to Cleisthenes." In *Defining Citizenship in Archaic Greece*, edited by A. Duplouy and R. Brock, 145–60. Oxford: Oxford University Press.

Jacoby, F. 1923–1958. *Die Fragmente der griechischen Historiker*. 3v. in 14 vols. Berlin: Weidmann.

Jacoby, F. 1949. *Atthis. The Local Chronicles of Ancient Athens*. Oxford: Clarendon Press.

Jameson, M. H. 1977. "Agriculture and Slavery in Classical Athens." *Classical Journal* 73: 122–41.

Jameson, M. H. 1980. "Apollo Lykeios in Athens." *Archaiognosia* 1: 213–36.

Jameson, M. H. 1992. "Agricultural Labor in Ancient Greece." In *Agriculture in Ancient Greece: Proceedings of the Seventh International Symposium at the Swedish Institute in Athens, 16–17 May 1990*, edited by B. Wells, 135–46. Skrifter utgivna av Svenska institutet i Athen 4° 42. Stockholm: Swedish Institute at Athens.

Jameson, M. H. 2002. "On Paul Cartledge, 'The Political Economy of Greek Slavery.'" In *Money, Labour and Land: Approaches to the Economies of Ancient Greece*, edited by P. Cartledge, E. E. Cohen, and L. Foxhall, 167–74. London: Routledge.

Jeffery, L. H. 1962. "The Inscribed Gravestones of Archaic Attica." *Annual of the British School at Athens* 57: 115–53.

Jeffery, L. H. 1976. *Archaic Greece: The City-States c. 700–500 B.C.* New York: St. Martin's Press.

Jeffery, L. H. 1990. *The Local Scripts of Archaic Greece: A Study of the Origin of the Greek Alphabet and Its Development from the Eighth to the Fifth Centuries B.C.* Rev. ed. with a supplement by Alan Johnston. Oxford: Oxford University Press.

Johnston, A. W., and R. E. Jones. 1978. "The 'SOS' Amphora." *Annual of the British School at Athens* 73: 103–41.

Johnstone, L., and R. J. Graff. 2018. "Situating Deliberative Rhetoric in Ancient Greece: The Bouleutêrion as a Venue for Oratorical Performance." *Advances in the History of Rhetoric* 21: 2–88.

Johnstone, S. 2011. *A History of Trust in Ancient Greece*. Chicago: University of Chicago Press.

Jones, J. E., A. J. Graham, and L. H. Sackett. 1973. "An Attic Country House Below the Cave of Pan at Vari." *Annual of the British School at Athens* 68: 355–452.

Jones, J. E., L. H. Sackett, and A. J. Graham. 1962. "The Dema House in Attica." *Annual of the British School at Athens* 57: 75–114.

Jones, N. F. 1987. *Public Organization in Ancient Greece: A Documentary Study*. Memoirs of the American Philosophical Society 176. Philadelphia: American Philosophical Society.

Jones, N. F. 1999. *The Associations of Classical Athens: The Response to Democracy*. New York: Oxford University Press.

Kakavogiannis, E. C. 2005. *Μέταλλα εργάσιμα και συγκεχωρημένα: η οργάνωση της εκμετάλλευσης του ορυκτού πλούτου της Λαυρεωτικής από την Αθηναϊκή δημοκρατία*. Δημοσιεύματα του Αρχαιολογικού Δελτίου 90. Athens: Υπουργείο Πολιτισμού.

Kallipolitis, V. G. 1963. "Ἀνασκαφὴ τάφων Ἀναγυροῦντος." *Ἀρχαιολογικὸν Δελτίον* 18 A: 115–32.

Kallipolitis, V. G. 1965. "Ἀνασκαφὴ τάφων Ἀναγυροῦντος." *Ἀρχαιολογικόν Δελτίον* 20 Bi: 112–16.

Kalogeropoulos, K. 2013. *Τὸ Ἱερο της Ἀρτεμιδος Ταυροπολου στις Αλες Αραφηνιδες (Λουτσα)*. Πραγματείαι της Ακαδημίας Αθηνών 71. Athens: Γραφείον Δημοσιευμάτων της Ακαδημίας Αθηνών.

Kampourelli, V. 2016. *Space in Greek Tragedy. Bulletin of the Institute of Classical Studies* Supplement 131. London: Institute of Classical Studies.

Karakasi, K. 2003. *Archaic Korai*. Los Angeles: J. Paul Getty Museum.

Karakatsanis, P. 1986. *Studien zu archaischen Kolossalwerken*. Europäische Hochschulschriften, Archäologie 9. Frankfurt: Peter Lang.

Karouzou, S. 1956. *The Amasis Painter*. Oxford Monographs on Classical Archaeology 4. Oxford: Clarendon Press.

Karusos, C. 1961. *Aristodikos: Zur Geschichte der spätarchaisch-attischen Plastik und der Grabstatue*. Stuttgart: W. Kohlhammer.

Kavvadias, G., and A. P. Matthaiou. 2014. "A New Attic Inscription of the 5th cent. B.C. from the East Slope of the Acropolis." In *Ἀθηναίων επίσκοπος· Studies in Honour of Harold B. Mattingly*, edited by A. P. Matthaiou and R. K. Pitt 51–72. Athens: Ελληνική Επιγραφική Εταιρεία.

Kearns, E. 1985. "Change and Continuity in Religious Structures after Cleisthenes." In *CRUX: Essays in Greek History Presented to G. E. M. de Ste. Croix on his 75th Birthday*, edited by P. Cartledge and D. Harvey, 189–207. London: Duckworth.

Kearns, E. 1989. *The Heroes of Attica. Bulletin of the Institute of Classical Studies* Supplement 57. London: Institute of Classical Studies.

Kearns, E. 1990. "Saving the City." In *The Greek City from Homer to Alexander*, edited by O. Murray and S. R. F. Price, 323–44. Oxford: Clarendon Press.

Keesling, C. M. 2003. *The Votive Statues of the Athenian Acropolis*. Cambridge: Cambridge University Press.

Keesling, C. M. 2005. "Patrons of Athenian Votive Monuments of the Archaic and Classical Periods." *Hesperia* 74: 395–426.

Keesling, C. M. 2015. "Solon's Property Classes on the Athenian Acropolis? A Reconsideration of *IG* 1.3.831 and *Ath. Pol.* 7.4." In *Cities Called Athens: Studies Honoring John McK. Camp II*, edited by K. F. Daly and L. A. Riccardi, 115–36. Lewisburg: Bucknell University Press.

Kienast, D. 2005a. "Die Funktion der attischen Demen von Solon bis Kleisthenes." *Chiron* 35: 69–100.

Kienast, D. 2005b. "Die Zahl der Demen in der Kleisthenischen Staatsordnung." *Historia* 54: 495–8.

Kim, H. S. 2001. "Archaic Coinage as Evidence for the Use of Money." In *Money and Its Uses in the Ancient Greek World*, edited by A. Meadows and K. Shipton, 7–21. Oxford: Oxford University Press.

Kindt, J. 2012. *Rethinking Greek Religion*. Cambridge: Cambridge University Press.

Kindt, J. 2016. *Revisiting Delphi: Religion and Storytelling in Ancient Greece.* Cambridge: Cambridge University Press.

Kirk, G. S. 1985. *The Iliad: A Commentary. Vol. 1: Books 1–4.* Cambridge: Cambridge University Press.

Kissas, K. 2000. *Die attischen Statuen- und Stelenbasen archaischer Zeit.* Bonn: Rudolf Habelt.

Kissas, K. 2008. *Archaische Architektur der Athener Akropolis: Dachziegel—Metopen—Geisa—Akroterbasen.* Deutsches Archäologisches Institut Archäologische Forschungen 24. Wiesbaden: Reichert Verlag.

Kistler, E. 1998. *Die "Opferrinne-Zeremonie": Bankettideologie am Grab, Orientalisierung und Formierung einer Adelsgesellschaft in Athen.* Stuttgart: Franz Steiner Verlag.

Klein, N. 2015. "The Architecture of the Athenian Acropolis Before Pericles: The Life and Death of the Small Limestone Buildings." In *Cities Called Athens: Studies Honoring John McK. Camp II,* edited by K. F. Daly and L. A. Riccardi, 137–64. Lewisburg: Bucknell University Press.

Kluiver, J. 2003. *The Tyrrhenian Group of Black-Figure Vases: From the Athenian Kerameikos to the Tombs of South Etruria.* Studies of the Dutch Archaeological and Historical Society New Series 1. Amsterdam: Dutch Archaeological and Historical Society.

Knapp, A. B. and S. W. Manning. 2016. "Crisis in Context: The End of the Late Bronze Age in the Eastern Mediterranean." *American Journal of Archaeology* 120: 99–149.

Konijnendijk, R. 2018. *Classical Greek Tactics: A Cultural History.* Mnemosyne Supplementum 409. Leiden: Brill.

Kosmopoulou, A. 2002. *The Iconography of Sculptured Statue Bases in the Archaic and Classical Periods.* Madison: University of Wisconsin Press.

Kotsonas, A. 2016. "Politics of Periodization and the Archaeology of Early Greece." *American Journal of Archaeology* 120: 239–70.

Kotsonas, A. 2017. "Sanctuaries, Temples and Altars in the Early Iron Age: A Chronological and Regional Accounting." In *Regional Stories: Towards a New Perception of the Early Greek World. Acts of an International Symposium in Honour of Professor Jan Bouzek, Volos 18–21 June 2015,* edited by A. Mazarakis Ainian, A. Alexandridou, and X. Charalambidou, 55–67. Volos: University of Thessaly Press.

Kourou, N. 1997. "A New Geometric Amphora in the Benaki Museum: The Internal Dynamics of an Attic Style." In *Greek Offerings: Essays on Greek Art in Honour of John Boardman,* edited by O. Palagia, 43–53. Oxford: Oxbow Books.

Kourou, N. 2002. *Attic and Atticizing Amphorae of the Protogeometric and Geometric Periods.* Athens, National Museum, Fascicule 5; Corpus Vasorum Antiquorum, Grèce, Fascicule 8. Athens: Academy of Athens.

Koutsoumpou, M. 2017. "Beyond Athens and Corinth. Pottery Distribution in the Seventh-Century Aegean: The Case of Kythnos." In *Interpreting the Seventh Century BC: Tradition and Innovation. Proceedings of the International Colloquium*

Conference Held at the British School at Athens, 9th–11th December 2011, edited by X. Charalambidou and C. A. Morgan, 160–72. Oxford: Archaeopress.

Kraay, C. M. 1956. "The Archaic Owls of Athens: Classification and Chronology." *Numismatic Chronicle* 6: 43–68.

Kraay, C. M. 1968. "An Interpretation of *Athenaion Politeia* Chapter 10." In *Essays in Greek Coinage Presented to Stanley Robinson*, edited by C.M. Kraay and G.K. Jenkins, 1–9. Oxford: Clarendon Press.

Kraay, C. M. 1976. *Archaic and Classical Greek Coins*. Berkeley: University of California Press.

Kreuzer, B. 2013. "Reading the François Vase: Myth as Case Study and the Hero Exemplum." In *The François Vase: New Perspectives. Papers of the International Symposium Villa Spelman, Florence 23–24 May 2003*, edited by H. A. Shapiro and A. Lezzi-Hafter, 1: 105–17. 2 vols. Akanthus Proceedings 3. Kilchberg: Akanthus.

Kroll, J. H. 1981. "From Wappenmünzen to Gorgoneia to Owls." *American Numismatic Society Museum Notes* 26: 1–32.

Kroll, J. H. 1998. "Silver in Solon's Laws." In *Studies in Greek Numismatics in Memory of Martin Jessop Price*, edited by R. H. J. Ashton and S. Hurter, 225–32. London: Spink.

Kroll, J. H. 2008a. "Early Iron Age Balance Weights at Lefkandi, Euboea." *Oxford Journal of Archaeology* 27: 37–48.

Kroll, J. H. 2008b. "The Monetary Use of Weighed Bullion in Archaic Greece." In *The Monetary Systems of the Greeks and Romans*, edited by W. V. Harris, 12–37. Oxford: Oxford University Press.

Kroll, J. H. 2012. "The Monetary Background of Early Coinage." In *The Oxford Handbook of Greek and Roman Coinage*, edited by W. Metcalf, 33–42. Oxford: Oxford University Press.

Kron, U. 1976. *Die zehn attischen Phylenheroen: Geschichte, Mythos, Kult und Darstellungen. Mitteilungen des Deutschen Archäologischen Instituts, Athenische Abteilung* Beiheft 5. Berlin: Mann Verlag.

Kübler, K. 1954. *Die Nekropole des 10. bis 8. Jahrhunderts*. 2 vols. Kerameikos Ergebnisse der Ausgrabungen 5. Berlin: Walter de Gruyter.

Kuhrt, A. 1988. "Earth and Water." In *Achaemenid History III: Method and Theory*, edited by A. Kuhrt and H. Sancisi-Weerdenburg, 87–100. Leiden: Nederlands Instituut Voor Het Nabije Oosten.

Kunisch, N. 1997. *Makron*. Forschungen zur antiken Keramik, II. Reihe, Kerameus 10. Mainz: Philipp von Zabern.

Kunze-Götte, E. 1992. *Der Kleophrades-Maler unter Malern schwarzfiguriger Amphoren: eine Werkstattstudie*. Mainz: Philipp von Zabern.

Küpper, M. 1989. "Frühattische 'Stempelidle' von Kiapha Thiti." In *Kiapha Thiti: Ergebnisse der Ausgrabung III.2 (Eisenzeit)*, edited by H. Lauter and D. K. Hagel, 17–29. Marburg: Selbstverlag der Philipps-Universität.

Kurke, L. 1993. "The Economy of *Kudos.*" In *Cultural Poetics in Archaic Greece*, edited by C. Dougherty and L. Kurke, 131–64. New York: Oxford University Press.

Kurtz, D. C., and J. Boardman. 1971. *Greek Burial Customs.* Ithaca: Cornell University Press.

Kyle, D. G. 1987. *Athletics in Ancient Athens.* Leiden: Brill.

Kyle, D. G. 1996. "Gifts and Glory: Panathenaic and Other Greek Prizes." In *Worshipping Athena: Panathenaia and Parthenon*, edited by J. Neils, 106–36. Madison: University of Wisconsin Press.

Kyrkou, M. 1997. "Η Πρωτοαττική πρόκληση. Νέες κεραμικές μαρτυρίες." In *Athenian Potters and Painters: The Conference Proceedings*, edited by J. H. Oakley, W. D. E. Coulson, and O. Palagia, 423–34. Oxbow Monograph 67. Oxford: Oxbow Books.

Kyrtatas, D. 2011. "Slavery and Economy in the Greek World." In *The Cambridge World History of Slavery: Volume 1: The Ancient Mediterranean World*, edited by K. Bradley and P. Cartledge, 91–111. Cambridge: Cambridge University Press.

Lalonde, G. V., M. K. Langdon, and M. B. Walbank. 1991. *Inscriptions: Horoi, Poletai Records, Leases of Public Lands.* Athenian Agora 19. Princeton: American School of Classical Studies at Athens.

Lambert, S. D. 1993. *The Phratries of Attica.* Ann Arbor: University of Michigan Press.

Lambert, S. D. 1997. "The Attic Genos Salaminioi and the Island of Salamis." *Zeitschrift für Papyrologie und Epigraphik* 119: 85–106.

Lambert, S. D. 1999. "The Attic 'Genos.'" *Classical Quarterly* 49: 484–9.

Lambert, S. D. 2000. "The Sacrificial Calendar of the Marathonian Tetrapolis: A Revised Text." *Zeitschrift für Papyrologie und Epigraphik* 130: 43–70.

Lambert, S. D. 2002. "The Sacrificial Calendar of Athens." *Annual of the British School at Athens* 97: 353–409.

Lambert, S. D. 2018. "Individual and Collective in the Funding of Sacrifices in Classical Athens: The Sacrificial Calendar of the Marathonian Tetrapolis." In *Feasting and Polis Institutions*, edited by F. van den Eijnde, J. Blok, and R. Strootman, 149–80. *Mnemosyne* Supplementum 414. Leiden: Brill.

Lang, M. L. 1976. *Graffiti and Dipinti.* Athenian Agora 21. Princeton: American School of Classical Studies at Athens.

Lang, M. L., and M. Crosby. 1964. *Weights, Measures, and Tokens.* Athenian Agora 10. Princeton: American School of Classical Studies at Athens.

Langdon, M. K. 1976. *A Sanctuary of Zeus on Mt. Hymettus. Hesperia* Supplement 16. Princeton: American School of Classical Studies at Athens.

Langdon, S. 2003. "Views of Wealth, a Wealth of Views: Grave Goods in Iron Age Attica." In *Women and Property in Ancient Near Eastern and Mediterranean Societies*, edited by D. Lyons and R. Westbrook, 1–27. Cambridge, MA: Center for Hellenic Studies.

Langdon, S. 2008. *Art and Identity in Dark Age Greece, 1100–700 B.C.E.* Cambridge: Cambridge University Press.

Laughy, M. H. 2018. "Figurines in the Road: A Protoattic Votive Deposit from the Athenian Agora Reexamined." *Hesperia* 87: 633–79.

Laurens, A. -F. 1995. "Les ateliers de céramique." In *Culture et cité: l'avènement d'Athènes à l'époque archaïque*, edited by A. Verbanck-Piérard and D. Viviers, 161–83. Paris: de Boccard.

Lauter, H. 1985a. *Der Kultplatz auf dem Turkovuni*. Attische Forschungen 1; *Mitteilungen des Deutschen Archaeologischen Instituts, Athenische Abteilung*, Beiheft 12. Berlin: Mann Verlag.

Lauter, H. 1985b. *Lathuresa: Beiträge zur Architektur und Siedlungsgeschichte in spätgeometrischer Zeit*. Attische Forschungen 2. Mainz: Philipp von Zabern.

Lauter, H., and H. Lauter-Bufé. 1975. "Die vorthemistokleische Stadtmauer Athens nach philologischen und archäologischen Quellen." *Archäologischer Anzeiger* 1–9.

Lavelle, B. 2005. *Fame, Money and Power: The Rise of Peisistratos and "Democratic" Tyranny at Athens*. Ann Arbor: University of Michigan Press.

Lazenby, J. F. 1993. *The Defence of Greece*. Warminster: Aris and Phillips.

Leão, D. F., and P. J. Rhodes. 2015. *The Laws of Solon: A New Edition with Introduction, Translation and Commentary*. London: I. B. Tauris.

Lear, A., and E. Cantarella. 2008. *Images of Ancient Greek Pederasty: Boys Were Their Gods*. London: Routledge.

Lempidaki, E. 2013. "Η λατρεία της Αθηνάς Νίκης στην Ακρόπολη των Αθηνών. Από την Αθηνά την Νίκη στη Νίκη Άπτερο." In *ΘΕΜΕΛΙΟΝ: 24 μελέτες για τον δάσκαλο Πέτρο Θέμελη από τους μαθητές και τους συνεργάτες του*, edited by E. P. Sioumpara and K. Psaroudakis, 367–93. Athens: Εταιρεία Μεσσηνιακών Αρχαιολογικών Σπουδών.

Lévêque, P., and P. Vidal-Naquet. 1996. *Cleisthenes the Athenian: An Essay on the Representation of Space and Time in Greek Political Thought from the End of the 6th Century to the Death of Plato*. Translated by D. A. Curtis. Atlantic Highlands: Humanities Press International.

Lévy, E. 1978. "Notes sur la chronologie athénienne au vie siècle." *Historia* 27: 513–21.

Lewis, D. M. 1988. "The Tyranny of the Pisistratidae." In *The Cambridge Ancient History. Volume IV. Persia, Greece, and the Western Mediterranean c. 525 to 479 B.C.*, edited by J. Boardman, N. G. L. Hammond, D. M. Lewis, et al., 287–302. 2nd ed. Cambridge: Cambridge University Press.

Lewis, D. M. 1997. "Cleisthenes and Attica." In *Selected Papers in Greek and Near Eastern History*, edited by P.J. Rhodes, 77–98. Originally published in *Historia* 12: 22–40 (1963). Cambridge: Cambridge University Press.

Lissarrague, F. 1987. *Un flot d'images: une esthétique du banquet grec*. Translated by A. Szegedy-Maszak as *The Aesthetics of the Greek Banquet: Images of Wine and Ritual*, Princeton: Princeton University Press. 2016. Paris: A. Biro.

Lissarrague, F. 1989. "The World of the Warrior." In *A City of Images: Iconography and Society in Ancient Greece*, edited by C. Bérard, 39–51. Translated by D. Lyons. Princeton: Princeton University Press.

Lissarrague, F. 1990. *L'autre guerrier: archers, peltastes, cavaliers dans l'imagerie attique.* Images à l'appui 3. Paris: La Découverte.

Lissarrague, F. 2013. *La cité des satyres. Une anthropologie ludique (Athènes, VIe–Ve siècle avant J. -C.).* Paris: Éditions EHESS.

Liston, M. 2017. "Human Skeletal Remains." In *The Early Iron Age: The Cemeteries*, edited by J. K. Papadopoulos and E. L. Smithson, 503–60. Athenian Agora 36. Princeton: American School of Classical Studies at Athens.

Lohmann, H. 1993. *Atēnē: Forschungen zu Siedlungs- und Wirtschaftsstruktur des klassischen Attika.* Cologne: Böhlau.

Loraux, N. 1986. *The Invention of Athens: The Funerary Oration in the Classical City.* Translated by A. Sheridan. Cambridge, MA: Harvard University Press.

Loraux, N. 1993. *The Children of Athena.* Translated by C. Levine. Princeton: Princeton University Press.

Lynch, K. M. 2009. "Erotic Images on Attic Vases: Markets and Meanings." In *Athenian Potters and Painters Volume II*, edited by J. H. Oakley, W. D. E. Coulson, and O. Palagia, 159–65. Oxford: Oxbow Books.

Lynch, K. M. 2011. *The Symposium in Context: Pottery from a Late Archaic House Near the Athenian Agora. Hesperia* Supplement 46. Princeton: American School of Classical Studies at Athens.

Lynch, K. M., and S. Matter. 2014. "Trade in Athenian Figured Pottery and the Effects of Connectivity." In *Athenian Potters and Painters Volume III*, edited by J. H. Oakley, 107–15. Oxford: Oxbow Books.

Mac Sweeney, N. 2013. *Foundation Myths and Politics in Ancient Ionia.* Cambridge: Cambridge University Press.

Mac Sweeney, N. 2015. "Introduction." In *Foundation Myths in Ancient Societies: Dialogues and Discourses*, edited by N. Mac Sweeney, 1–19. Philadelphia: University of Pennsylvania Press.

MacDowell, D. M. 1963. *Athenian Homicide Law in the Age of the Orators.* Manchester: Manchester University Press.

MacDowell, D. M. 1978. *The Law in Classical Athens.* Ithaca: Cornell University Press.

MacKay, E. A. 2010. *Tradition and Originality: A Study of Exekias.* BAR International Series 2092. Oxford: Archaeopress.

Maish, J. P. 2008. "Observations and Theories on the Technical Development of Coral-Red Gloss." In *Papers on Special Techniques in Athenian Vases: Proceedings of a Symposium Held in Connection with the Exhibition "The Colors of Clay: Special Techniques in Athenian Vases," at the Getty Villa, June 15–17, 2006*, edited by K. Lapatin, 83–94. Los Angeles: J. Paul Getty Museum.

Manville, P. B. 1990. *The Origins of Citizenship in Ancient Athens.* Princeton: Princeton University Press.

Marchiandi, D. 2003. "L'Accademia. Un capitolo trascurato dell' 'Atene dei Tiranni'." *Annuario della Scuola archeologica di Atene e delle Missioni italiane in Oriente* 81: 11–81.

Mark, I. S. 1993. *The Sanctuary of Athena Nike in Athens: Architectural Stages and Chronology. Hesperia* Supplement 26. Princeton: American School of Classical Studies.

Marwitz, H. 1961. "Ein attisch-geometrischer Krater in New York." *Antike Kunst* 4: 39–48.

Matthäus, H. 1999. "The Greek Symposion and the Near East: Chronology and Mechanisms of Cultural Transfer." In *Proceedings of the XVth International Congress of Classical Archaeology, Amsterdam, July 12–17, 1998. Classical Archaeology Towards the Third Millennium: Reflections and Perspectives*, edited by R. F. Docter and E. M. Moormann, 1: 256–60. 2 vols. Allard Pierson Series 12. Amsterdam: Allard Pierson Museum.

Mattusch, C. C. 1988. *Greek Bronze Statuary from the Beginnings Through the Fifth Century B.C.* Ithaca: Cornell University Press.

Mauzy, C. 2009. "A Pictorial History of the Agora Excavations." In *The Athenian Agora: New Perspectives on an Ancient Site*, edited by J. M. Camp and C. Mauzy, 87–112. Mainz: Philipp von Zabern.

Mazarakis Ainian, A. 1995. "New Evidence for the Study of the Late Geometric–Archaic Settlement at Lathouriza in Attica." In *Klados: Essays in Honour of J.N. Coldstream*, edited by C. Morris, 143–55. London: Institute of Classical Studies.

Mazarakis Ainian, A. 1997. *From Rulers' Dwellings to Temples: Architecture, Religion and Society in Early Iron Age Greece (1100–700 B.C.).* Jonsered: Paul Åströms Förlag.

Mazarakis Ainian, A. 2011. "A Necropolis of the Geometric Period at Marathon: The Context." In *The "Dark Ages" Revisited: Acts of an International Symposium in Memory of William D.E. Coulson, University of Thessaly, Volos, 14–17 June 2007*, edited by A. Mazarakis Ainian, 2: 703–16. 2 vols. Volos: University of Thessaly Press.

McDonnell, M. 1991. "The Introduction of Athletic Nudity." *Journal of Hellenic Studies* 111: 182–93.

McGlew, J. F. 1993. *Tyranny and Political Culture in Ancient Greece*. Ithaca: Cornell University Press.

Meiggs, R., and D. M. Lewis. 1988. *A Selection of Greek Historical Inscriptions to the End of the Fifth Century B.C.* 2nd ed. Oxford: Clarendon Press.

Melitz, J. 2018. "A Model of the Beginnings of Coinage in Antiquity." *European Review of Economic History* 21: 83–103.

Mertens, J. R. 2006. "Attic White Ground: Potter and Painter." In *The Colors of Clay: Special Techniques in Athenian Vases*, edited by B. Cohen, 186–93. Los Angeles: J. Paul Getty Museum.

Mertens, J. R. 2010. *How to Read Greek Vases*. New Haven: Yale University Press.

Meyer, M., and N. Brüggemann. 2007. *Kore und Kouros: Weihegaben für die Götter.* Vienna: Phoibos.

Mikalson, J. D. 1975. *The Sacred and Civil Calendar of the Athenian Year*. Princeton: Princeton University Press.

Miles, M. M. 1998. *The City Eleusinion*. Athenian Agora 31. Princeton: American School of Classical Studies at Athens.

Mills, S. 1997. *Theseus, Tragedy, and the Athenian Empire*. Oxford: Clarendon Press.

Mirhady, D. C. 2007. "The Dikasts' Oath and the Question of Fact." In *Horkos: The Oath in Greek Society*, edited by A. H. Sommerstein and J. Fletcher, 48–59. Exeter: Bristol Phoenix Press.

Missiou, A. 2011. *Literacy and Democracy in Fifth-Century Athens*. Cambridge: Cambridge University Press.

Moles, J. L. 2002. "Herodotus and Athens." In *Brill's Companion to Herodotus*, edited by E. Bakker, I. de Jong, and H. van Wees, 33–52. Leiden: Brill.

Mommsen, H. 2009. "Die Entscheidung des Achilleus auf dem Nearchos-Kantharos Akr. 611." In *Shapes and Images, Studies on Attic Black Figure and Related Topics in Honour of Herman A.G. Brijder*, edited by E. M. Moormann and V. V. Stissi, 51–61. *BABESCH Bulletin antieke beschaving* Supplement 14. Leuven: Peeters.

Moore, M. B. 2000. "Ships on a 'Wine Dark Sea' in the Age of Homer." *Metropolitan Museum Journal* 35: 13–38.

Moore, M. B. 2016. "Sophilos, Inscriptions, and the Funeral Games for Patroklos." In *Epigraphy of Art: Ancient Greek Vase-Inscriptions and Vase-Paintings*, edited by D. Yatromanolakis, 185–202. Oxford: Archaeopress.

Moore, M. B., and M. Z. Pease Philippides. 1986. *The Athenian Agora XXIII. Attic Black-Figured Pottery*. Princeton: American School of Classical Studies at Athens.

Moreno, A. 2007. *Feeding the Democracy: The Athenian Grain Supply in the Fifth and Fourth Centuries B.C.* Oxford: Oxford University Press.

Moretti, L. 1957. *Olympionikai: i vincitori negli antichi agoni olimpici*. Rome: Accademia Nazionale dei Lincei.

Morgan, C. A. 2021. "Northwestern Greece." In *The Oxford History of the Archaic Greek World*, edited by P. Cartledge and P. Christesen. New York: Oxford University Press.

Morgan, C. H. 1935. "The American Excavations in the Athenian Agora. Eighth Report. The Terracotta Figurines from the North Slope of the Acropolis." *Hesperia* 4: 189–213.

Morin, D., ed. 2020. *Ore Resources, Mining and Territory in the Aegean: The Ancient Mining Complex of Thorikos*. Fouilles de Thorikos–Opgravingen von Thorikos V. Leuven: Peeters.

Morin, D., and A. Photiades. 2005. "Nouvelles recherches sur les mines antiques du Laurion (Grèce)." *Pallas* 67: 327–58.

Morris, I. 1987. *Burial and Ancient Society: The Rise of the Greek City-State*. Cambridge: Cambridge University Press.

Morris, I. 1988. "Tomb Cult and the 'Greek Renaissance': The Past in the Present in the 8th Century." *Antiquity* 62: 750–61.

Morris, I. 2002. "Hard Surfaces." In *Money, Labour, and Land: Approaches to the Economies of Ancient Greece*, edited by P. Cartledge, E. E. Cohen, and L. Foxhall, 8–43. London: Routledge.

Morris, S. P. 1984. *The Black and White Style: Athens and Aigina in the Orientalizing Period*. Yale Classical Monographs 6. New Haven: Yale University Press.

Morrison, J. S., J. F. Coates, and N. B. Rankov. 2000. *The Athenian Trireme: The History and Reconstruction of an Ancient Greek Warship*. 2nd ed. Cambridge: Cambridge University Press.

Mosley, D. J. 1973. *Envoys and Diplomacy in Ancient Greece. Historia* Einzelschriften 22. Wiesbaden: Franz Steiner Verlag.

Mountjoy, P. A. 1995. *Mycenaean Athens*. Studies in Mediterranean Archaeology and Literature 127. Jonsered: Paul Åströms Förlag.

Mountjoy, P. A. 1999. *Regional Mycenaean Decorated Pottery*. 2 vols. Rahden: Verlag Marie Leidorf.

Moustaka, A. 2009. "Disiecta Membra: Early Terracotta Images on the Athenian Acropolis." In *Athens–Sparta: Contributions to the Research on the History and Archaeology of the Two City-States*, edited by N. E. Kaltsas, 41–50. Athens: Εθνικό Αρχαιολογικό Μουσείο.

Müller, D. 1997. *Topographischer Bildkommentar zu den Historien Herodots. 2. Kleinasien und angrenzende Gebiete mit Südostthrakien und Zypern*. Tübingen: Wasmuth.

Müller, K. 1922. "Die Lyseasstele." *Archäologischer Anzeiger*: 1–6.

Munn, M. H., and M. L. Zimmerman-Munn. 1989. "Studies on the Attic-Boiotian Frontier: The Stanford Skourta Plain Project, 1985." *Boeotia antiqua* 1: 73–127.

Munn, M. H., and M. L. Zimmerman-Munn. 1990. "On the Frontiers of Attica and Boiotia: The Results of the Stanford Skourta Plain Project." In *Essays in the Topography, History, and Culture of Boiotia*, edited by A. Schachter, 33–40. *Teiresias* Supplements Online 3. Montreal: McGill University.

Murray, O. 1990. "Cities of Reason." In *The Greek City from Homer to Alexander*, edited by O. Murray and S. R. F. Price, 1–25. Oxford: Clarendon Press.

Murray, O. 2018. *The Symposion—Drinking Greek Style: Essays on Greek Pleasure, 1983–2017*. Oxford: Oxford University Press.

Murray, S. C. 2017. *The Collapse of the Mycenaean Economy: Imports, Trade and Institutions 1300–700 BCE*. Cambridge: Cambridge University Press.

Mussche, H. F. 1998. *Thorikos: A Mining Town in Ancient Attika*. Fouilles de Thorikos II. Ghent: Ecole archéologique belge en Grèce.

Mylonas, G. 1975. *Τὸ Δυτικὸν Νεκροταφεῖον τῆς Ἐλευσῖνος*. Βιβλιοθήκη της εν Αθήναις Αρχαιολογικής Εταιρείας 81. Athens: Η εν Αθήναις Αρχαιολογική Εταιρεία.

Nagy, G., and M. Noussia-Fantuzzi, eds. 2015. *Solon in the Making: The Early Reception in the Fifth and Fourth Centuries*. Trends in Classics Supplementary Volume 7. Berlin: Walter de Gruyter.

Neer, R. 1995. "The Lion's Eye: Imitation and Uncertainty in Attic Red-Figure." *Representations* 51: 118–53.

Neer, R. 2002. *Style and Politics in Athenian Vase-Painting: The Craft of Democracy, ca. 530–460 B.C.E.* Cambridge: Cambridge University Press.

Neils, J. 1992. "The Panathenaia: An Introduction." In *Goddess and Polis: The Panathenaic Festival in Ancient Athens*, edited by J. Neils, 12–27. Princeton: Princeton University Press.

Neils, J. 2008. "'Women are White': White Ground and the Attic Funeral." In *Papers on Special Techniques in Athenian Vases: Proceedings of a Symposium Held in Connection with the Exhibition "The Colors of Clay: Special Techniques in Athenian Vases," at the Getty Villa, June 15–17, 2006*, edited by K. Lapatin, 61–72. Los Angeles: J. Paul Getty Museum.

Nevett, L. C. 2010. *Domestic Space in Classical Antiquity*. Cambridge: Cambridge University Press.

Niemeier, W. -D. 2002. *Die Kuros vom Heiligen Tor: überraschende Neufunde archaischer Skulptur im Kerameikos in Athen*. Mainz: Philipp von Zabern.

Niemeyer, H. G. 1964. "Attische Bronzestatuetten der spätarchaischen und frühklassischen Zeit." *Antike Plastik* 3: 7–32.

Nylander, C. 1962. "Die sog. mykenischen Säulenbasen auf der Akropolis in Athen." *Opuscula Atheniensia* 4: 31–77.

Oakley, J. H. 2004. *Picturing Death in Classical Athens: The Evidence of the White Lekythoi*. Cambridge: Cambridge University Press.

Ober, J. 1993. "The Athenian Revolution of 508/7 B.C.: Violence, Authority, and the Origins of Democracy." In *Cultural Poetics in Archaic Greece: Cult, Performance, Politics*, edited by C. Dougherty and L. Kurke, 215–32. Princeton: Princeton University Press. Reprinted in J. Ober, *The Athenian Revolution: Essays on Ancient Greek Democracy and Political Theory*, Princeton: Princeton University Press (1996), 32–52.

Ohly-Dumm, M. 1984. "Sosias und Euthymides." In *Ancient Greek and Related Pottery. Proceedings of the International Vase Symposium in Amsterdam, 12–15 April 1984*, edited by H. A. G. Brijder, 165–72. Allard Pierson Series 5. Amsterdam: Allard Pierson Museum.

Ohly, D. 1953. *Griechische Goldbleche des 8. Jahrhunderts v. Chr.* Berlin: Mann Verlag.

Oliver, I. C. 2017. "The Audience of Herodotus: The Influence of Performance on the *Histories*." PhD diss., University of Colorado at Boulder.

Orrells, D. 2015. *Sex: Antiquity and its Legacy*. London: I. B. Tauris.

Osborne, R. 1985. *Demos. The Discovery of Classical Attika*. Cambridge: Cambridge University Press.

Osborne, R. 1987. *Classical Landscape with Figures: The Ancient Greek City and its Countryside*. London: George Philip.

Osborne, R. 1988a. "Death Revisited; Death Revised. The Death of the Artist in Archaic and Classical Greece." *Art History* 11: 1–16.

Osborne, R. 1988b. "Social and Economic Implications of the Leasing of Land and Property in Classical and Hellenistic Greece." *Chiron* 18: 279–323.

Osborne, R. 1989. "A Crisis in Archaeological History? The Seventh Century in Attica." *Annual of the British School at Athens* 84: 297–322.

Osborne, R. 1992. "'Is It a Farm?' The Definition of Agricultural Sites and Settlements in Ancient Greece." In *Agriculture in Ancient Greece*, edited by B. Wells, 21–7. Göteborg: Paul Åströms Förlag. Reprinted with endnote in R. Osborne *Athens and Athenian Democracy*, Cambridge: Cambridge University Press (2010): 127–38.

Osborne, R. 1993. "Competitive Festivals and the *Polis*: A Context for Dramatic Festivals at Athens." In *Tragedy, Comedy and the Polis. Papers from the Greek Drama Conference: Nottingham, 18–20 July 1990*, edited by A. H. Sommerstein, S. Halliwell, J. Henderson, et al., 21–37. Bari: Levante Editori. Reprinted with an endnote in R. Osborne, *Athens and Athenian Democracy*, Cambridge: Cambridge University Press (2010), pp. 127–38.

Osborne, R. 1994a. "Archaeology, the Salaminioi and the Politics of Sacred Space in Archaic Attica." In *Placing the Gods: Sanctuaries and Space in Ancient Greece*, edited by S. E. Alcock and R. Osborne, 143–60. Oxford: Oxford University Press.

Osborne, R. 1994b. "Looking on Greek Style. Does the Sculpted Girl Speak to Women Too?" In *Classical Greece: Ancient Histories and Modern Archaeologies* edited by I. Morris, 81–96. Cambridge: Cambridge University Press.

Osborne, R. 1995. "The Economics and Politics of Slavery at Athens." In *The Greek World*, edited by A. Powell, 27–43. London: Routledge.

Osborne, R. 1996. "Pots, Trade and the Archaic Greek Economy." *Antiquity* 70: 31–44.

Osborne, R. 1997a. "Law and Laws: How do We Join Up the Dots?" In *The Development of the Polis in Archaic Greece*, edited by L. G. Mitchell and P. J. Rhodes, 74–82. London: Routledge.

Osborne, R. 1997b. "Review of H. Lohmann, Ατήνη. *Forschungen zu Siedlungs- und Wirtschaftsstruktur des klassischen Attika*." *Gnomon* 69: 243–7.

Osborne, R. 1998. *Archaic and Classical Greek Art*. Oxford: Oxford University Press.

Osborne, R. 2001. "Why did Athenian Pots Appeal to the Etruscans?" *World Archaeology* 33: 277–95.

Osborne, R. 2002. "Archaic Greek History." In *Brill's Companion to Herodotus*, edited by E. Bakker, I. de Jong, and H. van Wees, 497–520. Leiden: Brill.

Osborne, R. 2007a. "Did Democracy Transform Athenian Space?" In *Building Communities: House, Settlement and Society in the Aegean and Beyond: Proceedings of a Conference Held at Cardiff University, 17–21 April 2001*, edited by R. Westgate, N. Fisher, and J. Whitley, 195–9. British School at Athens Studies 15. London: British School at Athens.

Osborne, R. 2007b. "Projecting Identities in the Greek Symposion." In *Material Identities*, edited by J. Sofaer, 31–52. Oxford: Blackwell.

Osborne, R. 2007c. "Sex, Agency and History: The Case of Athenian Painted Pottery." In *Art's Agency and Art History*, edited by J. Tanner and R. Osborne, 179–98. Oxford: Blackwell.

Osborne, R. 2008. "Putting Performance into Focus." In *Performance, Iconography, Reception: Studies in Honour of Oliver Taplin*, edited by M. Revermann and P. Wilson, 395–418. Oxford: Oxford University Press.

Osborne, R. 2009. *Greece in the Making, 1200–479 BC*. 2nd ed. London: Routledge.

Osborne, R. 2010. *Athens and Athenian Democracy*. New York: Cambridge University Press.

Osborne, R. 2014. "Intoxication and Sociality: The Symposium in the Ancient Greek World." In *Cultures of Intoxication*, edited by A. McShane and P. J. Withington, 34–60. *Past and Present* Supplements 9. Oxford: Oxford University Press.

Osborne, R. 2018a. "Homeric Imagery." In *An Age of Experiment: Classical Archaeology Transformed 1976–2014*, edited by L. C. Nevett, J. Whitley, S. E. Alcock, et al., 75–85. Cambridge: McDonald Institute for Archaeological Research.

Osborne, R. 2018b. "Imaginary Intercourse: An Illustrated History." In *How to Do Things with History: New Approaches to Ancient Greece*, edited by D. Allen, P. Christesen, and P. Millett, 313–38. New York: Oxford University Press.

Osborne, R. 2018c. *The Transformation of Athens: Athenian Painted Pottery and the Creation of Classical Greece*. Princeton: Princeton University Press.

Osborne, R. 2018d. "A World of Choice: Taking Archaic Greek Diversity Seriously." In *Visual Histories of the Classical World: Essays in Honour of R. R. R. Smith*, edited by C. M. Draycott, R. Raja, K. Welch, et al., 3–14. Studies in Classical Archaeology 4. Turnhout: Brepols.

Osborne, R. 2019a. "Unruly Women and Greek Sanctuaries. Gendered Expectations and Their Violation." In *Die Grenzen des Prinzips: die Infragestellung von Werten durch Regelverstöße in antiken Gesellschaften*, edited by K. -J. Hölkeskamp, J. Hoffmann-Salz, K. Kostopoulos, et al., 25–45. Stuttgart: Franz Steiner Verlag.

Osborne, R. 2019b. "Why Athens? Population Aggregation in Attica in the Early Iron Age." In *Coming Together: Comparative Approaches to Population Aggregation and Early Urbanization*, edited by A. Gyucha, 135–48. Albany: State University of New York Press.

Osborne, R. 2020a. "Collapse and Transformation in Athens and Attica." In *Collapse and Transformation: The Late Bronze Age to Early Iron Age in the Aegean*, edited by G. Middleton, 137–44. Oxford: Oxbow Books.

Osborne, R. 2020b. "The Scale of Benefaction." In *Benefactors and the Polis: The Public Gift in the Greek Cities from the Homeric World to Late Antiquity*, edited by M. Domingo-Gygax and A. Zuiderhoek, 96–112. Cambridge: Cambridge University Press.

Osborne, R. 2021a. "How, and Why, the Athenians Painted Different Myths at Different Times." In *Texts and Intertexts in Archaic and Classical Greece*, edited by A. Kelly and H. L. Spelman. Cambridge: Cambridge University Press.

Osborne, R. 2021b. "Production, Urbanization and the Rise of Athens in the Archaic Period." In *Making Cities: Economies of Production and Urbanization in Mediterranean Europe*, edited by M. Gleba, B. Marin Aguilera, and B. Dimova, 77–87. Cambridge: McDonald Institute for Archaeological Research.

Osborne, R. 2022. "What is a Region?" In *Regions and Communities in Early Greece (1200–550 BCE). Proceedings of the International Conference at Tübingen University,*

14th–16th December 2018, edited by M. Rönnberg and V. Sossau, 89–104. Tübinger Archäologische Forschungen 35. Verlag Marie Leidorf: Rahden.

Osborne, R. Forthcoming. "Agricultural Productivity and the Athenian Economy." In *Athens: Economy and Democracy*, edited by D. Jew, R. Osborne, and S. von Reden.

Osborne, R., and A. Pappas. 2006. "Writing on Archaic Greek Pottery." In *Art and Inscriptions in the Ancient World*, edited by Z. Newby and R. Leader-Newby, 131–55. Cambridge: Cambridge University Press.

Osborne, R., and P. J. Rhodes, eds. 2017. *Greek Historical Inscriptions, 478–404 BC*. Oxford: Oxford University Press.

Ousterhout, R. 2005. "'Bestride the Very Peak of Heaven': The Parthenon After Antiquity." In *The Parthenon from Antiquity to the Present*, edited by J. Neils, 293–330. Cambridge: Cambridge University Press.

Padgett, J. M. 2017. *The Berlin Painter and His World: Athenian Vase-Painting in the Early Fifth Century B.C.* Princeton: Princeton University Art Museum.

Paga, J. 2010. "Deme Theaters in Attica and the Trittys System." *Hesperia* 79: 351–84.

Paga, J. 2015. "The Monumental Definition of Attica in the Early Democratic Period." In *Autopsy in Athens: Recent Archaeological Research on Athens and Attica*, edited by M. M. Miles, 108–25. Oxford: Oxbow Books.

Paga, J., and M. M. Miles. 2016. "The Archaic Temple of Poseidon at Sounion." *Hesperia* 85: 657–710.

Palagia, O. 2016. "Towards a Publication of the Piraeus Bronzes: The Apollo." In *Proceedings of the XVIIth International Congress on Ancient Bronzes, Izmir*, edited by A. Giumlia-Mair and C. Mattusch, 137–44. Monographie Instrumentum 52. Autun: Mergoil.

Palagia, O., and Y. Maniatis. 2015. "Naxian or Parian? Preliminary Examination of the Sounion and Dipylon Kouroi." In *Interdisciplinary Studies on Ancient Stone: ASMOSIA X. Proceedings of the Tenth International Conference of ASMOSIA (Association for the Study of Marble & Other Stones in Antiquity), Rome, 21–26 May 2012*, edited by P. Pensabene and E. Gasparini, 593–607. Rome: Bretschneider.

Palaiokrassa-Kopitsa, L. 2017. "Cult in Attica: The Case of the Sanctuary of Artemis Mounychia." In *Interpreting the Seventh Century BC: Tradition and Innovation. Proceedings of the International Colloquium Conference Held at the British School at Athens, 9th–11th December 2011*, edited by X. Charalambidou and C. Morgan, 245–59. Oxford: Archaeopress.

Palaiokrassa-Kopitsa, L., and E. P. Vivliodetis. 2015. "The Sanctuaries of Artemis Mounichia and Zeus Parnessios. Their Relation to the Religious and Social Life in the Athenian City-State until the End of the 7th Century B.C." In *Pots, Workshops and Early Iron Age Society: Function and Role of Ceramics in Early Greece, Proceedings of the International Symposium (Université Libre de Bruxelles, 14–16 November 2013)*, edited by V. Vlachou, 155–80. Études d'archéologie 8. Brussels: CReA-Patrimoine.

Palaiokrassa, L. 1989. "Neue Befunde aus dem Heiligtum der Artemis Mounichia." *Mitteilungen des Deutschen Archäologischen Instituts, Athenische Abteilung* 104: 1–40.

Palaiokrassa, L. 1991. *Το ιερό της Αρτέμιδος Μουνιχίας.* 2 vols. Athens: Η εν Αθήναις Αρχαιολογική Εταιρεία.

Paleothodoros, D. 2009. "Archaeological Contexts and Ionographic Analysis: Case Studies from Greece and Etruria." In *The World of Greek Vases*, edited by V. Nørskov, L. Hannestad, C. Isler-Kerenyi, et al., 45–62. Analecta Romana Instituti Danici Supplementum 41. Rome: Quasar.

Papadimitriou, N. 2017. "Συνοίκησις in Mycenaean Times? The Political and Cultural Geography of Attica in the Second Millennium BCE." *CHS Research Bulletin* 5, no. 2. https://research-bulletin.chs.harvard.edu/2017/09/11/sunoikisis-mycenaean/.

Papadimitriou, N., and M. B. Cosmopoulos. 2020. "The Political Geography of Attica in the Middle and Late Bronze Age." In *Athens and Attica in Prehistory: Proceedings of the International Conference, Athens, 27–31 May 2015*, edited by N. Papadimitriou, J. C. Wright, S. Fachard, et al., 373–85. Oxford: Archaeopress.

Papadopoulos, J. K. 1980. *Xoana e Sphyrelata. Testimonia delle Fonti Scritti.* Rome: Bretschneider.

Papadopoulos, J. K. 2003. *Ceramicus Redivivus. The Early Iron Age Potters' Field in the Classical Athenian Agora. Hesperia* Supplement 31. Princeton: American School of Classical Studies at Athens.

Papadopoulos, J. K. 2017. "Burial Customs and Funerary Rites." In *The Early Iron Age: The Cemeteries*, edited by J. K. Papadopoulos and E. L. Smithson, 575–688. Athenian Agora 36. Princeton: American School of Classical Studies at Athens.

Papadopoulos, J.K., and E. L. Smithson. 2002. "Cultural Biography of a Geometric Amphora: Islanders in Athens and the Prehistory of Metics." *Hesperia* 71: 182–93.

Papadopoulos, J.K., and E. L. Smithson, eds. 2017. *The Early Iron Age: The Cemeteries.* Athenian Agora 36. Princeton: American School of Classical Studies at Athens.

Papadopoulos, J. K., E. L. Smithson, and S. Strack. 2017. "Four Cemeteries: A Catalogue of Tombs and Their Contents." In *The Early Iron Age: The Cemeteries*, edited by J. K. Papadopoulos and E. L. Smithson, 35–502. Athenian Agora 36. Princeton: American School of Classical Studies at Athens.

Papangeli, K., S. Fachard, and A. R. Knodell. 2018. "The Mazi Archaeological Project 2017: Test Excavations and Site Investigations." *Antike Kunst* 61: 153–63.

Papaspyridi-Karouzou, S. 1963. *Ἀγγεῖα τοῦ Ἀναγυροῦντος.* Athens: Η εν Αθήναις Αρχαιολογική Εταιρεία.

Papazarkadas, N. 2011. *Sacred and Public Land in Ancient Athens.* Oxford: Oxford University Press.

Parikh, T. 2020. "The Material of Polytheism in Archaic Greece: Understanding Greek Religion through Patterns of Dedicatory Practice and Thought." PhD diss., University of Cambridge.

Parisi, V. 2014. "Terrecotte votive e pratiche rituali nell'Atene di VII secolo a.C." In *Gli Ateniesi e il loro modello di città. Seminari di storia e archeologia greca I*, edited by L.M. Caliò, E. Lippolis, and V. Parisi, 23–35. Thiasos monografie 5. Rome: Quasar.

Parker, R. 1991. "The *Homeric Hymn to Demete*r and the *Homeric Hymns*." *Greece and Rome* 38: 1–17.

Parker, R. 1996. *Athenian Religion: A History*. Oxford: Clarendon Press.

Parker, R. 2005. *Polytheism and Society at Athens*. Oxford: Oxford University Press.

Parker, R. 2017. *Greek Gods Abroad: Names, Natures, and Transformations*. Sather Classical Lectures 72. Berkeley: University of California Press.

Patterson, C. 1998. *The Family in Greek History*. Cambridge, MA: Harvard University Press.

Patterson, C. B. 1981. *Pericles' Citizenship Law of 451–50 B.C.* New York: Arno Press.

Payne, H., and G. M. Young. 1936. *Archaic Marble Sculpture from the Acropolis*. London: Cresset Press.

Pearson, L. 1942. *The Local Historians of Attica*. Philadelphia: American Philological Association.

Pébarthe, C. 2006. *Cité, démocratie et écriture: histoire de l'alphabétisation d'Athènes à l'époque classique*. Culture et cité 3. Paris: de Boccard.

Pedley, J. G. 1978. "Cycladic Influence in the Sixth Century Sculpture of Attica." In *Athens Comes of Age: From Solon to Salamis. Papers of a Symposium Sponsored by The Archaeological Institute of America, Princeton Society and The Department of Art and Archaeology, Princeton University*. 53–71. Princeton: Archaeological Institute of America.

Pelling, C. B. R. 2009. "Bringing Autochthony Up-to-Date: Herodotus and Thucydides." *Classical World* 102: 471–83.

Petrakos, B. 1999a. *Ο δήμος του Ραμνούντος. Σύνοψη των ανασκαφών και των ερευνών 1813– 1998*. 2 vols. Athens: Η εν Αθήναις Αρχαιολογική Εταιρεία.

Petrakos, B. 1999b. *Ο δήμος του Ραμνούντος: σύνοψη των ανασκαφών και των ερευνών: (1813– 1998) 1. Τοπογραφία*. Athens: Η εν Αθήναις Αρχαιολογική Εταιρεία.

Petrakos, B. 2013. *Πρόχειρον Αρχαιολόγικον 1828–2012: Μέρος 1: Χρονογράφικο*. Athens: Η εν Αθήναις Αρχαιολογική Εταιρεία.

Petropoulakou, M. and E. Pentazos. 1973. *Αττική, οικιστικά στοιχεία—Πρώτη έκθεση*. Αρχαίες ελληνικές πόλεις 21. Athens: Athens Center of Ekistics.

Philippson, A. 1952. *Die griechischen Landschaften. Eine Landeskunde. Band 1: Der Nordosten der griechischen Halbinsel. Teil III: Attika und Megaris*. Frankfurt: Klostermann.

Photos-Jones, E., and J. Ellis-Jones. 1994. "The Building and Industrial Remains at Agrileza, Laurion (Fourth Century BC) and Their Contribution to the Workings at the Site." *Annual of the British School at Athens* 89: 307–58.

Picard, O. 2001. "La découverte des gisements du Laurion et les débuts de la chouette." *Revue belge de numismatique et de sigillographie* 147: 1–10.

Pickard-Cambridge, A. W. 1946. *The Theatre of Dionysus in Athens*. Oxford: Clarendon Press.

Pierrot, A. 2015. "Who Were the Eupatrids in Archaic Athens?" In *'Aristocracy' in Antiquity: Redefining Greek and Roman Elites*, edited by N. Fisher and H. van Wees, 147–68. Swansea: Classical Press of Wales.

Plommer, W. H. 1960. "The Archaic Acropolis: Some Problems." *Journal of Hellenic Studies* 80: 127–59.

Porter, S., J. Roffe, C. Armstrong, et al. 1817. *The Unedited Antiquities of Attica, Comprising the Architectural Remains of Eleusis, Rhamnus, Sunium, and Thoricus*. London: W. Bulmer.

Pratt, C. 2015. "The 'SOS' Amphora: An Update." *Annual of the British School at Athens* 110: 213–45.

Pretzler, M. 2007. *Pausanias: Travel Writing in Ancient Greece*. London: Duckworth.

Prevedorou, E. -A., and J. E. Buikstra. 2019. "Bioarchaeological Practice and the Curation of Human Skeletal Remains in a Greek Context: The Phaleron Cemetery." *Advances in Archaeological Practice* 7: 60–7.

Price, S. R. F., and L. Nixon. 2005. "Ancient Greek Agricultural Terraces: Evidence from Texts and Archaeological Survey." *American Journal of Archaeology* 109: 665–94.

Pritchard, D. 2004. "Kleisthenes, Participation, and the Dithyrambic Contests of Late Archaic and Classical Athens." *Phoenix* 58: 208–28.

Privitera, S. 2013. *Principi, pelasgi e pescatori: l'Attica nella tarda età del Bronzo*. Paestum: Pandemos.

Psoma, S. 2016. "Choosing and Changing Monetary Standards in the Greek World during the Archaic and Classical Periods." In *The Ancient Greek Economy: Markets, Households, and City-States*, edited by E. M. Harris, D. M. Lewis, and M. Woolmer, 90–115. Cambridge: Cambridge University Press.

Rackham, O. 1983. "Observations on the Historical Ecology of Boeotia." *Annual of the British School at Athens* 78: 291–351.

Raubitschek, A. E. and L. H. Jeffery. 1949. *Dedications from the Athenian Acropolis: A Catalogue of the Inscriptions of the Sixth and Fifth Centuries B.C.* Supplementum Inscriptionum Atticarum 7. New York: Archaeological Institute of America.

Reese, D. S. 1989. "Faunal Remains from the Altar of Aphrodite Ourania, Athens." *Hesperia* 58: 63–70.

Reusser, C. 2002. *Vasen für Etrurien: Verbreitung und Funktionen attischer Keramik im Etrurien des 6. und 5. Jahrhunderts vor Christus*. Akanthus Crescens 5. Zurich: Akanthus.

Rhodes, P. J. 1972. *The Athenian Boule*. Oxford: Clarendon Press.

Rhodes, P. J. 1975. "Solon and the Numismatists." *Numismatic Chronicle* 15: 1–11.

Rhodes, P. J. 1976. "Pisistratid Chronology Again." *Phoenix* 30: 219–33.

Rhodes, P. J. 1981. *A Commentary on the Aristotelian Athenaion Politeia*. Oxford: Clarendon Press.

Rhodes, P. J. 2006. "The Reforms and Laws of Solon: An Optimistic View." In *Solon of Athens: New Historical and Philological Approaches*, edited by J. Blok and A. P. M. H. Lardinois, 248–60. *Mnemosyne* Supplementum 272. Leiden: Brill.

Rhodes, P. J. and R. Osborne, eds. 2003. *Greek Historical Inscriptions: 404–323 BC*. Oxford: Oxford University Press.

Richardson, N. J. 1974. *The Homeric Hymn to Demeter*. Oxford: Clarendon Press.

Richardson, N. J. 2011. "The 'Homeric Hymn to Demeter': Some Central Questions Revisited." In *The Homeric Hymns: Interpretative Essays*, edited by A. Faulkner, 44–58. Oxford: Oxford University Press.

Richter, G. M. A. 1961. *The Archaic Gravestones of Attica*. New York: Phaidon.

Richter, G. M. A. 1968. *Korai: Archaic Greek Maidens. A Study of the Development of the Kore Type in Greek Sculpture*. London: Phaidon.

Richter, G. M. A. 1970. *Kouroi: Archaic Greek Youths. A Study of the Development of the Kouros Type in Greek Sculpture*. London: Phaidon.

Ridgway, B. S. 1993. *The Archaic Style in Greek Sculpture*. 2nd ed. Chicago: Ares Publishers.

Rihll, T. E. 1991. "Ἑκτήμοροι: Partners in Crime." *Journal of Hellenic Studies* 111: 101–27.

Rihll, T. E. 2011. "Classical Athens." In *The Cambridge World History of Slavery: Volume 1: The Ancient Mediterranean World*, edited by K. Bradley and P. Cartledge, 48–73. Cambridge: Cambridge University Press.

Robertson, M. 1992. *The Art of Vase Painting in Classical Athens*. Cambridge: Cambridge University Press.

Rocco, G. 2008. *La ceramografia protoattica. Pittori e botteghe (710–630 a.C.)*. Internationale Archäologie 111. Rahden: Verlag Marie Leidorf.

Rolley, C. 1994. *La sculpture grecque I. Des origines au milieu au Ve siècle*. Paris: Picard.

Romano, I. B. 1982. "The Archaic Statue of Dionysos from Ikarion." *Hesperia* 51: 398–409.

Rombos, T. 1988. *The Iconography of Attic Late Geometric II Pottery*. Studies in Mediterranean Archaeology and Literature Pocketbook 68. Partille: Paul Åströms Förlag.

Rönnberg, M. 2019. "Zur Chronologie und kulturhistorischen Bedeutung frührarchaischer attischer 'Stempelidole.'" *Mitteilungen des Deutschen Archäologischen Instituts, Athenische Abteilung* 134.

Rönnberg, M. 2021a. *Athen und Attika vom 11. bis zum frühen 6. Jh. v. Chr. Siedlungsgeschichte, politische Institutionalisierungs- und gesellschaftliche Formierungsprozesse*. Tübinger Archäologische Forschungen 33. Rahden: Verlag Marie Leidorf.

Rönnberg, M. 2021b. "Reinterpreting the Diachronic Variations in the Numbers of Burials Known from Early Iron Age Athens." *Journal of Greek Archaeology* 6: 146–66.

Rönnberg, M. 2022. "Internal Colonisation. Village Fission and the Emergence of Local Cults in Attica." In *Regions and Communities in Early Greece (1200–550 BCE). Proceedings of the International Conference at Tübingen University, 14th–16th December 2018*, edited by M. Rönnberg and V. Sossau, 69–88. Rahden: Verlag Marie Leidorf.

Root, M. C. 1988. "Evidence from Persepolis for the Dating of Persian and Archaic Greek Coinage." *Numismatic Chronicle* 148: 1–12.

Rosenthal, P., D. Morin, R. Herbach, et al. 2013. "Mining Technologies at Deep Level in Antiquity: The Laurion mines (Attica, Greece)." In *Mining in European History and Its Impact on Environment and Human Societies—Proceedings for the 2nd Mining in European History Conference of the FZ HiMAT, 7.–10. November 2012, Innsbruck* edited by P. Anreiter, K. Brandstätter, G. Goldenberg, et al., 89–95. Innsbruck: Universität Innsbruck.

Rosivach, V. 1987. "Autochthony and the Athenians." *Classical Quarterly* 37: 294–306.

Rosivach, V. 1993. "Agricultural Slavery in the Northern Colonies and in Classical Athens: Some Comparisons." *Comparative Studies in Society and History* 35: 551–67.

Roy, J. 1998. "The Threat from the Piraeus." In *Kosmos: Essays in Order, Conflict, and Community in Classical Athens*, edited by P. Cartledge, P. Millett, and S. von Reden, 191–202. Cambridge: Cambridge University Press.

Rung, E. 2015. "The Language of the Achaemenid Imperial Diplomacy towards the Greeks: The Meaning of Earth and Water." *Klio* 97: 503–15.

Ruppenstein, F., and A. Lagia. 2007. *Die submykenische Nekropole: Neufunde und Neubewertung*. Kerameikos Ergebnisse der Ausgrabungen 18. Munich: Hirmer.

Ruschenbusch, E. 1966. *ΣΟΛΩΝΟΣ ΝΟΜΟΙ. Die Fragmente des solonischen Gesetzeswerkes mit einer Text- und Überlieferungsgeschichte. Historia* Einzelschriften 9. Wiesbaden: Franz Steiner Verlag.

Ruschenbusch, E. 2010. *Solon: Das Gesetzeswerk—Fragmente*. Stuttgart: Franz Steiner Verlag.

Ryan, F. X. 1994. "The Original Date of the δημος πληθυων Provisions of *IG* I³ 105." *Journal of Hellenic Studies* 114: 120–34.

Sallares, R. 1991. *The Ecology of the Ancient Greek World*. Ithaca: Cornell University Press.

Sapirstein, P. 2014. "Demographics and Productivity in the Ancient Athenian Pottery Industry." In *Athenian Potters and Painters Volume III*, edited by J. H. Oakley, 175–86. Oxford: Oxbow Books.

Sassù, A. 2014. "Depositi votivi e funzioni cultuali collettive nell'Atene di VII secolo a.C." In *Gli Ateniesi e il loro modello di città. Seminari di storia e archeologia greca I*, edited by L. M. Calio`, E. Lippolis, and V. Parisi, 37–50. Thiasos monografie 5. Rome: Quasar.

Sassù, R. 2014. "La ricchezza di Atene: l'Acropoli e le risorse della polis." In *Gli Ateniesi e il loro modello di città. Seminari di storia e archeologia greca I*, edited by L. M. Calio`, E. Lippolis, and V. Parisi, 107–18. Thiasos monografie 5. Rome: Quasar.

Sato, N. 2015. "'Aristocracy' in Athenian Diplomacy." In *'Aristocracy' in Antiquity: Redefining Greek and Roman Elites*, edited by N. Fisher and H. van Wees, 203–26. Swansea: Classical Press of Wales.

Scafuro, A. 2006. "Identifying Solonian Laws." In *Solon of Athens: New Historical and Philological Approaches*, edited by J. Blok and A. P. M. H. Lardinois, 175–96. *Mnemosyne* Supplementum 272. Leiden: Brill.

Scheidel, W. 2003. "The Greek Demographic Expansion: Models and Comparisons." *Journal of Hellenic Studies* 123: 120–40.

Schilardi, D. 2011. "Αριστοκρατικές ταφές από το Γεωμετρικό νεκροταφείο της Κηφισιάς." In *The "Dark Ages" Revisited: Acts of an International Symposium in Memory of William D.E. Coulson, University of Thessaly, Volos, 14–17 June 2007*, edited by A. Mazarakis Ainian, 2: 675–702. 2 vols. Volos: University of Thessaly Press.

Schlörb-Vierneisel, B. 1975. "Eridanos—Nekropole I. Gräber und Opferstellen hS 1–204." *Mitteilungen des Deutschen Archäologischen Instituts, Athenische Abteilung* 81: 4–111.

Schmalz, G. C. R. 2006. "The Athenian Prytaneion Discovered?" *Hesperia* 75: 33–81.

Schnapp, A. 1989. "Eros the Hunter." In *A City of Images: Iconography and Society in Ancient Greece*, edited by C. Bérard, 71–88. Translated by D. Lyons. Princeton: Princeton University Press. Translation of "Eros en chasse" in *La cité des images: Religion et société en Grèce ancienne*, Paris: Fernand Nathan (1984), pp. 67–84.

Schnapp, A. 1997. *Le chasseur et la cité: chasse et érotique dans la Grèce ancienne*. Paris: Albin Michel.

Scholl, A. 2006. "ΑΝΑΘΗΜΑΤΑ ΤΩΝ ΑΡΧΑΙΩΝ: die Akropolisvotive aus dem 8. bis frühen 6. Jahrhundert v. Chr. und die Staatswerdung Athens." *Jahrbuch des Deutschen Archäologischen Instituts* 121: 1–173.

Schulze, B. 2004. *Die Votivtafeln der archaischen und klassischen Zeit von der Athener Akropolis*. Bellerophon 2. Möhnesee: Bibliopolis.

Schweitzer, B. 1971. *Greek Geometric Art*. London: Phaidon.

Seaford, R. 2003. *Money and the Early Greek Mind: Homer, Philosophy, Tragedy*. Cambridge: Cambridge University Press.

Sealey, R. 1960. "Regionalism in Archaic Athens." *Historia* 9: 155–80.

Seeberg, A. 1971. *Corinthian Komos Vases. Bulletin of the Institute of Classical Studies* Supplement 27. London: Institute of Classical Studies.

Seiler, F. 1986. *Die griechische Tholos: Untersuchungen zur Entwicklung, Typologie und Funktion kunstmaßiger Rundbauten*. Mainz: Philipp von Zabern.

Seltman, C. T. 1924. *Athens: Its History and Coinage Before the Persian Invasion*. Cambridge: Cambridge University Press.

Sgouritsa, N. 2007. "Myth, Epos and Mycenaean Attica: The Evidence Reconsidered." In *Epos: Reconsidering Greek Epic and Aegean Bronze Age Archaeology. Proceedings of the 11th International Aegean Conference—The Paul Getty Villa, 20–23 April 2006*, edited by S. P. Morris and R. Laffineur, 265–74. *Aegaeum* 28. Liège: Université de Liège.

Shapiro, H. A. 1989. *Art and Cult Under the Tyrants in Athens*. Mainz: Philipp von Zabern.

Shapiro, H. A. 1990. "Old and New Heroes: Narrative, Composition and Subject in Attic Black-Figure." *Classical Antiquity* 9: 114–48.

Shapiro, H. A. 1991. "The Iconography of Mourning in Athenian Art." *American Journal of Archaeology* 95: 629–56.

Shapiro, H. A. 1997. "Correlating Shape and Subject: The Case of the Archaic Pelike." In *Athenian Potters and Painters: The Conference Proceedings*, edited by J. H. Oakley, W. D. E. Coulson, and O. Palagia, 63–70. Oxbow Monograph 67. Oxford: Oxbow Books.

Shapiro, H. A. 2000. "Modest Athletes and Liberated Women: Etruscans on Attic Black-Figure Vases." In *Not the Classical Ideal: Athens and the Construction of the Other in Greek Art*, edited by B. Cohen, 313–37. Leiden: Brill.

Shapiro, H. A., M. Iozzo, and A. Lezzi-Hafter, eds. 2013. *The François Vase: New Perspectives. Papers of the International Symposium Villa Spelman, Florence 23–24 May 2003*. 2 vols. Akanthus Proceedings 3. Kilchberg: Akanthus.

Shear, J. L. 2021. *Serving Athena: The Festival of the Panathenaia and the Construction of Athenian Identities*. Cambridge: Cambridge University Press.

Shear Jr., T. L. 1994. "Ἰσονόμους τ' Ἀθήνας ἐποιησάτην: The Agora and the Democracy." In *The Archaeology of Athens and Attica under the Democracy*, edited by W. D. E. Coulson, O. Palagia, T. L. Shear Jr., et al., 225–48. Oxford: Oxbow Books.

Sickinger, J. 2003. "Archon Dates, Atthidographers, and the Sources of *Ath. Pol.* 22–26." In *Gestures: Essays in Ancient History, Literature, and Philosophy Presented to Alan L. Boegehold on the Occasion of His Retirement and His Seventy-Fifth Birthday*, edited by G. Bakewell and J. Sickinger, 338–50. Oxford: Oxbow Books.

Siewert, P. 1977. "The Ephebic Oath in Fifth-Century Athens." *Journal of Hellenic Studies* 97: 102–11.

Siewert, P. 1982. *Die Trittyen Attikas und die Heeresreform des Kleisthenes*. Vestigia 33. Munich: C. H. Beck.

Siewert, P. 2002. "Die wissenschaftliche Bedeutung der Bronze-Urkunden aus Olympia." In *Olympia 1875–2000: 125 Jahre Deutsche Ausgrabungen: Internationales Symposium Berlin 9.–11. November 2000*, edited by H. Kyrieleis, 359–70. Mainz: Philipp von Zabern.

Sinn, U. 1992. "Das befestigte Heiligtum der Athena und des Poseidon an der 'Heiligen Landspitze Attikas'." *Antike Welt* 23: 175–90.

Slater, W. 1976. "Symposium at Sea." *Harvard Studies in Classical Philology* 80: 161–70.

Smith, T. J. 2007. "The Corpus of Komast Vases." In *The Origins of Theater in Ancient Greece and Beyond: From Ritual to Drama*, edited by E. Csapo and M. C. Miller, 48–76. Cambridge: Cambridge University Press.

Smith, T. J. 2010. *Komast Dancers in Archaic Greek Art*. Oxford: Oxford University Press.

Snodgrass, A. M. 1977. *Archaeology and the Rise of the Greek State: An Inaugural Lecture*. Cambridge: Cambridge University Press. Reprinted in A. M. Snodgrass, *Archaeology and the Emergence of Greece, Collected Papers on Early Greece and Related Topics, 1965–2002*, Edinburgh: Edinburgh University Press (2006), pp. 198–220.

Snodgrass, A. M. 1980. *Archaic Greece: The Age of Experiment*. Berkeley: University of California Press.

Snodgrass, A. M. 1987. *An Archaeology of Greece: The Present State and Future Scope of a Discipline*. Berkeley: University of California Press.

Snodgrass, A. M. 1989–1990. "The Economics of Dedication at Greek Sanctuaries." *Scienze dell'antichità: storia, archeologia, antropologia* 3–4: 287–94. Reprinted in A. M. Snodgrass, *Archaeology and the Emergence of the Greece, Collected Papers on Early Greece and Related Topics, 1965–2002*, Edinburgh: Edinburgh University Press, pp. 256–68.

Snodgrass, A. M. 2000. *The Dark Ages of Greece: An Archaeological Survey of the Eleventh to the Eighth Centuries*. Reprint (with new introduction) of 1971 edition. Edinburgh: Edinburgh University Press.

Sommerstein, A. H., and A. Bayliss. 2013. *Oath and State in Ancient Greece*. Berlin: Walter de Gruyter.

Sørensen, L. W. 2001. "Archaic Greek Painted Pottery from Cyprus, Naukratis and Tell Defenneh." In *Naukratis: die Beziehungen zu Ostgriechenland, Ägypten und Zypern in archaischer Zeit. Akten der Table Ronde in Mainz, 25.–27. November 1999*, edited by U. Höckmann and D. Kriekenbom, 151–61. Möhnesee: Bibliopolis.

Sourvinou-Inwood, C. 1995. *"Reading" Greek Death to the End of the Classical Period*. Oxford: Clarendon Press.

Sourvinou-Inwood, C. 2003. *Tragedy and Athenian Religion*. Lanham, MD: Lexington Books.

Spivey, N. 1994. "Psephological Heroes." In *Ritual, Finance, Politics: Athenian Democratic Accounts Presented to David Lewis*, edited by S. Hornblower and R. Osborne, 39–52. Oxford: Clarendon Press.

Stahl, M. 1987. *Aristokraten und Tyrannen im archaischen Athen: Untersuchungen zur Überlieferung, zur Sozialstruktur und zur Entstehung des Staates*. Stuttgart: Franz Steiner Verlag.

Stanton, G. R. 1984. "The Tribal Reform of Kleisthenes the Alkmeonid." *Chiron* 14: 1–41.

Stanton, G. R. 1994. "The Trittyes of Kleisthenes." *Chiron* 24: 161–207.

Stanton, G. R., and P. J. Bicknell. 1987. "Voting in Tribal Groups in the Athenian Assembly." *Greek, Roman, and Byzantine Studies* 28: 51–92.

Stavropoulos, P. 1965. "Ἐρεχθεῖου 25 καὶ Ἐρεχθεῖου 21-23." *Ἀρχαιολογικὸν Δελτίον* 20 B1: 84–7.

Stein-Hölkeskamp, E. 1989. *Adelskultur und Polisgesellschaft: Studien zum griechischen Adel in archaischer und klassischer Zeit*. Stuttgart: Franz Steiner Verlag.

Stewart, A. 1983. "Stesichorus and the François Vase." In *Ancient Greek Art and Iconography*, edited by W. Moon, 53–74. Madison: University of Wisconsin Press.

Stewart, A. 1990. *Greek Sculpture: An Exploration*. 2 vols. New Haven: Yale University Press.

Stieber, M. 2004. *The Poetics of Appearance in the Attic Korai*. Austin: University of Texas Press.

Stoneman, R. 2010. *Land of Lost Gods: The Search for Classical Greece*. London: I. B. Tauris.

Strasser, J. -Y. 2010. "'Qu'on fouette les concurrents . . .' À propos des lettres d'Hadrien retrouvées à Alexandrie de Troade." *Revue des études grecques* 123: 585–622.

Stroszeck, J. 2014. *Der Kerameikos in Athen: Geschichte, Bauten und Denkmäler im archäologischen Park*. Möhnesee: Bibliopolis.

Stroud, R. 1968. *Drakon's Law on Homicide*. University of California Publications, Classical Studies 3. Berkeley: University of California Press.

Stroud, R. 1978. "State Documents in Archaic Athens." In *Athens Comes of Age, from Solon to Salamis*, edited by W. A. P. Childs, 20–42. Princeton: Archaeological Institute of America.

Stroud, R. 1979. *The Axones and Kyrbeis of Drakon and Solon*. University of California Publications, Classical Studies 19. Berkeley: University of California Press.

Stroud, R. 1998. *The Athenian Grain-Tax Law of 374/3 B.C. Hesperia* Supplement 29. Princeton: American School of Classical Studies at Athens.

Stuart, J., and N. Revett. 1762–1830. *The Antiquities of Athens: Measured and Delineated*. 5 vols. London: John Haberkorn.

Sturgeon, M. C. 2006. "Archaic Athens and the Cyclades." In *Greek Sculpture: Function, Materials, and Techniques in the Archaic and Classical Periods*, edited by O. Palagia, 32–76. Cambridge: Cambridge University Press.

Taylor, M. C. 1997. *Salamis and the Salaminioi: The History of an Unofficial Athenian Demos*. Archaia Hellas 5. Amsterdam: J. C. Gieben.

Taylor, M. W. 1981. *The Tyrant Slayers. The Heroic Image in Fifth Century Athenian Art and Politics*. New York: Arno Press.

Theocharaki, A. M. 2020. *The Ancient Circuit Walls of Athens*. Berlin: Walter de Gruyter.

Theodoropoulou-Polychroniadis, Z. 2015. *Sounion Revisited: The Sanctuaries of Poseidon and Athena at Sounion in Attica*. Oxford: Archaeopress.

Thomas, R. 1989. *Oral Tradition and Written Record in Classical Athens*. Cambridge: Cambridge University Press.

Thomas, R. 2019. *Polis Histories, Collective Memories and the Greek World*. Cambridge: Cambridge University Press.

Thompson, H. A. 1940. *The Tholos of Athens and Its Predecessors. Hesperia* Supplement 4. Athens: American School of Classical Studies at Athens.

Thompson, H. A. 1982. "The Pnyx in Models." In *Studies in Attic Epigraphy, History and Topography Presented to Eugene Vanderpool.* 133–47. *Hesperia* Supplement 19. Princeton: American School of Classical Studies at Athens.

Threatte, L. 2015. "The Phanodikos *Stele* from Sigeum." In *ΑΞΩΝ. Studies in Honor of Ronald S. Stroud*, edited by A. P. Matthaiou and N. Papazarkadas, 105–23. Athens: Ελληνική Επιγραφική Εταιρεία.

Tiverios, M. 1976. *Ο Λυδός και το έργο του.* Athens: Υπουργείο Πολιτισμού και Επιστημών.

Tölle-Kastenbein, R. 1986. "Kallirrhoe und Enneakrunos." *Jahrbuch des Deutschen Archäologischen Instituts* 101: 55–73.

Tölle-Kastenbein, R. 1994a. *Das archaische Wasserleitungsnetz für Athen und seine späteren Bauphasen.* Zaberns Bildbände zur Archäologie 19. Mainz: Philipp von Zabern.

Tölle-Kastenbein, R. 1994b. *Das Olympieion in Athen.* Cologne: Böhlau.

Tomlinson, R. A. 1990. "The Chronology of the Perachora Hestiatorion and Its Significance." In *Sympotica: A Symposium on the Symposion*, edited by O. Murray, 95–101. Oxford: Clarendon Press.

Torelli, M. 2007. *Le strategie di Kleitias: composizione e programma figurativo del vaso François.* Milan: Mondadori Electa.

Tosto, V. F. 1999. *The Black-Figure Pottery Signed ΝΙΚΟΣΘΕΝΕΣΕΠΟΙΕΣΕΝ.* Allard Pierson Series 11. Amsterdam: Allard Pierson Museum.

Traill, J. S. 1975. *The Political Organization of Attica: A Study of the Demes, Trittyes, and Phylai, and their Representation in the Athenian Council. Hesperia* Supplement 14. Princeton: American School of Classical Studies at Athens.

Traill, J. S. 1986. *Demos and Trittys: Epigraphical and Topographical Studies in the Organization of Attica.* Toronto: Victoria College.

Travlos, J. 1971. *Pictorial Dictionary of Ancient Athens.* London: Thames & Hudson.

Traill, J. S. 1988. *Bildlexikon zur Topographie des antiken Attika.* Tübingen: Wachsmuth.

Trendall, A. D., and T. B. L. Webster. 1971. *Illustrations of Greek Drama.* London: Phaidon.

True, M., and A. P. A. Belloli. 1987. *Papers on the Amasis Painter and his World.* Malibu: J. Paul Getty Museum.

Tsalkou, E. 2020. "Τμήμα υπομυκηναϊκού νεκροταφείου στα νότια της Ακρόπολης (Κουκάκι). Μια προκαταρκτική παρουσίαση." In *Athens and Attica in Prehistory: Proceedings of the International Conference, Athens, 27–31 May 2015*, edited by N. Papadimitriou, J. C. Wright, S. Fachard, et al., 575–87. Oxford: Archaeopress.

Tsingarida, A. 2009. "Vases for Heroes and Gods: Early Red-Figure Parade Cups and Large-Scaled Phialai." In *Shapes and Uses of Greek Vases (7th–4th centuries B.C.). Proceedings of the Symposium Held at the Université Libre de Bruxelles, 27–29 April 2006*, edited by A. Tsingarida and L. Bavay, 185–201. Études d'archéologie 3. Brussels: CReA-Patrimoine.

van Alfen, P. 2012. "The Coinage of Athens, Sixth to First Century B.C." In *The Oxford Handbook of Greek and Roman Coinage*, edited by W. Metcalf, 88–104. Oxford: Oxford University Press.

van den Eijnde, F. 2010. "Cult and Society in Early Athens. Archaeological and Anthropological Approaches to State Formation and Group Participation in Attica. 1000–600 BCE." PhD diss., University of Utrecht. Open Access version available at https://dspace.library.uu.nl/handle/1874/41789.

van den Eijnde, F. 2018. "Power Play at the Dinner Table: Feasting and Patronage Between Palace and Polis in Attika." In *Feasting and Polis Institutions*, edited by F. van den Eijnde, J. Blok, and R. Strootman, 60–92. *Mnemosyne* Supplementum 414. Leiden: Brill.

van Effenterre, H. 1976. "Clisthène et les mesures de mobilisation." *Revue des études grecques* 89: 1–17.

van Wees, H. 2006. "Mass and Elite in Solon's Athens: The Property Classes Revisited." In *Solon of Athens: New Historical and Philological Approaches*, edited by J. Blok and A. P. M. H. Lardinois, 351–89. *Mnemosyne* Supplementum 272. Leiden: Brill.

van Wees, H. 2013. *Ships and Silver, Taxes and Tribute. A Fiscal History of Archaic Athens*. London: I. B. Tauris.

van Wees, H. 2018. "Citizens and Soldiers in Archaic Athens." In *Defining Citizenship in Archaic Greece*, edited by A. Duplouy and R. Brock, 103–44. Oxford: Oxford University Press.

van Wees, H. 2019. "Thermopylae: Herodotus versus the Legend." In *Textual Strategies in Ancient War Narrative: Thermopylae, Cannae and Beyond*, edited by L. W. van Gils, I. J. F. de Jong, and C. H. M. Kroon, 19–53. Amsterdam Studies in Classical Philology 29. Leiden: Brill.

Vansina, J. 1985. *Oral Tradition as History*. Madison: University of Wisconsin Press.

Vionis, A. K., and G. Papantoniou. 2019. "Central Place Theory Reloaded and Revised: Political Economy and Landscape Dynamics in the Longue Durée." *Land* 8: 1–21.

Viviers, D. 1992. *Recherches sur les ateliers de sculpteurs et la cité d'Athènes à l'époque archaïque. Endoios, Philergos, Aristokles*. Brussels: Académie Royale de Belgique.

Vlachou, V. 2011. "A Group of Geometric Vases from Marathon: Attic Style and Local Originality." In *The "Dark Ages" Revisited: Acts of an International Symposium in Memory of William D.E. Coulson, University of Thessaly, Volos, 14–17 June 2007*, edited by A. Mazarakis Ainian, 2: 809–30. 2 vols. Volos: University of Thessaly Press.

Vlachou, V. 2015. "From Pots to Workshops: The Hirschfeld Painter and the Late Geometric I Context of the Attic Pottery Production." In *Pots, Workshops and Early Iron Age Society: Function and Role of Ceramics in Early Greece. Proceedings of the International Symposium Held at the Université Libre de Bruxelles 14–16 November 2013*, edited by V. Vlachou, 49–74. Études d'archéologie 8. Brussels: CReA-Patrimoine.

Vlachou, V. 2017. "Pottery Made to Impress. Oversized Vessels for Funerary Rituals. A View from Geometric Attica and Beyond." In Τέρψις: *Studies in Mediterranean Archaeology in Honour of Nota Kourou*, edited by V. Vlachou and A. Gadolou, 191–207. Études d'archéologie 10. Brussels: CReA-Patrimoine.

Vlassopoulos, K. 2010. "Athenian Slave Names and Athenian Social History." *Zeitschrift für Papyrologie und Epigraphik* 175: 112–44.

von Bothmer, D. 1985. *The Amasis Painter and His World: Vase-Painting in Sixth-Century Athens*. Malibu: J. Paul Getty Museum.

von Eickstedt, K. -V. 1991. *Beiträge zur Topographie des antiken Piräus*. Βιβλιοθήκη της εν Αθήναις Αρχαιολογικής Εταιρείας 118. Athens: Η εν Αθήναις Αρχαιολογική Εταιρεία.

von Reden, S. 1995. "The Piraeus—A World Apart." *Greece and Rome* 42: 24–37.

Wachter, R. 1991. "The Inscriptions on the François Vase." *Museum Helveticum* 48: 86–113.

Wachter, R. 2001. *Non-Attic Greek Vase Inscriptions*. Oxford: Oxford University Press.

Wade-Gery, H. T. 1958. *Essays in Greek History*. Oxford: Blackwell.

Wagner, C. 1997. "Dedication Practices on the Athenian Acropolis 8th to 4th Centuries B.C." PhD diss., University of Oxford.

Wallace, R. W. 1989. *The Areopagus Council to 307 B.C.* Baltimore: Johns Hopkins University Press.

Walter-Karydi, E. 2015. *Die Athener und ihre Gräber (1000–300 v. Chr.)*. Image and Context 14. Berlin: Walter de Gruyter.

Walton, M., E. Doehne, K. Trentelman, et al. 2008. "A Preliminary Investigation of Coral-Red Glosses Found on Attic Greek Pottery." In *Papers on Special Techniques in Athenian Vases: Proceedings of a Symposium Held in Connection with the Exhibition "The Colors of Clay: Special Techniques in Athenian Vases," at the Getty Villa, June 15–17, 2006*, edited by K. Lapatin, 95–104. Los Angeles: J. Paul Getty Museum.

Wannagat, D. 2015. *Archaisches Lachen: die Entstehung einer komischen Bilderwelt in der korinthischen Vasenmalerei*. Image and Context 3. Berlin: Walter de Gruyter.

Watson, J. 2010. "The Origin of Metic Status at Athens." *Cambridge Classical Journal* 56: 259–78.

Weber, M. 1974. "Zu frühen attischen Gerätfiguren." *Mitteilungen des Deutschen Archäologischen Instituts, Athenische Abteilung* 89: 27–46.

Wecowski, M. 2014. *The Rise of the Greek Aristocratic Banquet*. Oxford: Oxford University Press.

West, M. L. 2011. *The Making of the Iliad: Disquisition and Analytical Commentary*. Oxford: Oxford University Press.

West, S. 2011. "A Diplomatic Fiasco: The First Athenian Embassy to Sardis (Hdt. 5,73)." *Rheinisches Museum für Philologie* 154: 9–21.

Whatley, N. 1964. "On the Possibility of Reconstructing the Battle of Marathon and Other Ancient Battles." *Journal of Hellenic Studies* 84: 119–139. Reprinted in E. L. Wheeler (ed.), *The Armies of Classical Greece*, Aldershot: Ashgate (2007), pp. 301–31.

Wheler, G. 1682. *A Journey into Greece in Company of Dr. Spon of Lyons*. London: William Cademan.

Whitehead, D. 1986. *The Demes of Attica 508/7–ca. 250 B.C.* Princeton: Princeton University Press.

Whitley, J. 1991. *Style and Society in Dark Age Greece: The Changing Face of a Pre-Literate Society 1100–700 B.C.* Cambridge: Cambridge University Press.

Whitley, J. 1994a. "The Monuments that Stood Before Marathon: Tomb Cult and Hero Cult in Archaic Attica." *American Journal of Archaeology* 98: 213–30.

Whitley, J. 1994b. "Protoattic Pottery: A Contextual Analysis." In *Classical Greece: Ancient Histories and Modern Archaeologies* edited by I. Morris, 51–70. Cambridge: Cambridge University Press.

Whitley, J. 1996. "Gender and Hierarchy in Early Athens: The Strange Case of the Disappearance of the Rich Female Grave." *Mètis* 11: 209–32.

Whitley, J. 2001. *The Archaeology of Ancient Greece*. Cambridge: Cambridge University Press.

Whitley, J. 2002. "Objects with Attitude: Biographical Facts and Fallacies in the Study of Late Bronze Age and Early Iron Age Warrior Graves." *Cambridge Archaeological Journal* 12: 217–32.

Williams, D. 1983. "Sophilos in the British Museum." *Greek Vases in the J. Paul Getty Museum* 1: 83–113.

Williams, D. 1991. "Vase-Painting in Fifth-Century Athens. 1.The Invention of the Red-Figure Technique and the Race Between Vase-Painting and Free Painting." In *Looking at Greek Vases*, edited by T. Rasmussen and N. Spivey, 103–18. Cambridge: Cambridge University Press.

Williams, D. 1995. "Potter, Painter and Purchaser." In *Culture et cité: l'avènement d'Athènes à l'époque archaïque. Actes du colloque international, organisé à l'Université libre de Bruxelles, du 25 au 27 avril 1991*, edited by A. Verbanck-Piérard and D. Viviers, 139–60. Brussels: de Boccard.

Williams, D. 1996. "Refiguring Attic Red-Figure." *Revue archéologique*: 227–52.

Williams, D. 2009. "Picturing Potters and Painters." In *Athenian Potters and Painters Volume II*, edited by J. H. Oakley, W. D. E. Coulson, and O. Palagia, 306–17. Oxford: Oxbow Books.

Wilson, P. 2007. "Performance in the *Pythion*: The Athenian Thargelia." In *The Greek Theatre and Festivals: Documentary Studies*, edited by P. Wilson, 150–82. Oxford: Oxford University Press.

Winkler, J. J. 1990. *The Constraints of Desire: The Anthropology of Sex and Gender in Ancient Greece*. London: Routledge.

Winter, F. 1893. "Übersicht über die auf der athenischen Akropolis gemachten Funde von Terrakotten." *Archäologischer Anzeiger* 1893: 140–7.

Winter, N. A. 1993. *Greek Architectural Terracottas from the Prehistoric to the End of the Archaic Period*. Oxford: Clarendon Press.

Winters, T. F. 1993. "Kleisthenes and Athenian Nomenclature." *Journal of Hellenic Studies* 113: 162–5.

Wolff, C. 2010. *Sparta und die peloponnesische Staatenwelt in archaischer und klassischer Zeit*. Munich: Herbert Utz Verlag.

Wood, E. M. 1988. *Peasant-Citizen and Slave: The Foundations of Athenian Democracy*. London: Verso.

Yatromanolakis, D. 2016. "Soundscapes (and Two Speaking Lyres)." In *Epigraphy of Art: Ancient Greek Vase-Inscriptions and Vase-Paintings*, edited by D. Yatromanolakis, 1–42. Oxford: Archaeopress.

Young, R. S. 1942. "Graves from the Phaleron Cemetery." *American Journal of Archaeology* 46: 23–57.

Zosi, E. 2012. "An Enigmatic Female Burial." In *'Princesses' of the Mediterranean in the Dawn of History*, edited by N. Stampolidis, 146–57. Athens: Μουσείο Κυκλαδικής Τέχνης.

Index